THE
VIRTUES
OF
LIBERALISM

THE
VIRTUES
OF
LIBERALISM

James T. Kloppenberg

OXFORD
UNIVERSITY PRESS

OXFORD
UNIVERSITY PRESS

Oxford   New York
Athens   Auckland   Bangkok   Bogotá   Buenos Aires
Calcutta   Cape Town   Chennai   Dar es Salaam
Delhi   Florence   Hong Kong   Istanbul   Karachi
Kuala Lumpur   Madrid   Melbourne   Mexico City
Mumbai   Nairobi   Paris   São Paulo   Singapore
Taipei   Tokyo   Toronto   Warsaw

and associated companies in
Berlin   Ibadan

Copyright ©1998 by Oxford University Press, Inc.

First published in 1998 by Oxford University Press, Inc.
198 Madison Avenue, New York, New York 10016

First issued as an Oxford University Press paperback, 2000

Oxford is a registered trademark of Oxford University Press

Library of Congress Cataloging-in-Publication Data
Kloppenberg, James T. 1951–
The virtues of liberalism / James T. Kloppenberg.
p. cm.
Includes index.
ISBN 0-19-512140-6; 0-19-514056-7 pbk.
1. Liberalism—United States.   I. Title
JC574.2.U6K58   1998
320.51'0973—dc21   97-50589

3 5 7 9 8 6 4 2
Printed in the United States of America
on acid-free paper

FOR
MARY
———

PREFACE

A UTHORS PUBLISHING COLLECTIONS of previously printed essays wrestle with competing impulses. On the one hand, it is tempting to rewrite the essays completely to reflect changes in perspective, to register the impact of new scholarship, and (most tantalizing of all) to respond to critics. On the other hand, it is tempting merely to reprint the essays and move on to other projects. Here I have decided to follow a middle course, revising some essays and leaving others alone.

Another temptation is to exaggerate the unity and coherence of the pieces being brought together to form a whole. These essays were written, over the span of a decade, for different purposes; thus, although each stands alone, they sometimes echo each other. I can only hope such similarities will reinforce the arguments that overlap rather than disturb readers who proceed through the book systematically. All the essays deal with aspects of American political thought, but they do not present a single consecutive argument. Although most of the essays cover considerable spans of time, they are arranged here to proceed more or less chronologically, moving gradually from a focus on the eighteenth century to the present.

Since some of the essays (notably chapters 2 and 6) have attracted commentary and criticism, to alter them would be to throw a curve ball to readers who are already familiar with the essays and might reasonably expect to find the arguments they considered valuable (or vulnerable). Chapter 2, "The Virtues of Liberalism: Christianity, Republicanism, and Ethics in Early American Political Discourse," was originally published in the *Journal of American History* in 1987. One of several essays written by historians attempting to break the logjam that clogged studies of early American politics and culture in the 1980s, it is an effort to clarify as well as complicate the relations between distinct sources of American political thought and practice. Chapter 6, "Democracy and Disenchantment: From Weber and Dewey to Habermas and Rorty," was published in 1994 in a volume edited by Dorothy Ross, *Modernist Impulses in the Human Sciences*. It extends and sharpens one of the central arguments I advanced in *Uncertain Victory: Social Democracy and Progressivism in European and American Thought, 1870–1920* (1986) about hermeneutics and democracy that some critics of the book misunderstood and links that argument with contemporary debates swirling around the work of Jürgen Habermas and Richard Rorty.

Three of these essays (chapters 3, 4, and 9) fall into a second category: they are considerably revised. Chapter 3, "Knowledge and Belief in American Public Life," was originally published in 1995 in *Knowledge and Belief in America: Enlightenment Traditions and Modern Religious Thought*, a volume edited by William M. Shea and Peter A. Huff. The essay surveys the tangled connections between eighteenth-century Enlightenment ideals of reason and diverse traditions of religious faith in American philosophy and politics. Chapter 4, originally entitled "Republicanism in American History and Historiography," appeared in 1992 as a companion piece with an article by Maurice Agulhon, "'*Républicain' à la française*," in *La Revue Tocqueville/The Tocqueville Review*. The essay explores methodological and substantive issues related to the ideas of republicanism that powerfully influenced writing about eighteenth- and nineteenth-century American political culture during the 1970s and 1980s, ideas that contributed to a reassessment of, and widespread confusion about, the meanings of liberalism in America. An earlier version of Chapter 9, "Why History Matters to Political Theory," appears in a volume edited by Ronald Walters, *Scientific Authority and Twentieth-Century America* (1997). The essay deals with the current reorientation of thinking about politics and social science by exploring the rise and consequences of a (sometimes implicitly) pragmatist historical sensibility among contemporary philosophers and political theorists.

Two essays (chapters 5 and 8) appear with only minor changes because they have been published quite recently. Chapter 5, "Life Everlasting: Tocqueville in America," examines the strange career of *Democracy in America* in the United States from its first American publication in 1838 to the present. Published in *La Revue Tocqueville/The Tocqueville Review* in 1996, it too originally accompanied an essay by a distinguished French historian, in this case Françoise Mélonio, who provided a précis of her outstanding book *Tocqueville et les français* (1993). Chapter 8, "Political Ideas in Twentieth-Century America," appeared in the *Encyclopedia of the United States in the Twentieth Century* (1995), edited by Stanley Kutler; it connects issues in contemporary political discourse with the broader sweep of twentieth-century political thought and reform.

Finally, chapter 7, "Deliberative Democracy and the Problem of Poverty in America," appears in print here for the first time. It was written to serve as the introductory essay for the volume *Self and Community in America*, edited by Willi Paul Adams and Winfred Fluck. I presented earlier, more and less wide-ranging versions of this essay, under the title "Elusive Consensus: Shaping the Welfare States in Britain, France, and the United States Since World War II," seven times at universities and academic conferences from 1989 to 1993, as I tried to learn from specialists in several disciplines why American liberals in the 1940s failed in their efforts to implement generous programs of social provision of the sort that came to be identified with social democratic governments in northern Europe. Now that the U.S. Congress has acted on President Bill Clinton's promise to "end welfare as we know it," it is instructive to recall the efforts of those who tried instead to end poverty as we know it, and to understand why their experiment with deliberative democracy failed. The virtues of liberalism shaped their aspirations; the explanation of their defeat lies elsewhere.

ACKNOWLEDGMENTS

THIS BOOK FOCUSES on the multi-stranded discourse of liberal theorists and political activists. These essays thus deal with contributions to American public life. But these thinkers and reformers sought to make possible for all Americans lives of moral excellence to be pursued in the private sphere as well as the public sphere, lives that would enrich others, and be enriched in turn, through personal interaction as well as through political activity.

Among the greatest joys of academic life is sustained contact with remarkable people. During the years I have worked on the conference papers from which these essays grew, I have relied on many scholars, some of whose work is noted in the acknowledgments to the essays that follow. Here I want to thank in particular three friends whose contributions as counselors and exemplars transcend their help as exacting critics of my work: David A. Hollinger, Timothy Peltason, and Richard Wightman Fox.

My colleagues at Brandeis, especially Morton Keller, David Hackett Fischer, Jacqueline Jones, and Jane Kamensky in History, and Mark Hulliung, Jeffrey Abramson, and Sidney Milkis in Politics, have earned my admiration for their scholarship and my gratitude for their friendship and generosity. I am also grateful to Peter Hansen, Darra Mulderry, and Jennifer Ratner, graduate students in American history at Brandeis, who have contributed to this project through their research and through our discussions of the ideals that animate their own scholarly projects. Indispensable help came in other forms, too: Guggenheim and Bernstein fellowships and ACLS and Mazer Fund research grants.

Other associations outside the academy have brightened my life and, just as importantly, helped shape my understanding of American culture. These include the vibrant parish of St. John the Evangelist; the bracing worlds of youth soccer, basketball, and baseball in greater Boston; and the neighborhood where our family has been lucky to make its home.

As a son and brother I have depended on the sustaining love of my parents,

George A. and Zona B. Kloppenberg, and the support of George F. and Joseph R. Kloppenberg. As the father of Annie and Jay I have been blessed with two kind and loving children whose energetic embrace of life is my answer to cynics who ask how and why hope should survive the evidence of cruelty.

It is fitting to dedicate this book, which explores ideals of justice and the design of liberal democratic institutions, to Mary Cairns Kloppenberg. She has turned such abstractions into realities by founding and guiding child care centers at Stanford University and McLean Hospital and by directing the exemplary early-childhood and after-school programs of the Wellesley Community Children's Center. As the families served by these centers over the last twenty years testify, she has enriched thousands of lives by embodying daily the virtues of love, generosity, and wisdom. My own debts to her exceed words. On this the twenty-fifth anniversary of our marriage, with the "undying admiration" she has earned from Annie, Jay, and me, I dedicate this book to her with love.

Wellesley, Massachusetts   J. T. K.
July 1, 1997

CONTENTS

THE
VIRTUES
OF
LIBERALISM

ONE

INTRODUCTION

Rethinking America's Liberal Tradition

America!
Land created in common,
Dream nourished in common,
Keep your hand on the plow! Hold on!
If the house is not yet finished,
Don't be discouraged, builder!
If the fight is not yet won,
Don't be weary, soldier!
The plan and the pattern is here,
Woven from the beginning
Into the warp and woof of America:
ALL MEN ARE CREATED EQUAL.

—Langston Hughes,
"Freedom's Plow"[1]

This book issues the summons of Langston Hughes to American liberals: "KEEP YOUR HANDS ON THE PLOW! HOLD ON!" For fifty years now the ideas and policies of American liberalism have been on the defensive, first against charges of communism or socialism, more recently against charges of moral as well as economic apostasy. The time has come to reconsider the ideals that inspired generations of Americans to see the rich potential of political engagement as well as the value of private pursuits, to acknowledge the importance of public deliberation about the meanings of our shared standards of liberty and justice for all. The time has come to proclaim again what James Madison termed the "necessary

3

moral ingredient" in all calculations—both public and personal.[2] The time has come to rediscover the virtues of liberalism.

Liberals need not surrender to conservative polemicists or self-proclaimed realists our nation's longstanding commitment to the ideal of equality as well as the ideal of individual freedom. We need not surrender the resources of our culture's diverse religious faiths to those who invoke divine authority to legitimate their own greed or their own narrow cultural preferences. We need not surrender to postmodernists our philosophical heritage of pragmatism, a tradition that hearkens back not only to William James and John Dewey but beyond them to Thomas Jefferson and James Madison, and ultimately to Aristotle, to proclaim the importance of continuously testing our principles in open, democratic debate, practical activity, and social experimentation rather than simply taking their truth for granted.

Our nation has flourished because we have not permitted those with power to silence those who challenged them, whether the former brandished dogmas of religion, race, ethnicity, gender, culture, or economics. Force, as Madison insisted, must never be the measure of right; we must not allow currently fashionable doctrines of selfishness to masquerade as virtue or rationality. We must instead recover a different set of ideals grounded not in fables but rooted in our history, which inspired earlier Americans to seek and, when necessary, to demand justice from those who tried to justify the inequalities that shielded their own privileges. We must recover the virtues of liberalism.

From the seventeenth century onward, Americans have struggled to align our personal interests with our ideals, not merely vice versa. We have struggled to create laws and institutions that would accommodate and regulate our pursuit of various goods in various domains, including but not limited to the worlds of cultural expression, work, politics, community, home, family, and faith. Such pursuits sometimes collide, which makes their coordination both difficult and necessary for any culture. Americans have sought to achieve that coordination through democracy. Beneath our democratic procedures, though, lie deeper commitments to substantive values that justify and sustain our laws and institutions, and to virtues that are immanent in the principles—if too often betrayed in the practice —of liberalism.

Virtue has returned from the margins to the center of cultural controversies in the United States at the end of the twentieth century. In contemporary moral philosophy, virtue ethics is usually contrasted to two different traditions descended from Immanuel Kant and Jeremy Bentham. Kant proclaimed a universal moral law, the categorical imperative, which all persons must internalize and obey from a sense of duty. Bentham countered with a utilitarian ethic: each person should maximize the greatest good, understood as the satisfaction of the desire for pleasure, of the greatest number. Virtue ethics, by contrast, descends from Aristotle through Aquinas and emphasizes the importance of nurturing a certain kind of character rather than attending exclusively to a universal rule or the consequences of particular acts. From a historian's perspective, however, the standard contrast between Kantian, utilitarian, and virtue ethics overlooks the ways in which these traditions have blended in American culture. Most Americans have embraced versions of Christianity that proclaim "a duty-based virtue ethics, according to which our duty is to manifest certain virtues, such as love."[3]

Whereas many moral philosophers persist in asserting that we must choose between Kantian and utilitarian ethics, others have returned our attention to the ideas of eighteenth- and nineteenth-century mediators, such as Adam Smith and Henry Sidgwick, who sought different paths between Kant and Bentham. Some emphasized, as Smith did, the moral sense of sympathy, a concept not incompatible with Christianity that was central to the Enlightenment in Scotland and America. Others such as Sidgwick sought to integrate the principles of justice (from Kant), prudence (from Bentham), and rational benevolence (which reflected the demands of reason on desire); his *Methods of Ethics* profoundly shaped the ethical ideas of America's greatest twentieth-century philosophers, William James and John Dewey. Sidgwick's, James's, and Dewey's anguished writings reflect the difficulties people face in everyday life when they try to resolve ethical dilemmas, difficulties similar to the challenge cultures face when they confront and try to reconcile apparently contradictory demands to protect individual freedom and advance the cause of equality and justice. If "the highest ethical life," in James's words, "consists at all times in the breaking of rules which have grown too narrow for the actual case," we might do well to seek an alternative to both Kantian and utilitarian approaches in the cultivation of virtue. Given the range of virtues available to us—from the patience of Job to the magnificence and well-bred insolence of Aristotle, from the propriety Mencius prized to the meekness Jesus preached in the Beatitudes—we suffer from a surfeit of options.[4]

Because liberalism is generally understood today, as it was understood in the seventeenth and eighteenth centuries by those we now identify as its early champions, to have emerged as an alternative to the ruinous wars of religion, both liberals and non-liberals often assume the incompatibility of liberalism and religion. Historically and conceptually, that is a mistake. Historically, early liberals from Locke through Jefferson and Madison were devout (if sometimes unconventional) Christians. Conceptually, moreover, central virtues of liberalism descend directly from the cardinal virtues of early Christianity: prudence, temperance, fortitude, and justice.

Liberals elevated individual freedom over the acceptance of imposed hierarchy. They conceived of freedom, however, not as license but as enlightened self-interest, not as the ancient vice of egoism but as "self interest properly understood," in the phrase of Alexis de Tocqueville. Exercising liberal freedom requires the disposition to find one's true good and to choose the proper means to it, which is the meaning of prudence. Liberals elevated the production and consumption of material goods over the acceptance of poverty and asceticism. They conceived of the good life, however, not as gluttony but as moderation in the enjoyment of pleasures and as a proper respect for the different preferences of others, which is the meaning of temperance. Liberals elevated the private life over the earlier demand of theocrats and republicans that individual citizens can find fulfillment only in, and thus must sacrifice themselves for, the good of the church or the state. They conceived of the liberal polity, however, as a legal and moral order necessary not only to protect them from each other and adjudicate their conflicts but also to enable them to achieve their goals. The liberal polity could survive only through the faithfulness of its citizens and their persistent loyalty to it—and to its proce-dures of resolving disputes through persuasion rather than force—regardless of the difficulties that might arise, which is the meaning of fortitude. Finally, lib-erals elevated the rights of every citizen over the privileges and preferences of an elite. They conceived of such rights, however, as bounded by the firm command that individuals must render to God and to their neighbors what is their due, which is the meaning of justice.

It would be possible to expand this list of inexact parallels by tracing other standard liberal commitments to those central to the Judeo-Christian tradition. The liberal virtues of law abidingness, honesty, and moderation, for example, echo certain of the commandments handed down through Moses. The liberal vir-tues of tolerance, respect, generosity, and benevolence likewise extend St. Paul's admonition to the Colossians that they should practice forbearance, patience, kindness, and charity. One might argue that even the theological virtues of faith, hope, and love, which Christians understand with reference to their deity, bear more than a faint resemblance to the liberal virtues of trusting others, resolutely resisting cynicism, and attempting to find ways to help others flourish. Of course there are differences, since the desire to shield religious dissenters from perse-cution helped launch liberalism in the first place, and those who long for religious homogeneity will always be uneasy with the toleration of diversity that liberals champion. But notwithstanding the protests of dogmatists on both sides of the religious-secular divide, the discrepancies between their versions of virtue are no more striking than the similarities.

Given the compatibility between Christian virtue ethics and the virtues of lib-eralism, it is tempting to draw up a more elaborate or definitive list of liberal vir-tues, to follow in the footsteps of earlier champions of virtue ethics such as Aris-totle and Aquinas. Some philosophers and political theorists have done just that in recent years.[5] But resisting that temptation is essential to the purpose of this book, both because this is not principally a prescriptive but a historical account and because disagreement, deliberation, and experimentation are essential to lib-eralism, not unfortunate accidents.

Overlooking the frequency and inevitability of discord and the importance of reaching tentative, provisional accommodations between apparently irreconcil-able points of view would be false to the history as well as the theory of liberal democracy in America. The essays that follow examine and illustrate how the virtues of liberalism have evolved and how their meanings have altered because of dissent, conflict, and the changes of mind and heart that result. Conceived his-torically, no static portrait or definition of liberalism would be accurate for all times even in this one place. To cite just three examples, American liberals' ideas about the desirability of religious and cultural diversity, about the rights and appropriate spheres of activity of women and members of different racial and ethnic groups, and about the role of government in regulating economic and social activity have all developed as new experiences and understandings have transformed old patterns of behavior and belief. That disposition to entertain criticism and accept change, a defining characteristic of liberalism, is itself grounded in the ancient Judeo-Christian virtue of humility.

The diverse and historically shifting virtues of American liberalism derive from various sources, religious and non-religious; they have manifested themselves in complex and changing practices of cultural expression, politics, economics, and social activity. Balancing commitments to popular sovereignty, regulated market exchange, and distinct cultural traditions, American liberals have sought to mediate their differences and maintain their equilibrium with varying degrees of success. The point of this volume is to make clear that, historically, the reconciling and balancing of competing values, which seems so elusive in the polarized culture of the United States at the end of the twentieth century, has been another defining feature of the liberal and democratic traditions in America. These traditions have not reflected the false dichotomies of our current debates but instead demonstrate the necessity and even the desirability of holding in suspension, and deliberating about the meaning and implications of, values that may seem incommensurable in theory but that inspire practices capable of sustaining and enriching our lives. The principles we need are to be found right in front of our eyes in the virtues of liberalism: in the deliberate and delicate balancing of freedom against responsibility, of the desire for individual wealth and security against the importance of social equality, and of the genuinely constitutive commitments to religious traditions or other cultural ideals against the awareness of the sometimes incompatible values of other Americans.

The desire to resolve those tensions, or to strike a permanent balance among those conflicting ideals, has been a perennial feature of American culture, but it is a desire we must learn to overcome or at least to keep under control. The yearning for resolution has often sprung from utopian reformers seeking social justice through dramatic social or political transformation. But as the last two decades have demonstrated, such yearnings can as easily emerge from free-market utopians whose dogmatic faith in capitalism leads them to distrust all public authority and to dismiss all invocations of responsibility, equality, and justice as illegitimate intrusions into the otherwise benign workings of the marketplace. The consequences of such capitalist utopian fervor can be as ruinous as the consequences of revolutionary egalitarian ideologies that have trampled individual rights, personal security, and religious faith. Liberalism and democracy go hand in hand, not because they can carry us beyond ideology or beyond history but precisely because the clear-eyed study of their connections in history can signal not only the dangers of utopianisms left and right but also the fruitfulness of compromise and the value of balance—together with the inevitable frustrations such moderation brings along with it. As England and France both have demonstrated in recent years, alternatives to free-market panaceas no longer require formulaic returns to rigid forms of socialist orthodoxy. The dissolution of the Soviet Union, the transformation of Eastern Europe, and the end of the cold war can make possible new forms of liberalism and social democracy attuned to the necessity of balancing commitments to liberty, equality, and fraternity with commitments to rights, security, and religious traditions. Although not always, American liberalism at its best has shown precisely those characteristics, along with the chastened realization that choices among such values always exact a price. One of America's most perceptive liberal democrats, William James, observed that whenever we must choose in practice between conflicting values, "some part of the ideal is butchered." Only through trial and error, experiment and evaluation, can our culture find ways to sustain with less butchery our commitments to different ideals. We will never escape the necessity of choosing nor the tragic cost of the choice itself.[6]

The virtues of liberalism in American history have been political, economic, and social, which explains both their enduring appeal and the vulnerability of contemporary liberalism to diverse forms of criticism. Liberal ideas are simultaneously attacked today by conservatives outside the university and by radicals inside it. These different critics ascribe to liberalism distinctly different meanings that often rest on misunderstandings of the complex historical dynamics that have shaped American politics and culture.

Liberalism today is under siege, assaulted by diverse enemies and abandoned by many of its friends. William Jefferson Clinton, the first Democrat reelected President since Franklin Delano Roosevelt, distanced himself from the liberal traditions of his own party. Although reelected with an overwhelming majority in the electoral college, Clinton nevertheless found himself facing a Congress under conservative control: not only did Republicans constitute a majority in the U.S. Senate, the election of 1996 marked the first time since 1930 that the Republican Party enjoyed back-to-back majorities in the House of Representatives. In the closing years of the twentieth century, fewer than 20 percent of American voters identify themselves as liberals.

More often hurled as an epithet these days than waved as a banner, liberalism attracts critics from all sides. Champions of both political parties, by contrast, enthusiastically sing the praises of virtue. From William Bennett's *The Book of Virtues* to Michael Lerner's *The Politics of Meaning*, commentators from right to left are trumpeting the importance of old-fashioned standards of moral excellence and personal obligation.[7] With Democrats fleeing and Republicans demonizing "liberal" ideas, with Jeremiahs competing to drum up support for individual responsibility by calling for personal "virtue," it may seem perverse to speak of the "virtues of liberalism." That is why it is necessary.

I use *virtues* in the plural for three reasons. First, I want to emphasize that there is no singular standard of human excellence in liberalism; indeed, considered historically, there is no singular liberalism in America. Second, by calling attention to the virtues of liberal ideas, I mean to stress the positive value of their diverse contributions to American culture as well as the attractiveness of virtue ethics and their compatibility with liberalism. Despite the current barrage of criticism directed against liberal ideas and political programs, they have widened the political, economic, and cultural options available to Americans. Finally, I highlight the multiple virtues of liberalism to signal the multiple dimensions of every human life: in their families, community activities, worlds of work, and places of worship no less than in their distinctly political participation, Americans have sought and even occasionally achieved forms of moral excellence facilitated by liberal institutions. Moreover, these different meanings can neither be collapsed into each other nor separated neatly from each other. The abstract ideals associated with these spheres may be analytically distinct and perhaps even incompatible, but in the lives of most persons at most times they have overlapped. The virtues of liberalism have been embodied historically in forms of life that cannot be described, let alone evaluated, on a single scale.

Such diversity makes clear why, conceived historically, the virtues of liberalism cannot be adequately understood at the level of definition or abstract theory. Only historical accounts can show how real people juggled, or balanced, or held in suspension the sometimes seemingly incommensurable virtues of liberalism, or, alternatively, how they struggled with, or were caught in the collisions between, the ideals of liberty, equality, and toleration that liberals have proclaimed. Only historical analysis can reveal whether, or to what extent, the problems identified or the solutions proposed by political theorists have connected with the lives people have led and the choices they have been forced or enabled to make. American political thought has taken shape in the practice of politics in its largest sense. America's important liberal theorists have occupied themselves with the writing of constitutions, laws, judicial decisions, and political commentaries, not with the production of great systems of political philosophy. If we separate liberal principles in America from their manifestations in American political discourse and practice, we will misunderstand their meanings and significance.

That insight is as old as the nation itself. On October 30, 1787, three days after publication of the first essay in *The Federalist*, the most often cited statement of American liberal political theory, James Madison recommended combining a historicist commitment to the particularity of all vital political discourses, a pragmatist commitment to testing the workability of political ideas in practice, and a democratic commitment to deliberation as the method of resolving political disputes. In a letter to Archibald Stuart, Madison expressed his belief that "if any Constitution is to be established by deliberation and choice, it must be examined with many allowances and must be compared, not with the theory which each individual may frame in his own mind, but with the systems which it is meant to take the place of and with any other which there might be a probability of obtaining."[8] Madison himself manifested the historical, pragmatist, and deliberative sensibility he described. Those are among the principal characteristics of American liberalism as theory and practice to be examined in this book.

To most Americans today, by contrast, "liberalism" carries two distinct meanings. First, it refers to the New Deal– or later New Frontier– or Great Society–inspired initiatives to bring about greater social equality through reliance on the federal government. It comprises a set of programs championed in recent years by politicians such as Hubert Humphrey, Walter Mondale, Edward Kennedy, and Michael Dukakis, a string of aspirants to the presidency whose candidacies are said to have foundered because the public identified them as "liberals." Second, most Americans associate "liberalism" with calls for greater personal freedom to be secured through government intervention. These demands for greater tolerance of diversity began with campaigns for abolition and women's rights, reemerged in the civil rights movement, and expanded into a broader agenda encompassing challenges to the obstacles associated not only with race but also with gender, sexuality, age, and physical or mental disability. Since the word *liberal* has long meant both generosity and tolerance, the former since the fourteenth century, the latter since the eighteenth, this common understanding of the dual meanings of "liberalism" has a solid foundation.

Within the academy, "liberalism" usually has a different range of meanings with an equally long lineage. These meanings derive from the tradition of political theory originating with John Locke in the late seventeenth century; extending through the Enlightenment to our own day thanks to the efforts of thinkers such as James Madison, John Stuart Mill, and Oliver Wendell Holmes Jr.; and culminating in the influential work of the contemporary American philosopher John Rawls. For most academics who write on social and political theory, "liberalism" is this rarefied discourse with its emphasis on individual rights, specifically property rights, and its focus on protecting individuals from political schemes that would limit their freedom, considered to be the value most prized by liberals. Academics who are cultural radicals dismiss the pleas for toleration that most Americans associate with liberals as a transparent rationalization of liberals' deeper preference for a narrow ideal of rationality descended from the eighteenth-century Enlightenment. Beneath liberals' gestures toward tolerating diversity, according to this critique, lie their abiding desires to preserve the prerogatives of Eurocentric, white, male elites. Paradoxically, this way of understanding these concepts emphasizes liberals' purported efforts to shield the economic freedom of individuals from the intrusiveness of state authority and their efforts to preserve Western standards of order and rationality. Not only is this view of liberalism distinct from, it is almost exactly opposite, that of most Americans outside universities who excoriate liberals.

For the last thirty years at least, liberalism has thus been under attack simultaneously from the political Right and the academic Left. Republican Party loyalists accuse liberals of being overly interested in using government to achieve equality and insufficiently sensitive to individual property rights. Academic radicals accuse liberals of being insufficiently sensitive to egalitarian aspirations and overly interested in protecting individual property rights. Conservative critics charge liberals with glorifying diversity by celebrating toleration; critics in the academy fault liberals for trivializing difference by pretending to tolerate forms of cultural diversity that they secretly wish to silence. Perhaps it is not surprising that with enemies like these, liberalism at the end of the twentieth century seems to have few friends.

That is unfortunate. The essays collected in this volume—essays written for a variety of purposes—establish why the critiques of both the Republican Party and the academic Left rest on misunderstandings of the multiple roles played by liberal ideas in American history. American liberals have been guilty of the sins of omission and commission that enrage contemporary critics. As dissidents from the left have made clear, centuries passed before the ranks of decision makers expanded to include nonwhites, women, and the poor. As conservatives have made equally clear, some champions of liberalism have exaggerated the capacity of reason, which can be thin and brittle, and the ability of self-righteous reformers, who can be blind and deaf, to solve social problems by empowering themselves. But the resources for responding to those critiques are to be found within liberalism itself. Liberalism is neither essentially exclusionary nor essentially naive. When critics have challenged liberals' broad-mindedness and hard-headedness, they have invoked virtues that liberals themselves should cherish; expanding the reach of democracy and evaluating the effectiveness of government policies should be obsessions of American liberals. Only when radicals or conservatives claim that liberalism lacks the depth to answer their charges do legitimate critiques become caricatures, exaggerated portraits of liberalism that conveniently overlook crucial aspects of the ideas being targeted for scorn.

These essays recover the multidimensional nature of the political ideals and programs often described as "liberal," which stretch back into colonial America and continue into the present. The multiple theories and practices of liberalism have been inspired and informed by, and carry forward, too-seldom understood conceptions of virtue that are less distant from the current concerns of either Republican Party loyalists or cultural radicals in the academy than the rhetoric of either group would suggest. American history, in short, reveals dimensions of American political thought and activity that have been conveniently forgotten, ignored, or misrepresented by conservative and radical critics: the virtues of liberalism.

These essays emphatically do *not* attempt to rehabilitate, or refine, the account of American history advanced by Louis Hartz in *The American Liberal Tradition* (1955), an exceedingly influential book that was mistaken in its general argument about American consensus and in almost every one of its particular arguments as well.[9] Hartz claimed, with impressive energy and dazzling allusive brilliance, that because America lacked a feudal tradition, and because Americans had the good fortune to enjoy a large measure of equality, their shared commitment to the primacy of individual freedom kept them from worrying about the questions of equality and social justice that have convulsed European nations since the eighteenth century. Hartz's account, despite its appeal to champions and critics of American politics from the Right and the Left, misses almost everything important about the social and political conflicts that have racked American history. It helped spawn mirror-image mythological misunderstandings of America that have inspired both conservatives' and radicals' equally overstated critiques of liberal ideas and politics in America. Those who seek heroes (or villains) in the American past among those who cherished property and scorned government, and those who seek villains (or heroes) among those who cherished a narrowly ethnocentric ideal and suppressed diversity, will continue to find in Hartz's narrative a comforting morality play that satisfies their thirst for melodrama. American history, like liberal discourse itself, is more complicated.

This volume represents a preliminary report of a work in progress, a larger comparative study of European and American democracy that will endeavor to replace Hartz's conception of property rights as the central value in American politics with a broader treatment of the emergence and transformation of autonomy and popular sovereignty—the complex ideals that underlie the changing practice of democracy on both sides of the Atlantic. In that story some of the particular issues discussed in these essays will receive less detailed treatment; others will come more sharply into focus. My goal in bringing together these essays at this moment is to indicate the reasons why the critiques of American conservatives and American radicals, of commentators within and outside the academic community, too often miss their mark because they fail to acknowledge the complicated, multidimensional history of American ideas and political activity, a history that reveals the diverse and dynamic virtues of liberalism. But if liberalism has been so often misunderstood, readers may wonder, why worry about preserving it? If responding to criticism from the left requires invoking democratic principles of equality and inclusion, and responding to criticism from the right requires invoking ancient virtues such as prudence and fortitude, why not abandon the term "liberalism" altogether? Why not concede its weaknesses and start over with something less vulnerable to attacks from left and right? This is a serious and legitimate question. There are good reasons why liberals might want to change our focus to democracy, and to the gradual evolution from political democracy to social democracy. I intend to explore those reasons in another book. But there are equally good reasons for illuminating the resources of liberalism itself: without an adequate appreciation of those resources, we have an impoverished and inaccurate understanding of the rich mixture of democratic and liberal virtues that have helped shape our history and can help guide us into the future.

Democracy is distinguishable from liberalism. Unless the principle of majoritarianism is tempered with principles such as autonomy and toleration, democracy can become tyranny, as political theorists ancient and modern have acknowledged. Nor is the multifaceted liberalism of American history merely a version of conservatism. Liberalism includes not only a legitimate concern with rights, or respect for the virtues of prudence and temperance as brakes on the hubris of reason, but an equally important thirst for justice. Almost fifty years ago, at a meeting of the State Department Policy Planning Staff, Reinhold Niebuhr, a quintessential liberal, observed that the problem with American conservatives and the business community "is that they do not really deal with the problem of freedom in the community, freedom and justice, because they believe that justice flows automatically from freedom." To the contrary, liberty itself, although a precious condition, is not a virtue. As Niebuhr pointed out, justice should be the aim of free persons and free nations: "There is no such thing as freedom as the sole end of life."[10] If liberalism meant nothing more than celebrating freedom, it would indeed be inadequate. If democracy always meant something more than simple majoritarianism, and if champions of America's religious traditions always tolerated diversity and embraced difference, democracy and religiosity might have provided Americans everything we need. But instead it has been an imperfect and changing amalgamation of liberal virtues, democratic procedures, and religious ideals that has inspired Americans in our still unfinished quest for justice.

From John Winthrop's shipboard address to the band of Puritans bound for the New World in 1630 through Bill Clinton's acceptance speech at the Democratic Party's national convention in the summer of 1996, Americans in public life have sought to balance deep commitments to liberty and to community. As the distance separating Winthrop's austere Calvinism from Clinton's rather less stringent standard of propriety makes clear, however, the meanings associated with both terms have changed even as public proclamations of their importance have persisted. Americans have long understood that efforts to balance freedom and fraternity have required trying to reconcile in practice ideals that seemed contradictory. Winthrop identified the problem in his address aboard the *Arabella* in 1630. He began by noting the divinely ordained and irremediable "Condicion of mankinde," in which "some must be rich and some poore, some high and eminent in power and dignitie; others meane and in subjection." Despite the resentment such inequality might engender, however, the community required a sustaining "Bond of brotherly affection." Tempering the fact of hierarchy was a commitment to justice; tempering the fact of misfortune was a commitment to mercy; tempering the fact of indolence was a commitment to prudence.[11] Yet Winthrop acknowledged that members of the community would be tempted to magnify the importance of their own well-being and distrust their neighbors. Although hardly a liberal—for him social hierarchy was fixed and religious truth known, ideas of equality and dissent intolerable—Winthrop nevertheless did identify the balancing act that his heirs have been required to perform. Americans' yearning for harmony has been frustrated by the realization, which dawned throughout the colonies as early as the middle of the seventeenth century, that freedom makes diversity and disagreement the inevitable features of liberal community.

In the abstract, tradeoffs between freedom and equality may appear inescapable, but in practice they are connected. Individuals cannot exercise freedom unless they are afforded equal protection under law from others who would restrict their choices. Likewise, no significant political thinker in the American tradition has valued equality without valuing freedom, if only because freedom has always been considered one of the most important goods to be made available equally among citizens.[12]

The idea that "liberalism," because of its emphasis on rights, prohibits government from intervening to regulate individual freedom in order to achieve greater equality has no historical foundation. Liberal theorists from Locke to Rawls have acknowledged that the idea of unrestricted freedom is chimerical and that government has a legitimate role to play in regulating the ownership and use of property. Although Isaiah Berlin is one of this century's most accomplished historians of ideas, his familiar distinction between negative and positive freedom— between freedom "from" government intrusion and freedom "to" take steps that Berlin worried might slide smoothly into oppressing others—has done much mischief in recent political thought. Freedom from state power (negative freedom) makes no difference unless individuals are thereby freed to achieve their desired goals (positive freedom). Berlin's leap from suspicion of efforts to ensure individuals' capacity to act (which the state might facilitate in various ways ranging from providing schools to providing roads) to his conclusions regarding the lurking danger of authoritarianism reflects the power that fears of totalitarianism exerted over Berlin's generation rather than the necessary conceptual—or historical—limits of liberalism.[13]

Participating in the marketplace, enjoying the fruits of one's enterprising activity, and nevertheless not only worrying about inequality but acting to regulate the conditions of economic life have long been American preoccupations. Puritans fled England for the New World because they refused to surrender their religious principles, but their dedication to righteous living translated into material success that made them uneasy. Winthrop cited biblical injunctions when he counseled "liberallity" toward the least fortunate members of the community; despite their emphasis on hard work and their acceptance of hierarchy as a natural part of God's plan, the Puritans nevertheless acknowledged from the outset the need to care for the poor and check the appetites of the rich.[14]

During the eighteenth century, as chapters 2, 3, and 4 make clear, Christian ideas of charity, bolstered by the English common law tradition, the idea of natural law, and ideas of duty drawn from Scottish moral philosophy combined with liberal and republican ideas to legitimate public regulation of individuals' economic activity on behalf of the common good. Although Americans fought a war to establish their independence from England, and although they disagreed about the shape their own institutions should take, they did not dispute the legitimacy of government intervention in social and economic activity. In the new nation, courts at the state and local level did not hesitate to regulate the economy on behalf of "the people's welfare," a maxim regularly invoked to justify circumscribing the rights of property holders. When uses of property threatened public safety, public access to roads, ports, or waterways, public morality, public health, or the legitimate interests of consumers, American courts asserted their authority to protect the common good.[15]

American democracy worked, Alexis de Tocqueville understood, because Americans neither inherited nor constructed walls dividing their private lives from public authority in the way that liberalism, at least as some commentators conceive of it, is sometimes said to require. Instead, as I indicate in chapter 5, Tocqueville understood that the roughly equal conditions Americans enjoyed, within which individuals were able to pursue their richly textured associational and religious lives, made possible the emergence of "self interest properly understood." This was a uniquely democratic virtue, which Tocqueville distinguished sharply from the vice of egoism that simple individualism might otherwise mirror. Its preservation required not only the indispensable community and religious institutions that political scientists now treasure as "civil society" but also a degree of social and economic equality that existed nowhere else in the world in the 1830s. That equality sprang not from the mythical magic of the market but instead from specific legal and political decisions rooted in the quintessentially American—and liberal—cultural ideal of a well regulated society.

Slavery, the most obvious contradiction to that ideal, mocked Americans' claims to cherish freedom or equality. But effective challenges to slavery eventually matured in the 1850s. Their power derived from the religious, republican, and liberal ideas that pervaded northern political culture, which reformers transformed by infusing Christian universalism with the "heightened emotional style" of Evangelical Protestantism and the idea of sympathy drawn from Scottish philosophers such as Adam Smith and Francis Hutcheson. These ideas found expression in various reform organizations until they coalesced in the Republican Party, which nominated Abraham Lincoln to oppose a system that degraded free and enslaved Americans alike. Lincoln's authority rested on his ability to extend the biblical ideals of individual freedom and equality to African Americans and to amalgamate those values with his devotion to a newly sanctified American national ideal. Although the scars left by slavery endure, Lincoln began the still unfinished healing process by redefining the national purpose and reestablishing the boundaries of tolerance.[16]

Much of nineteenth-century American political discourse demonstrates the folly of counterposing liberal "rights talk" against egalitarian ideals as if they were incompatible. From writers in the Jeffersonian tradition such as Ethan Allen, William Manning, and John Taylor to champions of natural rights republicanism such as Tom Paine, Joel Barlow, and Robert Coram, through Jacksonians such as Thomas Skidmore to the many late nineteenth-century land reformers entranced by Henry George, influential American political commentators simultaneously challenged the legitimacy of existing distributions of property and wholeheartedly endorsed the legitimacy, even the sanctity, of every individual's right to land ownership. This loose American tradition of natural rights republicanism—or liberal egalitarianism—shows how supple the ideas of freedom and equality were in practice; its long-term vitality indicates that claims for government intervention need hardly originate from somewhere outside the conceptual limits of liberalism.[17]

Viewed historically, the boundaries between religious, ethical, and political ideals, and those between liberal, republican, socialist, and social democratic ideas, have proved considerably more permeable in practice than some contemporary political theorists might suppose. Biblical injunctions against selfishness, greed, and cruelty have undergirded civic invocations of the ideals of freedom, equality, and justice, and Americans' failure to measure up to the standards of the Judeo-Christian tradition has provided ammunition not only for preachers but also for political activists, and not without results. In the wake of systematic campaigns of violence against blacks and unprecedentedly harsh codes of racial segregation imposed in the South in the 1890s, W. E. B. Du Bois wrote, in *The Souls of Black Folk* (1903), "Deeply religious and democratic as are the mass of the whites, they feel acutely the false position in which the Negro problems place them. Such an essentially honest-hearted and generous people cannot cite the caste-leveling precepts of Christianity, or believe in equality of opportunity for all men, without coming to feel more with each generation that the present drawing of the color-line is a flat contradiction to their beliefs and professions." Although Du Bois himself came to doubt the potency of religious precepts against the hard fact of racism, a later generation of civil rights activists led by Martin Luther King Jr. fueled their crusade with precisely the biblical principles Du Bois invoked. Combining shared religious and political ideals, they eventually succeeded in persuading white Protestants, Catholics, and Jews to join them; that alliance changed the nation's laws if not always its citizens' behavior. Although the ecumenical commitment to racial justice across religious lines, to which even Malcolm X committed himself before his assassination, remains fragile, and the racial divisions between Americans remain the nation's most serious problem, the absolutely crucial part played by religious communities in forging fragile coalitions across the color line is now beyond doubt.[18]

The writings of most of the influential American political thinkers in the last hundred years likewise illustrate the flexibility of liberals facing the unprecedented challenges of an urban industrial nation. Chapters 6, 7, and 8 explore the ideas of thinkers who challenged the brief, late nineteenth-century identification of liberalism with laissez-faire. Although the reign of laissez-faire endured only a short time, that moment enshrined in the imagination of twentieth-century conservatives an Edenic myth of a stateless America that has inspired a flood of antigovernment rhetoric ever since. Liberals quickly exposed the mythic quality of laissez-faire fantasies by pointing out the continuous engagement of government with American business, which flourished in the nineteenth century thanks to government subsidies, charters, and laws that restricted the freedoms of some inhabitants of the nation so that others could prosper. Insisting on the interdependence of American society and the incoherence of the concept of atomistic individuals, American philosophers and social theorists, notably John Dewey, whose ideas are examined in chapter 6, launched a new crusade to extend equality to all citizens.

Twentieth-century American reformers followed these thinkers' lead. Progressives established the principle of graduated taxation and experimented with the idea of government regulation through independent commissions. Premised on the ideas of scientific inquiry and pragmatic truth testing, such flexible institutions showed initial promise but were quickly captured by the forces they were designed to control. The New Deal, initially a hastily conceived potpourri of programs designed to counter the effects of a devastating economic depression, developed into a more comprehensive program of social security that now protects most Americans from slipping into poverty in old age. Moreover, Roosevelt tried, as I explain in chapter 7, to introduce an extensive safety net by framing it in familiar language as a "second bill of rights." Although his effort failed, the programs made available to World War II veterans, especially expanded educational funding, launched the nation into a twenty-five-year era of decreasing inequality by helping to lift millions of white- and blue-collar workers and their families into the middle class.

Those years of intoxicating growth ended in the mid-1970s, when U.S. domination of the world economy skidded to a halt. That economic crisis, ominously, coincided with an ignominious defeat in Vietnam, a series of scandals that discredited and finally brought down Richard Nixon's presidency, and an uneasy truce in the stormy, decade-long cultural trench warfare waged over contested issues of race, gender, and personal expression.

Only at that point, and for a combination of reasons, did suspicion of government activity itself move from the margins of political discourse to the center of the Republican Party. The Great Society programs of the 1960s, although they had established the crucial egalitarian principle of government-funded health care through the Medicare and Medicaid programs, sparked a backlash. Their gestures toward providing racial justice through economic reforms, understandable at a time when the limited effects of civil rights legislation were becoming clear, backfired in explosive ways. Great Society programs interfered with the preferences of lower middle-class white home owners, who felt threatened by integration of their neighborhoods and their schools. Affirmative action guidelines challenged the hard-won control of job-training programs by white trade unions. Such threats provoked a volatile mix of resentment and anger that occasionally boiled over into violence but more often simmered until hardening into racial hatred.

The initiatives designed to achieve racial integration were conceived by idealists and implemented by social engineers whose commitments to political activity set them apart from the counterculture of the 1960s. Nevertheless, many Americans interpreted such programs as sharp departures from the Democratic Party's bread and butter, its New Deal heritage, and symbols of a new orientation. This new agenda seemed to signal a politics of liberation, and it provoked a deep cultural and political struggle. It appeared to align the federal government with forms of cultural subversion that did not originate in the black community, where cultural conservatism fed by various forms of religious devotion remained strong, but that nevertheless came to be associated with African Americans by conservatives who automatically associated drugs, sexual promiscuity, and rock music with a longstanding distrust of blacks and other marginalized groups. Hollywood and Madison Avenue contributed far more to glamorizing cultural radicalism than did those who suffered the consequences of the backlash it provoked.[19]

From that polarization arose the futile culture wars we inherit at the end of the twentieth century, in which rightwing talk-show hosts and academic radicals fling at each other increasingly stylized and pointless attacks and the public turns away in disgust from everyday electoral politics. Political discourse descends toward the level of the thirty-second attack ads that alienate voters from their targets without inspiring them to vote for their sponsors. Dispirited citizens confront a set of false choices about symbolic issues that are tangential to their genuine concerns. Opinion polls indicate that the public is far more willing to compromise on such issues as abortion, welfare, gun control, and crime than are politicians, with the result that the public's common sense finds little outlet in managed elections controlled by rival elites who respond only to the highly organized, well funded, and frequently dogmatic fringes of their parties.[20]

The puerile cynicism of American political commentary is fine for satirists, but it also infects the supposedly sophisticated commentary of major television and newspaper pundits. The assumption that all public servants—especially those in Washington—are fools or knaves erodes even the possibility that either party will succeed in mobilizing support for positive initiatives. Tax cutting and government bashing are the leitmotifs of Republicans such as Newt Gingrich, who take their inspiration from Ronald Reagan at his most Manichean: one evil empire down, one to go. Democrats are reduced to bashing Republicans for wanting to cut government programs slightly faster than they do—except for the most expensive (defense, Social Security, and Medicare), which benefit members of the middle class. Neither party will concede that government provides indispensable services that cost money. An infantile escapism seems to be seeping into public life. Although it would be folly to deny the presence of corruption, ineptitude, and good old chicanery in American politics past or present, our current disdain for politics is anomalous. Earlier generations of Americans acknowledged not only the potential corruption of government but also, more than occasionally, its potential as a force for good. A simple-minded optimism would be no improvement over the simple-minded cynicism liberals now wear as a shield against accusations of cornball sincerity. Detached from the stereoscopic vision that clarifies both the limits of what can be achieved through politics and the necessity of iron-willed determination in the face of those limits, liberalism can shrivel into sentimental whimpering or bland admonitions that Americans should be nicer to each other in shops and on sidewalks. Despite such risks, unhip reminders that earlier Americans occasionally found in public life sources of inspiration rather than comic relief might nevertheless be worthwhile.[21]

In recent years American political discourse has displayed a debilitating extremism. Too often, in popular commentary and in academic political theory, we contrast, soap-opera style, saints and sinners. The history of American political thought and activity suggests that we should take another tack. As these essays should make clear, most of our predecessors drew on multiple traditions to balance competing values in a genuinely conflict-ridden polity marked by disagreements over policy rooted in genuine differences of conviction. Those differences persist in the compromises that have been worked out because of the shared commitment to democratic procedures. From the Constitution and the Bill of Rights onward, we Americans have committed ourselves to the provisionality of our principles as well as our policies. Our fundamental laws enable and require us to reconsider our current course in light of our experience, just as Madison believed we should do. The government of the United States was thus committed to a kind of pragmatism and historical sensibility more than a century before Dewey, along with Charles Peirce, William James, and George Herbert Mead, counseled trading in dogmas for democratic experimentation. At no point—even, tragically, at the end of the Civil War—have the victories in American politics been complete, but neither have the defeats. Unsatisfying as that observation is, it testifies not only to the power of those with privilege but also to the continuing struggles waged by those committed to the ideals of equality and freedom for all citizens— those who have manifested in their writing and other forms of economic, political, and cultural activity the virtues of liberalism.

Many of us who came of age in America during the war in Vietnam urged our elders to stop seeing the world through a World War II–induced reflexive pro-Americanism. Can we now stop seeing our past through an equally distorting Vietnam-induced reflexive anti-Americanism? Can we acknowledge that indignation and cynicism too can obstruct critical understanding? In addition to facing the frequent sobering moments when power trumped justice, we should recover the signs of promise in our past. Historical analysis reveals not only the hard lessons of persistent inequality, and the evidence that undercuts one-dimensional characterizations of the limits or dogmas ascribed to liberals, but also the potential for instruction and even inspiration. For all of those reasons, as I argue in chapter 9, history matters to political theory.

"I find that the best virtue I have has in it some tincture of vice," wrote Michel de Montaigne in his *Essays*, and that perspective serves us well as we reflect on American politics. For the very reason that liberal and democratic ideas and institutions make possible the development of individual virtues, they also provide fertile conditions for the development of vices such as indifference and despair. "Moral absolutism," the Polish dissident Adam Michnik observes, "is a great strength for individuals and groups struggling against dictatorship," and so it has been for Americans struggling to forge a nation, fight a Civil War, and end systems of discrimination based on ascribed characteristics such as race, gender, sexuality, and disability. But, Michnik continues, "it is a weakness for individuals and groups" struggling to build democracies, because a democratic world is "eternal imperfection, a mixture of sinfulness, saintliness, and monkey business. That is why seekers of a moral state and of a perfectly just society do not like democracy." Against the vivid purity of moral absolutism, democracy, like liberalism, seems a muddy gray. "Yet only gray democracy, with its human rights, with institutions of civil society, can replace weapons with arguments."[22] Early nineteenth-century European visitors to the United States, not only but surely including Tocqueville, remarked repeatedly on the chaos and disorderliness of the American experiment in liberal democracy, where no voice was ever silent and no question was ever finally resolved. That messiness of course has made possible more than a few of the tinctures of vice Montaigne admitted, but it has also made possible the nurturing of virtues. If we think we can enjoy the latter without risking the former, we display the moral absolutism of dissidents without the maturity of shrewd liberal democrats such as Madison, Tocqueville, Lincoln, or King.

There is in the American record no better spokesman for the virtues of liberalism than the wise and wily grandfather of the protagonist in Ralph Waldo Ellison's *Invisible Man*. Notwithstanding the indisputable evidence of injustice, betrayal, and evil facing us as we examine the American cultural tradition, we should nevertheless heed his advice to "affirm the principle."[23] Like Langston Hughes's admonition to "KEEP YOUR HANDS ON THE PLOW! HOLD ON!" that is not the counsel of resignation but of resolution to persist despite obstacles. Such fortitude, requiring moral convictions without the luxury of moral absolutism, and such faith, requiring trust in the plan and pattern of democracy without the certainty that justice will result, are among the principal virtues of liberalism.

TWO

THE VIRTUES OF LIBERALISM

Christianity, Republicanism, and Ethics in Early American Political Discourse

HISTORIANS SOMETIMES FORGET that Dante reserved a special place in the Inferno for sowers of discord. Having spent their lives tearing apart families, communities, and religions, such lost souls spend eternity with a demon who slices their bodies in two. Their wounds do slowly heal, Dante tells us, but no sooner has "the gashed flesh reunited its grain" than their bodies are again split by the fiend's sharp sword. So it goes forever. A visitor from outside the circles of American colonial and early national history, observing the polemics in which partisans of competing interpretations carve each other up, might well wonder what students of American political culture have done to deserve a fate similar to the one Dante prescribed for schismatics. These disputes have continued to heat up through the mid-1980s.[1]

Readers who relish such controversies may be disappointed, but I do not intend in this essay to audition for the role of Dante's demon. Instead I hope to suggest a way out of our historiographical inferno by mapping what may appear to be a singularly unpromising escape route, a rediscovery of the virtues of liberalism. By examining the diverse sources of liberalism in the eighteenth century, I hope to demonstrate how and why liberal ideas could be joined with ideas from the different traditions of Protestant Christianity and classical republicanism at two decisive moments—when Americans were launching the Revolution and formulating the Constitution—and to suggest why the three streams have not always flowed together. In my conclusion, I will discuss the two themes of individual autonomy and popular sovereignty that were at the center of the American vision of politics during those years.

THE LAST THREE DECADES have yielded a wide variety of competing interpretations of the late eighteenth century. In the 1950s, Louis Hartz and Daniel Boorstin offered two verdicts on a common version of America's liberal tradition. In the

1960s, Bernard Bailyn and Gordon Wood explained why Americans were drawn to varieties of classical republicanism as they tried to separate from Britain and consolidate their revolution. In the 1970s, Henry F. May and Morton White led a squadron of intellectual historians who emphasized the importance of Scottish common sense philosophy in the complex of ideas that constituted America's version of the Enlightenment. Finally, in the 1980s, J. G. A. Pocock has reiterated and extended his earlier claims for the centrality of republicanism and the relative insignificance of John Locke's liberalism, while John Patrick Diggins has countered by resurrecting Hartz's search for an abusable past in a passionate indictment of an American liberalism that has lost its soul.[2]

Is this a trajectory of accumulating knowledge or a downward spiral of increasingly futile circularity? Have we learned anything from these competing interpretations, or do they simply cancel each other out? In light of the work that has been done since the 1960s in social and political history, it is possible to argue that at least a few conclusions remain standing when the smoke of rhetoric clears. Some of the grander claims appear untenable, other arguments appear increasingly solid, and certain methodological guidelines for studying ideas appear helpful. I will discuss these topics in reverse order.

First, it is now uncontroversial to conclude that the nonhistorical study of ideas is dead. Contributions from hermeneutics, from linguistically sensitive versions of Marxism, and from analytic philosophy have combined to demonstrate the fruitfulness of contextualist analysis and the uselessness of studying ideas detached from their historical settings. Moreover, despite some nostalgia for the promised neatness of structuralism, intellectual historians now tend to agree that, although patterns of discourse do provide frameworks for thought, such frameworks are historical rather than eternal. Discourse, in other words, shifts, often slowly, sometimes rapidly, but always unevenly, in response to the imaginative manipulation of language by creative thinkers confronting unprecedented problems. Prevailing theories of rationality suggest that individuals interpret the meaning of experience only slowly and imperfectly, because experience is always culturally mediated by the systems of symbols that render ideas and behavior significant. The meaning of the past emerges for historians in the same way, as we attempt to uncover progressively clearer understandings of what experience meant for earlier generations. Intellectual historians who insist on viewing the past from the angle of those who lived it tend to be equally impatient with the claims of Marxists and Whigs to understand grand patterns of development, because such patterns may distort our understanding by imposing meanings different from those that ideas had historically. Just as social historians have turned increasingly to the project of reconstructing the past as it was lived, so intellectual historians have tried to reconstruct ideas as they were thought, by trying to uncover what thinkers believed themselves to be doing—what they meant to be doing—when they wrote what they did.[3] This hermeneutical approach to historical inquiry does not rule out the attempt to find larger patterns of change. Indeed, that is precisely what I will try to do in this essay, as I sort through the various interpretations of early American political culture in search of a new perspective on some familiar problems. The hermeneutical approach merely requires that such interpretations be seen in terms of the meanings available in the past. These meanings are then examined critically in light of later developments, rather than through some lens designed to broaden or deepen perspectives in order to fit events into a preconceived pattern.

Shifting from method to content, it is possible to identify an emerging consensus among historians concerning the persistence of diversity in American patterns of thought and behavior during the colonial and early national periods. Partisans of both the republican and the liberal interpretations have identified strands of American political culture whose presence can no longer be convincingly denied. When Pocock all but dismisses liberalism, for example, or when Diggins dismisses republicanism, they ignore an increasingly impressive body of scholarship not merely suggesting, but showing, evidence of contrast and diversity. In this essay, after examining three different sources of colonial American ideas about virtue— religious, republican, and liberal—and suggesting inconsistencies within each source, I will indicate how their evident incompatibilities and quite different regional strengths could be muted precisely because of the tensions that persisted within each tradition.

Virtue in various forms lay at the heart of Christian doctrine. Between the discussion of the virtues in the *Summa theologica* of Thomas Aquinas and *The Nature of True Virtue* of Jonathan Edwards ran a string of less carefully constructed, but nonetheless powerfully influential, meditations on universal benevolence as the ideal of Christian ethical doctrine. Several of these meditations have recently attracted renewed attention through the work of Norman Fiering.[4] Outside New England, which is at the center of Fiering's vision, it seems likely that Christian concepts of virtue flowed through colonial American culture principally in the form of mainstream Anglicanism and a complementary secular literature. Other historians, again looking primarily at New England, have emphasized the importance of evangelicalism as a source of social and political unrest in eighteenth-century America. After a period in which both European and American historians tended to downplay the religious dimensions of eighteenth-century thought and presented it as a celebration of science and skepticism, recent work has concentrated on the persistence of either explicit or implicit religious ideals in the Enlightenment on both sides of the Atlantic, and especially on the corrosive effect of religious enthusiasm on prevailing patterns of deference. The "irrepressibly democratic dynamic in Protestant theology," to use Perry Miller's exuberant phrase for it, remained all too repressible in most American denominations until social tensions brought it bubbling to the surface in a variety of forms. The idea of the covenant, central to Puritan theology from the outset, contained a doctrine of participation that threatened hierarchical stability. Several recent studies have refined earlier hypotheses concerning the connection between the Great Awakening and the American Revolution. Although the pattern and timing varied by region and denomination, it seems clear that the dissenting tradition, which originally flourished in the eroding soil of community, was transplanted into a republican environment in which it continued to grow.[5]

Religion continued to contribute to the shaping of American culture in the eighteenth century, but the Christian notion of virtue was sufficiently expansive to contain contradictory ideas. Did the challenge to authority represented by the awakening involve the abrogation of all rules, or did New Light communities merely seek to reconstitute order on a purified foundation? Did the renewed emphasis on man's depravity signal the distance America had fallen from its lofty mission, or did it testify to the community's faithfulness to its original ideals? Did the commitment to God, "whom to serve is perfect freedom," require selfless obedience—or rather the individual's liberation from all merely earthly forms of authority? Different communities answered those questions in different ways, and their recognition of those disagreements only made their competing claims to Christian virtue more strident.

The presence of classical republicanism as a second tradition in American political discourse during the latter half of the eighteenth century is no longer in doubt. Reasonable people certainly will continue to disagree about the centrality or the pervasiveness of these ideas and to question who articulated republican arguments for what reasons and for how long. These are serious questions to which I will return. Classical republicans called for independent citizens to protect fragile civic virtue against the threat of corruption represented by the extension of executive power. Their ideal of a community, in which individuals define their interests in terms of the common good, figured prominently in the political literature produced in America, particularly between the end of the Seven Years' War and the ratification of the Constitution. A successful challenge to the work of Caroline Robbins, Bernard Bailyn, Gordon Wood, and others would not merely have to deny the legitimacy of their understanding of the role of ideas in historical change, it would also have to destroy the formidable mountain of evidence on which their arguments rest. Although republicanism was not the only vocabulary of virtue available to Americans concerned with political questions, it surely was one of the several vocabularies available to them.[6]

Yet just as the Christian ideal of virtue was both central and ambiguous, so the republican ideal of the virtuous citizen was fuzzy. Did classical republicans fear change and distrust popular government? Did they tolerate hierarchy, embrace Spartan simplicity, and encourage militarism? It would be a caricature of republicanism in Britain or America to identify those characteristics as essential to the classical tradition in all its many "court" and "country" forms. Yet one need look no further than Machiavelli to discover the problematical nature of an ideal inspired by the Renaissance fascination with *virtù*. Neither Montesquieu nor James Madison nor John Adams subscribed to a version of republican virtue that elevated the will to combat fortune above the individual's responsibility to adhere to the moral law. The powerful, although brief, appeal of republicanism as a weapon to be wielded against corruption seems clear enough. But its meaning for a nation attempting to establish itself on a foundation of natural rights, equality, and the pursuit of happiness proved a good deal murkier.[7]

The third tradition I want to consider is liberalism. Since the false trail left by Hartz has distracted us from the meanings of liberal virtue, Joyce Appleby's work has been especially valuable. As she has pointed out, liberalism first took shape in the battle against both the inherited patterns of social hierarchy and the economic ideas of mercantilism that together served as props for privilege in the seventeenth and eighteenth centuries. Diggins has quite properly insisted that unless we restore liberalism to our vision of American politics, the republican perception may become as static and one dimensional as the Hartzian view it set out to replace. But which liberalism should we recover? There is a liberal tradition that originated with Thomas Hobbes's hardheaded cynicism and developed into the market liberalism examined by Appleby and excoriated in C. B. Macpherson's study of possessive individualism. That liberalism failed to make rapid progress either in England or in America precisely because, in Appleby's words, it "rested upon a moral base so shallow as to threaten the whole complex of conventional religious precepts." Although such liberalism promised freedom, it "delivered most of the propertyless into the hands of a new master—the market." Given the persistence of both religious and republican ideas running directly counter to the "radical reductionism" of personality required for the acceptance of behavior motivated solely by economic considerations, the resistance this version of liberalism encountered in eighteenth-century England and America should occasion little surprise.[8]

But there was another liberal tradition, whose roots stretched to the sober Puritanism of Locke rather than the stark individualism of Hobbes. Largely through the work of John Dunn, we now have a portrait that rescues the historical Locke from Macpherson's cartoon. The persuasiveness of Dunn's argument derives largely from his insistence that we take Locke on his own terms, instead of imposing on him meanings gathered from the social consequences of capitalism. His concept of individual liberty dissolves if it is removed from the context of divinely established natural law, which encumbers the freedom of individuals at every turn with the powerful commands of duty. Locke's belief in a natural law discernible by reason led him to condemn the unregulated pursuit of self-interest that Hobbes considered natural and that later writers who celebrated a market economy sanctioned. "He that has not a mastery over his inclinations," Locke wrote in 1687, "he that knows not how to resist the importunity of present pleasure, or pain, for the sake of what, reason tells him, is fit to be donne, wants the true principle of Vertue, and industry; and is in danger never to be good for anything."[9]

The recent emphasis on the pervasiveness of Scottish common sense philosophy in the American Enlightenment has been as important as the recognition that natural law provided the screen on which Locke projected his political ideas. Locke's Christianity may have shielded him from the unsettling implications of his empiricist epistemology, but those implications became apparent in David Hume's skepticism. The attractiveness of such thinkers as Francis Hutcheson, Adam Ferguson, Thomas Reid, and Dugald Stewart for Americans can be explained by their ability to reassure anxious religious sensibilities. Different Scots appealed to different Americans, as Henry May and others have shown. Despite their disagreements, the Scottish philosophers did share a commitment to the accountability of the individual to the community, and that commitment appealed to Americans as much as did their comforting theories of knowledge. Even Hume, whose social ideas betrayed no trace of sentimentality, conceded that "a tendency to public good, and to the promoting of peace, harmony, and order in society does, always, by affecting the benevolent principles of our frame, engage us on the side of the social virtues." Hume derived this argument from imagination and custom rather than reason; thus his approach differed from those of writers who grounded moral sense on feelings, with Hutcheson, or on rational intuition, with Reid.[10]

The Scottish Enlightenment was dedicated to discovering methods by which a provincial culture could create forms of social virtue without having to rely on republican political institutions unavailable to a province that was, like America, uncomfortable with its status. Thus the Scots turned to local, cultural, and, most notably, economic forms of association as potential fields for the cultivation of virtuous community life. The most influential of their efforts, of course, identified the mysterious workings of an invisible hand capable of transforming even the activity of the least virtuous into socially constructive behavior. As students of Adam Smith, including Jacob Viner, Donald Winch, and Richard Teichgraeber, have emphasized, Smith did not seek to establish the workability of a market economy to make possible the unchecked exercise of self-interest in the pursuit of wealth. Smith aimed instead to make possible, through ingeniously anti-utopian methods, a world of both plenty and justice. Barriers restricting freedom and ensuring poverty would yield to market mechanisms facilitating general prosperity. Smith worked within two contexts, the tradition of natural law articulated by Grotius and Pufendorf and reworked by Smith's mentor Hutcheson and the tradition of political economy established in late seventeenth-century England by the critics of mercantilism. The cold comfort enjoyed by later generations liberated from what E. P. Thompson and others have called the "moral economy" of precapitalist England has caused us to lose sight of Smith's intent. Just as Locke's enterprise is misunderstood when his liberalism serves as the midwife of possessive individualism, so Smith's purpose is distorted when the market mechanism he envisioned as a means to a moral end is presented as itself the goal of political economy. This interpretation of the *Wealth of Nations* resolves the thorniest part of the Adam Smith problem by suggesting that Smith expected a market economy to make possible the virtue he examined in *The Theory of Moral Sentiments*: "How selfish soever man may be supposed, there are evidently some principles in his nature, which interest him in the fortune of others, and render their happiness necessary to him, though he derives nothing from it, except the pleasure of seeing it." This concept of benevolence, flowing from the springs of natural law that fed Locke's liberalism, as well as various streams of Protestantism in America, thus played as large a part in Smith's philosophy as it did in those versions of

Scottish common sense that figured more directly in eighteenth-century American thought.[11]

Yet just as religious and republican ideas contained ambiguities blurring implicit inconsistencies, so tension remained latent even in versions of liberalism oriented more toward ideals of virtue than toward simple acquisitiveness. Could Locke's theory of money as the symbol of tacit consent, for example, justify forms of property holding that threatened the natural right of the poor to survive? Were Locke's strictures against extravagant accumulation incompatible with the legitimacy he accorded any social arrangements that earned popular assent? Did the Scottish philosophers expect man's innate moral sense to provide a standard that would rule out any social order resting on exploitation, or did they suppose instead that the impulse toward benevolence would suffice as a brake on oppression regardless of the form of economic organization? Finally, by identifying the inadvertently beneficial effects of consumption, did Smith encourage the prodigality scorned by earlier generations devoted to the Protestant ethic? In every case it seems clear that a gap separated the intentions of liberal thinkers from the world of possessive individualism that eventually emerged. Nevertheless, the inversion of means and ends that accompanied the process Max Weber described as the replacement of substantive rationality by instrumental rationality did lead to the rise of a mentality giving priority to consuming over producing, and to wealth over virtue. Istvan Hont and Michael Ignatieff have shown how the development of the concept of property in the transformation of natural jurisprudence from Aquinas to Grotius, and then from Locke to Smith, steadily attenuated the legitimate claims of the poor on the rich. Ironically, only when widespread prosperity seemed at last a possibility did recognition of the residual rights of the poor disappear.[12]

Thus the ideas that sailed to America during the seventeenth and eighteenth centuries were rich in diversity and in ambiguity. Montesquieu was only confirming what contemporaries already knew when he distinguished, in *The Spirit of the Laws*, between three sorts of virtue—Christian, political, and moral. With neatness of a sort that usually makes historians uneasy, they conform to the ideas of virtue in the traditions of religious, republican, and Scottish common sense philosophy. Not only were those conceptions of virtue not clearly compatible, as Montesquieu pointed out, there were inconsistencies within each of the three traditions as well, as I have tried to make clear. When Americans feverishly debated their future in the second half of the eighteenth century, they had available to them three distinguishable, if not altogether discrete, vocabularies of virtue. Each was unsteady enough by itself, but when combined they became unpredictably explosive. In America, moreover, an "inadvertent pluralism" emerged from the interaction of diverse cultures and the experimentation encouraged by the existence of opportunity. Because the roots of recently transplanted traditions were comparatively shallow, testing new alternatives was an attractive option in the colonies. Perhaps for that reason different intellectual and cultural patterns tended to rearrange themselves, or even to merge, rather than remaining altogether separate.

Regional differentiation further enriched the blend of diverse ideas and experience. Although not without exceptions, the first settlers of New England embraced ideals of social cohesion and patterns of precommercial agriculture. The middle colonies, culturally and intellectually more heterogeneous, were from the beginning less stable socially, and they more rapidly developed economic diversification and commercial farming. The southern colonies, founded by adventurers and called to order by a planter oligarchy, lacked both the restraints imposed by piety and community in New England and the experience of flexibility and fragmentation in the middle colonies. Further complicating this already crazy quilt is the increasing emphasis social historians have placed on change and on religious, political, and socioeconomic diversity in colonial America. The explosion of research since the 1960s has demolished simple pictures of a stable prerevolutionary America, and it is now apparent not only how diverse were the patterns of experience in different regions but also how complicated were the processes of development. Established forms of behavior persisted uneasily alongside innovations, as experience altered the cultures the colonists brought with them from Europe. Ideas have different meanings in different contexts, and as various religious, political, and ethical assumptions encountered the social and economic realities of life in a new and rapidly changing world, the potential meanings of virtue grew exponentially.[13]

It was precisely this variety of ideas that enabled the colonists to converge in the 1760s in opposition to British efforts to reassert the Crown's authority. Because of the ambiguities of the traditions from which they drew, and because of the unsteadiness and the inconsistencies of the arguments they advanced, they were able to join together behind a banner of ideas stitched together from three different sources: religious, republican, and liberal. I will be able to suggest only briefly how these traditions figured in revolutionary thinking. While the most ambitious claims for a tight causal connection between religious enthusiasm and political rebellion have not survived careful scrutiny, historians have shown how Puritan millennialism in the north, and Baptist evangelicalism in the south, could join forces with more secular forms of radicalism. Through participation in symbolic communal activities, colonists were able to put aside their differences and unite—however briefly—against the British. The galvanizing effect on American thinking of the second set of ideas I have isolated—classical republicanism—needs little discussion. The pamphlets of the revolution spoke the language of civic humanism as clearly as they spoke the language of dissenting Protestantism, and the evidence that the two languages coexisted in revolutionary political discourse is incontrovertible. As for Locke and Scottish moral philosophy, it seems clear both that these ideas were not the entire story, as used to be argued, and that they were not irrelevant, as it was popular to contend in the 1970s. It should not surprise us that the intricacies of philosophers' arguments rarely surfaced in broadsides designed to arouse patriots to war. For those gentry who traveled the road to independence via what May called the Moderate Enlightenment, however, such ideas made a decisive difference. Moreover, understanding that central document of the Revolution, the Declaration of Independence, as Morton White has demonstrated more persuasively than Garry Wills, requires seeing it against the background of natural rights philosophy and Scottish common sense.[14]

In articles published over the last two decades, Appleby has given a distinctive twist to the argument for the importance of liberalism in American revolutionary ideology. She concedes that a "regenerative republicanism" was part of the ferment leading to rebellion, but she insists that "deliverance from the strictures of classical republicanism came from the ideology of liberalism, from a belief in a natural harmony of benignly striving individuals saved from chaos by the stability worked into nature's own design." This liberalism, she concludes, "not only justified a revolution against an intrusive sovereign, it also offered ordinary people an escape from the self-denying virtue of their superiors." These passages, from her essay "The Social Origins of American Revolutionary Ideology," illustrate that at times Appleby has carefully qualified the nature of the liberalism she imputes to American revolutionaries. Theirs was a liberalism rooted in the natural law tradition and informed by Scottish moral sense philosophy, precisely the liberalism White discovered in *The Philosophy of the American Revolution*.[15]

Thomas Jefferson was optimistic about the harmonious interaction of self-interested individuals only because he believed their inner moral gyroscopes would prevent them from oppressing one another. Jefferson was a liberal who defined self-interest as Locke's virtue rather than Hobbes's possessive individualism. In his meditation on the "foundation of morality in man," Jefferson distinguished benevolence from egoism. "Self-love, therefore, is no part of morality. ... It is the sole antagonist of virtue, leading us constantly by our propensities to self-gratification in violation of our moral duties to others. ... [N]ature hath implanted in our breasts a love of others, a sense of duty to them, a moral instinct, in short, which prompts us irresistibly to feel and to succor their distresses." Jefferson went on to describe the utility of this moral sense, but he defined utility in terms of benevolence rather than vice versa, and his ethics was thus unrelated to the utilitarianism of eighteenth-century philosophers such as Jeremy Bentham. Jefferson believed that his theories of moral sense and natural rights were consistent with the available empirical evidence about man, but they were grounded more solidly in Hutcheson's intuitionism than in the behavior of Virginia planters. Indeed, the contrast between those theories and actual politics illustrates what Diggins has called the "pathos of the Enlightenment," the distance separating principles from practice that explains the failure of such American revolutionaries as Jefferson to repudiate slavery.[16]

Jefferson was hardly the only American to embrace this conception of liberalism. The constraints it included, the characteristics that distinguished it from the laissez-faire liberalism that developed in the nineteenth century, must be kept in mind. As John E. Crowley has emphasized, economic life in America was generally discussed within a religious framework. Even Benjamin Franklin, that notoriously calculating embodiment of the spirit of capitalism, sought only the degree of comfort midway between destitution and extravagance, and he too offered religious rather than economic reasons for his activities. Also jostling alongside the natural rights liberalism that informed much economic argument were competing ideas drawn from the older English idea of "moral economy" and the new egalitarianism of Tom Paine, both of which figured prominently in the writings of urban artisans in the revolutionary years. Finally, Forrest McDonald has demonstrated, in his study *Novus Ordo Seclorum*, the presence of a wide range of additional limits, including the natural jurisprudential tradition, the English common law, and various colonial American legal practices, that further held in check the appearance of an unrestrained market capitalism. For all these reasons, it would be a mistake to exaggerate the attractiveness of purely individualistic, proto-capitalist behavior during the 1770s.[17]

Reflecting on the ideas present and absent in those years, I believe we ought to think of autonomy rather than freedom as the aim of the American Revolution—autonomy not only for the nation but for individuals as well. The concept of autonomy, in its everyday as well as its Kantian sense, is inseparable from the concept of self-government and inseparable from the nuances of restraint, law, and moral responsibility that may be missed in the ambiguity of freedom as an idea divisible into negative as well as positive forms. Americans sought independence as a nation to secure autonomy as individuals.[18]

The unity achieved during the Revolution dissolved quickly during the 1780s—almost as quickly as historical syntheses of the period have tended to dissolve. I will not attempt to bring order to the chaos of the critical period because that chaos reflected the persistence of the disagreements present in colonial America and suppressed, but hardly resolved, during the war for independence. Before examining the persistence of diversity and the intensification of ideological and regional disputes in the 1790s, however, I want to discuss one idea Americans could agree upon after securing autonomy through successful revolution. That idea was popular sovereignty, the location in the people themselves of the ultimate decision-making authority for the new nation. The American decision to appeal beyond the traditional rights of Englishmen to the rights of men, their decision to reject the definition of government as the sovereignty of an executive in a legislature, has been described by Pocock as "the most profound breach ever to have occurred in an anglophone political practice." Robert R. Palmer, J. R. Pole, Gordon Wood, and Forrest McDonald have all identified the doctrine of popular sovereignty as the decisive achievement of the American political imagination.[19]

It is clear that the idea of popular sovereignty grew from the colonial experience of self-government. It is sobering to realize, as Michael Kammen has pointed out, how poorly we understand what the colonists thought they were doing when they embarked on that venture by establishing representative institutions. Again regional variations must be acknowledged. Timothy H. Breen has shown how New England Puritans held the electorate responsible for the quality of government and demanded from citizens more than mere obedience. Even when political questions became increasingly secularized in the eighteenth century, arguments in New England continued to reflect a mixture of concerns about property and concerns about piety and responsibility. In Pennsylvania, the assembly claimed powers more extensive than those of any other colonial legislature; it resisted temptations to compare itself to the House of Commons because that might mean reducing its powers vis-à-vis the executive. Yet according to John M. Murrin, this swaggering legislature was probably less active in exercising its elaborate powers than any other colonial representative assembly. Finally, in Virginia, the activities of the assembly consolidated citizens' rights while stabilizing a system of exploitation. Even if, to follow Pole's revision of Edmund S. Morgan's formulation, American freedom served as a means of guaranteeing American slavery, it also served as a means of guaranteeing the survival of republicanism in practice as well as in theory. Despite differences in regional political habits, it was above all the experience of self-government that enabled the colonists to fight the war for independence, to survive the critical period, and to create the federal republic. Yet the growth of representative institutions in America was as accidental as the fragmented form national political authority finally assumed as the new nation sought to accommodate the competing demands of the states. The triumph of popular sovereignty represented a watershed in the theory as well as the practice of politics. As Martyn P. Thompson has pointed out, the tension between competing efforts to establish fundamental law on the basis of either history or reason dissolved once the foundation of governmental authority was located in the people. Instead of grounding law on either ancient custom, on the one hand, or the logical fiction of a contract, on the other, American proponents of popular sovereignty followed the lead of Montesquieu and Rousseau by replacing the idea of fundamental law with the idea of the public will as the legitimating principle of the republic. Its haphazard development notwithstanding, the idea of popular sovereignty, rooted firmly in experience, had a universal appeal. It seemed to represent at once the fulfillment of the Puritan concept of the covenant, the republican idea of a public-spirited citizenry, and the liberal idea of responsibly self-interested individuals exercising their right to self-government.[20]

All three of the traditions apparent in colonial American political thought persisted into the 1790s, but the relations among them altered as the tensions within each tradition changed. The ideal of austere Christian virtue that had inspired and haunted Edwards lingered in the form of the jeremiad. Increasingly, though, as the nineteenth century dawned, American Protestantism accommodated itself to a comfortable position as guardian of a new, more privatized virtue characterized above all by propriety, the centerpiece of what would become the genteel tradition. Evangelicals bemoaned the smug worldliness of Americans, and at least some of their enthusiasm assumed a militaristic form that enabled them to reenact, in style if hardly in substance, the glorious struggle of God's chosen people against the popish plots of King George and Archbishop Laud.

If religious divisions during the 1790s did not fit neatly into the emerging pattern of party alignments, neither did the divisions among those who remained drawn toward varieties of classical republicanism. Although John Adams and Alexander Hamilton continued to use the republican vocabulary, the bitterness of their rivalry makes it apparent that they did not always speak the same language or see the same future for Federalism.[21]

The Jeffersonians were no less contentious. In a review of Appleby's provocative *Capitalism and a New Social Order*, John Ashworth pointed out that many of the disputes concerning Jeffersonian ideology turn on questions of definition and selection. What is to count as republicanism? Which republicans were Jeffersonians, and vice versa? For Drew McCoy, James Madison serves as the archetypal Jeffersonian republican. For Lance Banning, John Taylor's pamphlets are "probably the most important source for an understanding of Republican thought in the middle 1790s." For Appleby, Taylor, a classical republican from the "country" mold, is not a Jeffersonian republican at all.[22]

If republicanism is defined as backward-looking elitism opposed to commerce and economic growth, then clearly many Jeffersonians were not republicans. As Banning concedes, any attempt to depict the "thought of Americans in the 1790s as encapsulated in the conceptual world of Montesquieu's civic humanism" would be a serious error. Proponents of the republican hypothesis, Banning protests, specifically deny "that either English oppositionists or Jeffersonian Republicans identified their enemies as those involved in manufacturing or commerce." McCoy's *The Elusive Republic*, as Banning accurately points out, emphasizes again and again the transformation of the republican tradition in the 1790s. Madison and his allies repudiated the ideal of a "Christian Sparta" and embraced commercial agriculture and economic growth as the salvation of the American republic. Although worried about the consequences of that growth, they worked diligently to make it happen. "Recent scholarship," Banning concludes, "often actually *insists* on American departures from received ideas, most especially on American hostility to privilege and American rejection of 'the distinctions of class and rank whose balancing played so central a role in classical republicanism.' This scholarship should not be condemned as though the authors claimed that an entire, unchanging, civic-humanist tradition persisted into the new republic. Such criticism charges it with errors never made." I suspect that partisans of the liberal hypothesis such as Appleby have derived a measure of satisfaction from such remarks, since their challenges to the more extreme formulations of the republican argument—for example, those Pocock continues to make on occasion—have now elicited such a useful clarification.[23]

Yet the ideal of civic virtue, although transformed by the experiences of fighting the Revolution, writing the Constitution, and facilitating the expansion of commercial agriculture, did persist in Jeffersonian discourse. A crucial passage from Madison's speech before the Virginia ratifying convention, June 20, 1788, underscores this point.

> I have observed, that gentlemen suppose, that the general legislature will do every mischief they possibly can, and that they will omit to do every thing good which they are authorised to do. If this were a reasonable supposition, their objections would be good. I consider it reasonable to conclude, that they will as readily do

their duty, as deviate from it: Nor do I go on the grounds mentioned by gentlemen on the other side—that we are to place unlimited confidence in them, and expect nothing but the most exalted integrity and sublime virtue. But I go on this great republican principle, that the people will have virtue and intelligence to select men of virtue and wisdom. Is there no virtue among us? If there be not, we are in a wretched situation. No theoretical checks—no form of government can render us secure. To suppose that any form of government will secure liberty or happiness without any virtue in the people, is a chimerical idea. If there be sufficient virtue and intelligence in the community, it will be exercised in the selection of these men. So that we do not depend on their virtue, or put confidence in our rulers, but in the people who are to choose them.

Madison's argument illuminates his ideas on the relation between the structure of the federal republic and the necessity of a virtuous citizenry. As this passage indicates, Madison was a realist but not a cynic. *The Federalist* No. 10 and No. 57 likewise suggest that Madison considered the separation of powers a necessary, but not sufficient, condition to ensure what he called "the common good of the society."[24]

This idea of civic virtue did not die with the ratification of the Constitution, as Ralph Ketcham demonstrates in his study of presidential leadership in the early republic. Ketcham emphasizes the classical sources of the idea of the president as a nonpartisan patriot king, exercising leadership by appealing to citizens' moral sensibilities rather than pandering to narrow conceptions of self-interest. Of course something was gained when the chaotic democracy of Andrew Jackson replaced that more refined conception of what politics ought to be about, but something, namely the republican ideal of civic virtue, was also lost.[25]

If the idea of a common good continued to animate the republicanism of at least some Jeffersonians—and some Federalists—during the last decade of the eighteenth century, did the third tradition, the tradition of liberalism based on responsibility rather than cupidity, also survive? At least for a short time, for what might be called a Jeffersonian moment, it did, and its memory has lingered into the present. This liberalism is not to be confused with the liberal tradition that served as Hartz's whipping boy or with Macpherson's possessive individualism, and it also seems somewhat different from the economic individualism to which Appleby has directed our attention. Recovering the virtues of this liberalism is important if we wish to understand the peculiar vitality of American democratic theory. As Appleby argued persuasively in *Capitalism and a New Social Order*, Jeffersonians in the 1790s sought to effect two related revolutions, both premised on the idea of equality. The first was economic. It was to be accomplished by an expansion of commercial farming that would bring greater prosperity and equality of opportunity. The second was political. It was to be accomplished by dismantling the politics of deference and encouraging the active political participation of all men. The surprising congruence between these two aims and the aims of McCoy's Madisonian republicans should be clear enough. As he wrote in *The Elusive Republic*,

American republicans valued property in land primarily because it provided personal independence. The individual with direct access to the productive resources of nature need not rely on other men, or any man, for the basic means of existence. The Revolutionaries believed that every man had a natural right to this form of property, in the sense that he was entitled to autonomous control of the resources that were absolutely necessary for his subsistence. The personal independence that resulted from the ownership of land permitted a citizen to participate responsibly in the political process, for it allowed him to pursue spontaneously the common or public good, rather than the narrow interest of the men—or the government—on whom he depended for his support. Thus the Revolutionaries did not intend to provide men with property so that they might flee from public responsibility into a selfish privatism; property was rather the necessary basis for a committed republican citizenry.[26]

If McCoy is right, and I think he is, and if Appleby is right, and I think she is, then McCoy's republicans and Appleby's liberals were all struggling to achieve autonomy as economic individuals and the right to equal political participation as citizens. When this revised republicanism is viewed in its postrevolutionary American context, and when this restrained liberalism is appreciated in its ethical and political as well as economic depth, as a way of thinking rooted in the natural jurisprudential tradition inherited by Locke and the Scottish moral philosophers, then at least the potential coexistence of the two traditions becomes apparent.

Liberal republicans, in Appleby's words, "endowed American capitalism with the moral force of their vision of a social order of free and independent men. The vision itself was grounded in the particular promise of prosperity held out to Americans at the end of the eighteenth century." Banning's charge that Appleby has exaggerated her portrait of republicanism by presenting it as backward looking and anti-egalitarian may be correct, but his own portrait of liberalism as a celebration of the "unrestrained pursuit of private interests" is also one-sided. His portrait depends, as Banning notes, on Macpherson's analysis of possessive individualism. That is certainly one face of liberal capitalism, the Hobbesian face that becomes more familiar as the nineteenth century progresses. But it is not the only face liberalism has worn. Appreciating the role earlier liberals played in a world breaking free from feudal hierarchies and mercantilist economic assumptions may help us understand why they considered themselves rebels with a moral cause.[27]

Unfortunately for this vision of historical harmony, time did not stand still with the election of Jefferson to the presidency in 1800. Instead, Dante's demon appeared, sword in hand. The continuing development of the contradictory religious, political, and economic tendencies apparent in the 1790s gradually destroyed the bonds that might have linked an optimistic and egalitarian republicanism to an ethically attuned and democratically alert liberalism. The latent inconsistencies between Locke's theory of rights and his theory of money, for example, and between Smith's moral philosophy and his political economy, became manifest when social and economic change upset their unsteady equilibrium. The masters and journeymen who had flocked to Jefferson's republicanism divided into capitalists and industrial workers, the Second Great Awakening challenged the notion of a self-regulating secular order driven by calculating but benevolent individuals, and southern Jeffersonians gradually retreated into the stronghold of interest politics to defend their peculiar institution.

Franklin wrote that "only a virtuous people are capable of freedom." The American record in the early nineteenth century suggests that a free people may be incapable of virtue. During those years the meaning of virtue lost its earlier religious, civic, and ethical significance and became a label for bourgeois propriety or feminine purity. When independence lost its identification with benevolence, when self-interest was no longer conceived in relation to the egalitarian standard Jefferson upheld—in his theory if not in his practice—then freedom itself, especially the freedom to compete in the race for riches without the restraint of natural law, became an obstacle in the way of justice. That process is, of course, the story of the nineteenth century, and the growing dissatisfaction with the societies spawned by such freedom fueled the reform movements that appeared on both sides of the Atlantic. But it is important to appreciate the sequence of these developments in order to understand the cunning of freedom. Laissez-faire liberalism was not present at the creation of the American republic but took shape over the course of the nation's first hundred years.[28]

The significance of ideas can change dramatically over time. The ideas of autonomy and popular sovereignty had explosive force in a world emerging from the assumptions and institutions of early modern European culture, but their meaning proved to be quite different when used to legitimate conditions in urban industrial America. We must avoid reading back into the struggles of the eighteenth century contending forces that did not appear until later.

My interpretation of the intermingling of religious, republican, and liberal themes in the political culture of America in the late eighteenth century, which emphasizes the distance between the ethical thrust of such ideas and the flattened discourse of much nineteenth-century individualism and democracy, rests primarily on my reading of the meaning of the ideas of autonomy and popular sovereignty. Autonomy meant the combination of personal independence and moral responsibility that was central to the ideas of John Locke and Adam Smith, James Madison and Thomas Jefferson. It was autonomy that Samuel Harrison Smith, co-winner of the American Philosophical Society's prize for an essay on the sort of education appropriate to a republic, seems to have been seeking. The new nation, Smith wrote, required educational works "defining correctly political, moral, and religious duty." Only if American educators could instill such feelings of responsibility would "the radical ideas we have already established, and which are in great measure peculiar to us," be sufficient to secure "the virtue and happiness of the United States." In short, autonomy meant balancing the radical ideas of freedom and equality with the demands of duty.[29]

Popular sovereignty meant the commitment to representative government as a form uniquely attractive because of its openendedness. Although few Americans seem to have echoed Jefferson's blithe endorsement of periodic revolutions to water liberty's tree, many did believe that the new nation should commit itself unwaveringly to the principle of change. The principle of popular sovereignty was consistent with that belief. In the words of James Wilson, "This revolution principle—that, the sovereign power residing in the people, they may change their constitution whenever they please—is . . . not a principle of discord, rancour, or war: it is a principle of melioration, contentment, and peace." That dimension of the doctrine of popular sovereignty in America comes into focus when the American conception of democracy as an endless series of provisional approximations of the public interest is contrasted with the ideas embodied in the French Revolution. In an essay published in 1971, Appleby recounted the strange career of unicameralism in France and America. She pointed out that the fear of perpetuating a hierarchical system prevented French revolutionaries from accepting the division of authority symbolized by a bicameral legislature. Americans were persuaded to accept that division, Wood has shown, not for the reasons advanced by John Adams—reasons reflecting longstanding assumptions about necessarily different social orders—but instead because both houses of the legislature, like the various levels of authority preserved in the federal structure, were grounded on the bedrock of popular sovereignty. The fragmentation of authority institutionalized by the U.S. Constitution reflected the reality and the ideals of a wildly diverse, pluralistic society.[30]

In France, by contrast, the violent twists and turns of the Revolution can best be understood as a search for unitary authority. The Terror was not a reflection of the ideas of Rousseau. Roger Masters has argued persuasively that the *Social Contract* should be read as a warrant for popular government in which the general will is nothing more ominous than the assertion of the people's sovereign authority embodied in a constitution expressing their fundamental purposes. Robespierre translated Rousseau's call for virtue into terror not because the *Social Contract* pointed in a direction different from Adams's *Thoughts on Government* or Jefferson's Declaration of Independence, but because in France the splintering of opinions that was a fact of life in America simply proved too great a threat to the Revolution. As François Furet made clear, the legacy of the ancien régime imposed on the Revolution an unavoidable burden. The Republic had to establish a unitary and authoritative "opinion" in place of the chaos of "opinions" that bubbled up from the contradictory pressures of popular protest. Although many of Rousseau's later interpreters have doubted that he thought the conflict between private virtue and public virtue could be ended through politics, Robespierre was confident that the French republic could accomplish precisely that. "Man is good, as he comes from the hands of nature," Robespierre proclaimed; "if he is corrupt, the responsibility lies with vicious social institutions." If constructing new institutions that would not merely make possible, but require, both private and public virtue was indeed the goal of the Revolution, then the Terror represents not an aberration but a logical extension of the desire to reconstitute absolute authority on the basis of the public will.[31]

The genius of Rousseau and Madison lay in their realization that the public spirit they sought was in tension with—Rousseau may even have considered it antithetical to—the personal independence of democratic man. Rousseau, in the *Social Contract*, and Madison, in his writings and speeches on the Constitution, were looking for different ways to ease that tension.[32] Both republics failed to find the solution these theorists sought. In France, as Robespierre's life and death showed, that tension was resolved in ways that threatened the survival of democratic individuals and elevated the power of public authority. In America, as Alexis de Tocqueville understood, that tension was resolved in ways that elevated the power of democratic individuals and threatened the survival of public authority.

In conclusion, American revolutionaries committed themselves to a pair of principles that held out a formidable challenge to the new nation. Gordon Wood is surely right that American political debate narrowed in the nineteenth century, and Joyce Appleby is also right that the Jeffersonian moment of an equal commitment to material and moral progress was short-lived. But the principles of autonomy and popular sovereignty had been enshrined, and they exerted a powerful hold on the American imagination. When the challenge of socialism emerged in the nineteenth century, it was not so much co-opted by a liberal consensus as it was preempted by the nation's own prior commitment to liberty and equality. While debate may have narrowed, the breadth and depth of the ideas of autonomy and popular sovereignty enabled American reformers for the next two centuries to expand it again by appealing to the stated ideals of the Republic.[33]

Taken together, and understood in all of their ethical and political dimensions, the ideas of autonomy and popular sovereignty were the virtues of liberal republicanism. It is one of the most familiar maxims of La Rochefoucauld that "our virtues are frequently but vices in disguise." In American politics, our vices have instead been virtues in disguise, because it was only by securing liberty and democracy in the eighteenth century that Americans became capable of developing the irresponsible individualism and the erosive factionalism of the nineteenth and twentieth centuries. Emphasizing the original meaning of these ideas may help explain the perennial appeal of Jefferson and Madison for Americans puzzled by the disjunction between the world we experience—a world of dependency and inequality—and the promise of autonomy and popular sovereignty. In sum, recovering these ideas may help us understand, even if it cannot help us recapture, the early alliance between the virtues of republicanism and the virtues of liberalism.

THREE

KNOWLEDGE AND BELIEF IN
AMERICAN PUBLIC LIFE

K NOWLEDGE IS NOT WHAT it used to be. Almost three decades have passed
since Thomas Kuhn first rocked the confidence of the scientific community
by explaining scientific revolutions in terms of paradigm shifts rather than as
straightforward advances in knowledge. Since that time, students of the human
sciences have followed Kuhn's lead, teaching us to speak less of progress than of
historicity, less of certainty than of undecidability, less of explanation than of
thick description, less of universals than of prejudices, forms of life, and communities of discourse. Foundations have evaporated across the disciplines; establishing authoritative claims has grown increasingly problematical as all knowledge has fallen under the scrutiny of a hermeneutics of suspicion. An erstwhile
Kantian such as John Rawls can join hands with a former Marxist such as Alasdair MacIntyre in denying even the possibility of disclosing timeless truths; postfoundationalists turn instead toward a choice among competing traditions, whose
claims "for us" should not be confused with any pretense to transcendental status. Where once the human sciences as fervently as the natural sciences aspired
to certain truths universally acknowledged, we can now only watch as knowledge
appears to recede beyond the horizon of inquiry.[1]

Belief, by contrast, may be making a modest comeback. The popular press
mirrors the scholarly community in paying renewed and even respectful attention
to the claims of faith. Divinity schools are flourishing, courses and books dealing with all sorts of religion proliferate, and even religious observance appears to
be slowly increasing in some denominations.[2] In this essay, I discuss three sets
of issues. First, I briefly review recent historical literature on the relation between
knowledge and belief in American public life from the eighteenth century to the
present. Second, I discuss the indigenous origins of postfoundationalism in the
writings of William James and John Dewey, and I examine their rather different
ideas concerning the role of faith in pragmatic conceptions of truth. Finally, I reflect on the continuing attractiveness of a particular, historically rooted concep-

tion of the proper relation between rationalism and religion in American culture. Since much recent poststructuralist thought challenges the very possibility of knowledge conceived within the framework of Enlightenment rationalism, it might seem self-evident that religion, the eighteenth-century philosophers' whipping boy, would be increasingly implausible. Perhaps paradoxically, that is not the case, for reasons I suggest later.

Historical Perspectives

In his contribution to a collection of essays entitled *Religion and Twentieth-Century American Intellectual Life*, theologian David Tracy contrasts "the two classic traditions of the American experiment." He characterizes the Enlightenment tradition as "fundamentally a tradition of reason based on argument." The other tradition, "the Puritan covenental tradition, is, like all religious traditions, grounded in conversation with particular religious classics."[3] Tracy argues that in America's public sphere both traditions mingled, and he calls for the continuation of exchanges between the community of inquiry pursuing the Enlightenment tradition of knowledge and the community of interpretation pursuing the religious tradition of belief. This formulation, although sensible, does not go far enough: until quite recently, it has been all but impossible to separate, even for purposes of analysis, the strands of rationalism and religion in American thought or American politics. "Our tradition," to invoke the phrase favored by postfoundationalists such as Richard Rorty, has been formed by continuously intertwined communities of inquiry and communities of interpretation.

For much of the twentieth century, prevailing historical interpretations of America emphasized either the progressive view of economic conflict or the consensus view of substantial agreement on the principles of liberal individualism. In either case, historians tended to assume that economic self-interest was the bedrock of American culture. When the new social history emerged in the 1960s to challenge prevailing conceptions, historians' focus shifted from elites to previously ignored groups. For a time the emphasis on economic questions persisted, but in the last two decades historians have gradually altered their perspective. Taking their cues increasingly from cultural anthropology and philosophical hermeneutics, historians have become more concerned with the phenomenology of historical experience. As they have sought to understand the past as it was lived, in addition to continuing their efforts to explain how the present emerged from it, historians have found themselves confronting everywhere the clear evidence of religiosity. As history has become increasingly a quest for meanings, as well as structures and causes, the role of religion has become more central, because it is impossible to interpret accurately the experience of earlier Americans unless we attend to religion as well as economics, politics, and society.[4] Paradoxically, now that philosophers and political theorists are turning deliberately to the American cultural tradition to inform a self-consciously hard-headed, skepti-

cal, and postfoundationalist approach to knowledge, they are learning from historians that the heart of their tradition is both rationalistic and religious. As I suggest in my conclusion, this realization poses awkward problems for both champions of Enlightenment and champions of religion.

The absence of an established church in America has made the clean separation of rationalist and religious traditions impossible. It is worth remembering,
though, that the separation of church and state has its origins not in secular distrust of religion but instead in Roger Williams's contempt for the effort by Massachusetts Puritans to sanctify their civil society. Williams insisted, following
Augustine's argument in *The City of God*, that no human institution could con-
strain belief. He wanted to keep religion unpolluted by law, not vice versa. Although Rhode Island quickly became a haven for the unorthodox and irreligious,
that was hardly Williams's aim.[5] The proliferation of religious denominations has
of course prevented the identification of faith with authority or autocracy that
sparked Enlightenment anticlericalism in Europe. It has also meant, just as cru-
cially, that all challenges to established ways of thinking or forms of social organization have attracted explicitly religious allies, whose participation sprang from
their faith and manifested itself in spirited political action. In the quick survey of
American reform that follows, I mean only to suggest the pivotal importance of
religion in effecting social change. It goes without saying that the opposition also
deployed religious arguments in every case; clearly neither progressives nor conservatives, neither radicals nor reactionaries, have had any persistent monopoly
over religious convictions or rhetoric. Witch-hunters, Indian fighters, Tories,
proslavery southerners, laissez-faire capitalists, imperialists, fascists, racists, and
cold warriors all believed God was on their side, and all attracted followers who
invoked their faith to justify their commitments. That should come as no surprise.
What may be somewhat more surprising, or at least deserves to be emphasized,
is the extent to which those who carried forward the Enlightenment principles of
liberty, equality, and fraternity—or sought to universalize the American rights
to life, liberty, and the pursuit of happiness—were motivated explicitly by, and
understood their activity primarily in terms of, their commitment to religious
principles. Those who would equate religion with reactionary politics reveal a
breathtaking ignorance of American history.

In *Albion's Seed*, the first volume of his ambitious cultural history of America,
David Hackett Fischer writes, "Of all the determinants which shaped the cultural
character of British America, the most powerful was religion. During the seventeenth century, the English-speaking people were deeply divided by the great
questions of the Protestant Reformation. These divisions in turn created a broad
spectrum of English denominations in the New World." Beneath the banners of
different Protestant denominations, various groups set off in various directions
socially and politically, and trying to arrange them on a single spectrum distorts
the multidimensional complexity of their variations. In the words of David Hall,
when studying colonial America the "imperative task is to detach religion from
a backward-looking communalism" because "modes of belief" changed along

with American society. "But we should not say," Hall insists, "that emerging capitalism determined the path of religious development. Though it was conditioned by social change and social forces, religion retained important powers of autonomy; religion was a mediating force."[6]

Although American partisans of Enlightenment in the eighteenth century shared their European counterparts' confidence in reason, in the New World Christianity provided the framework within which, rather than against which, the Enlightenment emerged. The pervasiveness of religion, whether manifested in varieties of orthodox or dissenting Protestantism or, in a few notable instances, reformulated by Deists, conditioned the reception of European ideas in America. Locke, Newton, Pope, and Montesquieu were especially revered, as were spokesmen for the radical Whig tradition, such as Algernon Sidney, and Scottish moral philosophers who followed Francis Hutcheson and Adam Ferguson. Skeptics such as Voltaire and Hume and free thinkers such as Thomas Paine (in his later years) exerted less widespread influence. Regardless of the tension between Enlightenment rationalism and Protestant Christianity, which seemed as undeniable to many philosophers as it seems to many critics today, in America the Age of Reason was nevertheless also an age of belief.

Despite some variations within each region, distinguishable forms of Enlightenment emerged in New England, the Middle Atlantic, and the South. In all three regions faith mediated the claims of reason. In New England, the tension between Calvinists' convictions regarding humanity's depravity and the experience of democracy, heightened by the Great Awakening of the mid-eighteenth century, could be eased if not altogether resolved through the idea of the moral sense. This innate capacity, according to Charles Chauncy and Jonathan Mayhew, enabled human beings, though flawed by sin, to discern the difference between right and wrong. Calm confidence in the human ability to identify and comply with the demands of morality, while hardly consistent with Puritan doctrine, became the backbone of the Scottish-inspired, and New England–dominated, genteel tradition that was to emerge in the early nineteenth century. Although Jonathan Edwards sympathized with some of the central efforts of the Enlightenment, he nevertheless denied the adequacy of reason to penetrate the mysterious depths of being revealed by God. By resisting the most expansive claims of reason, and by insisting on the reality of evil, Edwards counterposed themes from Augustinian Christianity to the domesticated religiosity that began making its peace with science through the efforts of Americans such as Benjamin Franklin. In Franklin's more heterogeneous, commercial, and urban Middle Atlantic region, such accommodations with the Arminian ideas of free will and perfectibility came more easily. Franklin scorned the Puritan divines' other-worldly fatalism, declaring, with Montesquieu, that we best serve God by serving his children. Franklin's fellow Philadelphians Benjamin Rush and James Wilson espoused a similar eclectic faith in divine providence, human reason, the moral sense of sympathy, and progressive social reform through education and democratic politics. In the South, champions of the Enlightenment such as Thomas Jefferson were members of the planter oligarchy whose religious views were generally unconventional forms of Anglicanism.[7]

As perhaps the central figure in eighteenth-century American culture, Jefferson embodies the commitments to Enlightenment rationalism, to the principles (if not always the institutionalized manifestations) of Christianity, and to Scottish commonsense morality that so many Americans shared. For that reason a brief sketch of Jefferson may illuminate the complex relations between knowledge and belief at the dawn of the new nation. In his home in Monticello, which embodies the contradictions of Jefferson's life and his legacy, Jefferson the architect even accomplished a goal that forever eluded Jefferson the statesman: he made slavery disappear. By locating the slave quarters out of sight, below the hillsides that surrounded the house, and by placing the stables, the kitchen, and the house servants' rooms beneath the terraces that extended beyond the house, Jefferson removed as much evidence as possible of the slave labor that lay at the foundation of his existence as an enlightened Christian planter and statesman.

Jefferson deliberately sited his mansion so that it faced westward, toward the wilderness that he believed would enable America to expand indefinitely as a republic of yeomen farmers; yet he just as deliberately derived its design from the antique architectural models of classicism. He cherished America's unsettled West; yet he laid on the entire nation a geometric grid that imposed the Enlightenment's vision of rational order, irrespective of the meandering flow of rivers and the unyielding features of the terrain. He wanted Monticello to reflect his enthusiasm for the finest fruits of the eighteenth-century Enlightenment in philosophy, science, and aesthetics; yet he made sure that such examples of refinement as a world-class library, a seven-day calendar clock, and a bust of Voltaire by the French sculptor Jean-Antoine Houdon were juxtaposed with elk and moose antlers, the head of a bison, the bones of a mastodon, and various Indians artifacts, all of which demonstrated the untamed grandeur of the New World.

Jefferson prided himself on his commitment to the newest advances in agriculture, smuggling a strain of rice from Italy, inventing a prize-winning plow, and experimenting with the latest ideas on crop rotation; yet he was unable to turn a profit as a farmer. He often railed against the dangers of manufacturing for a republic; yet he experimented with manufacturing nails and spinning cloth at Monticello, ventures that proved as unprofitable as his efforts at commercial farming. He criticized government spending and argued against encumbering future generations through profligate public expenditures; yet he refused to curtail his own lavish purchases and extravagant entertaining, which left him nearly bankrupt for much of his life and saddled his own heirs with a heavy burden of debt.

Jefferson privately expressed his hatred of slavery, and condemned it with such eloquence in his *Notes on the State of Virginia* that his words were frequently quoted by abolitionists; yet his own comfortable way of life depended on slave labor. He often professed his passionate opposition to miscegenation; yet he kept as slaves members of the Hemings family, all of whom were the children of the union of his father-in-law and one of his slaves, and one of whom, Sally, gave birth to children whose father was, according to various and hotly contested accounts, an Irish-born overseer of Monticello, Jefferson's nephew, or (least plausibly of all) Jefferson himself.

Such contradictions are not merely intriguing details that can be reconciled within some broader unity; instead they constitute the essentially inconsistent, even contradictory, nature of Jefferson's life and his thought. Despite the efforts of generations of commentators who have sought to reveal beneath the obvious dissonances a deeper harmony, no such harmony exists except through the creative efforts of historians devoted to muting some part of Jefferson and attending closely to another.

The urge to resolve Jefferson's contradictions is hardly surprising. As a symbol of the meaning and aspirations of the new nation, for Americans and for others, Jefferson has overshadowed every other figure. For that reason, efforts to construct a coherent image of his ideas have been a constant feature of American intellectual life from the eighteenth century to the present.[8]

Jefferson's public career began with his election to the Virginia House of Burgesses in 1768. His reputation as a writer was established when it became generally known that he had written the anonymous *Summary View of the Rights of British America* (1774). There he proclaimed, in words that have often been cited to demonstrate his commitment to the primacy of individual rights, "The god who gave us life, gave us liberty at the same time: the hand of force may destroy, but cannot disjoin them." But commentators sometimes neglect Jefferson's careful and characteristic placement of rights within the context of his deep and prior commitments to religious piety and to the democratic idea of popular sovereignty: "From the nature of things, every society must at all times possess within itself the sovereign powers of legislation."[9] Jefferson's dual emphasis on popular sovereignty and liberty, both of which he rooted in divine plan, ancient practice, and English tradition, helped provide fuel and a conceptual framework for the colonists' resentments. In the Declaration of Independence, drawing on a variety of ideological sources and rhetorical devices, he crafted an enduringly persuasive statement of the American case.

Jefferson likewise sought to secure the principle of religious freedom, which he introduced in 1777 and the Virginia General Assembly finally enacted in 1786. Because Jefferson's own religious faith was highly unorthodox, his critics branded him an unbeliever. He nevertheless considered himself both a foe of institutionalized Christianity and a fervent Christian; he later compiled extracts from the Gospels to piece together what he considered a pure version—before their corruption beneath layers of theology—of the ethical teachings of Jesus, "the most sublime and benevolent code of morals which has ever been offered to man."[10] In his embrace of Enlightenment rationality and science, his suspicion of superstition, the idiosyncratic eclecticism of his own genuine faith, and his desire to shield religious belief from government and vice versa, Jefferson embodied many of the characteristics that were to mark most of his fellow Americans' complex, continuing efforts to reconcile their misgivings about dogma and the consequences of religious intolerance with their commitments to the truth as well as the value of Protestant Christianity.

Regional and denominational differences mattered profoundly to Americans, but their significance shrank after 1763 relative to the increasing importance of the colonies' deteriorating relationship with England. The colonists understood that conflict in both imperial and religious terms. J. C. D. Clark has demonstrated that the conflicts among American denominations, and many Americans' shared mistrust of Anglicanism and hatred of Catholicism, helped unify the colonists against England. In an essay surveying the literature on religion and the Revolution, Ruth Bloch writes, "Far from having become secularized by the eighteenth century, the religious preoccupations that had always informed political ideology remained vitally important to Americans of the Revolutionary generation." During these crucial years, "ideological change occurred within a symbolic structure largely defined by the Calvinist experiential approach to salvation and providential understanding of the collective experience of God's people on earth." Forced by the pressure of war to create a new language for a new nation, colonial Americans refashioned and wove together the quite different vocabularies of Protestant Christianity, classical republicanism, and Scottish common sense philosophy to form a powerful, if ambiguous, discourse of virtue that served their purposes well. America's revolutionaries used religious, civic, and ethical conceptions of duty to express the commitments that sustained them until they had secured their independence and established a constitution for their new republic. Unfortunately, their new language could not contain the rapidly changing shape of the democratic and commercial culture that was beginning to develop.[11]

Yet perhaps the loose weave of the American language of politics explains both its initial success and its survival in the Constitution. The multiple meanings of the central words in the American lexicon, according to Harry Stout and Daniel Rodgers, enabled different Americans to read what they wanted into the language of the founding documents. That ambiguity helped keep the genuine conflicts among changing and competing social groups from ripping the nation apart. Moreover, the provision for amending the Constitution not only sealed the doctrine of popular sovereignty by preserving the people's effective power to shape their laws but further testified to the Founders' willingness to admit their own limitations.

Whereas the French Revolution would seek to fix forever the luminous principles of government disclosed by reason, the U.S. Constitution provided explicitly for the corrections that would inevitably be required. Donald Lutz has demonstrated that by far the most important template for the Bill of Rights was the Massachusetts Body of Liberties, compiled in 1641 by the Puritan minister Nathaniel Ward. Since at that time John Locke was only nine years old, confident assertions of the importance of Locke's *Letter Concerning Toleration* for the shaping of American rights consciousness may be in need of revision.

While the nature of the religiosity of Madison in particular, and the Founders in general, remains a difficult question, it is clear that their faith in reason was bounded by their awareness of their finitude. Thus the Bill of Rights in general reflects the Federalists' shrewd political instincts, which enabled them to allay the Antifederalists' fears, and also their piety. The First Amendment in particular, which guaranteed the separation of church and state, rested on a similar combination of calculation and sobriety. The First Amendment neither explicitly prevented state governments from being involved with religion nor authorized the promotion by government of a vague, nondenominational Christianity. The aim of the amendment, according to John F. Wilson, was simply to "neutralize religion as a factor that might jeopardize the achievement of a federal government." Not because faith was flagging, then, but precisely because it remained so powerful—and so protean—was the exclusion of government from religion, and vice versa, of such importance to the new republic.[12]

Precisely the fear that Antifederalists would impose religious tests figured prominently in Madison's shift from opposition to support of a Bill of Rights. As he explained to Jefferson in October 1788, Madison initially feared that the bills of rights being proposed would narrow the rights of conscience and lead to the establishment of official state religions. As early as 1785, Madison had opposed Patrick Henry's attempt to impose a tax in Virginia that would provide government support for religion. The "Memorial and Remonstrance against Religious Assessments" that he wrote on that occasion provides the most comprehensive account of his views both on the importance of religion and the importance of keeping it separate from civil authority. Far from contending that religion should be kept separate because he feared religion would corrupt the public sphere, Madison feared that politics would corrupt religion. Preserving the purity of faith could not be trusted to sinful civic authorities. Religion, Madison wrote in the "Remonstrance," is a "duty toward the Creator. It is the duty of every man to render to the Creator such homage, and such only, as he believes to be acceptable to Him. This duty is precedent, both in order of time and in degree of obligation, to the claims of civil society. Before any man can be considered as a member of civil society, he must be considered as a subject of the Governor of the Universe. . . . We maintain, therefore, that in matters of religion no man's right is abridged by the institution of civil society, and that religion is wholly exempt from its cognizance." Madison supported the First Amendment not to facilitate the eventual emergence of a secular society in which self-interest might be given free rein, unincumbered by the intrusions of religion. He sought to prevent encroachments by civil authority in a sphere he considered privileged, where no legitimate claims could be made by the state against the individual. Madison believed that only by securing the right to freedom of conscience, and preventing the establishment of religious tests or state-sponsored religions envisioned by prominent Antifederalists, could piety, which he judged the most important source of virtue, be preserved.[13]

When the volatile blend of faith, civic virtue, and enlightened self-interest that had fueled the Revolution began to run out, the role of religion in American culture changed. *The Federalist*, the writings of John Adams on the Constitution, and the efforts of evangelical denominations and the New England clergy represent alternate strategies designed to solve a widely perceived problem: the virtue of individual citizens might no longer be adequate to sustain the public life of the Republic after the crises of the Revolution and founding had passed. As hierarchies fell and economic opportunities rose, a new species of individualism began to appear throughout America. Harnessing that new energy, finding ways to turn it to the public interest, was a project shared by religious and political elites of various persuasions.[14]

The dramatic rise of varieties of evangelical Christianity accompanied the transformation of American culture from the 1770s through the 1830s. Civic virtue no longer seemed adequate to religious leaders, and they began calling Americans away from economic and political diversions to confront their sinfulness. Whereas historians twenty-five years ago routinely characterized early nineteenth-century Americans as "unchurched," and implied that they were increasingly irreligious as well, more recent interpretations stress the persistent religiosity of the new nation. Americans were, to use the title of Jon Butler's study, floating into a new world of democracy and capitalism "awash in a sea of faith." Americans were confident that the exercise of reason would enable them to fulfill their divinely ordained historical mission. Christianity provided the frame of reference for worldly forms of political, economic, and scientific activity. Rationalism and religion seemed fully compatible. "Educated Evangelicals," James Turner argues, "no less than the eighteenth-century infidels they abhorred, hitched their wagon to the rising star of science." In the estimation of Lyman Beecher, Evangelicalism was "eminently a rational system"; by that he meant, Turner notes, "nothing more nor less than the rationality of science."[15]

As American political life became increasingly boisterous in the 1820s and 1830s, religious issues remained central to debates about rational policy choices. The democratization of American culture proceeded within the dual contexts of enthusiasm for science and enthusiasm for evangelical Christianity, and the various reformist crusades of the antebellum years thus cannot be understood in narrowly secular terms. They manifested neither merely elitist attempts to impose order on unruly multitudes nor merely the efforts of ambitious and uncultivated Americans to remove the last vestiges of privilege. In the words of Daniel Walker Howe, "it was the explosive combination of humanitarianism plus Christianity that gave the world the evangelical movement and its attendant reforms." In antebellum America, "it was the institutional and emotional resources of Christianity that typically empowered humanitarian reform." Criticism of all these reforms as veiled efforts to achieve social control confuses their effect with their cause, and neglects the widespread support from all classes for measures such as temperance and antislavery. Opponents of Indian removal, and champions of compulsory education and penal reform, shared a commitment to positive freedom; only by ignoring the Whigs' greater sympathy for the causes of feminism and abolitionism can their politics of self-control be judged more coercive than the laissez-faire politics of Jacksonians. The cultural and economic conflicts of these years were real enough, but only if we view the Whigs' crusades through the prism of their Christianity can we move beyond easy cynicism toward an understanding of their motivation. It is not enough to affirm, as the ethnocultural interpretation of American politics enables us to do, that political affiliation was tied to ethnicity and religion. We must also stop assuming that the hidden economic dimensions of these conflicts were somehow more "real" than the surface moral and religious issues. Democracy, Alexis de Tocqueville wrote, throws the individual back forever upon himself alone, and "there is danger that he may be shut up in the solitude of his own heart." Without the resources provided by religion, Tocqueville argued, democratic individuals find themselves damned to a civic hell. He believed that the process of democratization he witnessed, and chronicled, skirted that inferno precisely because Americans' worldviews were not so much comfortably capitalist as they were uncomfortably Christian. The transformation of American society during these years of rapid economic change is clear, but its meaning for those who experienced it will remain opaque unless we acknowledge the importance of religion as well as science in their conception of progress.[16]

Groups suffering from oppression likewise found in Christianity not only consolation, although that was certainly part of its appeal, but also inspiration for resistance and social action. Campaigns against slavery, alcohol, and prostitution, and campaigns for women's rights, Sunday schools, and female missionary societies, enlisted women in communal activities that strengthened their organizational abilities and heightened their sense of solidarity as women. The public culture was impoverished when virtue was shunted into a separate female sphere, but women succeeded in keeping alive ideals of benevolence and compassion that became increasingly endangered as the nineteenth century wore on. Religion provided a similar combination of consolation and empowerment for antebellum black culture. Jon Butler may be right about white southerners' efforts to extinguish the African roots of black religiosity, yet the forms of Christianity that emerged among blacks in the nineteenth century were as distinctive as they were powerful. To cite only the most familiar examples, Nat Turner was a Baptist preacher who believed he was responding to God's call to battle, Harriet Tubman's heroic efforts were inspired by a deep religious commitment to freedom, and Sojourner Truth showed how feminism and antislavery both could be rooted in a passionate spirituality. Whether one judges the consequences as salutary or unfortunate, it is clear that religion was central to the experience of women and blacks in nineteenth-century America.[17]

The centrality of religion likewise explains Lincoln's commanding power for his contemporaries and his uniquely enduring stature. Although his own religiosity was as idiosyncratic as Jefferson's, Lincoln became increasingly drawn to a profound, heterodoxically Christian supernaturalism during the final decade of his life. His responses to Stephen Douglas in their debates, as J. David Greenstone, John P. Diggins, and Andrew Delbanco have argued in very different ways, derive their power from biblical authority as much as from political principles.

Lincoln's writings and speeches, both before and after his election as president, carried forward another set of themes in addition to the classical republican emphasis on civic duty and the liberal emphasis on individual rights. Lincoln expressed as well an Augustinian awareness of the human capacity for evil and the possibility of redemption. As was true in the eighteenth century, the most powerful arguments in American public discourse during the nineteenth century were those grounded on both faith and reason. Commitments to the Union (and the Confederacy) were inspired by, and justified in terms of, a cosmology of sacred sacrifice and salvation rather than either republican sacrifice and glory or calculating sacrifice and personal profit. The horror of slavery for Lincoln extended beyond its "monstrous injustice" for slaves, and beyond its threat to the Union, to the fundamental challenge slavery represented to the sanctity of all human life. Yet again as was true in the eighteenth century, Lincoln's deepest convictions were chastened by his acknowledgment, in the Second Inaugural Address, that "The Almighty has His own purposes." Thus not only his resolve to fight, but also his commitment to reconciliation, drew on his unconventional but unmistakable Christian faith.[18]

In the Gilded Age, not only did ethnocultural identity continue to be among the most important determinants of political partisanship, but religious principles also continued to undergird the efforts of many reformers. Leon Fink has pointed out that the Knights of Labor used religious as well as economic arguments to mobilize workers. The religious imagery of the populists is familiar, although recent historians eager to appropriate the populists for their own purposes have chosen to overlook the importance of evangelical Christianity for agrarian radicals. The imagery and convictions of William Jennings Bryan were those of a prophet and a crusader, not those of a secular socialist, and his widespread appeal throughout rural America depended on his ability to tap the wellsprings of Protestant fervor as well as economic discontent. The social gospel moved gradually from the periphery to the center of American Protestantism, and by the first decade of the twentieth century the commitment to progressive reform had become orthodox in many denominations. Moreover, the pre–World War I alliance between such partisans of the social gospel as Walter Rauschenbusch and such social scientists as Richard T. Ely suggested that, from their perspective, scholarship, faith, and political activism were natural partners. If social problems are rooted in the sin of greed, as Rauschenbusch argued in *A Theology for the Social Gospel*, then progress toward their solution would require repentance in addition to institutional reform. To achieve the latter, the work of professional organizations such as the American Economic Association, which Ely helped to establish and tried unsuccessfully to steer toward social activism, should be directed toward helping scholars bring knowledge to bear on questions of justice. Both Rauschenbusch and Ely sought to shift their contemporaries' attention away from the fixation on inevitability that they thought incapacitated too many laissez-faire economists and mainstream Protestants, who interpreted the social scientific and sacred scriptures as authorizing the quiet acceptance of conditions that could not be changed. Interpretations that would collapse all of American progressivism into Protestantism seem to me overdrawn, but the centrality of religion to certain varieties of progressive reform, such as the work of social settlements and the efforts to regulate economic activity and working conditions, is undeniable.[19]

Jane Addams, arguably the most influential progressive social reformer, traced her "passionate devotion to the ideals of democracy" to the lives of the first Christians, who "boldly opposed . . . the accepted moral belief that the well-being of a privileged few might justly be built upon the ignorance and sacrifice of the many." Without the continuing efforts of self-consciously Christian communities, she wrote, the world might easily "slip back into the doctrines of selection and aristocracy." Firm as her own faith was, Addams learned from experience that religious observance could not be made part of the communal life at Hull House. For a time, she wrote,

> we made an effort to come together on Sunday evenings in a household service, hoping thus to express our moral unity in spite of the fact that we represented many creeds. But although all of us reverently knelt when the High Church resident read the evening service and bowed our heads when the evangelical resident led in prayer after his chapter, and although we sat respectfully through the twilight when a resident read her favorite passages from Plato and another from Abt Vogler, we concluded at the end of the winter that this was not religious fellowship and that we did not care for another reading club. So it was reluctantly given up.

The residents at Hull House "could not come together for religious worship because there were among us Jews, Roman Catholics, English Churchmen, Dissenters, and a few agnostics," all of whom "found unsatisfactory the diluted form of worship which we could carry on together."

In this case, as in so many others in American history, the toleration of difference, and the consequent separation of religious observance from public life, derived not from indifference toward religion but instead precisely from respect for its integrity under conditions of diversity. Addams knew that the vibrancy of the many faiths represented at Hull House would only be smothered under the soft blanket of official interfaith services, and for that reason she preferred to let each resident worship, or not, as each saw fit. In a pattern that has become standard in American culture, the prospect of shared community evaporated in the face of diversity.[20]

The years since World War I have witnessed the partial unraveling of the ties that bound much of progressivism to religious commitment. Two parallel trends, the rise of a self-conscious devotion to objectivity among social scientists and the rise of an equally self-conscious aspiration to realism among political liberals, combined with the triumph of religious fundamentalism in some Protestant denominations to weaken the links between religion and reform. The effect of the Scopes trial in particular, in the words of Garry Wills, "sealed off from each other, in mutual incomprehension, forces that had hitherto worked together in American history. Bryan's career had been the sign of the possible integration of progressive politics and evangelical moralism." Clarence Darrow's humiliation of

Bryan in Tennessee not only put on the defensive the fundamentalism that Darrow and H. L. Mencken loathed, it also ended the alliance between evangelical Christianity and reformist politics that had been a feature of American politics since the Great Awakening of the eighteenth century. During the 1920s both liberal social science and fundamentalism seemed to move, in oddly opposite ways, toward newer versions of orthodoxy that sought to freeze the present into the eternal.[21]

Paradoxically, this transformation of American academic and political culture may have been responsible for both the short-term successes of the moderate New Deal and the long-term failures of the truncated American welfare state. The sobering experiences of the Depression and two global wars intensified the commitments of many American intellectuals and politicians to resisting naïveté in both its religious and its ideological forms. Although this realism could take the shape of Reinhold Niebuhr's austere neo-orthodoxy, it more often manifested itself in smug dismissals of faith and celebrations of science. Scholars who had learned to examine the functional role of religion from a variety of psychological, sociological, or anthropological perspectives frequently assumed that regardless of its therapeutic value, its social utility, or its meaning-giving quality, religion is illusory. Secular cultural critics emerged to play the part often filled in the nineteenth century by theologians, explaining to the educated bourgeoisie what is to be done, and what is to be thought, about matters of ultimate concern.[22]

At the same time, both liberal and conservative politicians nevertheless continued to rely, with increasing sophistication (and at times with quite unnerving cynicism), on appeals to the millions of Americans who still conceived of their public commitments in terms of their religious faith. As the separation of knowledge from belief has become more and more apparent in the American academic community, equally deep rifts have emerged within most religious denominations concerning social and political issues. Progressive Protestants tracing their lineage from Ely or Rauschenbusch make common cause with Catholics descended from Father John Ryan or Dorothy Day, while conservatives invoke different but equally lively traditions grounded in their favorite biblical commands. Thus despite the apparent acceleration of the secularization process in the last fifty years, religion remains an inextricable part of public life in late twentieth-century America. It is as impossible to understand the civil rights movement without Vernon Johns or Martin Luther King Jr., the antiwar movement without Robert Drinan or William Sloane Coffin, the farm workers movement without Cesar Chavez, or the Rainbow Coalition of the late 1980s without Jesse Jackson, as it is to understand earlier American reform movements in isolation from the religious activists who helped give them their shape and their energy. Critics may decry that affiliation of religion with politics. Adolph Reed, for example, has challenged the wisdom of Jesse Jackson's decision to rely on religious metaphors rather than interest-group politics. One might respond to such arguments that interest-group politics is the problem rather than the solution, that the rise of interest-group liberalism has been responsible for the demise of progressive political action in

America, and that minorities in any democracy are better off appealing to justice than to interest, but that is beside the point. I want to insist only that religion continues to be a central factor in American public life.[23] By itself, of course, religion does not explain American politics, especially now that electoral politics appears to be devolving into a species of marketing that competes in banality, if not imagination, with the advertising of athletic shoes. But American politics can be neither understood nor explained without attending to the persistence, as well as the transformation, of religious belief.

Pragmatic Truth and Religious Faith

Viewed strictly as an empirical question, then, it is clear that knowledge and belief have been inseparable in American public life from the colonial period though the present. The second question I want to raise, however, is a good bit more difficult to answer: is the postfoundationalism that attracts the allegiance of many contemporary scholars compatible with religious faith? I approach this question by concentrating on answers given by two twentieth-century American thinkers, William James and John Dewey, postfoundationalists *avant la lettre*. The choice of James and Dewey is hardly arbitrary, since their writings are central to the renewed interest in pragmatism apparent in much contemporary American philosophy, cultural criticism, and political theory.

James's ideas about religion have two different aspects, the phenomenological and the pragmatic. The pragmatic dimensions are familiar from James's *The Will to Believe* and *The Varieties of Religious Experience*. James argued that religious questions, like other questions that cannot be answered by empirical tests, should be addressed from a particular perspective: we should inquire what practical difference the answers to such questions make. His investigations into the consequences of religious beliefs revealed that faith can have a profound influence on individual lives, and that influence itself seemed to James worth emphasizing. But beyond and beneath the invocation of the pragmatic test lay James's own personal crisis and his recovery through an act of will. That familiar incident provided the experiential ground for James's life-long quest to understand the multiple dimensions of consciousness. From his *Principles of Psychology* to his *Pluralistic Universe*, James consistently opposed all dualisms and all dogmatisms. He understood that separations between mind and body, subject and object, fact and value, knowledge and action, and natural and supernatural conformed only to the conventional categories of Western thought. Experience—amorphous, plastic, shimmering, and slippery as it was—escaped whatever conceptual nets philosophers and psychologists might devise to capture it.

James's own quirky religiosity was consistent with his conception of immediate experience as the intersection of self with nonself in the fluid and ever-changing encounters of an attending individual consciousness. Just as his ethics stood not on bedrock but rather on his preference for a "strenuous" rather than an "easy-going"

morality, a preference based on pragmatic judgment rather than logical demon-
stration of its superiority, so his faith stood on a felt fact, which he described in
the conclusion of *The Varieties of Religious Experience* as "*the fact that the conscious person is continuous with a wider self through which saving experiences
come.*" The impulse toward something beyond the self, something "more" with
which we seek union, the desire for consolation in the face of persistent feelings
that the self and its limits do not circumscribe the realm of the possible, were for
James adequate warrants for belief. As an empirical scientist he was sensitive to
charges that his "'piecemeal' supernaturalism" lacked substance, but he responded without apology: "Humbug is humbug, even though it bear the scientific
name, and the total expression of human experience, as I view it objectively"—
that is, as a scientific naturalist—"invincibly urges me beyond the narrow 'scientific bounds.' Assuredly, the real world is of a different temperament—more intricately built than physical science allows." For James, the claims of knowledge
could not topple the fact of belief, because the latter was rooted in the mysterious
court of last appeal, the phenomenology of personal experience. A truly radical empiricism, James insisted, must leave open the possibility of faith, and also the possibility that the object of that faith might exist.[24] In his sensitivity to the inadequacy of language to express the depth and breadth of experience, in his resolute
refusal to admit the possibility of closure for any knowledge claims, and in his resistance to the grander claims of scientific rationality, James stands as a champion
of ideas cherished by many contemporary dissident intellectuals.

In James's writings, the relation between religion and knowledge is never
quite clear, possibly because his ideas always seem to slide just outside the frame
of his texts. That deliberate elusiveness was a matter of principle for James; it
accounts in part for both his charm and his continuing significance. "It is perhaps
an advantage," Alfred North Whitehead wrote of James, "that his system of philosophy remained so incomplete. To fill it out would necessarily have made it
smaller." By contrast, Whitehead wrote, we should consider the work of John
Dewey: "In carrying out the philosophy of William James, I think he enormously
narrowed it. With James the consciousness of the ever-present complexity and
possibility in human experience is always implicit in his writing. Dewey is without it."[25] From the perspective of some commentators, Dewey appeared to lack
that consciousness precisely because, after he shifted from his early Congrega-
tionalist faith to his mature naturalism, he seemed to rule out the possibility of
unscientific discourse, unconventional modes of experience, and traditional forms
of religiosity. James and Dewey thus apparently offered two alternative judgments concerning the compatibility of knowledge and belief. But that appearance
is illusory.

Like James, Dewey believed we should begin thinking about religion by reflecting on its concrete consequences, and he argued that those consequences, not
any theological or metaphysical claims, constitute its importance. So troubled
was Dewey by doctrine that he refused even to use the word *religion*, preferring
instead the adjective *religious* to express his conception of an attitude that always

springs from human experience and should never be allowed to settle into institutionalized form. In his most sustained discussion of the religious, *A Common Faith*, Dewey insisted that "it denotes nothing in the way of a specifiable entity, either institutional or as a system of beliefs." The religious was not limited to mystical or supernatural faith; to the contrary, Dewey defined religious belief as "the unification of the self through allegiance to inclusive ideal ends." These ideal ends can be aesthetic, scientific, political, or moral; they can relate to any realm in which the individual seeks to relieve experienced tension through unification with an ideal. For Dewey, such ideals are not necessarily associated with any deity; the decision to seek harmony with them springs from individual choice rather than from achieving any mystical union with, or dispensation of grace from, something supernatural. But that conception of the religious did not prevent Dewey from endorsing the value of faith. As Stephen Rockefeller makes clear in his comprehensive study of Dewey's religiosity, for Dewey moral action as well as political activity must emanate from belief in the possibility of achieving ideals that extends beyond any evidence. In the words of John E. Smith, for Dewey "God is the *function* which this active union of ideal and actual performs in human experience as it develops against the background of a natural environment." Religion has no existence independent of the human community's struggle to achieve what Dewey called "the democratic idea."[26]

For Dewey, democracy embodies the religious; efforts to realize "the great community," to use his phrase from *The Public and Its Problems*, constitute the most sublime religious project. Whereas James conceptualized such struggles for unity as quests for some ineffable beyond, Dewey explicitly rejected such notions as distractions from the hard work of aesthetic, scientific, political, or moral praxis. The young Dewey's antidualistic Hegelianism carried over into his mature naturalism. The passionate commitment to overcoming dualisms persisted, but in place of *Geist* Dewey invoked science. The community of inquiry, extended to politics and society through the diffusion of democratic principles, took over for abstract reason as the motor driving history. For Dewey, the religious originated in human striving, and its proper target remained the sanctification of this world rather than the achievement of salvation in another. If Dewey's mysticism remained earth-bound, however, it was not without romantic, or even unconventionally religious, aspirations. As the ideals of democratic intelligence and instrumentalism "find adequate expression in social life," Dewey wrote in *Reconstruction in Philosophy*, "they will . . . color the imagination and temper the desires and affections. . . . Then they will take on religious value. The religious spirit will be revivified because it will be in harmony with men's unquestioned scientific beliefs and their ordinary day-by-day activities. . . . And when the emotional force, the mystic force one might say, of communication, of the miracle of shared life and shared experience is spontaneously felt, the hardness and crudeness of contemporary life will be bathed in the light that never was on land or sea."[27]

Neither James nor Dewey, then, saw a necessary conflict between knowledge and the authentically religious—at least as they understood the latter in their quite different ways. Yet both men distrusted institutionalized religion and both detested dogmatism. James was willing to entertain the possibility that some realm beyond our own might exist, whereas Dewey's conception of religious ideals generated by human striving evidently did not admit that possibility, even though he refused to accept the label "atheism" for his position. Important as that difference is, it seems equally important to acknowledge that both James and Dewey deployed their religious ideas, just as they deployed all pragmatic knowledge, for ethical purposes. Both faith and reason were part of the pragmatic project, and both were to be judged by their consequences.

If pragmatism need not necessarily rule out undogmatic varieties of religious belief, as the writings of James and Dewey suggest, what might be the consequences of such belief for politics? If our ideals are to derive from experience rather than dogma or metaphysics, if we are to learn from "our tradition" rather than from abstract principles, as some neopragmatists such as Richard Rorty advise, what are we to make of a tradition that has been marked, as I have indicated, by the deep penetration into public life of religious doctrines and rationalist principles of just the sort we are urged to discard? "Strong poets," to use the term Rorty borrows from Harold Bloom, might respond by changing the subject. In *Contingency, Irony, and Solidarity*, Rorty calls for the creation of a culture that would be "enlightened, secular, through and through. It would be one in which no trace of divinity remained, either in the form of a divinized world or a divinized self. Such a culture would have no room for the notion that there are nonhuman forces to which human beings should be responsible." Having discussed his recent writings elsewhere, I will not elaborate here the reasons why Rorty's liberal utopia seems to me neither liberal, utopian, nor consistent with the ethics of pragmatism as conceived by James or Dewey. Instead I want merely to suggest that Rorty's recent proclamations of contingency and irony seem to me incapable of yielding the solidarity he seeks, because by authorizing the narcissistic self-absorption of strong poets he encourages precisely the cultivation of inwardness that James and Dewey rejected.[28]

Nothing other than the creativity of isolated individuals remains when postmodernists declare the death of Enlightenment rationality and religious faith, as Giles Gunn has pointed out in a recent essay.[29] Although both James and Dewey likewise appreciated the artificiality of language as a system of signs, they also believed that interpersonal communication nevertheless remains a possibility. In James's words, "All human thinking gets discursified; we exchange ideas; we lend and borrow verifications, get them from one another by means of social intercourse. All truth thus gets verbally built out, sorted up, and made available for everyone. Hence, we must *talk* consistently just as we must think consistently: for both in talk and in thought we deal with kinds. Names are arbitrary, but once understood they must be kept to." We can acknowledge the arbitrariness of signifiers, James insisted, without being incapacitated by that knowledge or freed from our responsibility to communicate with each other. Likewise Dewey recognized the instability of language without denying its pragmatic potential. Through our use of symbols, Dewey argued, we communicate and weigh the meaning of shared experience. Through that process we learn to understand one another, and from that understanding emerges a "community of interest and endeavor." Dewey appreciated the difficulty of such "communicative action," to use the phrase Jürgen Habermas applies to this process.[30] Solving such problems, moreover, is a continuing process, never ending in the closure postmodernists dread but instead forever opening up new possibilities—and new problems to be discussed and addressed. In marked contrast to the social tests of truth emphasized by James and Dewey, celebrations of ironic subjectivity not only beg the questions raised by James's strenuous ethics and Dewey's democratic community but they also concede the political field to those with power who would shape public opinion by cynically manipulating a kinder and gentler imagery.[31]

Yet the solvent of historical criticism is indeed corrosive, and it is not clear that a faith chastened by its awareness of contingency can still have the consequences James and Dewey respected. Nietzsche reflected on this difficulty with some satisfaction. Historical study reduced faith to "pure knowledge about Christianity, and so has annihilated it." All living things need "to be surrounded by an atmosphere, a mysterious circle of mist: if one robs it of this veil, if one condemns a religion, an art, a genius to orbit as a star without an atmosphere, then one should not wonder about its rapidly becoming withered, hard and barren."[32] Santayana put the point more succinctly: the pragmatists' gods are demonstrable only as hypotheses, but as hypotheses they are no longer gods. What sustenance can a culture take from its traditions once they have been dissected? As I suggest briefly in my conclusion, one possible response to that challenge can be drawn from a strand of the discourse of American public life as it has developed from Edwards and Madison to James and Dewey.

Rethinking Knowledge and Belief

In the bracing climate of postfoundationalist criticism, several strategies have been suggested to protect faith from skepticism. To those for whom religion is not, in James's phrase, a live option, and to those whose faith remains solid, such discussions may seem pointless; others face these questions with attitudes that range from idle curiosity to urgency. If faith has indeed died for us, can we will it back to life by pretending ourselves back to innocence? This is the counsel of Daniel Bell in *The Cultural Contradictions of Capitalism*, but such a functionalist appeal seems born of desperation rather than conviction. Can we select a therapeutic religion from a faith court of congregations marketing sin-free affirmations of the self? To pose the question is to answer it, since such transparent consumerism parodies religious faith. Can we instead deepen and redeem our dominant cultural norms of utilitarian and expressive self-interest by recovering submerged but still vital traditions of both civic republicanism and religion? In *Habits of the Heart*, Robert Bellah and his associates recommend that project, ar-

guing that the republican and biblical communities of memory can deliver us
from our culture's individualist excesses. While that might seem an attractive
prospect, even roughly consistent with the account of the shaping of American
political culture I have sketched, there are reasons to resist its appeal; as H. Richard Niebuhr periodically reminded his brother Reinhold, that strategy compromises religion without sanctifying politics.[33]

Politics has suffered as much as religion from the disenchantment the twentieth century has brought. In contrast to Dewey's hope that secularization would
lead to the transfer of religious energies into political action, these energies have
either dissipated or been directed toward private pleasures. The citizen, as well
as the believer, has tended to disappear, as the secular state finds itself stagger-
ing under the weight of what Habermas calls the "legitimation crisis." Welfare
states can generate loyalty only by using instrumental rationality to achieve economic prosperity. Although technical considerations alone are permitted to influence decision making in such a depoliticized culture, the persistence of other
norms and goals leads to resistance by dissident groups whose aspirations cannot
be reconciled with those of the state system. According to Habermas, such efforts
to combat the "colonization of the life-world" make use of cultural resources inherited from traditional, noninstrumental forms of reasoning and interaction.[34]
This much of Habermas's critique, which I find persuasive as an updating of Max
Weber's analysis of democratic culture under conditions of disenchantment and
rationalization, illuminates the inadequacy of Bellah's solution. Merging the vocabularies of religion, republicanism, and individual expressiveness cannot be
achieved, since the forms of reasoning—and, just as important, the conceptions
of the capacity of reason—are irreconcilable. When the demands of religious
faith and the demands of instrumental rationality collide, as they inevitably do
now that religion does not provide, as it did in the eighteenth century, the context surrounding the exercise of reason, something must give way. For Bellah,
presumably, religious commitments would triumph, but only at the cost of sacri-
ficing individuals' responsibilities as republican citizens and their desire to
achieve personal fulfillment as they conceive it for themselves.

Instead we must be content to hold in suspension and resist efforts to unite the
claims of faith and the claims of reason, because both the public and the religious
communities of discourse are diminished when they collapse into one another. In
the pluralistic and contentious culture that America has always been, the commitment to the separation of church and state has been grounded and validated
in experience. A faith deep enough to have consequences is fierce enough to need
restraint. That realization, as old as Montaigne's *Essays* and Locke's *Essay Concerning Toleration*, is fundamental to the American tradition, and it continues to
offer the strongest response to urgings from across the political spectrum to bring
the full force of religious fervor to the debates of the public sphere.[35]

This tradition of endorsing restraint in the face of diversity has characterized
the thinking of those whose contributions to American public discourse I emphasized in the first section of this essay. Jefferson and Madison differed on impor-

tant issues, but they shared the commitment that manifested itself in the Virginia Statute for Religious Freedom. Their passion for the principles embodied in the founding documents, on the one hand, and for the separation of religion from politics, on the other, likewise animated Lincoln's condemnation of slavery as the denial of everything for which he and his nation claimed to stand. Although Lincoln understood the force of the arguments from expediency that had bolstered defenses of slavery, he responded in a vocabulary altogether different from that of the rational pursuit of self-interest. The language of the Enlightenment seemed to Lincoln inadequate to the task facing him: the consecration of great sacrifice for the sake not of material advantage but of universal principles. A faith such as Lincoln's, alert to the perils of expecting too much from politics, and perched between skepticism and fanaticism, is sturdy enough to survive the toxin of instrumental rationality.

The faith of William James was similarly immune to disenchantment. James perceived clearly what Charles Taylor has made the central theme of his brilliant *Sources of the Self*: all the choices that confront us in the modern era exact a price. The conflict between the insistent demands of Enlightenment rationality and the persistent yearnings for a source of values beyond our subjectivity does not disappear simply because reason cannot yield answers to all our questions. Although an "irremediable flatness" appeared to James to be replacing "the rare old flavors" of life, he remained committed to the possibility that something lay beyond the thin and tasteless broth of modernity. As Taylor points out, the Enlightenment drew on the accumulated resources of the Judeo-Christian conception of *agape* to fund its commitments to autonomy, equality, and benevolence. As I have tried to indicate here, voices in the American tradition have sought to keep alive both the discourse of religion and the discourse of reason, and to keep them distinct, so that the conversation between them can continue, so that knowledge and belief can engage each other in spirited disagreement as well as forge the occasional fertile alliance. For individuals, the "solid meaning of life is always the same eternal thing," James claimed, "the marriage, namely, of some unhabitual ideal, however special, with some fidelity, courage, and endurance; with some man's or woman's pains."[36]

For the public culture, however, collapsing the ideal into the everyday, or defining the everyday as the ideal, risks confusing our aspirations with our achievements. By identifying his democratic goal with the process of inquiry itself, Dewey sometimes slipped into that confusion; by advocating the fusion of religious and political commitments, or the erasure of religion to clear the field for secular rationality, contemporary critics run a similar risk. The cost of silencing the claims of reason can be enormous, as the most cursory glance at religious oppression indicates. But the cost of denying what Taylor calls "the deepest and most powerful spiritual aspirations that humans have conceived" may be even higher. A better strategy can be derived from the experience of our tradition and the commitment to tolerance expressed in sermonic terms by Madison after he retired from the presidency:

Ye States of America, which retain in your Constitutions or Codes, any aberration from the sacred principle of religious liberty, by giving to Caesar what belongs to God, or joining together what God has put asunder, hasten to revise and purify your systems, and make the example of your Country as pure and compleat, in what relates to the freedom of the mind and its allegiance to its maker, as in what belongs to the legitimate objects of political and civil institutions.[37]

The contributions of both reason and faith to American public life have been, and continue to be, as crucial as they are disconcerting to those who believe that one or the other of them threatens to undermine all that is precious. Yet both the insistence on tolerating religion and the insistence on restraining it are necessary for precisely the same reasons they are painful.[38]

Champions of religion and Enlightenment rationality should acknowledge that the American political and cultural tradition has been shaped by the constant interaction of religious and secular passions and ideals. Skeptical rationalists should be chastened by the knowledge that reason itself is a blunt instrument, incapable of prying open the recesses of experience and aspiration. Fervent believers should remember the injunctions of St. Paul and St. Augustine concerning the folly of trying to leap the gulf dividing the city of man from the city of God. Both such a skepticism and such a faith, sensitive to the limits of human knowledge and to the inaccessibility of divine wisdom, are potentially compatible with the uncertainties of postfoundationalism. Whether these delicately balanced, self-consciously tentative commitments can still inspire action, or whether they can even survive in a culture impatient with the notion of finitude and quick to greet all yearnings with the promise of instant gratification, remains to be seen.

FOUR

PREMATURE REQUIEM

Republicanism in American History

GIVEN THE UNPREDICTABILITY of human affairs, historians need a rich appreciation of paradox. Unlike so many other commentators on America,
who have sought to unmask either the greatness or the venality of the people or
their leaders, or the triumphs or tragedies flowing from America's political, economic, or social institutions, Tocqueville understood that conflicting values have
been held in suspension in American culture. In this essay I will offer an overview
of the ways in which historians have used the concept of republicanism to explain
the development of democracy in America; it may be easier to understand the apparent inconsistencies of these accounts if they are viewed through the series of
spectroscopic lenses provided by Tocqueville's analysis.

Anglo-American civilization, Tocqueville observed, reflects the shaping influence of "two perfectly distinct elements which elsewhere have often been at war
with one another but which in America it was somehow possible to incorporate
into each other, forming a marvelous combination. I mean the *spirit of religion* and
the *spirit of freedom*."[1] Beneath this unstable fusion lay at least two deeper paradoxes: in the South, the freedom of citizens rested on the institution of slavery,
while in New England the freedom of citizens rested on the enforcement of social
conformity. Equality and hierarchy, liberty and oppression, individuality and obedience—these were among the incompatible values that Americans managed
magically to embrace. What made that cultural juggling act possible? Why did
America not immediately dissolve into a host of squabbling factions?

Answering those questions reveals both the appeal and the inadequacy of the
concept of republicanism as the master analytical framework for American history. Unlike French history, which has been characterized by dramatic and recurrent changes of regime along the way to the eventual consolidation of republican
government, America has enjoyed a comparatively placid and continuous course
of political development since the original break from England. Yet to read many
American historians writing in the last three decades, one might infer that conflicts

as cataclysmic as those racking modern European nations have likewise marked the American past. Whereas earlier generations of historians fastened on notions such as the covenant to explain America's peculiar status as a "redeemer nation," or on America's supposedly unique "liberal tradition" to account for the centrality of economic divisions and/or the absence of socialism or fascism, more recently historians have focused attention on the presence and persistence in America of another set of ideas, those derived from classical republicanism. Imported from the civic humanism of Renaissance Italy via the publicists of the English dissenting tradition, republicanism served as an attractive ideology for Americans seeking to justify their desire to separate from Great Britain and establish an independent nation.[2] Since the central themes of republicanism entered American historiography principally through analyses of the American Revolution, that event serves as a convenient point of entry for addressing the broader question of the role republicanism has played in shaping American culture.

A large literature exists concerning the issue of republicanism in the American Revolution, and a detailed discussion is beyond the scope of this essay. Some of the ambiguities of republicanism, though, can be suggested by briefly contrasting two of the seminal studies that established the centrality of republican ideas in late-eighteenth-century American thought: Bernard Bailyn's *The Ideological Origins of the American Revolution* and his student Gordon Wood's *The Creation of the American Republic, 1776–1787*.[3] Bailyn was at pains to explain the apparent incongruity between Britain's fairly modest attempt to spread out the costs of maintaining its empire and the American colonists' exaggerated reaction, their shrill insistence that British colonial policies after 1763 represented nothing less than the leading edge of a worldwide conspiracy against liberty. The answer to this puzzle, disclosed by Bailyn's meticulous analysis of the pamphlets Americans wrote in protest against British policy, lay in the ideology of republicanism that Americans adopted from British Whigs and magnified into a rationale for their own self-interested campaign to achieve independence. American pamphleteers, according to Bailyn, drew arguments from the left and right margins of British political dissent to provide the ideological framework that "would most specifically determine the outbreak and character of the American Revolution."[4]

Wood, by contrast, in his analysis of the discourse of American revolutionaries stressed the ethical impulses that found expression in the language of republicanism. Whereas the ideological origins uncovered by Bailyn seemed to rest on hazy and exaggerated fears of power, the arguments examined by Wood appeared to be rooted in solid commitments to the republican ideal of civic virtue. If a modern politics of self-interest eventually replaced the classical republican concern with moral commitment, Wood argued, that change represented not merely a shift in the vocabulary of self-justification but also a profound transformation of values in American culture. In short, for Bailyn the irrationality of the colonists' perceptions explained the appeal of republican rhetoric; for Wood its appeal lay in its capacity to express Americans' deep allegiance to republican ideals.

As that contrast suggests, disputes over the meaning and significance of republicanism in American history can be both methodological and substantive. At the level of methodology, some historians have dismissed ideas as mere smoke-screens for interests. If we want to understand the significance of words, they advise, we should look behind the rhetoric to see what those who used them were trying to accomplish. Others have insisted that the words we choose are important because they are the means by which we constitute ourselves as humans; our language reflects our desire to communicate with and persuade others, not merely our desire to manipulate or mislead them. Indeed, the very notions of "manipulation" and "misleading" themselves rely on contrasting standards of sincerity and veracity that conceptions of language as purely instrumental appear to undercut.

At the substantive level, historians have characterized a wide variety of positions as republican, and republicanism has frequently been distinguished from liberalism, but the adequacy of those characterizations has been the subject of considerable debate. It is clear that eighteenth-century American republicans feared centralized executive power and trusted the capacity of autonomous, public-spirited citizens to preserve civic virtue by participating in local politics. Stated in those terms, republicanism represents an alternative to the liberal emphasis on individual rights as the central value in American culture, and its appeal to Americans looking for something other than individualism is not difficult to understand. But beyond that basic republican commitment to civic virtue, much is in dispute. Inasmuch as republicans scorned those who were dependent, it can be argued that unpropertied workers, women, and slaves were excluded from republican considerations of justice. Inasmuch as republicans celebrated sacrifice and feared that change meant either greater glory or decline, it can be argued that they authorized national expansion through military conquest, that they disapproved of interest groups of any kind, and that they prized austerity over improving standards of living. Stated in those terms, republicanism appears to be a celebration of hierarchy, patriarchy, and militarism, and a denial of the importance of privacy and prosperity, hardly an amalgam likely to inspire the fervor of contemporary egalitarians or communitarians.

Is it possible to untangle these strands? I believe it is, and I have attempted in a series of essays to explain how we can understand the important role republican ideas have played in American history by rethinking both the methodological and the substantive problems that seem unavoidable when the issues are stated as binary opposites: *either* ideas as rhetoric *or* ideas as conviction; *either* republicanism *or* liberalism.[5] Instead we must appreciate that both the instrumental and constitutive dimensions of language are inescapable. It is true that we do things with words, but what we do when we speak or write cannot be reduced simply to self-interest. Our projects as individuals and members of various communities are not entirely our own but rather emerge through the interaction of our minds with our cultural environments, and those projects frequently assume an importance for us that transcends calculations of personal advantage. As historians we must understand, then, both the strategic significance of the arguments Americans have used and why those arguments were considered persuasive. In short, we must examine the force of words as weapons and the appeal of words as expressions of genuine commitment, because it is impossible in most instances to separate speakers' calculations of their words' effect from their belief in their persuasiveness.

In a similar way we must avoid reifying "republicanism" and "liberalism" and appreciate that both traditions comprised a multitude of arguments developed in different contexts to solve different problems and to articulate different ideals. Beyond complicating our use of the terms themselves, this strategy involves placing both the arguments for civic virtue and the arguments for individual rights within the overarching context of the religiosity that has been so persistent and so pervasive in American culture. Whereas in France, for example, republicans from the eighteenth century through the present have consistently challenged the authority of religion both as embodied in the institution of the Roman Catholic Church and as a way of thinking that bolstered pre-republican ideologies, in America religiosity from the outset simultaneously served the double function of subverting authority and reconstituting it. The dynamics of orthodoxy and dissent, religious fervor and diversity, from the outset gave American culture its distinctive shape, as Tocqueville understood. The alliance between monarchy and church hierarchy made opposition to Catholicism an important part of French republican ideology until well into the twentieth century. In America, however, the situation was dramatically different. Rather than standing against organized religion, America's revolutionaries relied upon, and framed their arguments within the boundaries of, religious faith. Historians who have investigated the relation between religion and politics in the American Revolution agree that religious concerns remained paramount. For the generation that struggled to forge a new nation, the question of personal salvation always hovered beyond and above questions of freedom and justice, no matter how important those were.[6] Contemporary historians may find religion tangential to their own concerns, but when they project that cosmology back to eighteenth-century America they are looking through a filter that distorts the worldviews they seek to understand.

When placed within the framework of Protestant Christianity, republican ideas take on a rather different set of meanings. Alongside the Aristotelian conception of man as a political animal and Renaissance conceptions of civic virtue must be placed the stark challenges of Augustinian Christianity. If America was to be a republic, it was to be, in Samuel Adams's phrase, a "Christian Sparta," and the qualifier carried enormous weight.[7] The language of religion, which strikes many twentieth-century historians as a diversion, was pivotal in enlisting the allegiance of eighteenth-century Americans to the republican cause. Thomas Paine was an American hero when he sprinkled *Common Sense* with biblical allusions, endorsed religious diversity, and declared "the Almighty hath implanted in us these inextinguishable feelings for good and wise purposes"; he became a pariah when he attacked Christianity in *The Age of Reason*.[8]

Much the same was true of ideals such as freedom and property rights that we now associate with the ideology of liberalism. Important as these values were, for most Americans their attractiveness was mediated by nagging concerns with sinfulness and guilt, which led most Americans to conceive of self-interest and material success within boundaries imposed by standards of righteousness. Unlimited wealth, irresponsible exercises of liberty, and disregard for ethical concerns lay outside the acceptable realm of propriety. While the entrepreneurial ethos was certainly alive in eighteenth-century America, and the gap between the gentry and the majority of people was real, so too were the brakes on excess. Calvinism, the lingering idea of "moral economy," the tradition of natural law, and the various formal and informal restraints imposed by British common law and colonial American legal practices all combined to restrict the flow of liberal ideas within a fairly narrow channel defined by religious convictions and conventions.[9]

As Americans celebrate the two hundredth anniversary of the ratification of the Bill of Rights, it is instructive to consider the passage of the provision of the First Amendment that guarantees the federal government will not restrict the free exercise of religion, because that process reveals the centrality of religious considerations in American constitutionalism. First, the provision for amending the Constitution itself testifies to the founding generation's awareness of their inability to legislate finally and decisively the framework of government for their republic, a reflection not only of their hard-headed political sense but also of their awareness of their limited capacity to discern timeless principles of justice. Second, the most important model for the Bill of Rights was the Massachusetts Body of Liberties (1641), a document that reflects the religious preoccupations of the devout Puritan minister Nathaniel Ward. Third, the First Amendment was designed neither to promote nor preclude the establishment by state governments of an official religion; it simply removed the question from consideration by the federal government.[10]

Indeed, James Madison's fear that Antifederalists would impose religious tests may have been the decisive factor prompting him to shift from opposition to support of the Bill of Rights. As I pointed out in chapter 3, Madison feared that the bills of rights being proposed would narrow the rights of conscience and lead to the establishment of state-sponsored religions. To reiterate, Madison considered religious belief

> a duty toward the Creator. It is the duty of every man to render to the Creator such homage, and such only, as he believes to be acceptable to Him. This duty is precedent, both in order of time and in degree of obligation to the claims of civil society. Before any man can be considered as a member of civil society, he must be considered as a subject of the Governor of the Universe. . . . We maintain, therefore, that in matters of religion no man's right is abridged by the institution of civil society, and that religion is wholly exempt from its cognizance.

Madison endorsed the First Amendment because he feared the corrosive effects of politics on piety. Although liberal pluralists have tried for the last fifty years to enlist Madison on behalf of more secular crusades, his conviction that republican politics requires virtue, and that virtue requires religious belief, distinguishes his rationale for the separation of church and state from that of many contemporary civil libertarians.[11] Whereas in France, religion and republicanism faced each other as adversaries, in America their union made possible the achievement of the central document solidifying a whole range of individual liberties, the Bill of Rights. It is difficult to envision a much clearer indication of the ways in which both liberalism and republicanism blended, and functioned together within the context of religious faith, than the framing and ratification of the First Amendment to the Constitution. As Tocqueville noted, in America the "spirit of religion and the spirit of freedom" did indeed form a "marvelous combination."

To recapitulate, republicanism appealed to Americans in the eighteenth century because certain themes central to the classical republican tradition resonated with American ideas and experience, notably the emphasis on autonomous citizens participating in public affairs. Insofar as those ideas overlapped with the Lockean idea of responsible freedom and the Christian idea of the covenant formed by God's people, it was possible for Americans to think of themselves simultaneously as republicans, liberals, and Christians, although of course those categories are ours rather than theirs. In the absence of rigid traditions requiring differentiation by bloodlines, classes, or creeds, it was possible in nineteenth-century America as well for diverse interpretations of these ideas to coexist and for loose and fluid coalitions to form and dissolve as different issues appeared and vanished. In a study that illustrates the ever-changing nature of these affiliations, John Brooke demonstrates through a microscopic analysis of Worcester County, Massachusetts, from 1713 through 1861 that different social, economic, and religious groups adopted rhetorics that we might label liberal and republican at different times for different purposes. Moreover, the (republican) ideas of virtue and community on the one hand, and the (liberal) ideas of freedom and voluntarism on the other, could be and were used equally well by insurgents and conservatives depending on the purpose for which, and the context within which, they were used. Brooke's evidence shows that liberal and republican vocabularies, along with the competing varieties of religiosity that formed the shifting framework surrounding political and economic debates, persisted throughout the period from 1713 to 1861. Unfortunately Brooke's somewhat schematic treatment tends to reify the categories of republicanism and liberalism that his evidence does so much to destabilize. His study does illustrate, sometimes more than he acknowledges, how intricately and even inextricably these ideas were interwoven into the pattern of eighteenth- and nineteenth-century American culture, thereby illuminating the enduring appeal and potency of these traditions as arsenals for public debate.[12]

A thorough account of the debates among American historians concerning the role of republicanism vis-à-vis liberalism in the nineteenth century is impossible here. But a brief discussion of some of the conflicting interpretations of recent years may reveal just how contested the concept of republicanism has become in the years since Bailyn and Wood established its presence in American discourse. *The Federalist Papers*, which social scientists offered in the mid-twentieth cen-

tury as the founding document for liberal pluralism, has been interpreted as an in-
genious justification for institutions that could produce civic virtue despite the
frailties of a republican citizenry. Historians persuaded by Madison's celebrated
speech at the Virginia Ratifying Convention on June 20, 1788, argue that the Federalists included some true republicans who "put confidence" in what Madison
called "this great republican principle, that the people will have virtue and intelligence" sufficient to choose wisely those who will hold positions in government.
Only the virtue of the people, Madison insisted, not their leaders nor the institutional form of their government, can secure a republic.[13] For those unpersuaded
by Madison's passionate appeal, the Antifederalists seem the true patriots out to
preserve civic virtue in the face of commerce, centralized authority, and the corruption embodied in the Federalist gentry.

That division, and the historiographical split concerning its significance,
echoes through analyses of antebellum history. If the Federalists' schemes seemed
to Jeffersonians to threaten the republic by undercutting the autonomy of independent craftsmen and farmers, to the Federalists themselves the desire for a
strong standing army, stable elites, and the suppression of selfish individualism
seemed a straightforward republican program. Jeffersonians likewise invoked the
magic of civic virtue to legitimate their alternative policies, and some historians
have interpreted their efforts as the genuine embodiment of republican ideas. Yet
the diverse coalition that followed Jefferson included such a wide variety of people, espousing such a wide range of programs, that any simple characterization
distorts their complex amalgamation of different values. As Robert Shalhope has
written,

> The assault on Federalism that joined such men as John Taylor of Caroline, the south-
> ern slaveholding planter, Matthew Lyon, the aggressive man on the make on the
> Vermont frontier, William Findley, the self-made political leader from western
> Pennsylvania, Benjamin Austin, the urban agitator, the radical British emigrés
> Joseph Priestley and Thomas Cooper, and the simple Massachusetts farmer William
> Manning produced no quintessential Republican. Rather a variety of elements
> throughout the nation—agrarian and urban entrepreneurs resentful of the power
> and prestige of urban merchants who controlled the Atlantic trade; ambitious, un-
> connected individuals no longer willing to defer to entrenched elites; radical re-
> publicans innately suspicious of the tyranny of a centralized government; old re-
> publicans fearful lest the advent of widespread commercial development bring a
> loss of American virtue; groups caught up in the egalitarianism spawned by the
> Revolutionary attack on the corporatism of the old order; independent producers
> frustrated with the elite control and social restraints characteristic of an ordered,
> paternalistic hierarchy—joined to form Republican coalitions.[14]

If the Jacksonians incorporated equally diverse self-styled republicans who
feared banks as breeders of corruption and "venturous conservatives," to use
Marvin Meyers's phrase, who ranged from backwoods frontiersmen to urban artisans who shared only a desire to secure autonomy for themselves, so could the
Whigs think of themselves as legitimate heirs of the "country tradition" of re-

publicanism thanks to their emphasis on duty rather than rights, on organic unity rather than conflict, and on hierarchical order rather than indiscriminate leveling. Neither Jacksonians nor Whigs succeeded in laying exclusive or altogether convincing claim to the republican heritage, in part because of the diversity of their constituencies and the hybrid nature of their programs, and in part because of the internal inconsistencies and instabilities originally present in the republican tradition itself. The categories of liberalism and republicanism are inadequate to deal with the rapidly shifting social and economic order that was beginning to emerge in the new nation; for the 1830s and 1840s those categories are even less appropriate. The terminology of the eighteenth century lingered, but the meanings attached to such highly charged words—as well as the world in which they were spoken—changed. Many Americans came to identify freedom increasingly with freedom from interference and restraint. Others came to identify virtue increasingly with women who were safely cordoned off from the hurly-burly of the public sphere. Whereas John Locke and Adam Smith had conceived of political rights and economic exchange within the contexts of religious duty and ethical life, some Americans were beginning to think of freedom as something independent of social responsibility. Whereas eighteenth-century American republicans concerned themselves with maintaining the vitality of the political realm, by the mid-nineteenth century some guardians of virtue separated female purity from the pollution of politics.[15] Lincoln's Republican Party succeeded in part because he was able to revitalize older, fading republican ideals of autonomy and ethical citizenship by linking them with appeals to the property rights of free men and appeals to biblical injunctions against injustice. Champions of the Confederacy, on the other hand, likewise believed they stood firmly on a quite different conception of autonomous and honorable service to their republic and homage to biblically justified forms of hierarchy.[16]

In the aftermath of the Civil War, republican echoes continued to reverberate, although perhaps more faintly. The rise of laissez-faire liberalism made references to civic virtue or the public good, conceived as something separate from individual interest, seem quaint if not irrelevant. E. L. Godkin tried to keep republican themes alive in the *Nation* during the early 1870s, but as the decade wore on he shifted to the new language of expertise, specialization, and Anglo-Saxon superiority as the only effective response to the new ethos of greed. Public-spirited individuals could nurture civic virtue only when they aimed to create and preserve a unitary common interest; in the face of unvarnished self-interest, and the conflicts between interest groups that were coming to be seen as inevitable, republican discourse became increasingly archaic. In a splendid analysis, Kevin Thornton points out that the ideals of sacrifice and responsibility proclaimed in the *Nation* as late as 1867 were being subjected to ridicule by Godkin himself only a decade later. The earlier ethical idea of "republican simplicity" had become an impediment to progress and prosperity defined as success in the marketplace; in Thornton's apt image, Cincinnatus was becoming Dale Carnegie.[17]

If the self-styled "best men" frequently abandoned republicanism during the

1870s, so too did many workers. As Philip Ethington demonstrates, historians who have tried to find in the ideas of the American labor movement a successor to eighteenth-century republicanism have misunderstood both the process of labor organizing and the thrust of republican ideology. Whereas the working-men's parties depended on creating, or at least bringing to consciousness, labor-ers' sense of themselves as a distinctive group with particular interests, republi-cans traditionally denied legitimacy to any interest groups that defined themselves independently of the ostensibly singular public interest. By replacing the lan-guage of virtue with the language of class, workingmen's parties contributed to the transformation of American public life. To simplify a complex process, for many workers the ethical and political categories that dominated republican dis-course were displaced by the economic and social categories of interest-group liberalism. Satisfying the desires of individuals, rather than channeling those de-sires toward civic virtue, became the purpose of politics. Given the emergence of self-interest as a positive value, as something no longer requiring either apology or identification with the common good, efforts to employ republican rhetoric were doomed. Whether the attempt to assume the mantle of virtue—and to char-acterize the opposition as corrupt—was made by Denis Kearney in San Fran-cisco, or by the Knights of Labor, or by Texas Populists, it would fail to mobilize a population that was beginning to think in terms of the interests of private indi-viduals rather than the duties of a republican citizenry.[18]

In twentieth-century America, scattered republican themes continue to rattle around in political rhetoric, but they fit poorly into the dominant discourse of rights. During the progressive period, a small and exceptional group of American thinkers and reformers attempted to keep alive the notion of a common good that would emerge from the active participation of all citizens in democratically orga-nized communities. Their conception of knowledge as uncertain, and of politics as egalitarian and open-ended, however, seemed to most Americans shapeless and naive in the wake of World War I. By 1920 their crusade had come to an end.[19]

The next generation of reformers, the creators of the New Deal, replaced the idea of the public interest with a full-blown theory of interest groups. If the pref-erences of different groups, although often contradictory, could somehow be made to seem part of a broad and ill-defined agenda, it might be possible to cre-ate a powerful political coalition. Occasionally the Democratic Party has tried to refashion the republican ideal of citizenship by using themes of justice and equal-ity, but more frequently its appeals have focused on the ideas of family, ethnic-ity, race, labor, and government activity, all of which rely on somewhat narrow self-definitions that make forging a simple majority—to say nothing of a unified republican citizenry—difficult if not impossible.[20]

The Republican Party, by contrast, has in recent years more successfully pack-aged itself for national consumption, in part, oddly enough, by incorporating themes from the tradition of classical republicanism that Americans on the left have tried to adopt as their own. Republican candidates claim to fear the central-ization of power in the federal government as a source of corruption. They defend hierarchy, distrust interest groups, scorn dependency, celebrate valor in battle, fear that change is evidence of decline, prefer patriarchy to the chaos of sexual equality, and even find virtue in austerity—at least for those without tax shelters. Notwithstanding the element of caricature in that portrait, it should serve to suggest how peculiar is the attempt by some American historians and political theorists to locate in classical republicanism a left-leaning alternative to the program of the Republican Party. Few contemporary American politicians in either party have any apparent interest in, or evident familiarity with, the notion of civic virtue. Yet it should be clear that Republicans have at least as legitimate a claim to certain aspects of the republican tradition as do Democrats, who worry about satisfying as many particular interest groups as possible by according legitimacy to demands for government programs as a question of individual rights.

Perhaps the growing awareness among academics that republicanism now seems a decidedly unattractive and inappropriate foundation for progressive politics helps to explain the current retreat from interpretations that emphasize the role of republican ideas in American history. Jennifer Nedelsky's much discussed *Private Property and the Limits of American Constitutionalism: The Madisonian Framework and Its Legacy* challenges the significance of republicanism and emphasizes the central role played in American law by the desire to protect private property.[21] Robert Bellah and his associates, who in 1985 stressed the potential of republicanism as a counterweight to the corrosive force of "expressive individualism" in their celebrated *Habits of the Heart*, scarcely mention the republican tradition in their successor volume, *The Good Society*, published in 1991.[22] Daniel Rodgers, in an incisive discussion of republicanism in the *Journal of American History*, argues that the language of republicanism appealed to intellectual historians primarily because they were looking for a way to respond to the new social history of the 1960s. Though Rodgers convincingly demonstrates why interpretations stressing republicanism now seem unbalanced, his own insistence that ideas must be studied solely from the perspective of their instrumental value strikes me as similarly lopsided.[23]

Pendulums swing back and forth, and these recent studies indicate that republicanism now seems rather less central to historians than it did a decade or two ago. Yet it would be a mistake to swing to the opposite extreme, either substantively (with Nedelsky) or methodologically (with Rodgers). A more fruitful course lies in the recognition that Americans have always drawn upon a variety of sources to fashion the arguments they want to make. At times those arguments have been "republican," if we must characterize invocations of virtuous citizens and the public good as republican. At times they have been "liberal," if we must characterize invocations of individual freedom and rights as liberal. Frequently they have been "religious," if we pay attention to the almost obsessive piety of American public discourse. But almost always they have been hybrids of these and other languages and traditions. Likewise most participants in public discourse have simultaneously expressed their beliefs—and thereby constituted themselves and their culture—and at the same time calculated the effectiveness of their words as weapons. In a brilliant study of American law that challenges both the liberal and the republican readings of American constitutional and economic development, William Novak demonstrates that beneath the thin layer of federal law, the states' lower courts drew on a wide variety of resources to elaborate and enforce the doctrine *salus populi*, the people's welfare. What Novak terms "the common law vision of a well-regulated society" does not fit neatly with either the republican or the liberal tradition, but in all its complexity it fits very well indeed with the rich texture of American legal practice in the new nation's first century.[24]

My point is not to dissolve the question of the role of republicanism in America but merely to insist that we return republican ideas to their appropriate location, not as statements of universal principles equally appropriate for Athens or Rome, Florence or London, but as a discourse embedded in particular historical disputes. In an essay reflecting on the U.S. Constitution, Bailyn has struck precisely the balance I have in mind. Leading federalists, he insists,

> would have been astonished to hear that they were initiating a change from something scholars would later call "civic humanism" or "classical republicanism" to another, something that would be called "liberalism," or that they were chiefly interested in preserving patrician rule derived from the older tradition. They were neither more nor less determined to protect private property as a foundation of personal freedom and to advance economic enterprise than their predecessors and opponents, and they were no less committed to the need for disinterested "virtue" in government. Both they and their opponents were working within the broad pattern of political thought inherited from the early days of the Revolution, but the urgencies the federalists felt led them to reassess the impediments to the creation of a national state which they found embedded in that enveloping tradition.[25]

That "broad pattern of political thought" included, among other elements, republican, liberal, and religious ideas; we can understand these traditions only if we see how they changed as they were blended together in response to the "urgencies" of particular situations.

Yet it would be a mistake to assume, as a result of our awareness that the meanings of ideas are transformed as they are put to use, that words are nothing more than vehicles for asserting our individual preferences, and that beneath lofty rhetoric lies the bedrock of personal interest. An impressive body of scholarship from a wide range of disciplines indicates the inadequacy of self-interest as an explanation for human behavior. In the midst of a culture dominated by "rights talk," Mary Ann Glendon finds that the starkness, simplicity, absoluteness, and hyperindividualism of our political and legal discourse do not reflect "the more complex ways of speaking" that Americans use when they interact with each other at home, in school, in the workplace, or in other "communities of memory and mutual aid." Acknowledging this disjunction does not require a romantic leap of faith. It requires only the recognition that we must make the analytical move "beyond self-interest," to use the title of a richly informative cross-disciplinary collection edited by Jane Mansbridge, if we want to understand the complexity of human motivation.[26] Republican, liberal, and religious ideas have appealed to Americans for a variety of reasons, just as different historians have been attracted to these ideas for a variety of reasons. Awareness of the inadequacy of any one of these as a master analytic unlocking the secrets of the past need not blind us to their interaction and their persistence in the historical development of American culture.

FIVE

LIFE EVERLASTING

Tocqueville in America

D*emocracy in America* is not a classic text—at least if one accepts Mark Twain's definition of a classic as a book everyone wants to have read but no one wants to read. By that measure John Locke's *Essay Concerning Human Understanding* might be a classic, or perhaps G. W. F. Hegel's *Phenomenology of Spirit* or William James's *Principles of Psychology*. But by Twain's standard *Democracy in America* emphatically is not a classic, because it is a book that people continue to read and reread, a book that continues to engage readers and repay their efforts, a book cited and endorsed by both Newt Gingrich and Bill Clinton at their parties' National Conventions in the summer of 1996. It is also a book everyone wants to write about, judging from the hundreds of books and articles on Tocqueville and his ideas flowing from European and American writers in many different disciplines.

The topic of this essay—the status of Tocqueville in America—has generated so much attention that merely summarizing what has already been written on the subject could fill a short book.[1] Instead I will trace only in barest outline the shifting varieties of interpretation and levels of interest in Tocqueville among Americans, then hazard a tentative explanation of the current obsession with him, which may be the only thing Pat Buchanan and Hillary Clinton have in common.

Americans' continuing fascination with *Democracy in America* is easy to understand; Tocqueville himself was the first to explain it. In a letter to his friend Eugène Stoffels, made available to American readers in John Bigelow's introduction to his 1899 edition of *Democracy in America*, Tocqueville stated his goal: he wanted to show his readers that the reality of popular government was neither so grand as its friends' estimates nor so awful as its enemies' fears. He sought to demonstrate, he wrote, that democracy has none of the elevated features with which [its champions'] imagination would endow it; and, moreover, that such a government can not be maintained without certain conditions of intelligence, of private morality, and of religious belief that we [French], as a nation, have not reached, and that we must labour to attain before grasping their political results. To those for whom the word democracy is synonymous with destruction, anarchy, spoliation, and murder, I have tried to show that under a democratic government the fortunes and rights of society may be respected, liberty preserved, and religion honoured; that though a republic may develop less than other governments some of the noblest powers of the human mind, it yet has a nobility of its own; and that, after all, it may be God's will to spread a moderate amount of happiness over all men, instead of heaping a large sum upon a few by allowing only a small minority to approach perfection.[2]

That passage, which echoes the concluding words of Tocqueville's second volume, signals the essential tension in *Democracy in America*, the ambivalence that gives Tocqueville's analysis its richness and makes possible the multiple readings offered by his many interpreters.

"I please many persons of opposite opinions," Tocqueville continued to Stoffels in a revealing admission, "not because they penetrate my meaning, but because, looking only to one side of my work, they think they find in it arguments in favour of their own convictions. But I have faith in the future, and I hope that the day will come when all will see clearly what now only a few suspect."[3] Whether or not that latter day has come, Tocqueville was right about the reasons for his enthusiastic initial reception in America. Many of the early reviewers of the book, like many of those with whom he spoke during his travels, were members of the American gentry about whom Daniel Walker Howe has written brilliantly in *The Political Culture of the American Whigs*. "Ordered liberty" was these ambivalent republicans' principal value.[4] Their complex combination of a longing for stability together with an appreciation of the republican principles of liberty and equality strongly resembled Tocqueville's own sensibility. Since these proto-Whigs were among the most important of Tocqueville's sources, and since they were prominent among his reviewers, there is nothing surprising in the congruence between his account and their perceptions, which also accounts for the initial enthusiasm of his early American interpreters.

The first American edition of *Democracy in America* was published in 1838 with a preface written by the Whig attorney and New York state assemblyman John C. Spencer, who had discussed America with Tocqueville during his visit. Spencer emphasized the multidimensionality of Tocqueville's analysis and identified it as one of the two main sources of the immediate flurry of interest in the book in the United States. Tocqueville, Spencer wrote, "has discussed many subjects on which very different opinions are entertained in the United States; but with an ability, a candour, and an evident devotion to the cause of truth, which will commend his views to those who most radically dissent from them. Indeed, readers of the most discordant opinions will find that he frequently agrees with both sides, and as frequently differs from them."[5] If there was not always something in Tocqueville for everyone to like, there was at least something every American reader was likely to find intriguing.

The second reason for Americans' initial enthusiasm is more straightforward. Tocqueville's account was distinctive, as John Bigelow admitted candidly in his 1899 introduction, because "it was the first book written about the United States by any European of repute that was not conceived in a spirit of disparagement and detraction."[6] Frances Trollope, to cite only one prominent example, was disgusted by the fruits of democracy. She detested Americans' hypocrisy as slaveholders who proclaimed their love of liberty; their table manners, which made every trip to the dinner table a nightmare; and especially their proclamations of equality, which the most ignorant and untalented made with the greatest fervor.[7] In one of the most entertaining sections of his study of American democracy, *Self-Rule*, Robert Wiebe catalogs the numerous travelers' accounts of America written by Europeans in the early nineteenth century. He concludes that in the great chain of being, the typical portrait placed American citizens somewhere between pigs and dogs.[8] No wonder Tocqueville's account stood out. It was, in the words of the review published in the *United States Magazine and Democratic Review*, "decidedly the most remarkable and really valuable work that has yet appeared upon this country from the hand of a foreigner. . . . The difference between M. Tocqueville and our common herd of travellers, is, that when he speaks of the principles of government he knows what he is talking of." In other words, Tocqueville alone could distinguish democratic activity in America from the behavior of barnyard animals.[9]

Democracy in America was wildly praised and widely adopted as a textbook in the schools popping up like mushrooms across America. But toward the turn of the twentieth century the book fell out of fashion—and out of print. Robert Nisbet has argued, and Wilfred McClay has recently concurred, that Tocqueville's account disappeared because his positive assessment of American democracy was drowned in a flood of equally enthusiastic celebrations.[10] I think that assessment misses the mark. It was instead the prevalence of conflict that submerged Tocqueville's *Democracy*. Conflict caused Americans to doubt the wisdom of Tocqueville's analysis, because they interpreted *Democracy in America* as stressing an underlying national consensus on basic values. By the end of the nineteenth century, the evidence of discord had become inescapable.

It is generally agreed that this interpretation of Tocqueville, which highlights his identification of what Americans had in common, accounted for his dramatic revival in the America of the 1940s and 1950s. It also accounts for the somewhat tiresome recitation by more recent American historians of all the conflicts in American society in the 1830s to which Tocqueville supposedly paid insufficient attention. In much the same way, the obvious breakdown of American consensus explains the temporary disappearance of Tocqueville in the years from the outbreak of the Civil War until the outbreak of World War II.

This was a period marked by dramatic and violent disagreements among

Americans on a wide variety of issues, including not only the questions of slavery and race relations that lay behind the Civil War and hovered over the postwar years but also the destruction of American Indian cultures, the influx of immigration and the resulting controversy over religious and ethnic diversity, and the related struggles between labor and management, and between rural America and the emerging urban majority, over the economic as well as political meanings of democracy in America.

The almost complete lack of interest in Tocqueville among the most prominent progressive historians such as Frederick Jackson Turner and Charles Beard—historians struggling to make sense of their conflict-ridden nation—confirms this somewhat unconventional explanation of Tocqueville's eclipse. Confirmation of a different sort comes from noting that Henry Adams, arguably the least representative American historian writing at the end of the nineteenth century, was almost alone in declaring himself a disciple of Tocqueville.[11] Although not quite a rule of American culture, it is nearly always true that wherever Henry Adams stood, at any stage of his life, scarcely anyone else could be found.

The resurgence of American interest in Tocqueville of course dates from the publication of George W. Pierson's landmark study *Tocqueville and Beaumont in America* in 1938 and the subsequent republication of several editions of *Democracy in America* in the mid- to late 1940s.[12] This wave crested twice, initially carrying the arguments of Tocqueville's first volume into American political discourse, then extending the subtler arguments of his second volume into broader and deeper assessments of American society and culture.

The first wave was launched by the emergence of what came to be called totalitarian governments in Europe. Americans in the 1930s and 1940s were searching for explanations of how European democracies such as Germany and Italy could have gone so wrong, and how the Soviet Union could have devolved so rapidly from a utopian experiment into a dangerous dystopia. *Democracy in America* seemed to offer a clue—or rather many clues. The first was Tocqueville's warning that the quest for equality could lead to the tyranny of the majority, in which the voices of dissent were stifled by an oppressive conformism, an all-powerful centralized government, or a combination of the two that seemed ominously familiar in the 1940s, especially after European refugee intellectuals began arriving in America.

When Dwight Macdonald published his essay "A Theory of Mass Culture" in 1953, he brought into sharp focus the scattered anxieties that had been expressed in various writings by European and American social and cultural critics such as Erich Fromm, Hannah Arendt, Theodor Adorno, and Leo Lowenthal. Critiques of MacDonald, such as Daniel Bell's in *The End of Ideology*, tried to place the argument in a broader historical framework and to separate the critique of conformity from the often Marxist presuppositions—the ideology, to use Bell's term—behind it. Such analysts were turning away from the confident radicalism of the preceding decades toward something else. Whereas American thinkers in the first half of the twentieth century might have looked toward Jefferson or perhaps Marx for inspiration, a new generation of intellectuals looked instead to the less comforting but apparently more incisive wisdom of thinkers such as Max Weber, who made his first appearance in English translation in the 1940s; Karl Mannheim, who called in *Ideology and Utopia* for replacing faith in all-encompassing philosophical systems by reliance on the critical intelligence of independent intellectuals; and especially Tocqueville, who began making cameo appearances everywhere. The first president of the United States to quote Tocqueville was Dwight D. Eisenhower; since then his words have appeared in the speeches of every president.[13]

Tocqueville played starring roles in books such as Louis Hartz's *The Liberal Tradition in America*, published in 1955, and Marvin Meyers's *The Jacksonian Persuasion*, published in 1956. Sandwiched between those was political scientist Clinton Rossiter's apt (and typical) observation in 1955: "No book on an American subject is thought complete these days without a few insightful words from Alexis de Tocqueville," to which Rossiter then added a few insightful words from Tocqueville to nail down the point. Hartz's widely accepted notion of a liberal tradition could have been taken almost without modification from the opening pages of *Democracy in America* (although it could hardly have been sustained by a more careful reading of both volumes). Meyers brilliantly portrayed Jacksonian America as a land of "venturous conservatives" whose paradoxical invocations of the past and bold departures from it could best be explained through Tocqueville's nuanced and multidimensional analysis. In short, arguments drawn from *Democracy in America* were ubiquitous in the works of American social scientists during the 1950s. As the idea of American democracy emerged as a normative concept in both the critical and celebratory studies of American consensus produced in the early years of the cold war, Tocqueville was everywhere.[14]

Perhaps Tocqueville's deepest impact registered in sociology, thanks initially to the dramatic success of David Riesman's argument in *The Lonely Crowd* (1953), hailed by academic specialists and the popular press alike as the key to understanding modern America. Riesman littered his book with quotations from Tocqueville, whose insights into the dangers lurking beneath prosperity framed and informed the book's analysis. Beyond the shift from nineteenth-century "inner-directed" to post–World War II "other-directed" individuals, Riesman held out an ideal of "autonomy" for those strong enough, and far-seeing enough, to embrace the ironic sensibility he seemed to derive from, and to identify with, the wisdom of Tocqueville. The defense against mass culture, and the shield that protected America from the tyranny of the majority, could be found through careful study of *Democracy in America*.[15]

Throughout the 1950s and the long 1960s, which ended only in 1974 with the resignation of Richard Nixon and America's withdrawal from Vietnam, Tocqueville was a staple in the curriculum of American universities. For conservatives such as Robert Nisbet at Berkeley (or Vincent Starzinger at Dartmouth College, where I first encountered *Democracy in America* as a student), Tocqueville was a sober prophet who saw through the promise of material prosperity and egalitarian ideals to the hollowness at the core of modern democratic cultures that had lost touch with the values of tradition and authority. For members of the New Left, whom I also encountered at Dartmouth and as a graduate student at Stanford, Tocqueville was the scourge of conformism, a sober prophet who saw through the promise of material prosperity and egalitarian ideals to the invisible oppression that Herbert Marcuse was laying bare in books like *One Dimensional Man* and *Essay on Liberation*.[16]

Tocqueville's odd stature as a sage revered by conservatives and radicals alike merely confirmed the accuracy of his own early assessment in the letter to Stoffels already quoted. He was still attractive to "many persons of opposite opinions," as he put it, because they were "looking only to one side" of his work and finding there "arguments in favour of their own convictions." That tendency has continued for a century and a half, and there is no reason to suspect that it will soon come to an end.

Tocqueville's eternal life in America is due partly to the *lack* of congruence between his ideas and those prevailing in American politics at any time, which makes possible his adoption by disparate guardians eager to embrace him for their own purposes. By his own admission he was neither simply a democrat nor simply an aristocrat. He fits only awkwardly into our categories of Hamiltonian or Jeffersonian, republican or democrat, conservative or liberal. For that reason we characterize him, as Meyers did, as a "venturous conservative," or as Roger Boesche has done recently, as a "strange liberal," or as Alan Kahan has done even more recently, as an "aristocratic liberal."[17] But for reasons Tocqueville himself made clear, such characterizations are inadequate: recall his admission that he had "faith in the future" and his hope that eventually "all will see clearly what now only a few suspect." Has that day come?

At the considerable risk of appearing to pull a rabbit from a hat, in my conclusion I will attempt to show clearly what only a few of Tocqueville's interpreters have suspected. It is possible to see what Tocqueville was driving at, to see both sides of his argument, by looking carefully at what remains constant in both of the quite different volumes of his *Democracy*. It is by now a commonplace that these two volumes differed considerably from one another in their tone, and even in their arguments, largely because of developments in France between Tocqueville's completion of volume one in 1835 and his completion of volume two in 1840. The first volume focuses on his fear that majority tyranny will stifle dissent; the second that there will be no dissent to stifle but only conformity. The first volume worries that uncontrolled passions will lead to tyranny; the second that there will be no passions to control but only torpor. The first volume registers no concern with industrialization; the second expresses Tocqueville's alarm (following his visit to England) about the dangers of a new industrial aristocracy, and so on.

Given those differences, what, if any, are the threads connecting the two volumes? There are at least two. First, the characteristic of American democracy that has impressed commentators on Tocqueville from the earliest to the most recent is the importance of voluntary associations. Participation in such associations prepares Americans for civic life by prompting them to focus on solving concrete problems as members of community groups of all kinds, from the most benevolent and/or ambitious to the most self-serving and/or trivial. Serving on juries leads them to imagine themselves in each other's shoes.[18] All of these experiences prevent "self interest properly understood," to use that crucial phrase of Tocqueville's, from degenerating into the old-fashioned egoism that earlier moralists abhorred or the equally unattractive, newfangled individualism that Tocqueville portrays as a danger in volume two. Both egoism and individualism were inimical to democracy.

Why did Tocqueville think voluntary associations, service on juries, and all kinds of participation in public affairs mattered so much? He certainly did not consider Americans uniquely virtuous. In fact, he refused even to associate "self interest properly understood" with virtue, in either its republican or its Christian forms.[19] But he did identify it closely with the practice of deliberation and the ethic of reciprocity, which he believed associational life fosters and which makes democracy work. The *experience* of associational life inclines Americans toward benevolence, or sympathy, whether they are virtuous or not. Even at the end of volume two, where Tocqueville confessed his anxiety about the threat of government centralization in democratic cultures lacking this practice of deliberation and the ethic of reciprocity that undergirds it—democratic nations such as France—he emphasized this feature of American democracy:

> It is through political associations that Americans of every station, outlook, and age day by day acquire a general taste for association and get familiar with the way to use the same. Through them large numbers see, speak, listen, and stimulate each other to carry out all sorts of undertakings in common. Then they carry these conceptions with them into the affairs of civil life and put them to a thousand uses.

In America, he wrote in the concluding pages of volume two, "interest as well as sympathy prompts a code of lending each other mutual assistance at need. The more similar conditions become, the more do people show this readiness of reciprocal obligation."[20]

This ideal of reciprocity, which underlay the exercise of deliberation in voluntary associations and in public life that was central to what Tocqueville meant by democracy, provides the thread of continuity between the two volumes of *Democracy in America*. It is reciprocity that prevents a tyrannical majority from stifling dissent through the decentralization of authority in volume one; it is reciprocity, or sympathy, that prevents the decline of "self interest properly understood" into egoism or selfish inwardness in volume two. Tocqueville valued associational life for the same reasons James Madison did, reasons seldom grasped by pluralists in the 1950s but now more sharply in focus thanks to the later work of Marvin Meyers and the work of Drew McCoy and Lance Banning. Madison, like Tocqueville, believed that as a result of participating in common projects, people learn something that transcends the simple clash of competing interests envisioned by political scientists writing about pluralism. Through the process of confronting and filtering different ideas, clashing interests, and divergent ideals, people in associations can learn to see things from other points of view. To translate this very old insight into the hip lexicon of contemporary cultural studies, encountering the other teaches people how to think dialogically, to appreciate the instabilities and complexities of judgment. That hope underlay Madison's commitment to federalism, just as it underlay Tocqueville's stubborn refusal to dismiss the possibility that democracy in America might survive despite the dangers it faced.[21]

A similar hope animates the writings of a diverse group of contemporary thinkers who likewise do not fit comfortably into the standard categories of American politics. Just as Tocqueville's analysis was attractive to readers of various persuasions but also somewhat unsettling—or "strange," to use Boesche's word again—so contemporaries who look to deliberation, and who embrace an ethic of reciprocity, do not fit our standard categories. Several of these writers, some of whom are called communitarians because they share Tocqueville's enthusiasm for the potential of association and his concerns for what happens to democracy when participation in community life vanishes and unbounded individualism triumphs, cluster around the journal *The Responsive Community*.

They include those associated with Robert Bellah in the project that became *Habits of the Heart*;[22] Harvard law professor Mary Ann Glendon, who has savaged the absurdities of *Rights Talk*, to use the title of her unclassifiable book;[23] historians such as Thomas Bender, whose studies of community and public life have helped keep alive Tocqueville's own insights into American democracy;[24] those political activists allied with Senator Bill Bradley who share the reasons for his dissatisfaction with both the Democratic and the Republican Parties; and political theorists such as William Galston, who served for several years as a domestic advisor in the Clinton White House; Jane Mansbridge, who has shown the breadth of social scientists' dissatisfaction with the reductionist attribution of all human behavior to self-interest; and Jean Bethke Elshtain, who argues in her recent book *Democracy on Trial* that Americans' growing cynicism about politics, the absence of civic mindedness, and a destructive obsession with rights have sapped the mutual respect, empathy, and understanding that are necessary for the survival of a democratic community.[25] Such thinkers write in the spirit of Tocqueville, most of them explicitly acknowledge their debt to him, and all of them show that they have grasped both sides of his argument in *Democracy in America* because of the attention they pay to associational life and to the other common thread connecting both of Tocqueville's volumes, the importance of religious faith.

This dimension of Tocqueville's argument is more important than most American commentators in the last fifty years have appreciated. I will explain why indirectly, by turning to a phrase made familiar by the political scientist Robert Putnam in his widely read essay "Bowling Alone." Putnam, like the scholars and activists just mentioned, worries that America is losing the rich associational life that impressed Tocqueville. Such densely textured public life, according to Putnam's study of Italian politics over the last few centuries, *Making Democracy Work*, also explains the difference between the relatively stable cultures of northern Italy and the chaos of the south. When Americans stop participating in voluntary associations such as little leagues, parent-teacher associations, Rotary clubs, and so on, civic life is impoverished. While the number of people bowling in America is rising, Putnam points out, the number of bowling leagues, and bowling teams, is falling. Thus we confront the haunting anomie of "bowling alone."[26]

But the associational life of such voluntary organizations is not always so warm and cuddly. When it became known that the primary suspect in the bombing of the federal building in Oklahoma City in the spring of 1994, Timothy McVeigh, and his friends, James and Terry Nichols, often went bowling together, it was clear American society would have been better off had each of them gone bowling alone. From that detour I return to the importance of religious faith for Tocqueville's analysis.

It is not clear that Tocqueville himself was religious; that vexed question may never be answered more thoroughly than it was by André Jardin in his biography of Tocqueville.[27] Nor is it clear that all of those identified as communitarians today are religious. But many of them endorse Tocqueville's judgment that nineteenth-century American democracy worked because of a shared commitment to the ethic of reciprocity and an orientation toward a future in which virtue would be rewarded and vice punished. From Toqueville's perspective, the principal historical contribution of Christianity had been its revolutionary commitment to "the equality, the unity, the fraternity of all men," a commitment distinct from the prior acceptance of human inequality as inevitable. Moreover, Tocqueville insisted that even though some slaveholders and their apologists professed a belief in Christianity, such ideas disgusted Christians who took seriously the brotherhood of all races. Hypocrisy, however common, should not blind us to the ideals being mocked: "my heart rebels daily at seeing the little gentlemen who pass their time in clubs and wicked places, or great knaves who are capable of any base action as well as of any act of violence, speak devoutly of *their holy religion*. I am always tempted to cry out to them: 'Be pagans with pure conduct, proud souls, and clean hands rather than Christians in this fashion.' "[28] Acknowledging the difference between Christian principles and the hypocrisy of some who call themselves Christians, as Tocqueville did, might make it possible to distinguish between murderous voluntary associations such as the Ku Klux Klan, the Mafia, and those wings of the militia movement currently attracting members like Timothy McVeigh, and associations committed to activities premised on an ethic of love rather than resentment.

Tocqueville argued in *Democracy* that the close connection between civic life and religious faith, which took various forms in the wildly diverse tapestry of America's ethnic communities, was possible in America only because the separation of church and state prevented an opposition from growing between individual liberty and religious institutions of the sort that an official state religion created in France and other European nations. In a democratic age, Tocqueville insisted, religion alone could draw people away from the materialism that might otherwise obsess them, thereby keeping alive the precious sense of mutual obligation that animated community life. "Despotism may be able to do without faith," Tocqueville reasoned, "but freedom cannot."[29]

In recent decades historians have underestimated the significance of this argument for the importance of religious faith, which Tocqueville advanced with reference to Pascal's wager. Historians have faulted Tocqueville for underestimating the importance of revivalism and for paying too much attention to the exceptional views of New England Unitarians.[30] That observation may be accurate. Yet it should not obscure the central importance of religion in Tocqueville's analysis. Religious faith was inextricably intertwined with associational life in the structure of his argument: as his emphasis on the Puritan concept of the covenant at the beginning of volume one makes clear, he believed that Americans' practice of association embodied the ethic of reciprocity that derived from their common Christian heritage. He also saw, as we should see just as clearly, that although such an ethic in principle elevates benevolence, in practice it could and did serve to justify slavery—or lynching, or assassination—activities driven by hatred instead of sympathy. Not by invocations of religiosity, then, but by the precise nature of the activities undertaken ostensibly under its inspiration, should the value of all forms of community organizing be judged.

I cannot claim too much originality for this argument. Indeed, my emphasis on the dual importance of voluntary associations and religious faith merely echoes Tocqueville's own, and that of his early American interpreters, as John Spencer pointed out in 1838 in his preface to the first American edition of *Democracy in America*. Tocqueville's great achievement, Spencer concluded, derived from the connection between his "views of religion . . . [and] the democratic principle, which he steadily keeps in view." This insight, in Spencer's words, "cannot fail to confirm the principles already so thoroughly and universally entertained by the American people."[31] In other words, Tocqueville's sense of the mutual dependence of American democracy and American religiosity corresponded with Americans' understanding of themselves, a judgment I think most historians of nineteenth-century America now would share.[32]

The dual emphasis on voluntary associations and the civic value of religious faith, which enables us to bridge the gap between the first and second volumes of Tocqueville's *Democracy* and to see both sides of his argument, does help to account for the renewed intensity of engagement with Tocqueville that is apparent in much public debate in America today. Although that interest is hardly limited to those I have termed communitarians, their analyses are especially incisive because, like Tocqueville's, their ideas are less congruent with our rickety partisan categories of conservatism and liberalism than with the elusive and multidimensional realities of American democracy, which remain at least as complicated now as they were when Tocqueville first came to America.

Inasmuch as emphasizing the importance of reciprocity in *Democracy in America* helps focus attention on aspects of Tocqueville's analysis blurred by treatments that emphasized only his interest in individual freedom and voluntarism, it can serve to remind us of the delicate balance that characterizes his work and explains its perennial appeal. But exaggerating his emphasis on the ethic of reciprocity as the keystone of democracy would distort his arguments as much as ignoring that issue did several decades ago. If focusing on deliberation obscures the persistent realities of unequal wealth and power in America, for example, it will advance our understanding of one aspect of Tocqueville's argument only by blinding us to another: he not only emphasized the habits of the heart but also advanced a hard-headed assessment of the unsentimental calculations of self-interest that such habits must struggle to restrain and redirect. Only within the relatively equal social and economic conditions of antebellum America could the practice of deliberation and the ideal of reciprocity flourish. Under the more common conditions of inequality, Tocqueville feared, democratic behavior and democratic goals would wither.

The tendency to overlook this aspect of *Democracy in America* allows sentimental communitarians and supply siders alike to imagine that pockets of vibrant associational life can stand in for the egalitarian reality Tocqueville himself stressed. Thus Newt Gingrich, addressing the Republican Party National Convention in San Diego on August 13, 1996, praised the contributions of churches and neighborhood organizations and concluded that nothing less than "the moral case for lower taxes" is to be found in Tocqueville's *Democracy in America*. Simplification for simplification, that claim rivals the worst excesses of communitarians who imply that Tocqueville shows us how regular block parties can moderate the pathological violence of gangs.

Although only interpretations as multidimensional as Tocqueville's own can help us resist the persistent temptation to capture him and enlist his book for narrow partisan crusades, shrill and one-sided arguments attract more attention than such nuanced readings. Not only will competing American interpreters continue to champion various Tocquevilles for various purposes but new strains will no doubt also sprout from America's fertile soil. If the Tocqueville who warned us about the dangers of totalitarianism has died with the cold war, for example, others in addition to the communitarians' partisan of deliberative democracy will doubtless take his place.

We need only remember that, at one end of our cultural spectrum, the president who quoted Tocqueville most frequently was Ronald Reagan, whose speech writers, like Gingrich, detached Tocqueville's emphasis on civil society from his emphasis on the ideal of reciprocity. At the opposite end, we are about to see the appearance of the first study arguing that Tocqueville, with his sensitivity to multiple causation, his tolerance for paradox, and his capacity to embrace conflicting values and hold in suspension contradictory ideas, should at last be recognized as an early postmodernist who has too long remained in shadow.[33] The life of Tocqueville in America, already reflecting the circuitous path of democratic theory and practice over a century and a half, seems destined to continue indefinitely. That interest persists, however, for reasons that owe more to Americans' irresistible urge to simplify Tocqueville's ideas than to a willingness to acknowledge his ambivalence or to keep in focus the multiple dimensions of his complex analysis of American democracy.

SIX

DEMOCRACY AND DISENCHANTMENT

From Weber and Dewey to Habermas and Rorty

THE CULTURE OF MODERNISM springs from the unsettling but liberating experience of uncertainty. When knowledge is recognized as contingent, standards that seemed stable start to wobble, convictions that felt solid start to crumble, and revolutionary forms of expression emerge. Thus in the late nineteenth and early twentieth centuries writers of imaginative literature began to address questions of consciousness itself, as well as the world outside the mind. Poets began to experiment with radically new forms as well as strange and unfamiliar material. Painters began to deconstruct, rearrange, and ultimately ignore the world of perceived objects in favor of excursions into uncharted territory, culminating finally with the fateful plunge into pure abstraction.

In philosophy and social theory, modernism took various forms that may appear less dramatically new and also perhaps even more diverse than were the manifestations of a new sensibility in the arts. Without disputing the range of the ideas that emerged in the explosion of late nineteenth-century thought, or claiming that these thinkers represented the "essence" of modernism, in this essay I explore the writings of Max Weber and John Dewey, two theorists whose ideas have played an important part in twentieth-century debates but whose perspectives are usually considered so distinct that comparison is fruitless. To the contrary, I will argue that their similarities as well as their differences illuminate several of the persistent themes and tensions in twentieth-century thought, and that important controversies in contemporary critical theory recapitulate to a striking degree the issues that engaged these pioneer modernists.

In 1904, Max Weber visited the United States for the first and last time. Given Weber's reputation for pessimism, and given the tendency of European intellectuals to malign the United States, one might reasonably expect that Weber found little to like about the American version of the flattened, utilitarian *Zivilisation* that German critics were fond of contrasting to their own more refined *Kultur*. When Freud traveled to America in 1909, for example, the experience turned his stomach. He later complained that his American journey caused the deterioration of both his digestive system and his handwriting. As he told Ernest Jones, in a judgment expressing the sentiment of countless Europeans before and since, "America is a mistake; a gigantic mistake, it is true, but none the less a mistake."[1]

Measured against that standard, Weber's response to America seems surprisingly moderate. Of course the smell of New York's streets and the impersonality of its dwellings disgusted him, as did Chicago's stockyards, an "ocean of blood" serving only to break the monotony of the "endless human desert" of the city itself. Characterizing Chicago with an unnerving image that only a student of urban sociology could love, Weber wrote that "the whole tremendous city . . . is like a man whose skin has been peeled off and whose intestines are seen at work." Notwithstanding such remarks, though, Weber found his American travels exhilarating and even therapeutic. He embarked on the journey after six years of almost complete mental incapacitation, and the lecture he delivered at the Universal Exposition in St. Louis was his first public performance since the mental collapse that followed his father's death in 1897. In contrast to Freud, whose experience illustrates how travel can narrow the mind, Weber reflected at the end of his stay that the trip had widened his scholarly horizons and improved his state of health. To the surprise of everyone traveling with him, Weber found America to be the tonic he needed. As he put it, in what might serve as the motto of conference goers everywhere, "Stimulation and occupation of the mind without intellectual exertion simply is the only remedy."[2]

In his travels Weber met a number of Americans who impressed him favorably, notably the social activist Jane Addams and the socialist Florence Kelley. He did not, however, meet the philosopher John Dewey, who was packing up and moving from Chicago to New York while Weber was traveling in the opposite direction during the fall of 1904. During the last eight decades, the paths of Dewey and Weber have continued not to cross. Despite the avalanche of studies by and about Dewey and Weber, which with the ongoing publication of their complete writings will doubtless soon bury even the most conscientious researchers, there has not yet been—at least to my knowledge—any effort besides my own to compare the ideas of these two seminal thinkers. That may not appear surprising. The evident dissimilarities between the hard-headed partisan of German power politics and the soft-hearted American populist make their comparison seem singularly unpromising. Yet their reputations as quintessential representatives of anti-democratic German *Kultur* and democratic middle-brow American pragmatism have obstructed our understanding of their ideas. Several recent interpreters have argued that Weber (no less adamantly than Dewey) proclaimed himself a partisan of democratic institutions and the Kantian ideal of individual autonomy. His pessimistic assessment of the prospects for democratic government sprang from his analysis of the unavoidable tension between instrumental and substantive rationality in a disenchanted world, not from any simple elitist or antipopular predispositions. Conversely, Dewey appreciated fully the distance separating the reality of welfare capitalism from his social democratic ideal. He worked to nurture citizens' critical intelligence not because he naively trusted the people but because he was so suspicious of those who presumed to lead and instruct them.[3]

In this chapter I will argue, first, that Weber's modified neo-Kantianism and Dewey's instrumentalism have a good deal in common at the levels of epistemology and ethics; and second, that their ideas about the limits of knowledge in the modern world have surprising, and surprisingly similar, implications for political theory, implications masked by their contrasting assessments of the potential for democratic practice in their own nations and by their quite different judgments of the threats to freedom represented by bureaucratic and popular forms of domination. I will conclude by linking their ideas with the recent work of Jürgen Habermas and Richard Rorty, two other apparently dissimilar thinkers whose adversarial positions can be shown to rely in quite unexpected ways on the work of Weber and Dewey. Now that historians, sociologists, and philosophers have begun to wonder about the consequences of a pragmatic hermeneutics,[4] it may be instructive to examine in that light the writings of two earlier thinkers who encountered the problem of constructing a democratic political culture on the quicksand of instrumentalist logic.

While Weber was struggling to recover from his breakdown, he began working on the nature and limits of knowledge in the *Geisteswissenschaften*, an endeavor that might seem more likely to cause than to cure mental exhaustion. Although these methodological essays were conveniently misinterpreted by sociologists seeking Weber's imprimatur for their own efforts to construct a value-free social science, a large and growing literature has established during the past decade Weber's reliance on *Verstehen*, or understanding, as the indispensable tool for social inquiry. Because human experience is meaningful, social analysis cannot escape the hermeneutic circle; interpretations of meaning can yield only partial and provisional knowledge. A relentless critic of positivism and of scientists' pretensions to provide solid foundations for modern culture, Weber was impatient with claims that empiricism could yield objective knowledge about human values. An antifoundationalist *avant la lettre*, Weber now attracts the attention not only of scholars interested in Dilthey but of those interested in Nietzsche as well.[5]

If perceptions of Weber as a partisan of objectivity in social science are both widespread and mistaken, so the popular image of Dewey as a scientific naturalist distorts his ideas. It is true that Dewey's appreciation of the link connecting language, meaning, and interpretive understanding surfaced only occasionally in his writings. "Consciousness in a being with language denotes awareness of perceptions of meanings," he wrote in *Experience and Nature*. "It is the perception of actual events, whether past, contemporary, or future, *in* their meanings." Interpretation, requiring recognition of the relation between text (or individual, or culture) and context, is integral to the study of human knowledge and action, because people think, express themselves, and act within a universe of meanings that exist outside them and which they nevertheless help to shape. In his chapter "Meaning" in *How We Think*, Dewey expressed an insight strikingly similar to that informing Weber's hermeneutics. "All knowledge, all science, thus aims to grasp the meaning of objects and events," Dewey argued. "This process always consists in taking them out of their apparent brute isolation as events, and finding them to be part of some larger whole *suggested by them*, which, in turn, *accounts for, explains, interprets* them; i.e., renders them significant."[6]

This emphasis on interpretation, on the search for meaning lodged in the relation of all objects of analysis to their contexts, reveals an intriguing aspect of Dewey's thinking. Dewey considered himself a naturalist by the time he wrote these passages, and they show the extent to which even in his post-Hegelian stage Dewey remained as critical of positivist versions of science as did Weber. Dewey did not intend by offering science as the paradigm for inquiry to minimize the importance of interpretation as a means of knowing. To the contrary, he emphasized that science, like all other forms of knowledge, aims at understanding the meaning of the phenomena toward which it is directed. He consistently repudiated the claim that science reveals information about the world that is privileged in some way. Instead he stressed the continuity between philosophical inquiry and natural science, both of which are experimental enterprises attempting to provide useful hypotheses by inquiring of the world and finding answers that enable us to cope successfully with reality.

It is important to emphasize this point, because Dewey continues to be misunderstood as a partisan of the scientism that has beguiled so many American social scientists, a form of reductionism that Dewey repeatedly and explicitly repudiated. Dewey's fundamental conception of experience, first advanced in "The Reflex Arc Concept in Psychology" in 1896 and elaborated again and again throughout his career, emphasized the qualitative dimension of human experience. Knowledge, for Dewey, cannot be separated from the purposes and plans we bring to experience as thinking and valuing creatures. In "Nature and Its Good" (1909), Dewey wrote that though nature itself, "till it produces a being who strives and who thinks in order that he may strive more effectively," has no purposes to fulfill—"has no mind of its own," in Dewey's phrase—things are otherwise where humans are concerned.

> But when the sentient organism, having experienced natural values, good and bad, begins to select, to prefer, and to make battle for its preference; and in order that it may make the most gallant fight possible picks out and gathers together in perception and thought what is favorable to its aims and what hostile, then and there Nature has at last achieved significant regard for good.

The process of valuing, then, is inextricably connected with life as humans live it, and social science goes wrong when it loses sight of that fundamental dimension of human experience.[7]

In the lectures Dewey delivered in China in 1919–20, he argued that science "can describe and record natural phenomena, but it cannot guide them or change them according to human ideals. But social philosophy cannot stop with mere recording and description; it must direct with thoughtful understanding the conclusions and recommendations which grow out of the records and descriptions of science." Thus description is not independent of value judgments in social inquiry; instead "the relationship between the social sciences and social philosophy is thus one of interpenetration." This conviction lay behind Dewey's spirited responses to the wide-ranging critiques of democracy advanced in the 1920s by psychologists, sociologists, political scientists, and journalists including Beardsley Ruml, Harry Elmer Barnes, Charles Merriam, Harold Lasswell, and especially Walter Lippmann. Unless this philosophical foundation is acknowledged, Dewey's opposition to the hard-boiling of American social science seems either quirky or incomprehensible.[8]

Dewey resisted the impulse toward scientism that flowed through American social analysis in the 1920s because he had an especially acute understanding of the nature and limitations of knowledge derived from all scientific inquiry. Although contemporary critics generally derive that appreciation from the work of Thomas Kuhn, it was available to early twentieth-century thinkers through the efforts of critical positivists such as Karl Pearson, Ernst Mach, Henri Poincaré, and Pierre Duhem.[9] Dewey was appalled that such critiques had so little impact on social science. In *The Public and Its Problems* (1927), he devoted considerable attention to this issue despite its apparent distance from his principal interest, which was to answer Lippmann's critique of democracy in *Public Opinion* (1922). But the methodological discussions in *The Public and Its Problems* are hardly the distraction they might appear; James Gouinlock is correct to characterize this book, rather than Dewey's *Logic: The Theory of Inquiry* (1938), as "the culmination of Dewey's instrumentalism."[10]

In *The Public and Its Problems*, Dewey criticized the faulty public conception of natural science as the house of Truth rather than Opinion, emphasizing that "the glorification of 'pure' science" is merely "a rationalization of an escape; it marks a construction of an asylum of refuge, a shirking of responsibility. The true purity of knowledge exists not when it is uncontaminated by contact with use and service. It is wholly a moral matter." From Dewey's point of view, the infatuation of America's Martin Arrowsmiths with the purity of research and their fear of the contamination of applied practice was the problem rather than the solution, and he saw its consequences spreading throughout the culture. "To make physical science a rival of human interests is bad enough, for it forms a division of energy which can ill be afforded. But the evil does not stop there. The ultimate harm is that the understanding by man of his own affairs and his ability to direct them are sapped at their root when knowledge of nature is disconnected from its human function."[11] Natural science, like any form of inquiry, is a human affair; it cannot exist apart from cultural values any more than social science can.

Dewey was an enthusiastic partisan of Albert Einstein and Werner Heisenberg for a similar reason. They revealed that physics, like philosophy, is a human enterprise, reflecting human values and conforming to human desires. In *The Quest for Certainty* (1929), Dewey offered an intellectual history of philosophers' efforts to gain just the kind of certain knowledge that he, as a pragmatist, considered illusory. The scientific revolution, Dewey argued, was but a halfway revolution until its work was completed by the even more revolutionary work of twentieth-century physics. When the structure of matter itself was shown to be comprehensible only in terms of our own artificial conceptual apparatus, the grail of unchanging laws disappeared once and for all. Completing the work begun by the generation of critical positivists, Heisenberg's uncertainty principle, Dewey believed, invalidated claims to certainty derived from the sciences and illegitimately extended to social knowledge. To replace such discredited scientism, in both the natural and the social sciences, Dewey nominated pragmatism, the commitment to open-ended and ever-expanding communities of inquiry operating on democratic principles to investigate problems in all the spheres of experience ranging from the nature of the atom to the nature of justice. Following the earlier revolutions of astronomy in the sixteenth and the seventeenth centuries, and Kant's philosophical revolution of the eighteenth century, Dewey dubbed this integration of the natural sciences into the same field of inquiry as the human sciences a third Copernican Revolution. First the earth was displaced by the sun as the center of our planetary system, then knowledge was shown to conform to the structure of human faculties. "The new center," Dewey concluded, "is indefinite interactions taking place within a course of nature which is not fixed and complete, but which is capable of direction to new and different results through the mediation of intentional operations."[12]

Whereas Dewey's contemporary critics from the right rebuked him for emphasizing the indefinite and incomplete nature of the world as he conceived it, his more recent critics on the left challenge him for facilitating social control through references to direction and results. But Dewey's point, which is difficult to keep in focus amid the clatter of criticism from both sides, is that all knowledge is uncertain, all claims to authority are suspect, and all candidates for truth must submit to searching investigation by democratically constituted communities of inquiry. Neither a nihilist nor a partisan of social control, Dewey insisted on the value-laden and interpretive nature of all quests for knowledge.[13]

Dewey and Weber not only shared the conviction that meaning is central to all human knowledge but also understood the depth of the crisis resulting from the awareness of the historicity of meanings. Both Weber and Dewey believed that human motivation must be understood in terms of cultural desires as well as physical needs. Standing beside the material interests emphasized by Marx, Weber argued, were "ideal interests," the values that give meaning to social action. When those values came unstuck from their moorings in religion and metaphysics, the phenomenon Weber dubbed disenchantment, cultures faced the unprecedented challenge of generating their own sets of meanings from within themselves.[14]

Scanning the horizon for candidates to accomplish this task, Dewey and Weber both identified scientific inquiry as the likely successor to faith. Thinking, Dewey argued in *Studies in Logical Theory*, does not arise in response to abstract problems of logic, but in specific situations in which we encounter concrete obstacles. In response we formulate plans of purposive action in order to change the condition of the world around us. Scientific method, as the most successful example of how such intelligence operates, for that reason should replace religion and philosophy as the model for pragmatic reasoning. Weber contended that of the various forms of rationality he identified, instrumental reasoning was the variety best suited to the disenchanted modern world. None of the other forms of rational action was appropriate. Value-rational action was governed by belief in the "value for its own sake" of some behavior, without concern for the means or the prospects of achieving that end. Affectual action was governed by emotional states, and traditional action by "ingrained habituation."[15] Only instrumentally rational action was calculated to achieve identifiable ends through available means. Like Dewey's pragmatic, scientific intelligence, Weber's instrumental rationality was a way of getting things done. Both forms of reasoning, it should be noted, were value-neutral in the sense that they stipulated no ends or goals beyond the achievement of results. Providing purposes was a different matter, a cultural project that could not be avoided or taken for granted.

Were Weber and Dewey then partisans of technocracy, as their critics have charged? Did they assume that the only problems left for disenchanted cultures were problems of technique? These are among the most controversial questions in the literature surrounding both thinkers. Although they recognized the appeal of instrumental reasoning as an analytical tool, both Weber and Dewey insisted that individuals must choose their own substantive values on other than strictly scientific grounds. Weber put the point bluntly and memorably in his lecture "Science as a Vocation" (1919):

> After Nietzsche's devastating criticism of those "last men" who "invented happiness," I may leave aside altogether the naive optimism in which science—that is, the technique of mastering life which rests upon science—has been celebrated as the way to happiness. Who believes in this?— aside from a few big children in university chairs or editorial offices . . . Tolstoy has given the simplest answer [to the question of the meaning of science], with the words: "Science is meaningless because it gives no answer to our question, the only question important for us: 'What shall we do and how shall we live?'" That science does not give an answer to this is indisputable.[16]

Their search for the substantive values that might anchor instrumental reason led Dewey and Weber beyond the competing ethical systems of Kant and Bentham. In "Self-Realization as the Moral Ideal," Dewey outlined the concept of character growth that would serve as his norm. Dewey contended that rather than judging an act moral "only when done from consciousness of duty," as Kant would have it, we should say that such an act "is immoral (because partial) as long as it is done merely from a sense of duty, and becomes moral when done for its own concrete sake." In other words, both the motives of the actor and the consequences of the act must be considered in assessing it. What standard of judgment did Dewey recommend? In contrast to the efforts of intuitionists and utilitarians to find universally applicable rules for determining the right and the good, Dewey maintained that "the object of moral principles is to supply standpoints and methods which will enable the individual to make for himself an analysis of the elements of good and evil in the particular situation in which he finds himself." Asserting the uniqueness of each situation, Dewey admitted in *Reconstruction in Philosophy*, may seem "not merely blunt but preposterous." Yet his instrumentalist method dictated nothing more specific than shifting the burden of morality from rules to critical intelligence. That procedure, Dewey insisted, "does not destroy responsibility; it only locates it."[17]

Dewey based his instrumentalist ethics on his democratic ideal: he relied on each individual to use his own moral judgment responsibly and on the community to ride herd over outlaws. He argued that the sole restriction on individual choices lay in the challenge of testing them in the long run in a social context. Only guidelines drawn from past experience and validated in future experience furnish us with ethical standards. Ethics can thus be but a method of inquiry, whose specific content varies as individuals collectively alter their ethical choices over time in response to new situations. We must reflect on the results of our actions in order to evaluate their moral content, and only in a democracy, Dewey believed, can collective ethical estimates be effectively translated into positive legal codes. Although a formal, prescriptive ethics is impossible, the need for a substantive ethics remains. As we encounter difficult choices, Dewey advised, we can best discern the path toward self-realization by applying the instrumentalist method. Each individual must shoulder the burden of responsibility without hoping that a universal rule will make his choice easier.

Weber likewise acknowledged the conflict between deontological and utilitarian ethics, but he was less confident it could be resolved. In "The Meaning of 'Ethical Neutrality,'" he pointed out that two incommensurable values collide in ethical judgment. We can, as Kant instructed, esteem more highly what Weber termed "the intrinsic value of ethical conduct—the 'pure will' or the 'conscience.'" Alternatively, we can take into account the utilitarians' concern for "the responsibility for the predictable consequences" of an action. According to Weber, this is a choice "not only of alternatives between values but of an irreconcilable death-struggle, like that between 'God' and the 'Devil.' Between these, neither relativization nor compromise is possible." In the jumble of our daily activities we generally blend these considerations, Weber admitted, but the logical problem remains.[18] Compared with Weber's stark conception of ethical dilemmas, Dewey's reliance on the ideal of self-realization may appear either fuzzy or evasive.

Having thus placed the weight of personal responsibility, albeit in quite different ways, squarely on the shoulders of individuals who lacked the comfort of religion or the support of metaphysics, Dewey and Weber turned their attention to the possibilities of politics. Could such responsible individuals, through political activity, somehow manage to construct a culture based on substantive values that would replace the ideas of divine will and natural law? How could the form of modern law, premised on the doctrines of freedom, equality, and justice, be propped up when the traditional sources of legitimation, the philosophical foundation of constitutionalism, had crumbled? Could the practice of popular government survive without the ideals that had given it life?

Both Dewey and Weber considered American democracy uniquely successful. They also agreed on the reasons why the United States had nurtured democratic institutions and Germany had not. In his lecture in St. Louis, Weber adumbrated several of the explanations historians have offered to account for popular government in America, including the absence of a feudal past and the presence of free land, the luxury of prosperity, and the even greater luxury of safe borders. But he also suggested another argument, which he developed at length in *The Protestant Ethic and the Spirit of Capitalism*. Owing to its Calvinist heritage and its historical circumstances, America afforded individuals the opportunity to participate actively in small-scale, egalitarian organizations at the community level, organizations that nourished democratic values and institutions. While Weber hoped such "'club' associations," as he called them, would flourish in Germany, he realized that the depth of the authoritarian tradition made such mass participation extremely unlikely. Moreover, he considered the future of pluralist democracy problematical even in the United States, because he believed that the logic of instrumental rationality contradicts the logic of democracy. The unpredictability of the electorate undermines the values of consistency and efficiency central to large-scale corporations and large-scale government. For that reason popular participation in setting goals or determining ends would necessarily disappear. Even the United States, which Weber admitted "still bears the character of a polity which, at least in the technical sense, is not fully bureaucratized," was bound to change. "The greater the zones of friction with the outside and the more urgent the needs for administrative unity at home become, the more this character is inevitably and gradually giving way formally to the bureaucratic structure."[19] Faced with a choice between the strict calculability of a professionalized administration or the spirited but capricious will of the people, cultures operating according to the principles of instrumental reason would inevitably opt for bureaucracy over democracy.

Here Dewey disagreed. Democracy is uniquely suited to the twentieth century, he argued, because the democratic community replicates the community of broadly conceived scientific inquiry that serves as the prototype for instrumental reasoning. Free and creative individuals, in democratic as in scientific communities, collectively test hypotheses to find out what works best. These communities set their own goals, determine their own tests, and evaluate their results in a spirit of constructive cooperation. To the extent that democratic communities do not conform to the model of collaborative scientific communities, Dewey insisted, they demonstrate merely their own failure to reach what they must continue to consider their goal. In *The Public and Its Problems*, Dewey confronted the challenge to democracy posed in *Public Opinion*; Dewey's argument there also constitutes his most direct answer to Weber's pessimistic assessment of the fate of popular participation in the urban industrial world. Dewey acknowledged "the void left by the disintegration of the family, church, and neighborhood," but he argued that "there is nothing intrinsic in the forces which have effected uniform standardization, mobility and remote invisible relationships that is fatally obstructive" to the community activities that nourished democratic culture. By preserving the vitality of "local community life" and infusing that democratic spirit into the public life of the entire nation, Dewey argued, it would be possible to create what he called "the great community,"[20] an ideal that blurred the standard distinction between *Gemeinschaft* and *Gesellschaft*. Participation and communication, Dewey insisted, must remain the goal of democracy.

Weber conceded that democracy might succeed in certain circumstances. Democracy requires small, local, egalitarian organizations, staffed by rotating administrations of amateurs, which disappeared as interdependent social and economic organizations of great size and complexity replaced well-integrated and harmonious communities. In direct democracies, participation was an end in itself as well as a means, and for that reason efficiency mattered less than maintaining civic virtue. But with a few notable exceptions, such as the Greek and Italian city-states and the Swiss cantons, democratic communities quickly collapsed, and frequently, as in Switzerland, the appearance of participation masked the reality of elite domination. Even in apparently undeveloped regions of America such as the Oklahoma Territory, Weber reported after his visit, traditional forms of local life were under attack. "With almost lightning speed," he wrote, "everything that stands in the way of capitalistic culture is being crushed."[21]

Weber did not of course believe that socialism offered an alternative to the inevitable domination of popular impulses by a professionalized bureaucracy. To the contrary, "the steel frame of modern industrial work" would impose its logic even if the management of the economy were integrated into the state bureaucracy. Working conditions in the state-owned Prussian mines and railroads, Weber pointed out, did not differ appreciably from those in private industries. Now it is surely true that there are bureaucracies and bureaucracies, and Weber many have begged important questions by offering the notoriously rigid Prussian civil service as prototypical. But his point concerned a structural problem. Whereas in a capitalist economy public and private bureaucracies could, at least in principle, check one another's excesses, in a socialist state they "would be merged into a single hierarchy. This would occur in a much more rational—and hence unbreakable—form." Weber dismissed democratic socialism, which Dewey briefly endorsed in the 1930s, as a utopian delusion. In the modern world, the pressure of instrumental reason would strangle popular participation in any economic scheme. In small groups, value-rational and instrumentally rational action might combine, but the insistence on abstract rules for the sake of equality, together with the prevalence of merely functional interactions characteristic of interdependent society, would gradually displace all forms of democratic participation.[22]

Because he identified bureaucratization with the larger process of rationalization, Weber denied that democracy could control the power of bureaucracy. The demand for specialized knowledge, which replaced the demand for what Weber called "magical means to master or implore the spirit," rendered democracy anachronistic. "Technical means and calculations," Weber wrote, now "perform the service" of providing meaning. One of the paradoxes of this period, as the differences between Weber and Dewey illustrate, concerns the contrast between, on the one hand, the emancipation of knowledge from dogma, which made possible an increasing emphasis on experience and volition, and on the other hand, the increasing reliance on bureaucracy, which, as the institutionalized form of that knowledge, used the techniques of science to usurp power from the individuals whose liberation, both intellectual and political, Weber and Dewey both wanted to make possible.[23]

Although Weber chose to play Daedalus to Dewey's Icarus, he nevertheless championed the democratic values that appeared from his description of modern politics to be in such peril. In an address he delivered in 1894, Weber proclaimed that the goal of political and social action must be to cultivate "personal responsibility, the deep aspiration for the moral and spiritual goals of mankind."[24] Although his commitment has seldom been acknowledged, Weber passionately affirmed the importance of struggling against the thrust of history for the values of personal liberty and popular government. Arguing against liberals waiting for the market and orthodox Marxists waiting for the revolution, Weber wrote, "It would be extremely harmful to the chances of 'democracy' and 'individualism' today, if we were to rely for their 'development' on the 'lawlike' operation of *material* interests." For those interests were pointing history in the opposite direction, toward industrial America's "benevolent feudalism" or toward Germany's "so-called 'welfare institutions,' " both of which in their separate ways threatened individual autonomy. "Everywhere," Weber wrote, "*the casing of the new serfdom* is ready." Merely the continuation of the economic, social, and political processes already in motion would end in that enslavement.

Weber expected the pressures threatening individuality to intensify, but he considered resistance possible. The further "parcelling out of the soul," to use his description of the consequences of disenchantment, could be halted only by "the resolute *will* of a nation not to allow itself to be led like a flock of sheep. We 'individualists' and supporters of 'democratic' institutions are swimming 'against the stream' of material developments. Anyone who wishes to be the weathervane of 'developmental trends' might as well abandon these outdated ideals as quickly as possible."[25] Weber himself, however, emphatically refused to abandon the ideals of individuality and democracy, despite their slim chances of survival in the face of rationalization.

As a scholar Weber felt obliged to identify the unique constellation of economic, social, political, and intellectual factors that led to the development of the liberal values he cherished, and he felt obliged to point out the differences between those circumstances and the circumstances of his own day. His aversion to wishful thinking did not, however, entail acquiescence in the demolition of freedom and popular government. Indeed, the concept of plebiscitary leader democracy that Weber developed in the wake of World War I must be understood in terms of his conviction that democracy in Germany could survive only in that unstable form. Given the precarious position of any German state in the postwar crisis, given the absence of any democratic tradition in Germany, and given the pressures of bureaucratization, Weber judged the personal charisma of a leader indispensable for a German republic. Of the three forms of legitimate domination, *viz.* traditional, rational, and charismatic, Weber believed that only the latter was appropriate in a postimperial Reich. Tradition had been annulled by the end of the empire. Rationality would lead inexorably to bureaucratization. But a charismatic leader, restrained, it must be remembered, by constitutional government, and deriving his authority from the consent of the governed, might be able to prevent the paralysis of the public will that Weber considered otherwise unavoidable in postwar Germany. While his concept of democracy understandably evokes a shudder in the wake of this century's lessons in charismatic domination, I believe Weber was willing to entrust such power to a democratically chosen leader precisely because he feared the numbing effects of bureaucracy more than he doubted the ability of the people to select responsible leaders.[26]

Weber was not disillusioned about the prospects for political action. In fact, he suggested in "Politics as a Vocation" that a unique form of ethical life might be possible in the public realm. He drew a distinction between the ethic of single-minded conviction, which can be equated roughly with Kant's categorical imperative, and the ethic of responsibility, which resembled utilitarianism. Given Weber's dramatic characterization of the conflict between these two approaches as a "death struggle," efforts to reconcile them might seem futile. Yet Weber seems to have considered a limited resolution possible in a particular kind of political practice. Although Weber failed to find in history or reason any foundation for ultimate standards, he did not conclude that all values are therefore equally legitimate. Ultimately, he believed, individuals must choose their values on the basis of accumulated social experience, without the consolation of certainty. However attractive the ethic of conviction may be, it is no longer possible for everyone in the modern era, because the absolute confidence that must inform such an ethic is no longer widely available. Neither religion nor science can any longer provide the content for a genuine and universal ethic of conviction.

Weber nevertheless believed passionately that a moral life requires more than simply instrumental adjustment to the world. The individual must be responsible for the consequences of his actions, for the religious flight from the world remains open to few in a secular age. Yet unless the individual acts in service to some ideal, he sinks into opportunism and forfeits the chance to give meaning to life. "Some kind of faith must always exist," Weber insisted, or else "the curse of the creature's worthlessness overshadows even the externally strongest political successes." Politics "is made with the head, but it is certainly not made with the head alone." Life must be fired by what William James called a will to believe, a faith in the validity of one's goals—even though that faith can have no foundation beyond individual conviction—if it is to have meaning and ethical significance. "It is immensely moving," Weber proclaimed, when an individual

> feels with his entire soul the responsibility for the consequences of his actions and thus acts according to the ethic of responsibility. At some point he says, "I cannot do otherwise. Here I stand." That is something genuinely human and stirring. For

each of us who is not spiritually dead, this situation must surely be a possibility. In that sense, the ethic of single-minded conviction and the ethic of responsibility are not absolute opposites but supplements, which together constitute a genuine man, a man who can have the "vocation for politics."[27]

This was obviously a "virtuoso ethic," whose difficulty made its general adoption impossible. Weber doubted that this desperate form of reason, without the buttress provided by religious faith, could sustain the commitment of any but exceptional individuals to such an ethics. We cannot escape the dilemma of choosing between competing values. Especially if we choose to enter the sphere of political activity, we are forced to decide, as William James put it, which of our ideals to butcher. Weber concluded that no universally applicable solution can be found in religion, science, or politics for the problem of ethics in an era of disenchantment.[28]

Dewey did not share Weber's mood of heroic pessimism. Four passages from Dewey's writings will suffice to illustrate his different assessment of the prospects for constructing a democratic culture. In his Presidential Address before the American Psychological Association in 1899, twenty years before Weber's "Politics as a Vocation," Dewey acknowledged the difficulty involved in reconciling the demands of conscience with the desire to achieve results. The modern age has brought with it a tremendous increase in our ability to shape nature to our purposes, Dewey declared. Despite that increased capacity, the realization of our aims grows increasingly "unassured and precarious. At times it seems as if we were caught in a contradiction; the more we multiply means the less certain and general is the use we are able to make of them." Yet Dewey remained undaunted. He admitted that science "will never tell us just what to do ethically, nor just how to do it. But it will afford us insight into the conditions which control the formation and execution of aims, and thus enable human effort to expend itself sanely, rationally, and with assurance."[29] So there can be no final resolution of the tensions between means and ends in any activity, just as there is no final resolution of political problems in a democracy. But Dewey, committed to a pragmatic approach to problem solving, nevertheless considered a measure of incremental progress possible if instrumental reasoning could be combined with the substantive values of freedom, equality, and justice.

One year after Weber suggested politics as a vocation for those few heroic individuals who might combine conviction and responsibility in the charismatic exercise of a virtuoso ethic, Dewey's *Reconstruction in Philosophy* appeared. In his concluding paragraph, Dewey wrote, "We are weak today in ideal matters because intelligence is divorced from aspiration," or, in Weber's terminology, because instrumental rationality is divorced from substantive rationality. When this separation is ended, Dewey predicted, when "philosophy shall have cooperated with the force of events and made clear and coherent the meaning of the daily detail, science and emotion will interpenetrate, practice and imagination will embrace. Poetry and religious feeling will be the unforced flowers of life." Beyond illustrating how Dewey occasionally managed in his prose to combine the worst excesses of Hegel and Fourier, that passage suggests Dewey's confidence that modern culture, if freed from illusions and directed toward solving the actual problems encountered in experience, would develop in the direction of democracy rather than toward bureaucratic domination.[30]

It is the nature of instrumental reason, Dewey believed, to resolve through communication and cooperative inquiry the problems we confront, and the tension between the two ethics of conviction and responsibility can therefore be resolved through the cultural project of democratic social reconstruction. We must keep in mind, Dewey counseled, the "basic moral and ideal meaning" of democracy. "It denotes faith in individuality, . . . faith in corresponding unique modes of activity that create new ends." Uncoerced egalitarian communication should determine the ends we seek, and pragmatic experimentation should be the means by which we strive to reach those goals. Whereas Weber feared that those principles of participation and instrumental reasoning contradicted one another, Dewey was convinced of their consistency. Dewey's vision of "moral democracy" involved "free and open communication, unself-seeking and reciprocal relationships, and the sort of interaction that contributes to mutual advantage."[31] In his estimation the domination and perversion of communication by those with power, not the inherent features of instrumental reasoning and the inevitability of bureaucratization, were the principal obstacles preventing the realization of his ideal.

As should be apparent from those passages, Dewey considered communication central to democratic culture. Unlike some more recent poststructuralist critics, Dewey looked to language as the means of solving the problems confronting his culture. Participation in social projects requires "*communication* as a prerequisite," Dewey wrote in *The Public and Its Problems*. "Only when there exist *signs* or *symbols* of activities and of their outcome can the flux be viewed as from without, be arrested for consideration and esteem, and be regulated." Mere physical phenomena exist in no particular form and have no meaning until "a new medium is interposed" as the phenomena are described, he explained, and thereby given meaning and significance by and for humans. Dewey elaborated on this point in an important passage that I will quote at length:

> Symbols in turn depend upon and promote communication. The results of conjoint experience are considered and transmitted. Events cannot be passed from one to another, but meanings may be shared by means of signs. Wants and impulses are then attached to common meanings. They are thereby transformed into desires and purposes, which, since they implicate a common or mutually understood meaning, present new ties, converting a conjoining activity into a community of interest and endeavor. Thus there is generated what, metaphorically, may be termed a general will and social consciousness: desire and choice on the part of individuals in behalf of activities that, by means of symbols, are communicable and shared by all concerned. A community thus presents an order of energies transmuted into one of meanings which are appreciated and mutually referred by each to every other on the part of those engaged in combined action.

Dewey realized the imprecision of such communication. He admitted that the emergence of "mutual interest in shared meanings . . . does not occur all at once nor completely. At any given time, it sets a problem rather than marks a settled achievement."[32]

Despite those concessions, Dewey insisted that communication, however imperfect, makes possible the continuing process of social problem solving that he understood as the essence of democracy. In *Experience and Nature*, Dewey speculated that language originated in the primitive human need to offer "mutual assistance and direction" in the face of dangers or difficulties. As Robert Westbrook writes, for Dewey "events and things took on their initial meanings in the course of these cooperative transactions; words and other signs became names—things with significance—when they established 'a genuine community of action.' Meaning, in brief, was symptomatic of a 'community of partaking.' "[33]

When presented in this form, the contrast between Weber and Dewey calls to mind the controversy swirling around the ideas of Jürgen Habermas. In *The Theory of Communicative Action*, Habermas sets up a distinction between the lifeworld, in which symbolically mediated interactions are oriented toward consensus modeled on the regulative concept of the ideal speech situation, and an economic realm in which strategic action is oriented toward efficiency modeled on the concept of instrumental rationality. Habermas has come to realize, as both Weber and Dewey did, that in the modern world the attraction of instrumental rationality has become nearly irresistible. The challenge, he believes, is to prevent what he calls the "colonization" of the lifeworld by an instrumental logic that focuses exclusively on technique and is oblivious to ends. We must not allow "an unleashed functionalist reason of system maintenance," in the phrase Habermas uses at the end of volume one of *The Theory of Communicative Action*, to dictate ends as well as means. Our values must derive from our understanding—and our experience—of communication and community. The paradox of rationalization, for Habermas, consists in the dissolution of authority under the corrosive pressure of disenchantment. Without the confidence provided by inherited and unquestioned normative guidelines, individuals find themselves in the modern world thrown back on their own intelligence. Robbed of security and certainty, they engage in rational communication to reach for themselves conclusions no longer available through appeals to, or the imposition of, traditional authority. The "cultural impoverishment of everyday communicative practice," Habermas argues, comes not from the erosion of that authority, which is progressive in that it contributes to the development of rational processes of decision making, but derives instead from "an elitist splitting-off of expert cultures from contexts of communicative action in daily life." Everyday communication provides occasions for spontaneous resistance to that process of colonizing the life-world, but the threat to its integrity remains in the persistence of the capitalist values and institutions that carry forward, and are carried forward by, rationalization.[34]

Habermas's efforts to construct a logic of the life-world, a portrait of the ideal speech situation in which communication successfully takes place, has drawn the fire of a number of critics, among them the American pragmatist Richard Rorty. Rorty has joined French poststructuralists in calling for the end of "philosophical metanarratives," which presume to establish a transhistorical reason capable of yielding a set of universal values. He chides philosophers to stop trying to float freely up to the realm of Abstract Truth by shedding the weight of history. In Rorty's words, "the moral justification of the institutions and practices of one's group—e.g., of the contemporary bourgeoisie—is mostly a matter of historical narratives . . . rather than of philosophical metanarratives" of the sort Habermas persists in seeking. In support of his argument Rorty has invoked the spirit of Dewey, whom he describes as "a postmodernist before his time" because Dewey concentrated on solving problems rather than constructing a model for human rationality.[35] In a recent critique of Habermas, in fact, Rorty uses the passage from Dewey's *Reconstruction in Philosophy* that I have quoted above, in which Dewey recommended that philosophers concentrate on "the meaning of the daily detail." As Dewey saw, Rorty writes, "the way to re-enchant the world, to bring back what religion gave our forefathers, is to stick to the concrete."[36]

But as I have tried to demonstrate by comparing Dewey to Weber, it was precisely Dewey's very abstract faith in the progressive quality of our efforts to solve concrete problems that gave him what Weber considered an unwarranted degree of confidence in democracy. For that reason I would argue that Habermas, the philosopher of the ideal speech situation, can more legitimately trace his roots to Dewey than can Rorty. As Dewey did, Habermas conceives of reason as purposeful and progressive, leading man in the direction of cooperation as a consequence of natural although not inevitable tendencies latent in human communication. Responding to Rorty's critique, Habermas has made exactly this point. Calling himself "a good pragmatist," he argues that he has "for a long time identified [himself] with that radical democratic mentality which is present in the best American traditions and articulated in American pragmatism."[37] Dewey remained committed to the possibility of democracy, as does Habermas, because he had confidence in the capacity of pragmatic reason to establish provisional social norms as well as techniques, and he considered that process the democratic project. "We cannot judge what is good or what is bad," Dewey wrote, "what is better or what is worse, unless we have criteria on which to base our judgments." Those criteria derived, Dewey insisted, not merely from personal choice, or "taste," but from collective experience. Experience yielded an ideal of "associated living" that Dewey invoked as the standard for political judgment. A social practice is "to be judged good when it contributes positively to free intercourse, to unhampered exchange of ideas, to mutual respect and friendship and love—in short, to those modes of behaving which make life richer and more worth living for everybody concerned; and conversely, any custom or institution which impedes progress toward these goals is to be judged bad." In the aftermath of the student uprising in Peking, it is worth noting that Dewey made those remarks in the lectures he delivered in China in 1919–20. Dewey was invited to the National University in Peking by his former student Hu Shih, who was among the most influential members of the May Fourth movement of the early twentieth century, the movement invoked in 1989 by student radicals calling once again for democratic reform. For

Dewey, instrumentalism, while incapable of providing universal rules to resolve all ethical questions (for the reasons I have discussed above), nevertheless did provide a philosophical foundation for political action of just the sort we have witnessed in Eastern Europe as well as Asia since 1989, the kind of foundation that Habermas seeks and Rorty rejects. For that reason, it seems to me that Richard J. Bernstein is right in suggesting that "Habermas is closer in spirit to Dewey than Rorty is."[38]

The argument Rorty advances against Habermas is, I believe, Weber's argument rather than Dewey's. Rorty denies that there is a philosophical foundation for democratic values such as freedom and equality; he recommends that we be content to profess such values for no reason other than that by our own lights they are the best available. Rorty's mistrust of metanarratives thus echoes Weber's doubt rather than Dewey's faith in the consistency between pragmatic reason and democratic action. Rorty affirms the ideals of liberal democracy, but, like Weber rather than Dewey, he finds no philosophical warrant for them. We adopt such values, as Weber insisted, for historical reasons, because they seem to us pragmatically true rather than consistent with the demands of reason.[39]

When Rorty recommends cultivating an ironic sensibility in the safe seclusion of the private sphere, however, he moves well beyond Weber's restrained partisanship toward a form of inwardness that Weber detected in some of his contemporaries and found troublesome. Like Nietzsche and Freud, Weber feared the flattening of experience that would accompany the inexorable process of rationalization. For that reason the increased democratization that Dewey sought seemed to Weber more likely only to intensify the impact of bureaucratization by universalizing the process of formal deliberation and the spread of depersonalized rules.

Yet Weber was equally suspicious of the cultivation of an aestheticized or sensualized sphere in which individual creative impulses might know no master and feel no restraint. Indeed, for Weber the iron cage of modernity and the lure of inwardness were linked. Weber suggested that this sort of "apolitical emotionalism may take the form of a flight into mysticism and an acosmistic ethic of absolute goodness or into the irrationalities of non-religious emotionalism, above all eroticism."[40] Those who opted for art, such as the members of the Stefan George circle, and those who opted for sensuality, such as some enthusiastic followers of Freud, slipped into easy retreat from the hard realities of a world that such escapism might temporarily elude but never transform. "The latest literati," Weber wrote disparagingly, "with their urge to brag about and to print their personal 'experiences'— erotical, religious, or what not—are the enemies of all dignity, no matter of what sort." Such self-indulgent seekers lost sight of the crucial value of critical distance, which is essential to intellectual life and cannot be preserved merely by "snobbishly setting one's self off from the 'far too many,' as is maintained by the various and misconceived 'prophecies' which go back to Nietzsche." Concluding with a passage that expressed his ambivalence yet sharply distinguished him from the antidemocratic aesthetes of his day, Weber wrote, "Perhaps the necessity of maintaining one's inner dignity in the midst of a democratic world can serve as a test of the genuineness of dignity."[41]

Rather than applauding the achievements of a liberal culture in which personal preferences for irony might be indulged without concern for the consequences, as Rorty occasionally advises us to do, Weber called for resistance to both routinization and the cultivation of purely private enthusiasms. In the modern age, even such apparently benign forms of associated life as choral societies might, by gratifying individuals' profound inner longings, contribute to the seductive but ominous "passive democratization" that Weber feared. The alternatives he offered required engagement in either the discipline of a vocation or the rigors of principled political action, neither of which could be pursued with the shoulder-shrugging imperturbability of Rorty's liberal ironism.

Dewey believed that the democratization of modern culture was a goal to be attained through political action, not a *fait accompli* to be celebrated and enjoyed. Weber, by contrast, saw veiled beneath the form of democracy a threat to the autonomy of individuals and the integrity of their deepest personal and cultural aspirations. Despite their surprising similarities, then, an important difference remains between Dewey's and Weber's assessments of the implications of disenchantment for democracy. The very spread of a thoroughgoing spirit of inquiry, of democratic communication and problem solving, which represented for Dewey the means to an undefined—and, because it would be in a constant state of development, undefinable—end of equality and justice, Weber judged likely to squash the spirit of individuality that the entire democratic project was originally intended to nourish. Though they shared a commitment to the democratic form of government as the most desirable alternative available, Dewey and Weber couched their preferences in dramatically different analyses of the broader cultural significance of democracy in the modern world.

When we reflect on the meanings of modernism, we should keep in mind two distinctions brought into focus by comparing the ideas of Dewey and Weber. First, we should remember the distance between the historical Dewey, a pragmatist committed to democracy as an ethical ideal, and the proto-liberal ironist that Rorty now describes accurately as his "hypothetical Dewey."[42] Second, we should remember the distance between the two forms of modernism represented by Weber's tragic sensibility and Dewey's indomitable democratic faith. Although both devoted their lives to scientific inquiry, both warned of the dangers of scientistic reductionism. Although both believed that the modern era promised an end to the enslavement of individuals by outmoded dogmas and inherited structures of authority, they reached strikingly different conclusions regarding the likely consequences for politics and society of the uncertainty that both considered the distinctive characteristic of modernism.

SEVEN

DELIBERATIVE DEMOCRACY AND THE
PROBLEM OF POVERTY IN AMERICA

DEMOCRACY HAS RECENTLY become an almost universally attractive ideal. But if everyone invokes democracy as an ideal, it is only because democracy means very different things to different people. For some it means nothing more than choosing political representatives through universal suffrage, then allowing those elected to make decisions as they see fit. For others democracy means universal participation in all forms of social and economic as well as political decision making. As attractive as it is in theory, the practice of democracy almost everywhere falls far short of its promise.

Democracy in the United States is in especially bad shape. In the 1996 presidential election in the United States only 48 percent of the electorate bothered to vote, the lowest total since 1924 and the second lowest since 1824. Exit polls revealed that even many of those who voted had little knowledge of the presidential candidates' positions on issues such as welfare reform, defense spending, and environmentalism. The public draws most of its information about politics from television, where anesthetizing images of uplifting fluff alternate with attack ads to poison public discourse. On the evening of the presidential election, only one of the major television networks broadcasting coverage of the election returns attracted as many viewers as the broadcast of the movie *Beethoven*, which is a film not about a gifted composer but about a very large dog.

Beyond concern about the lack of public participation in contemporary American democratic politics, there is widespread concern about the nature of the participation that does exist. During the debates between candidates Bill Clinton and Bob Dole, candidates whose relentless informality reflected and extended the striking decline of deference in American politics, one of the experiments with voter reaction illustrated the extent to which democratic politics and marketing are converging at the end of the twentieth century. Viewers of the debates at a number of sites, including the John F. Kennedy School of Government at Harvard University, sat at desks equipped with dials that enabled them to register their degree of approval or disapproval of every word each candidate spoke, each gesture he used, even each expression on his face. Not surprisingly, viewers responded positively to humor, smiles, and friendly strolls toward the audience of ordinary citizens who asked them questions. In other words, they responded positively to President Clinton, who, like an engaging television talk-show host or an alluring soap-opera character in the grip of uncontrollable appetites, could make them laugh when he laughed or choke up with emotion when tears welled up in his eyes, which was often. The political principles of President Clinton may be hard to identify, but at least a plurality of the American electorate seems to identify with him—or at least to find his ups and downs and zigzags endlessly entertaining.

Tempting as it is to address the theme of deliberative democracy and the problem of poverty in America by focusing on recent presidential elections, I will ask instead whether the *culture of democracy*, not the style of contemporary politics, can bridge the gap between self and community. Instead of discussing any further the dismal condition of democratic politics in America, I want to focus instead on the more intriguing possibility that democracy, conceived as a culture of deliberation rather than simply a means of electing political officials, might hold out more promise for reconciling individuals with each other.

In an essay entitled "Democratic Institutions and Moral Resources," German political theorists Claus Offe and Ulrich Preuss contrast their vision of deliberative democracy with two ideal types. On the one hand, they sketch an American tradition of liberal pluralism premised on the assumption of self-interested, atomistic individuals lacking any connection with community. On the other hand, they describe a French tradition of collectivism, premised on an all-encompassing vision of the common good, which trampled the rights of individual selves in its relentless quest for community. Both of these traditions, according to Offe and Preuss, have impeded the emergence of a genuinely democratic culture, a culture of deliberation that would mediate between the American liberal tradition with its atomistic, rights-bearing individuals, and the French communal tradition with its dangerous, authoritarian impulse toward the unitary general will of the community.[1] In recent years the ideal of deliberative democracy has attracted increasing attention on both sides of the Atlantic, and I will focus on it here briefly in relation to persistent debates over liberalism and republicanism in America, then in relation to two recent American political thinkers, Michael Sandel and Seyla Benhabib, then particularly in relation to the failure of Franklin D. Roosevelt's attempt, in the last three years of his life, to institute a generous American welfare state, which I will contrast to the relatively warm reception of the contemporaneous Beveridge Report in Great Britain. My aim is to demonstrate the possibilities and perils of deliberative democracy.

The question of reconciling the self with the community has been at the center of debates in American political theory, and in the history of American politics, for the last thirty years. Accounts of a liberal consensus on the paramount importance of individualism in America dominated the 1950s. Accounts of an American culture racked by wrenching struggles over race, class, and gender dominated the 1960s. Then another account emerged, which seemed to promise an alternative by locating in eighteenth- and nineteenth-century America a republican tradition that galvanized Americans around an ideal of civic virtue, an ideal of selflessness distinct from liberal individualism and distinct from narrow definitions of group identity and interest that propelled stories of consensus and social conflict alike. Soon various, exotic strains of republicanism sprouted across the landscape of American history. Not only were American revolutionaries searching for virtue, so too, it turned out, were southern Jeffersonians who praised independent yeomen farmers, northern Whigs who sought order and unity, and urban artisans who treasured their autonomy as craftsmen. By the mid-1980s, historians had found republican ideals animating Jacksonian Democrats who feared government, Lincoln Republicans who cherished the Union, Knights of Labor who defended workers' autonomy, Mugwumps who ferreted out corruption, populists who longed for a new commonwealth, and progressives who envisioned a public interest. The language of republicanism, all but unknown to American historians and political theorists for the first six decades of the twentieth century, seemed to be everywhere.[2]

Republican interpretations came from the left and the right, because these ideas seemed to offer a homegrown alternative to liberal individualism, a different American tradition that highlighted community instead of self. Given this well-established tendency of scholars to counterpose republicanism to liberalism in American political thought, it is perhaps not surprising that republican ideas dominate the most prominent study of American democratic theory published recently, a book by the political theorist Michael Sandel entitled *Democracy's Discontent: America in Search of a Public Philosophy*. Given Sandel's visibility as one of the most thoughtful and perceptive critics of John Rawls, *Democracy's Discontent* has received wide discussion not only inside the academic community but also beyond it. In contemporary American law, Sandel argues, judges treat the individual self as something separate from, and prior to, its freely chosen ends and interpret the Constitution as nothing more than a "neutral framework of rights within which persons can pursue their own ends," whatever those ends may be. This "procedural republic," Sandel argues in the second part of his book, represents a departure from the eighteenth- and nineteenth-century American tradition of civic republicanism that prized character and emphasized the importance of forming citizens to follow a path of virtue rather than freeing them to follow whatever path they choose.[3]

Sandel thus replaces the earlier emphasis on the sovereign liberal self with an almost equally distorted emphasis on the republican community. A better strategy would be to keep in focus both the continuous presence of rights talk and the continuous presence of competing ideals of the common good. How? The answer lies in acknowledging the importance of the tradition of democracy in America, because, until very recently, in American political discourse the claims of individual rights and the claims of a civic ideal have been made together more often than separately. American champions of liberalism, in other words, have tended to conceive of individuals as rights bearers who are restrained by moral and religious responsibilities to the community. American champions of republicanism, by the same token, have tended to conceive of the civic community as restrained by the need to secure, in the face of cultural and religious pluralism, the natural rights of individuals.

Our best strategy is to abandon the increasingly fruitless debates about liberalism and republicanism and turn instead toward democracy, in which the demands for both equal individual autonomy and popular sovereignty are always simultaneously an insistent presence. Although we should dismiss the argument of Offe and Preuss that the United States has been a culture of individualism that can be helpfully contrasted to a French culture of community, their ideal of deliberative democracy may nevertheless provide a useful analytical framework.

Among recent discussions of that conception of democracy, including those advanced in recent years by American pragmatists such as Richard J. Bernstein and Hilary Putnam, Seyla Benhabib has refined the ideals of deliberative democracy and discourse ethics most thoroughly developed by Jürgen Habermas and his allies on both sides of the Atlantic. Benhabib proposes to replace the unsustainable aspirations of Enlightenment rationalism with a more chastened universalism that nevertheless refuses to surrender to postmodernists' melodramatic proclamations of the death of man, the death of history, and the death of philosophy. In place of the Enlightenment notion of a "self-transparent and self-grounding reason," Benhabib proposes "a discursive, communicative concept of rationality." In place of a "disembedded and disembodied subject," she proposes that a human infant becomes "a 'self,' a being capable of speech and action, only by learning to interact in a human community." Finally, in place of the Kantian aspiration toward an Archimedean ethical standpoint located outside history and culture, Benhabib proposes that we conceive of a "moral point of view" as a "contingent achievement of an interactive form of rationality rather than as the timeless standpoint of a legislative reason."[4]

Benhabib's argument for the situated self culminates in a "radically proceduralist model of the public sphere." Incorporating feminist and postmodernist criticism of Habermas, she stresses the contingent status of every provisional agreement reached through such procedures. Although she concedes that postmodernist impulses toward diversity, heterogeneity, and otherness are important correctives to lingering vestiges of Enlightenment rationalism that can exclude and oppress the marginalized, she insists that feminists in particular cannot do without the "legal, moral, and political norms of autonomy, choice, and self-determination" that some self-proclaimed post-Enlightenment critics dismiss as incoherent. Alert to the insights of postmodernism but wary of its excesses, she denies that the procedures of discourse ethics and deliberative democracy will ever yield agreement. Instead she views the very concept of "the general interest" in politics more as "a regulative ideal and less as the subject matter of a substantive consensus." In ethics, even if we view "the universalizability procedure" as a commitment to reciprocity, as "a reversing of perspectives and the willingness to reason from the other's (others') point of view," that commitment hardly guarantees unanimous consent. Instead it only manifests "the will and the readiness to seek understanding with the other and to reach some reasonable agreement in an open-ended moral conversation." In politics, we should abandon the quest for a unitary public good and commit ourselves instead to ensuring that "collective decisions be reached through procedures which are radically open and fair to all."[5]

Although Benhabib's terminology is new, many of the ideas she champions are, in some respects at least, as old as the European presence in North America. From the seventeenth century to the present, it is possible to identify strands of deliberative democracy in the discourses of politics in America (and in Europe; this is not a strictly North American phenomenon). Such ideas did not *dominate* American politics, nor did they alone constitute a "genuinely" or "exceptionally" or even distinctively American idea of democracy such that the significance of all other competing ideas must be dismissed or diminished. This essay does not attempt to do for the ideas of deliberative democracy what critics accuse Louis Hartz of doing for liberalism or John Pocock for republicanism. I argue instead only that this conception of discursive democracy, historically grounded more often in Christian concepts of human fallibility and sinfulness than in our contemporary ideas of contingency and uncertainty, figured as one of several prominent conceptions in a democratic culture braided of many strands.

Moreover, adequately tracing the career of this cluster of ideas would require tracing social and political changes as well, because the history of ideas of democracy in America is woven into the hard facts of American conflict. Part of the difficulty involved in studying political ideas, of course, is the gap that usually separates theory from practice. Although it is beyond the scope of this essay, a more thorough investigation of these ideas would require examining not only philosophers' and political theorists' formulations but also the efforts to translate these ideas into political and cultural practice—and especially the *difficulties* such efforts always encountered, which will become apparent below in the discussion of Franklin Roosevelt's final crusade against poverty.

The idea of public deliberation arrived in America, together with the ideas of autonomy and popular sovereignty, on the first ships carrying settlers from England to the New World. It was institutionalized by Puritans in unruly New England town meetings, in the diverse and contentious political cultures that developed in the middle colonies, and within the lively representative assemblies that developed in the South. The idea that deliberation provides the most promising path toward justice was written into the constitutions of the states and the new nation, and its appeal shines through James Madison's defense of the decision to hold the Constitutional Convention behind closed doors. Those deliberating about the Constitution, Madison believed, should for this particular purpose be free from the constraints imposed by their constituencies' scrutiny. They should be free to learn from each other and to adapt their initial ideas after reflecting on the different ideas of others. This commitment to dialogue, descended from ancient practices, surely manifested an Enlightenment faith in reason of the sort some late twentieth-century postmodernists find objectionable. But inasmuch as it likewise reflected a sense of man's sinfulness shared by eighteenth-century American Christians of various denominations and a practical concern with negotiating differences to achieve provisional consensus shared by politically active Americans, it reflected the peculiarities of the American version of Enlightenment.

It would be a mistake to exaggerate eighteenth-century Americans' suspicion of reason or their commitment to decentered selves. Despite the enormous distance that separated them from Nietzsche, let alone Foucault, they did know, from experience as well as from philosophy and theology, that encounters with different points of view can teach the virtue as well as the necessity of dialogical thinking. As Bernstein, Benhabib, and others committed to radically proceduralist models of the public sphere have pointed out in their responses to postmodernists and their refinements of Habermas, diversity can help foster a commitment to communication and problem solving as well as illuminating the instability of the individual subject, the complexity of judgment, and the difficulty of reaching agreement through interaction among selves constituted discursively. Eighteenth-century Americans encountered "the other" with increasing frequency in their daily lives, and they created formal institutional arrangements to reflect their awareness of the need to acknowledge and accommodate difference.[6] The ideal as well as the practice of deliberation is deeply rooted in the American experience with democracy.

Intriguing variations on these ideas emerged in the nineteenth century, but in the remainder of this essay I want to fast-forward to the later years of Franklin D. Roosevelt's New Deal, because some of its principal initiatives reveal the persistence of the ideal of deliberation and the problems that ideal has encountered in democratic practice. The New Deal was designed to mitigate the effects of an underregulated economy that seemed stuck in a downward spiral, but its shape was so clearly determined by what was politically feasible that many commentators have doubted there was any coherence at all to Roosevelt's policies. Roosevelt's administration did inaugurate an enduring national system of contributory old-age pensions, a system initially limited in scope that has gradually expanded enough to raise most retired Americans above poverty. Beyond that achievement, however, the legislation passed during the 1930s and 1940s seemed to contemporaries, as it seems to historians today, haphazard and chaotic. That much of the story is familiar.

It is less well known that Roosevelt tried unsuccessfully, during the last three years of his life, to establish in the United States a social welfare state as extensive as any established in Europe in the late 1940s. Roosevelt announced his plan in his State of the Union Address on January 11, 1944, describing it in familiar terms as a "second bill of rights" because he wanted Americans to see these plans as securing rather than threatening their freedom. Roosevelt proposed programs ensuring that every American would have access to education, a job with a living wage, adequate housing, universal medical care, and insurance against old age, sickness, accident, and unemployment. This agenda was the culmination of

Roosevelt's effort to bring order to the chaos of the New Deal. Global warfare dominated the 1944 presidential election, and it has dominated historical accounts of these years as well. But the proposals of the second bill of rights surfaced periodically, especially in an address Roosevelt gave in Chicago on October 28, 1944, in which he delivered what he called "a well reasoned resume of his political and economic philosophy."[7] At the center of that philosophy were his plans for a decentralized and democratically administered American welfare state. Because the war preoccupied America until Roosevelt's death, and because the cold war transformed American politics afterwards, Roosevelt's plan for a second bill of rights, and his successor Harry Truman's plan for what he called a Fair Deal that incorporated some of the same ideas, went nowhere.

But the defeat of this plan was not inevitable—any more than the dissolution of the Soviet Union and the reunification of Germany at the end of the 1980s were inevitable—and the little-known story of the plan's emergence reveals dimensions of American political culture almost as significant as the fact that it failed.[8] Roosevelt's blueprints for postwar social policy originated in the efforts of the National Resources Planning Board, an agency Roosevelt created after the Executive Reorganization Act of 1939, and received their most elaborate expression in a report delivered to the president by his uncle Frederic Delano, chairman of the National Resources Planning Board, on December 4, 1941.

From its inception, the National Resources Planning Board (NRPB) enjoyed a precarious existence. Its relations with Congress, which distrusted all creatures of the executive branch, were nasty, its funding was poor, its reception by the news media was brutish, and its life was short. It was also immensely productive, of plans if not of policies that eventually came to fruition. During the four years the NRPB existed, from July 1, 1939, to August 24, 1943, the board produced 220 reports on everything from "Post-Defense Economic Development in Alaska" to "A Development Plan for Puerto Rico."[9] Its range extended from microscopic studies of local water problems to all-encompassing plans for national economic and social policy. The most ambitious of its reports was *Security, Work, and Relief Policies*, the comprehensive plan for the future that was submitted to Roosevelt on the eve of America's entry into the war. The NRPB, whose most influential member was the political scientist Charles Merriam, engaged the economist Eveline M. Burns as the Director of Research for this project. Her training at the London School of Economics, and her status as an authority on German as well as British social and economic policy, made the board's recommendations especially vulnerable to the predictable shrieks of socialism and fascism that greeted the report when it was finally published—after a lengthy delay that reflected Roosevelt's preoccupation with World War II as much as his perception of the political firestorm it would ignite—in 1943.

The first 362 pages of the report today make rather tedious reading, since they consist of detailed descriptions of existing policies concerning public assistance, health care, social insurance, and federal work programs. The second half of the report, on the other hand, outlines bold strategies for solving the problems previously described. Included in this sweeping program were "government provision of work for all adults who are willing and able to work," "assurance of basic minimum security through social insurance," "a comprehensive underpinning general public-assistance system providing aid on the basis of need," and "expansion of social services which are essential for the health, welfare, and efficiency of the whole population." Programs providing "disability insurance," "unemployment compensation," "old age and survivors insurance," and "a comprehensive general public-assistance program" were to be funded by progressive taxes on income rather than comparatively regressive taxes on consumption. In what proved to be a futile effort to forestall charges of fiscal irresponsibility, the committee argued that the nation could more easily afford to implement such programs than to ignore them.

> It is not the provision of these basic services that would threaten the security and prosperity of the nation, but it is, on the contrary, the failure to develop the purchasing power implied in these services that drags down our national income. . . . Operating at half capacity, . . . we cannot provide these services, nor can the national economy be operated effectively. On a high level income these services are not only possible but are indicated as indispensable even from a narrow economic point of view. From a broader democratic point of view these guarantees of minimum security are equally indispensable.[10]

A distinctive aspect of the NRPB plan has been overlooked in the literature surrounding its work. Critics at the time focused so much on the centralization of government authority they believed such a plan would bring that they overlooked one of the principal themes of the report—the need for "increased citizen participation." Particularly in the board's conclusion to its recommendations concerning the administration of social services, the report repeatedly emphasized public involvement. "It is highly important that efforts should be made to secure greater citizen participation in the programs operated by government."[11] Some historians see such language as rhetoric designed to stave off charges of totalitarianism. That judgment neglects the board's persistent emphasis on combining federal coordination of programs and local advisory bodies of citizens as the most desirable policy as well as the most effective strategy to win public support. The NRPB recommended specifically creating local boards that could report to administrators and to legislatures "concerning failures to attain the objectives of the program attributable to organizational or administrative defects," and it emphasized engaging the "lay public with the appeals machinery of the different programs." Cumbersome as such procedures might be, that was simply the price of democracy. Such provisions would "add to the duties of the administrator and may well involve less speedy action. But the gains through the enlistment of public support and understanding of the issues faced by the administrator will more than compensate for any slight delay." Such advantages would flow in both directions, as the desire for civic involvement that might motivate citizens to join such advisory bodies would be further bolstered by the experience. The board members had read their Tocqueville as well as their Madison.[12]

They had also read their Dewey. The NRPB arguments for citizen participation seem to me less a form of rhetorical self-defense than a self-conscious endorsement of an ideal of open-ended, deliberative democratic community. In the 1930s that ideal was most often linked with the philosopher John Dewey, whose work was well known by Merriam, who taught at the University of Chicago, and by Burns, who was Dewey's colleague at Columbia. In fact, the final paragraph of the NRPB discussion of "The Administration of Public Aid" could be a paraphrase of Dewey's arguments in books such as *The Public and Its Problems* (1927), *Individualism Old and New* (1930), or *Liberalism and Social Action* (1935):

> [L]ay participation will make great demands upon the individual citizens. . . . [T]hey must be prepared to take their duties seriously and to sacrifice time and effort to public service. The solution of the complex problems of public aid awaits the concentration of the best thinking of the country upon this aspect of our national life. It calls, too, for a willingness on the part of the population at large to subordinate cherished illusions and traditional values when they impede the attainment of our national objectives. Prominent among our postwar objectives is the assurance to our citizens of that minimum of security which keeps alive self-respect and initiative, which will permit a higher standard of living and give the opportunity to participate in the good things of life which our productive capacity makes possible. We look forward to the day when this objective will come to be regarded as one of the most challenging and significant of all the problems facing a great people.[13]

As the final phrase makes clear, the NRPB realized that day had not yet dawned. They did not know just how far away it was.

Howls of protest greeted the NRPB report when it was published. Critics could not decide which part of the report was most objectionable, the idea of a welfare state, the expansion of the authority of the federal government, or a third dimension of the report that endorsed the idea of a mixed economy and called for government planning. Again Merriam's staff tried to reassure the public that they were democrats rather than autocrats; again they failed.[14] "We recommend," they wrote in another report submitted in 1943, "that governmental *planning programs be decentralized*, as far as administratively practical, to the States, counties, cities and appropriate regional agencies. Only in this way can we keep our post-war planning and action programs close to the public."[15] But how much decentralization is "administratively practical"? How can programs designed to coordinate activities beyond the grasp of local governmental agencies remain "close to the public"? These were questions that might trouble even those sympathetic to the NRPB's Deweyan vision, and they suggest the difficulties that would ultimately bring down the NRPB and its ambitious plans for the postwar world. The references to democracy, decentralization, and citizen participation that run through the NRPB reports indicate the distinctiveness of the American plan for a welfare state and also suggest, paradoxically enough, the reasons why it failed. Regardless of whether the NRPB intended its democratic pronouncements to be taken as serious indications of its commitment to decentralization or intended them merely as a smokescreen, they testify to the persistent appeal of democratic and community-based approaches to economic and social problems. In order to understand the roots of that commitment, and its implications for shaping the welfare state, a brief glance backward is necessary.

The basic distinction between the deserving and nondeserving poor dates from the Middle Ages. Christian charity was to be extended to those of the poor who were resident, passive, and invalid, while those who were wandering, active, and healthy deserved to be scorned. The secularization of society beginning in the early modern era transformed the significance of poverty. Whereas it had been understood from a religious perspective as an experience that could sanctify both the givers and receivers of charity, poverty metamorphosed into a sign of moral failure that justified incarcerating the able-bodied poor. Workhouses, which emerged in the eighteenth century, further transformed the experience of poverty, adding to the former objective of isolating the poor a grander plan of converting them into citizens through the discipline of work. With industrialization and urbanization came a new category of poor, a class of highly mobile and unhealthy wage laborers who not only sustained but also threatened the lives of the urban bourgeoisie. Keeping the lid on this cauldron was the purpose of outdoor relief, of the mutual societies that emerged during the nineteenth century, and of the urban political machines that looked after those whose votes, incidentally, could be won by various kinds of public assistance.[16]

Convictions regarding the moral significance of work and the discreditable status of poverty persisted throughout this lengthy transformation, even though most of those who received outdoor relief in nineteenth-century America were widows, children, the aged, or the very sick. The equation of virtue with autonomy that derived in various ways from the traditions of Christianity, republicanism, and liberalism nevertheless continued, although that equation became increasingly problematical as the quality of industrial work deteriorated.[17]

The distinctiveness of the American experience with poverty stems not from that division between the deserving and the nondeserving poor, which was universal in the Atlantic world, but from the absence of a unified national policy to cope with it. Because Americans understood poverty to be a local problem, towns and cities developed a multitude of strategies to cope with it in the eighteenth and early nineteenth centuries. The first large-scale, nationwide program emerged with the Civil War pension system of the late nineteenth century, arguably the largest government program in the world at that time—a startling and paradoxical achievement for a nation generally characterized as lacking a fully developed state. Yet the shape of the pension system reflected the peculiarly American state of courts and parties. Because America democratized comparatively early, there was no existing state bureaucracy to administer a program as ambitious as the Civil War pension system grew to be. Because Republican Party leaders controlled the apparatus needed to run the system, they could and often did manipulate it as they chose. The pensions themselves, and the bureaucracy that administered the program, gave the G.O.P. carrots to offer those who might otherwise be attracted to the favors dispensed by the proto-welfare agencies generally operated at the local level under the aegis of Democratic Party machines. Thus, whether in the shape of the pension system or in the shape of local systems of caregiving, many Americans wanting or needing assistance came into contact with some agency of government.[18] Because political parties controlled these forms of assistance, however, they were especially vulnerable to criticism in a nation that cut its teeth on the fear of dependency and the belief that nothing threatens civic virtue more directly than the corruption of administration.

Thus before progressives could discover that business corrupts politics, to use Richard L. McCormick's characterization of the motor driving early twentieth-century reform, their predecessors the Mugwumps had already discovered that politics corrupts government. That conviction led many (although by no means all) late nineteenth- and early twentieth-century reformers to shy away from administration, which they deemed inherently corrupt, and to seek refuge in nostalgic invocations of a romanticized antistatist tradition. In their quest for social assistance for the poor, most progressives followed John Commons and the Wisconsin school of economists in emphasizing private schemes of social insurance. Only a minority of progressives believed, with Commons's colleague Richard Ely, that a social democratic state, funded by a system of graduated taxes, properly organized, and efficiently administered, might provide universal coverage, impossible to achieve through the private sector, without falling victim to Bismarck's autocracy or the corruption of American schemes tainted by patronage.[19]

Progressives who did not dismiss the possibility of state action hoped the experience of federal activism in World War I might lead to permanent expansion of the national government's role in the economy and the provision of social welfare. Across the political spectrum, though, postwar sentiment turned away from the state and toward various private-sector alternatives. Welfare capitalism and industrial democracy attracted more talk than action, but both generated more enthusiasm than calls for government planning and social insurance. While Herbert Hoover's ideal of an "associative state" differed from laissez-faire liberalism, the planning he envisioned was to be done at the instigation of, and on terms agreeable to, the private rather than the public sector.[20] Then came the New Deal.

Scholars have quarreled for five decades now about the thrust of Roosevelt's policies. The tumult will no doubt continue, because it is impossible to determine exactly what Roosevelt intended the New Deal to be. Congress, the Supreme Court, and the ebbs and flows of public support for his programs severely constrained Roosevelt's options. Debates about whether or not he believed in the social democratic programs of the New Deal, however, have begun to seem pointless. Evidence is accumulating that he not only read but also helped write the celebrated speech at the Commonwealth Club in the 1932 campaign, that he was an active member of the Brains Trust that framed the New Deal, and that his persistence in the face of mounting opposition during the years from 1934 to his death in 1945 testifies to his commitment to the welfare state. Recent work on the New Deal by Barry Karl, Alan Lawson, and Sidney Milkis in particular indicates that Roosevelt sought far more change than he got.[21] Charges that Roosevelt wanted nothing more coherent than popular support ignore many of the major initiatives of his presidency, all of which were risky and most of which significantly eroded his political base. He embarked on his Supreme Court packing plan, his doomed effort to purge conservative Congressmen from the Democratic Party, and, most important for my purposes here, his futile attempt to muster support for the policies recommended by the NRPB, not because such ideas were politically popular but because he considered them necessary. As more recent experience has shown, presidents intent on pleasing the American public learn to avoid such unpopular and expensive initiatives whenever possible.

Roosevelt was committed primarily to widening the door to economic opportunity and rigging the safety net that Harry Hopkins had been talking about since 1931.[22] He was a politician rather than a visionary, but he knew where he wanted the nation to go. He articulated his ideal most clearly in his 1944 State of the Union Address, a speech clearly based on the NRPB report delivered to him two years earlier, three days before the Japanese attack on Pearl Harbor on December 7, 1941, abruptly reordered his priorities. In this speech, which James Mac-Gregor Burns has accurately termed "the most radical speech of his life," Roosevelt proclaimed a second bill of rights, which included the right to a job, to food, clothing, housing, medical care, education, and "protection from the economic fears of old age, sickness, accident, and unemployment." This was, after all, no more than Roosevelt had asked, and Congress would deliver, in the G.I. Bill for veterans. But the president wanted to secure those benefits for all citizens, just as the NRPB had urged.[23]

He was in good company, just in the wrong country. Whereas in America the NRPB's report led many liberals to disown the board and Congress to dismantle it, the Beveridge Report won solid, bipartisan support for a similarly ambitious scheme in Great Britain. Roosevelt clearly felt cheated by fate. He complained to Frances Perkins that the British version ought properly to be called the Roosevelt Plan, and he very much resented the pressures that forced him first to postpone discussion of the welfare state and then to make its most visible proponent, Henry Wallace, a sacrificial lamb to propitiate Southern Democrats.[24] The mood in Britain was clearly very different.

In June 1941, Beveridge was appointed to direct a committee charged with cleaning up Britain's existing national insurance scheme. Displaying more ambition than respect for the wishes of his superiors in the Treasury, he transformed the committee into a one-man band announcing the need for a wholesale revision of the entire scheme of social services. According to his biographer Jose Harris, Beveridge almost immediately decided on the principal ideas that would appear in his final report. He aimed to banish from Britain "Five Giant Evils": want, disease, ignorance, squalor, and idleness. After he had formulated a tentative plan of attack, Beveridge began calling before the committee witnesses from various groups to discuss his ideas. He discovered a surprising degree of agreement. In his published report, he called for a comprehensive system of social insurance, with benefits guaranteed by right to all citizens; for a national health service; for family allowances; and for policies sustaining full employment.[25]

In striking contrast to the hostile reception from the Left and Right that the recommendations of the NRPB received in America, the Beveridge Report was an immediate hit. Astonishingly, it sold over 600,000 copies. None of the witnesses Beveridge had called from the business community had objected that his ideas violated the inviolable principles of the free market, and none of the conservative press condemned his published report. None of the Labourites called as witnesses had protested the dangers of creeping autocracy, and such fears did not surface in the publications of the Left that discussed his plans. Even the Communist Party lionized him. Although Beveridge himself was a member of the Liberal Party (as was John Maynard Keynes, the other British prophet of the postwar world), both the Conservative and Labour Parties endorsed his proposals. The only discouraging words came from grumpy ministers in the wartime coalition government, who wondered aloud how a nation struggling to survive might afford the lavish programs Beveridge proposed. Churchill warned the cabinet that "a dangerous optimism is growing about the conditions it will be possible to establish after the war. . . . I do not wish to deceive the people by false hopes and airy visions of Utopia and Eldorado." Churchill was still playing Cassandra. His government by then was rather more interested in hopes and visions—false, airy, or otherwise—than in continuing to confront the bleak features of the present.[26]

How can such near unanimity of opinion in Great Britain be explained? For twenty-five years a popular answer was that offered in 1950 by Richard Titmuss in his official study *Problems of Social Policy*. Titmuss wrote, "the mood of the people changed and, in sympathetic response, values changed as well. . . . Dunkirk, and all that evokes, was an important event in the wartime history of the social services. It summoned forth a note of self-criticism, of national introspection, and it set in motion ideas and talk of principles and plans."[27] Perhaps, but commentators have become increasingly suspicious of the "war-warmed" glow of Titmuss's own account. Constructing the welfare state in Britain—as elsewhere in Europe—was arduous economically and politically. Any residue of the widespread enthusiasm at first felt for the Beveridge Report quickly sank in the morass of inflation, shortages, and unemployment that ultimately enveloped Atlee's Labour government. Perhaps consensus carried Labour into power, but it could not dissolve the economic and political problems that eventually drove it out.[28]

Several features of the Beveridge Report deserve consideration because of their contrast to the NRPB report. As is true of the NRPB report, contemporaries writing about the Beveridge Report focused on certain themes while all but ignoring others. The first is the extent to which Beveridge's apparently radical scheme was advanced on the basis of familiar premises. "The state in organizing security," he wrote toward the beginning of his report, "should not stifle incentive, opportunity, responsibility; in establishing a national minimum, it should leave room for encouragement for voluntary action by each individual." In his conclusion, Beveridge distinguished his scheme from the social insurance programs of other European nations. Whereas others calibrated benefits to the level of contributions, which varied according to salary level, Beveridge insisted that both benefits and contributions remain uniform. "The flat rate of benefit treating all alike is in accord with British sentiment for equal treatment of all in social insurance, irrespective both of their previous earnings and of the degree of their risk of unemployment or sickness."[29] This provision sounds egalitarian, even altruistic. But Beveridge clinched his argument, on the closing page of his report, by pointing out that equal treatment would be achieved by setting benefits at a level low enough to encourage all citizens to continue contributing to their own supplementary insurance schemes as well. From the outset, then, Beveridge took for granted the precariousness of life for those who did not accumulate savings of their own. The minimum standard was to be austere as much by design as by necessity; the economic constraints, real as they were, mattered less to Beveridge than the moral reasons for encouraging prudence and foresight.[30]

Second, Beveridge felt no need, and made no effort, to defend his program against criticism of its centralized administration. Again, regardless of whether members of the NRPB are judged genuinely democratic or merely cagey, their report crackles with a rhetoric of participatory democracy altogether absent from the Beveridge Report. Beveridge discussed administration in considerable detail, but the question of the bureaucracy's problematical status vis-à-vis the public evidently concerned him not at all. A unified system would be more efficient and more cost-effective, Beveridge contended, and the public would find the programs less confusing. His section "Advice to Citizens" contained no discussion of citizen participation or appeal procedures. Instead Beveridge blithely assured the public that an official would be present in every local office to explain the program to them and answer their questions. Nothing more was deemed necessary, and no objections were raised on this issue.

The NRPB's concern with consultation and interaction seems never to have crossed Beveridge's mind. In a later report, *Full Employment in a Free Society*, Beveridge elaborated his view of British government in a passage illuminating the gulf separating his conception of representative democracy and the more Deweyan conception of the value of participation that animated the NRPB. "The constitution of Britain concentrates in the Government of the day the great power without which the problems of a great society cannot be solved. . . . Britain has a public service central and local, second to none in the world for efficiency, integrity and devotion to duty." Since our civil servants are neither Prussian autocrats nor American crooks, Beveridge reasoned, the British public need fear neither tyranny nor corruption. Even when Beveridge did indulge in a bit of democratic rhetoric, his words revealed an unself-conscious smugness altogether missing from the NRPB report. "The British people can win full employment while remaining free. But they have to win it, not wait for it. . . . It is not a thing to be promised or not promised by a Government, to be given or withheld as from Olympian heights. It is something that the British democracy would direct its

Government to secure, at all costs save the surrender of individual liberties."[31] The democratic responsibilities Beveridge envisioned for British citizens would begin and end with the ballot. After representatives had been selected and programs created, the government would take care of them itself. Administration must be left to a crackerjack corps of civil servants, not muddled by the intrusions of amateurs.

That predisposition likewise surfaced in Beveridge's call for government planning to sustain economic growth. "To look to individual employers for maintenance of demand and full employment is absurd. These things are not within the power of employers. They must therefore be undertaken by the State, under supervision and pressure of democracy, applied through the Parliament men." Once more, citizens are to apply pressure only through their elected representatives, not through direct involvement in the planning process itself.[32]

The British experience with the politics of poverty helps to explain Beveridge's approach to these problems just as clearly as American development helps to account for the shape of the NRPB report. The world of the workhouse is familiar from the nightmarish accounts in Dickens's novels, but less frightful alternatives emerged during the nineteenth century. An elaborate network of private charitable organizations developed, and mutual societies and union-sponsored programs provided other sources of relief. While the Charity Organization Society demanded moral reform almost as rigorously as the Poor Law did, the various worker-organized insurance plans offered less punitive solutions to the problems of short-term poverty. Perhaps as much as half the adult male population of England participated in such programs by the middle of the nineteenth century. But such plans survived only by turning away the worst risks. They thus cut adrift those most in need of assistance, who then had recourse only to the tender mercies of private or public Victorian "charity."

The Liberal Government that came to power in 1906 undertook the challenge of replacing the inadequate Poor Law system, and both trade unions and the struggling mutual societies reluctantly endorsed David Lloyd George's plan to provide pensions, public assistance, and insurance against ill health and unemployment. Until World War I shattered the optimism that undergirded the Liberal Party's philosophy of a new liberalism, the Liberals' program of social insurance and other progressive reforms seemed likely to succeed in integrating the working classes into a widening mainstream of British life. Although there were scattered protests concerning the potential intrusions by an alien bureaucracy into the sanctity of private life, by the 1920s the legitimacy of the National Insurance program, and the integrity and efficiency of its administration, were well established. When thoughts turned toward expanding the welfare state during World War II, the precedents of government-sponsored and centrally administered insurance programs were already in place.[33] Viewed in this context, the Beveridge Report can be seen as a logical extension rather than a radical departure, and the widespread support it attracted from across the political spectrum seems no more surprising than the abuse that greeted the NRPB report.

American resistance to further expansion of the welfare state and economic planning stands in stark contrast to the experience of European nations, and it has attracted the attention of a number of historically minded social scientists. The most persuasive of their accounts have recently paid attention to a dimension that has not always figured prominently in social science—the subjective side of social experience. Identifying institutions and structures is essential, but it is equally essential to remember that unless institutions and structures have meaning for individuals, they do not survive. American political, social, and economic institutions have changed over two centuries, and those changes have reflected the efforts of individuals, groups, classes, and the emergence of uncontrollable or at least uncontrolled forces such as urbanization and industrialization. Unless we attend equally to the phenomenology of historical experience and to the structural dimensions of social life, our explanations are bound to be incomplete.[34] Having noted that beneath these general characterizations lie the particular commitments and loyalties of individuals, I will briefly outline some of the features of American political culture that stood in the way of Roosevelt and his National Resources Planning Board.

The absence of a tradition of royal absolutism in the United States and the fact that democratization preceded the emergence of the state contributed to the rise and persistence of boisterous, vital, and diverse political cultures at the local and state levels. These jurisdictions have developed vested interests, cherished different aspirations, and exhibited often quite limited administrative competence, all of which have enormously complicated efforts at national reform. Moreover, America's two-party system and tradition of pluralism have meant that parties are coalitions lacking unity of identity and purpose—primitive creatures that rarely generate sufficient ideological loyalty to sustain ambitious political programs. These features of public life invite widespread participation at every level of decision making, and that degree of democratic engagement makes the creation of coherent national policies almost impossible. When Roosevelt tried to reorganize the executive branch of the federal government, pack the Supreme Court, purge the Democratic Party of conservatives who opposed the programs of his New Deal—or extend the federal government's role in social welfare or economic planning—he encountered opposition at every step. The traditions of decentralization, local government, and separation of powers are values that Americans cherish for a variety of high-minded as well as self-interested reasons. If "bringing the state back in" is to mean more than Hegel's revenge, students of American public life must appreciate that the flip side of the narrow-minded parochialism often associated with antistatist positions is the relatively autonomous, local democratic community, whether it offers the warm and nurturing intimacy of Tocqueville's acquaintance or the cold-blooded power politics of urban machines. The American distrust of bureaucracy springs from a longstanding association of virtue with autonomy and of dependency with corruption, and American champions of state activism must continue to contend with the variations on that theme that persist across the political spectrum.[35]

Roosevelt disliked John L. Lewis of the CIO as much as he disliked Sewell

Avery of Montgomery Ward, but he nevertheless fancied himself a friend of organized labor as well as, in his own words, the best friend America's capitalists had. Unfortunately for the New Deal, neither group reciprocated. Organized labor continued to migrate to the Democratic Party during the 1930s and 1940s, but beyond workers' votes, Roosevelt received little visible support for his more ambitious social and economic policies during World War II. Labor opted instead for collective bargaining, preferring the autonomy of private negotiations on fringe benefits to the universal programs urged by the NRPB report.[36]

Although some self-styled progressives saw the opportunities planning presented for corporate America, most business leaders distrusted Roosevelt's vision of a mixed economy. Farmers' organizations likewise grew cooler about Roosevelt's plans once prosperity returned to American agriculture. Southerners saw lurking behind every national program dangerous threats to the system of racial supremacy that they had no intention of surrendering. Lacking support from labor, business, farmers, or the South, Roosevelt found few to rally behind his second bill of rights. Even liberal economists, whose support Roosevelt had thought secure by the end of the 1930s, began shifting their allegiance from trust busting or regulation to Keynesian fiscal policy as the most promising strategy for achieving full employment. Pump priming through tax cuts appeared far more palatable—and more effective—than expensive public works projects. As Keynes's stock rose, enthusiasm for the plans of the NRPB fell.[37]

As fundamental as any other factor, though, was the economic boom that war brought to America. With prosperity came satisfaction, and satisfaction eroded reformist sentiment. Public sacrifice, at least on the scale that Titmuss and others considered adequate to account for the acceptance of the Beveridge Report in England, was largely absent in the United States. Although the suffering of Americans separated by the war cannot be denied, Americans were required to give up much less in the way of material goods than were the populations of some European nations. In the unsentimental formulation of Mark Leff, "What? Me Sacrifice?" was the characteristic American response to calls for solidarity. Confidence in business and commitment to the superiority of the American way of life soared during the war and peaked at the war's end. Roosevelt's (and later Truman's) postwar plans spelled change. Americans were ready to celebrate, not ready to reform.[38]

American political institutions, various economic characteristics, the crucial fact of racism, and the return of prosperity all presented obstacles to implementing the NRPB report. Beyond all of these, though, was another set of factors, the contingent, unpredictable political developments that likewise limited Roosevelt's options. First, both the successes and failures of his own initiatives constrained him. The Social Security system was safe, but its safety was secured by institutionalizing the longstanding division between the deserving and nondeserving poor. The American plan drew a line separating old-age pensions, funded by contributions, from welfare programs, which would remain discretionary, means-tested, and political lightning rods. By contrast, the problems involved in administering both the NRA and the WPA sobered Roosevelt, and his ambivalence about postwar economic planning derived at least in part from his doubts about the compatibility of democratic politics and government by central planning board—doubts that recent experience with planned economies have shown to be well founded. Other noninstitutional, nonstructural developments included the dramatic losses Democrats sustained in the midwar congressional elections in 1942. Just as the triumph of the Beveridge Report was confirming a wartime political truce in Britain, the New Deal coalition was losing control of Congress to an alliance of Southern Democrats and conservative Republicans. Whereas Britain's coalition government effectively suspended most partisan squabbling for the duration of the war, Roosevelt was granted no holiday from politics: When the NRPB report appeared, for example, it was quickly branded "socialist, fascist, and medieval," an omnibus charge that indicted the Roosevelt administration for moving at once too fast, too slow, too far to the left, and too far to the right. Roosevelt had reason to act cautiously in 1944: charges of dictatorship and collectivism were fighting words. Despite the best efforts of the NRPB to present its plans in democratic terms, and to couch them in the vocabulary of rights, in the supercharged atmosphere of wartime America all change was suspect, all government ominous.[39]

The confidence Americans felt in the free enterprise system was more than matched by the confidence and pride Britain felt in its government's resourcefulness in the face of the Luftwaffe. The Labour Party's participation in Churchill's government enabled Labour Ministers to establish their legitimacy and responsibility without identifying them too closely with the war itself. Ministers such as Ernest Bevin, Clement Atlee, Hugh Dalton, and Herbert Morrison succeeded in associating Labour with the Beveridge Report, and all that it promised, without appearing to be either disloyal or responsible for the hardships of the war. Hysterical protests against government tyranny, of the sort common in America, were mooted by the simple fact that the British government did manage the economy effectively during World War II, nationalizing industries and running the health service to see the nation through the emergency. Condemning such measures as "unBritish," as they were dubbed "unAmerican," was not an option.[40]

Moreover, Conservatives and Liberals had vied with Labour in their enthusiasm for the idea of the welfare state and planning even before the war. The renegade Tory Harold Macmillan favored the nationalization of the coal mines (a measure he opposed after the war). In 1936 he called for a new Centre Party, which would be "a fusion of all that is best in the Left and the Right." Macmillan also wrote a book, *The Middle Way* (1938), in which he argued the case for a national minimum, to be secured by a welfare state and financed through revenues derived from a comprehensive plan for a managed economy. Although Liberals differed on how extensive planning should be, contributors to the Liberal manifesto *The Next Five Years* (1935) agreed that government must broaden its horizons. During the war a Royal Commission headed by Sir Montague Barlow recommended a plan for allocating resources and locating industrial development, and in 1944 the Conservative Minister of Health, Henry Willink, proposed a plan for a permanent national health service. At times it seemed Liberals such as Beveridge and Conservatives such as Macmillan were trying to outflank Labour on the left. In the words of T. H. Marshall, whose postwar writings on the welfare state helped explain its emergence and legitimate its presence, by the end of the war the welfare state "could enjoy a ready-made consensus."[41] What to build on that consensus, not whether to accept it, was at issue in the elections of 1945. Churchill promised to remain rock-solid until Japan was defeated; Labour promised mass housing. Churchill miscalculated the public mood; Labour triumphed. But it is worth noting that both parties endorsed the Beveridge Report. Although they disagreed about nationalization, there was no point in discussing the welfare state and economic planning, which by 1945 had moved beyond controversy. They had become integral parts of the British conception of government, as they remain today despite the spirited efforts of the Conservative Party to dismantle costly social programs.[42]

The legacy of the New Deal was a pattern of social welfare programs bifurcated along two separate axes. The public system distinguished between Social Security, with benefits "earned" by contributions, and welfare, with "unearned" and means-tested benefits paid from general tax revenues. An equally split private system of employee benefits packages developed alongside this public system. Millions of workers contributed to company- or union-sponsored insurance plans, while others, usually those in the most marginal positions in the economy and thus most vulnerable, survived without any insurance at all. As such programs became increasingly comprehensive and generous, they cemented the commitment to the private sector of those who stood to benefit from them, while at the same time they eroded public interest in state-sponsored programs designed to assist those who lacked access to such insurance. Not only salaried members of the middle class but also unionized workers achieved levels of insurance that rivaled those of the most elaborate welfare states. Since these schemes remained private, however, participation in them was no more secure than the jobs workers held or the sectors of the economy in which they were employed.[43]

Despite, or perhaps, paradoxically, because of this doubly divided system, America's fragmented welfare system has expanded slowly and not surely. The Social Security system has become as generous as any pension plan anywhere; its benefits are indexed to inflation and set at a level that makes retirement for most Americans less perilous than it once was. Private benefits packages have become increasingly comprehensive. For those excluded from these contributory schemes, however, the situation has remained bleak. Studies of public opinion have found repeatedly that Americans are "operational liberals" and "ideological conservatives." In other words, they want existing programs to continue, although often not to expand, even as they proclaim themselves philosophically opposed to government assistance. Cross-national studies confirm the near universality of such contradictory positions, which underscores the persistence of distinctions long drawn between the deserving and nondeserving poor. To reiterate, the American scheme is unusual—although hardly unique—because it institutionalizes that division by separating contributory from noncontributory programs. Acknowledging that limitation, however, should not blind us to the steady expansion of the American Social Security system, which now covers over 90 percent of the workforce, or to the more recent creation of programs providing food stamps, Medicaid, and Medicare, which have further broadened the benefits available.[44]

Despite its successes, the American welfare state has remained on the defensive, assailed from the Right for wastefulness and from the Left for institutionalizing social control. Despite such criticism, the system survives, sustained by its own bureaucratic momentum and by the general belief that something (usually unspecified) must be done about poverty. To a degree, the perpetuation of the system reflects the accuracy of a prediction offered by one of its many architects, Joseph Harris, at a planning session for the federal Committee on Administrative management in 1936:

> We may assume that the nature of the problems of American economic life are such as not to permit any political party for any length of time to abandon most of the collectivist functions which are now being exercised. This is true even though the details of policy programs may differ and even though the old slogans of opposition to enlargement of governmental activity will survive long after their meaning has been sucked out.[45]

Not only have the "policy programs" of the New Deal and the "old slogans of opposition" both survived, as Harris anticipated, but so has the meaning of that opposition. Opposition to welfare, in other words, need not always be rooted in racism, although surely it often is. It can also derive from a legitimate fear that corruption of both parties—the one receiving and the one providing benefits—inevitably results under conditions of dependency. In such conditions, the reciprocity that should undergird democratic culture cannot be secured because of the asymmetry of the relationship.

Philosophers from Hugo Grotius and Thomas Hobbes to Robert Goodin and Jeremy Waldron have argued that everyone has the moral right to do what is necessary to survive. Thus the most solid, if not the most inspiring, defense of the welfare state may be among the most simple: Welfare, Waldron writes, "is a way of ensuring that no one should ever be in such abject need that he would be driven to violate otherwise enforceable rules of property." Beyond that rather modest justification, champions of the welfare state might add Joseph Raz's "autonomy principle," which requires, as a cost of freedom, making efforts "to secure the conditions of autonomy for all people." Together these principles provide a rationale for welfare that does not require altruism or a commitment to equality as a higher priority than liberty. In Robert Goodin's words, "If full participation in our societies is conditional upon a person's being a minimally independent agent, then morally we must not only serve the needs of those who are dependent upon us but also do what we can to render those persons independent." Viewed in this light, the welfare state can be defended, not as a form of soft-hearted humanitarianism, but as nothing more (or less) than a manifestation of a thoroughgoing commitment to autonomy for all citizens. Until or unless such arguments are made, the welfare state will continue to appear vulnerable to legitimate criticism from the Right as well as the Left.

The problem with America's welfare state, conceived in these terms, is not its generosity but its lack of generality. To quote Goodin again, "what was crucial in the shift from the old poor law state to the modern welfare state was the move (coming in 1911 in Britain, and 1935 in the United States) away from discretionary public charity and toward nondiscretionary entitlement rules. It is these nondiscretionary entitlement rules, more than anything else, that give the welfare state its peculiar moral flavor."[46] Thus it was not, as is often argued, the shift in rhetoric from responsibilities to rights that doomed America's welfare state.[47] Roosevelt's decision to follow the NRPB, and to frame the issue in terms of individual freedom, was not a fatal error but rather a sensible strategy that failed. It failed, moreover, not because it embodied a faulty conception of the purpose of welfare, but for the various political, economic, social, and circumstantial reasons already discussed. Americans were not prepared in the 1930s, and will not be prepared in the 1990s, to endorse principles they consider socialist. Michael Walzer has urged partisans of a universalist welfare state, a system that would extend its benefits to all citizens as a matter of right and without means testing, to stop trying to socialize the means of production and concentrate instead on trying to socialize the means of distribution. As socialist states have learned from decades of experience, public ownership is a disappointment. The challenge remains to find ways to maximize production while assuring that all citizens have access to the opportunities necessary for autonomous life.[48]

Equally attractive are the means Roosevelt's planners preferred. In the introduction to his comparative study of the welfare state, *In Care of the State*, Abram de Swaan writes, "it may well be that the collection and distribution of money transfers is handled best by the central state—for reasons of distributive justice—but that the adjudication of cases and the administration of human services is better left to small, self-managing cooperative bodies of citizens."[49] That sensible judgment resembles nothing I have encountered in the literature of the welfare state so closely as it resembles the final recommendations of the NRPB. Principled democrats distrust powerful state bureaucracies for good reasons, which Max Weber explored in his analysis of the elective affinities between the disenchantment of the world and the rise of rationalization. The principles of effective administration require predictable procedures and impersonal rules; the principles of democracy provide for change and innovation in response to public demand. The conflict between bureaucracy and democracy is inescapable, and only to the extent that participation can be built into administration, as the NRPB hoped and Walzer and de Swaan urge, can those conflicts be eased. They can never be eliminated.

It is impossible to explain the results of the American or British efforts to construct a welfare state by concentrating exclusively on social structures, long-term processes, political institutions, or cultural traditions. All of those factors played a part, yet they are necessary but not sufficient elements of an adequate explanation. In addition to such components, we must add—as historians always do—the contingent and unpredictable circumstances within which individuals made choices, the subjective dimension of these policy-making processes that the effort to construct analytical models may cause us to overlook. As studying the construction of welfare states in America and Britain reveals, history without a structural framework is shapeless, but institutional explanations without a phenomenology of historical experience are hollow.

The references to democracy, decentralization, and citizen participation that run through the NRPB report indicate both the distinctiveness of the American plan for a welfare state and the reasons why it failed. The democratic pronouncements of the NRPB testify to the persistent and powerful appeal in the United States of democratic and community-based approaches to economic and social problems. Yet it was the resistance of certain communities in the United States—notably the communities of white southerners who successfully blocked any initiatives that might destabilize a social order premised on racism and designed to preserve inequality—that eventually defeated these proposals. The wealthy white males who dominated the U.S. Congress deliberated on these ideas and rejected them because they threatened their own treasured forms of hierarchical community. The NRPB program for a generous, extensive, and democratic welfare state foundered for many reasons, but it did not fail simply owing to the absence of social democratic ideas similar to those that triumphed in Western Europe after 1945. Without a commitment to the ethic of reciprocity, deliberation within democratic institutions does not guarantee egalitarian results.

The American architects of a postwar welfare state tried hard to counter Americans' distrust of centralized authority by designing programs that would embody democratic ideals of civic participation at the local level. When Eveline Burns wrote a report comparing the provisions of the two plans, she concluded that

> it is doubtful whether there is anything in Beveridge's report more "revolutionary" (relative to its environment and time) than the NRPB reports' proposals for implementing two fundamental policies, namely, that it is the responsibility of government to provide jobs for all whom private industry cannot employ and that the national government has a responsibility to ensure minimum security for all.[50]

She was right. Roosevelt's second bill of rights represented an ambitious attempt to extend the principles of democracy from politics to the economy and to the field of social provision. His plan proved too ambitious—perhaps too "revolutionary"—to succeed against the obstacles it faced, obstacles that testify to the double-edged quality of democratic deliberation.

The ideal of deliberative democracy, most often associated today with Habermas's discourse ethic and assumed by many to be unknown in the liberal pluralist culture of the United States, does indeed have roots in the American past, and it has remained a vibrant part of American political culture throughout the twentieth century. But those who participate in public debate do not always reach conclusions that can be characterized as substantively democratic. The original Latin meaning of *deliberare* was "to weigh well," and deliberation of that kind requires a prior commitment to an ethic of reciprocity that Winthrop acknowledged in the seventeenth century, Madison in the eighteenth, Tocqueville in the nineteenth, and Dewey and his allies on the NRPB in the twentieth.

But it is equally important to recognize that the practice of politics in America has more often than not failed to correspond to that deliberative ideal, as the defeat of Roosevelt's second bill of rights, to cite just one example, makes clear. Americans with wealth and power have frequently proved themselves capable of manipulating formally democratic institutions to preserve privileges that some critics consider inconsistent with the democratic principle of equality. That realization should sober us as we think about deliberative democracy as a way of spanning the gap between self and community. Because not only has community sometimes provided the occasion for developing an ethic of reciprocity, as Tocqueville pointed out, such group loyalties have also been used to justify preserving inequalities and propounding varieties of racism. The asymmetry in all human relationships complicates efforts to achieve the ideal of reciprocity. Beginning with the most basic relationship between parents and children, the degree and kind of love and dependency vary: a father's children are more lovable to him, Aristotle observed, than is his own father. Such an imbalance is replicated in some form in nearly every human interaction. Moreover, not only do intimate relationships change over a lifetime for good reasons—even between the same people, as adult sons and daughters who are also fathers and mothers know—they often change for mysterious and apparently irrational reasons. Because desires and needs impinge on obligations and commitments subtly and unpredictably, even the most selflessly devoted seem occasionally demanding. Given such difficulties, approaching the ethic of reciprocity in social and political life is an enormous challenge. Given the greater asymmetry of most social and political relations, and the weaker bonds of attachment, it is no surprise that domination and resentment abound even in the best of circumstances.

In the absence of commitments to autonomy for all and an ethic of reciprocity, any group of three can yield a majority of two committed to enslaving the other one. Whether directed toward American Indians or African Americans or Asians or Hispanics within the United States, or toward other peoples beyond the nation's borders, such majoritarian racism has also been as American as apple pie. Historians who study those excluded from the mainstream of American democracy illuminate the problematical nature of attempts to incorporate diversity within any culture premised on assumptions about fundamental commonality—most notably, the willingness to abide by the will of the majority—that must underlie democratic institutions. The scope of democratic citizenship expanded during the eighteenth, nineteenth, and twentieth centuries largely owing to changing conceptions of the criteria appropriate for determining who should participate in the decision-making process, and on what terms. That struggle is not yet over.

The ideas that supplanted older versions of racial supremacy required acceptance of something like W. E. B. Du Bois's notion of "double consciousness," the effort to keep in balance—because it is not possible fully to reconcile—the competing demands of the self and the other. Such a democratic self is constituted by the tension between one's own awareness of membership in a particular community —whether racial or otherwise—and one's aspiration to membership in the larger, more cosmopolitan and transracial human community, a tension further deepened by the awareness that the "other" is multiple rather than singular. Those contradictory demands alert individuals—especially members of racial minorities, Du Bois argued—to the necessity of working to legitimate a cultural ideal beyond the summing of purely individual preferences. Only when the preferences of members of a majority are formed through interaction with and recognition of the different desires of members of minorities can the latter hope to escape oppression. Only by persuading all members of democratic cultures that their ideal must incorporate the "double consciousness" to which some members of racial minorities come naturally (albeit painfully), and to which other people come by embracing ethical imperatives such as the Christian law of love or political ideas such as the ethic of reciprocity, can we move toward the ideal of a "postethnic America" that David Hollinger has so attractively and persuasively laid out in the book that bears that title.[51]

American historians have a responsibility to be tough-minded about American democracy. We must remind our students and our readers that the struggle for democracy has been an uphill battle, and that merely preaching the values of deliberation, of being reasonable and learning to get along with each other, has never been sufficient to end injustice or secure a democratic culture. American historians also have an opportunity to reawaken, and to sharpen, the sense of democracy as an unfinished project in which we all participate, and to make available the knowledge of how democratic struggles have been fought, so that our students and our readers can see late-twentieth-century democratic cultures as products of those struggles, and see themselves as the potential creators of a different, and perhaps more fully more democratic, future.

EIGHT

POLITICAL IDEAS IN
TWENTIETH-CENTURY AMERICA

IN HIS INAUGURAL ADDRESS on January 20, 1993, William Jefferson Clinton declared categorically, "our greatest strength is the power of our ideas." But what are our ideas? Clinton himself identified democracy, freedom, responsibility, sacrifice, and religious conviction—the same themes he invoked throughout his campaign for the presidency. But the pundits were not impressed. Calls for sacrifice and responsibility, they assured savvy listeners and readers, mean only higher taxes and increased government spending.

It is tempting to deny any connection between theorists' ideas and political reality, but they are related to the changing social and political contexts in which they appear—the circumstances of their articulation. Of course, many factors shape public policy, including political institutions, social and cultural pressures, economic conditions, legal traditions, religious, ethnic, racial, and gender identities and conflicts, the nature and content of communications technology, international pressures and opportunities, and doubtless others. For both the producers and the consumers of political discourse, however, ideas have been, and continue to be, constitutive of political consciousness. Encountering, or engaging in, political discourse provides the occasion for citizens to reflect on their preferences and occasionally to reformulate their conceptions of what America is and what Americans ought to do. Such activities proceed within historical horizons that ought to be kept in focus.

Two features of contemporary American intellectual life complicate the historical analysis of political ideas in the twentieth century. First, a pervasive cynicism threatens to undercut any effort to take seriously the role of ideas in political life. The public suspects that hidden beneath politicians' lofty rhetoric lies personal calculation. Many scholars insist that language is merely strategic. Viewed from either perspective, political discourse appears less likely to express deeply held convictions than to reflect judgments concerning which symbols can be manipulated to greatest effect. Now that the electorate's responses to candidates' comments can be electronically monitored during the course of a campaign, as they were throughout the 1992 and 1996 presidential debates, each individual voter's reactions to word choices, quips, inflections, and facial expressions can be measured instantly. Candidates' presentations can be calibrated to the preferences of targeted segments of the population, rendering ever greater both the potential rewards for shrewd strategists and the risks run by those who express, naively, their genuine convictions. Taking ideas seriously runs counter to the popular and the scholarly suspicion that political discourse is a charade.

Second, contemporary debates in political theory tend to revolve around the categories of "liberalism," with its focus on individual rights, and "communitarianism," with its focus on social responsibility. Neither of these categories, however, adequately captures the complexities and dynamism of twentieth-century political debate in the United States. Such simplifications only reproduce the complementary demonologies of political partisans. In order to understand our political ideas, it is necessary to escape such unsatisfactory conceptual frameworks and return to the very different terms in which earlier generations of American thinkers conceived of the relation between freedom and community.[1]

Looking Backward: Political Ideas in Historical Perspective

Late nineteenth-century thinkers inherited from their predecessors a rich and complex mixture of ideas drawn from diverse sources and leavened by historical experience. From the Revolutionary era they derived ideals of virtue that blended together Christian notions of sinfulness and salvation, the public spiritedness and autonomy joined in the ideal of republican citizenship, and the concern for responsible individual freedom that was central to early liberal theory. From the antebellum years they inherited the Jacksonians' celebration of a boisterous democratic politics for white males, together with the formal exclusion of blacks and the less formal but equally significant creation of a separate, domestic sphere for white women. But earlier, more universal ideals did not disappear. Abolitionists, woman suffragists, labor radicals, and Whigs continued to invoke the standards of Christian, republican, and liberal justice against proclamations of the sanctity of white men's rights. Thanks largely to Lincoln's legacy, such ideals continued to resound powerfully in post–Civil War American political discourse.

Confronting a new, urban industrial world, and the excesses of the era that Charles Warner and Mark Twain christened *The Gilded Age*, late nineteenth-century American political thinkers slipped into varieties of Manichean thinking. Conservative champions of the ideas that have come to be known as Social Darwinism gloried in the mysterious process whereby progress emerged miraculously from conflict. Ranging from the romantic guild ideal of the Knights of Labor to the diverse forms of agrarian protest that coalesced as the populist crusade, and from Henry George's single tax to Edward Bellamy's magical postindustrial utopia in *Looking Backward*, radical thinkers gravitated toward what

Walter Lippmann, writing in *Drift and Mastery* in 1914, termed "the panacea habit of mind."[2] All these thinkers shared Bellamy's nostalgic yearning for the world America had left behind; like his protagonist, Julian West, they were "looking backward" even as they envisioned futures in which harmonious communities would replace the strident competition of their world. Those who were to follow them looked toward the future rather than the past.

Progressive Democracy: An Age of Reform, 1900–1917

When Theodore Roosevelt succeeded the assassinated William McKinley as president in 1901, he brought with him a new spirit of activism to the national political scene. In response to the widespread perception of corruption in the public and private spheres, a perception that would be sharpened by the disclosures of muckraking journalists in the first few years of the new century, various social, economic, and political reforms had been bubbling up from the local and state levels in the 1890s. When Roosevelt ascended to the presidency, he used that bully pulpit to bring to national attention the reformist views he shared with many progressives. Although historians have discovered too many varieties of progressivism to make possible a simple characterization of a coherent movement, it is clear that a diverse array of new political ideas and reform proposals appeared in the first two decades of this century.

Several streams fed the flow of progressive thinking. The new social sciences, which emerged in the post–Civil War era and began to take shape around the turn of the century as the distinct disciplines we know today, contributed not only a wealth of new information but also a new way of thinking about social life. Sociologists Franklin Giddings, Albion Small, Charles Cooley, and E. A. Ross replaced atomistic individuals with selves constructed through the process of social interaction, and earlier ideas of independence with the concept of interdependence.[3] Economists John Commons, E. R. A. Seligman, and Richard T. Ely called for historical analysis to replace the timelessness of classical economics.

Ely drew on a wide range of social scientific research to advance arguments concerning economics, politics, and social reform. His *Outlines of Economics* went through six editions, and in the early decades of the twentieth century it was outsold, among economics books, only by Adam Smith's *The Wealth of Nations*. In his widely read *Socialism and Social Reform* (1894), Ely marshaled evidence from several social sciences in support of a typical progressive reform agenda. The United States could find a "golden mean" between stasis and revolution, Ely argued, if the nation took three steps. First, Americans must reduce the "waste" in their competitive economic system by achieving full employment and "wholesome" working conditions. Second, Americans must reduce the "extremes" of wealth and poverty by shaping distribution so that "all shall have assured incomes, but that no one who is personally qualified to render service shall enjoy an income without personal exertion." Third, Americans must commit themselves to "abundant public provision of opportunities for the development of our faculties," primarily by developing educational and recreational facilities. In his discussion of the design and implementation of such plans for what is now called the welfare state, Ely stressed the need for democracy and decentralization, two recurrent themes in American progressive and social democratic discourse. He also emphasized another common theme, the consistency between progressive reform and Americans' religious and ethical ideals. Religion, Ely insisted, is an "independent force, often sufficient to modify and even to shape economic institutions." Society "is not an automaton. That society has some option, some choice, and conscience to which an appeal can be made, is a fact, if there is any such thing as a fact at all."[4] For many social scientists of Ely's generation, evidence derived from empirical research went hand in hand with ethical commitment, and together they bolstered the case for democratic economic, social, and political reform.

Ely's style of argument points toward the second source feeding progressive political thinking, the social gospel. A reformist impulse swept through American Protestantism from 1890 to 1915, spreading gradually from moderate preachers such as Washington Gladden to more radical figures such as William Dwight Porter Bliss, who helped create the Society of Christian Socialists and also edited the comprehensive *Encyclopedia of Social Reform*. Most partisans of the social gospel combined, as did Ely and Bliss, a passion for social research with a commitment to social change, and they conceived of both within the framework of their religious faith. The most creative theorist of the social gospel movement was Walter Rauschenbusch, whose most important book, *Christianity and the Social Crisis* (1907), sold fifty thousand copies and was translated into eight languages. In *Christianizing the Social Order* (1912), Rauschenbusch singled out Ely as one of the "pioneers of the social gospel" whose spirit had "kindled and compelled" Rauschenbusch's own reformist sensibility. In his writings Rauschenbusch passionately denied the adequacy of competition as a principle for social organization, contrasting it to the principle of cooperation governing interaction in homes, schools, and churches. Reform could come only through steady, gradual democratic progress keyed to the ethical and religious ideal of cooperative life. But Rauschenbusch, perhaps more realistically than some of his progressive allies, cautioned his readers against expecting too much from society even if it were reformed: suffering, conflict, and tragedy, he warned, would persist as an inevitable part of the human condition.[5]

That nonutopian spirit likewise infused the work and the writings of Jane Addams, who shared with social scientists and social gospelers a commitment to reform, and whose example inspired the third source of progressivism, the social settlement movement. As Addams explained in *Twenty Years at Hull House* (1910), she established Hull House to provide herself and other young women with an opportunity to provide useful service. Her religious faith, combined with a faith in democracy that she considered complementary to her Christian principles, undergirded her commitment to working with the poor. Unlike many—usually male—progressives who preferred the universalistic approach of social insurance, women such as Addams valued the hands-on approach that was to become standard among social work professionals later in the twentieth century. But central commitments nevertheless linked social settlement workers with other Progressives. Together with social scientists such as Ely, who was a frequent visitor to Hull House, Addams believed that "the dependence of classes on each other is reciprocal." Together with social gospelers such as Rauschenbusch, she believed that "the things which make men alike are finer and better than the things that keep them apart, and that these basic likenesses, if they are properly accentuated, easily transcend the less essential differences of race, language, creed and tradition."[6]

Their common humanity might also enable individuals to transcend differences of gender, at least according to some feminists who believed that the ultimate triumph of "the woman movement" would result in unprecedented levels of social cooperation. Charlotte Perkins Gilman, the most creative and influential American feminist theorist, argued in *Women and Economics* (1898) that women's dependence on men had debased both sexes and had robbed society of the contributions independent women could make. Building on Gilman's influential arguments, some feminists sought to expand women's separate sphere to encompass the entire public realm, thereby bringing to political life the virtues of selflessness and sacrifice that had unfortunately been cordoned off from politics. In *The Man Made World, or Our Androcentric Culture* (1911), Gilman herself made such arguments explicit in an extended prescription of social reforms that complemented her earlier diagnosis of her culture's sickness. Gilman urged reformers to redirect "the mother instinct," the tireless devotion that mothers bring to the care of their children, from the narrow mother-child relation to the broader sphere of politics. If that mixture of love, care, and service could be transported from the home to public life, all Americans—male as well as female—might begin to appreciate their social nature as humans and apply the mother's spirit of loving service in place of the reigning male habits of dominance and mastery. If women were allowed to enter democratic politics, Gilman argued, they would bring with them a genuine impulse toward public service instead of the desire to exercise power arbitrarily from above. Then government authority might at last rest on consent and proceed by agreement rather than compulsion, as the people themselves gradually developed habits of cooperation to replace the earlier competition of male-dominated politics. So complete would be the transformation, Gilman concluded, that democratic government could do without the spirit of partisanship; political parties themselves would wither away.[7]

That confidence in the capacity of citizens to transcend their individual differences was a hallmark of much progressive thinking. Although it was consistent with all four sources already discussed, the ideal of the public interest also drew heavily on the fifth source of progressive political thinking, the philosophy of pragmatism. In his reconceptualization of experience, William James broke down the dualisms that had undergirded empiricist as well as rationalist philosophy, dualisms that had thereby contributed indirectly to the abstract and dogmatic theorizing characteristic of laissez-faire liberalism and revolutionary socialism. Proclaiming a radical theory of knowledge, James abandoned the philosophical quest for certainty, placing all ideas within their historical contexts and urging that an attitude of constant experimentation replace the search for timeless truths. Hermeneutical understanding, historically sophisticated and self-consciously aware of its provisionality, replaced certainty as James's standard for human knowledge.[8]

The contribution of pragmatism to the progressive-era search for a public interest that would transcend particularity is reflected in the writings of other feminists as well. Educational pioneer Lucy Sprague Mitchell studied with James while she was at Radcliffe, and later with John Dewey at Columbia. In her work as the first female dean at the University of California, and as founder of what was to become the Bank Street College of Education, she applied the principles of pragmatism to social reform. The too-little-known feminist philosopher Jessie Taft likewise attempted to apply pragmatic philosophy to social and political criticism. She studied at the University of Chicago with George Herbert Mead, and her book *The Woman's Movement from the Point of View of Social Consciousness* (1916) may have been the first philosophy dissertation written on feminist theory. She argued, as Gilman had done, that the purpose of the women's movement was less to emancipate women than to enable all people to "feel within themselves as their own the impulses and points of view of all classes and both sexes." Taft believed that women, particularly women educated in pragmatism and the social sciences, had a particularly clear view of social conflict because of their marginality. For that reason they could see that the fundamental transformation of gender roles, not mere institutional reforms or the achievement of woman suffrage, was a necessary precondition for effecting lasting social and political change.[9]

Such feminists were not alone in advancing political arguments from pragmatist foundations. W. E. B. Du Bois, who studied philosophy at Harvard, described himself as "a devoted follower of James at the time he was developing his pragmatic philosophy." Du Bois credited James with turning him away from "the sterilities of scholastic philosophy to realist pragmatism," and Albert Bushnell Hart for saving him from "the lovely but sterile land of philosophic speculation" and turning him toward "the social sciences as the field for gathering and interpreting that body of fact which would apply to my program for the Negro."[10] Du Bois's program, and the means he suggested for its achievement, bore a striking resemblance to the ideas of Gilman and Taft. As he wrote in *The Souls of Black Folk* (1903),

The history of the American Negro is the history of this strife—this longing to attain self-conscious manhood, to merge his double self into a better and truer self. In this merging he wishes neither of the older selves to be lost. He would not Africanize America, for America has too much to teach the world and Africa. He would not bleach his Negro soul in a flood of white Americanism, for he knows that Negro blood has a message for the world. He simply wishes to make it possible for a man to be both a Negro and an American, without being cursed and spit upon by his fellows, without having the doors of opportunity closed roughly in his face. This, then, is the end of his striving: to be a co-worker in the kingdom of culture.[11]

In that spirit Du Bois undertook to edit *Crisis*, the periodical published by the newly formed National Association for the Advancement of Colored People, and in its early years he was the only African American to serve as a national officer of the organization. His faith in the prospects for racial harmony would fade, but during the prewar years he shared the progressive confidence in the possibility of cooperative reform.

The mercurial Walter Lippmann and the stolid Herbert Croly were two other prominent progressive theorists inspired by pragmatism. Eventually their confidence in reform too would falter, but prior to World War I they helped articulate progressive ideas in a series of important books and in the *New Republic*, the journal they founded in 1914 together with the reform-minded economist Walter Weyl. Both Lippmann and Croly studied with James at Harvard, and both shared the common progressive belief that pragmatism provided a fruitful method for thinking about political as well as philosophical problems.

In his first book, *A Preface to Politics* (1913), Lippmann mocked those who set to work on politics "with a few inherited ideas, uncriticized assumptions, a foggy vocabulary, and machine philosophy." Instead Americans needed the flexibility only pragmatism and democracy together could provide. In *Drift and Mastery* (1914), Lippmann explained why radical philosophy and radical politics fit together. Now that our culture has lost confidence in authority, we must "substitute purpose for tradition." Just as the community of scientific inquiry reaches provisional agreement through testing hypotheses, so a democratic community must proceed through constant experimentation. The precise shape of the culture created by that process could not be delineated in advance. In *Drift and Mastery* Lippmann endorsed the full range of economic, social, and political reform measures advocated by most Progressives: "a minimum standard of life below which no human being can fall is the most elementary duty of the democratic state." Yet he emphasized that the democracy he had in mind could not be reduced to particular programs. "The day is past," he wrote in *Drift and Mastery*, "when anybody can pretend to have laid down an inclusive or a final analysis of the democratic problem. Everyone is compelled to omit infinitely more than he can deal with; everyone is compelled to meet the fact that a democratic vision must be made by the progressive collaboration of many people."[12]

If Lippmann's idea of "mastery" seemed vague, its imprecision was no worse —and no less deliberate—than was Croly's call for a "democratic St. Francis" at the conclusion of *The Promise of American Life* (1909). Owing largely to Theodore Roosevelt's enthusiastic endorsement of its call for a "new nationalism" to supplant the old shibboleths of small-scale democratic individualism, *The Promise* established Croly as the most influential theorist of progressivism. Whereas in *The Promise* Croly appeared to teeter unsteadily between science and mysticism, challenging every citizen to become "something of a saint and something of a hero," in *Progressive Democracy* he rooted his political ideas firmly in the philosophy of pragmatism. The resemblance between Lippmann's idea of mastery and Croly's conception of democracy as cooperative problem solving derives from their shared reliance on pragmatism. Democracy, Croly wrote, "assumes the ability of the human intelligence to frame temporary programs which will provide a sufficient foundation for significant and fruitful action. It anticipates that as a result of such action a progressive democracy will learn how to be progressively democratic."[13]

Although that formulation initially appears circular, it reflects instead Croly's incisive understanding that a genuinely democratic politics depends on a genuinely democratic culture, a culture not afraid of change. Croly urged Americans to unshackle their imaginations from the "presumably permanent body of constitutional law" and have the courage to experiment with "a social program which will not make any corresponding pretensions to finality." The only "permanent element in the life of the community will be derived," Croly concluded, from "the democratic faith and ideal."[14] Croly never doubted that conflicts faced in that spirit could be resolved.

All of the sources of progressive political thinking—social science, the social gospel, social settlements, feminism, and pragmatism—came together in the life and work of John Dewey. Dewey was the towering figure of twentieth-century American political thought, and his development, along with Lippmann's, provides a thread connecting many of the central debates that have occupied those involved in shaping American political discourse. Although Dewey is best known as a philosopher, his ideas cannot be separated from the broader cultural ferment of progressivism. He first established his reputation with his writings in psychology; in his work on education he applied ideas about experience and interaction from psychologists and sociologists. From his early address "Christianity and Democracy" (1892) to his unconventional *A Common Faith* (1934), Dewey grappled with the consequences of religious faith for politics. During his years at the University of Chicago around the turn of the century, Dewey was involved with the activities at Hull House. When he moved to Columbia University in New York in 1904, he became affiliated with Lillian Wald's Henry Street Settlement. Dewey dedicated his most strident call to political radicalism, *Liberalism and Social Action* (1935), to the memory of Jane Addams. According to his daughter Jane M. Dewey, whose biography of her father appeared in Paul Arthur Schilpp's *The Philosophy of John Dewey* (1939), Dewey enthusiastically supported "every cause that enlarged the freedom of activity of women," and Dewey attributed to the influence of Jane Addams his central, abiding conviction that "democracy is a way of life, the truly moral and human way of life, not a political institutional device."[15]

Consistent with that belief, Dewey's political writings yoked together epistemological, psychological, sociological, and especially ethical arguments to sustain a program for democratic reform. For Dewey democracy was, from first to last, an ethical project. As he wrote in *The Ethics of Democracy* (1888), and reiterated tirelessly throughout his career, "Democracy is an ethical ideal. . . . Democracy and the one, the ultimate, ethical ideal of humanity are to my mind synonyms."[16] But the precise meaning of democracy would for that very reason necessarily remain both fuzzy and elastic, since its shape could emerge only from the efforts of all citizens working together. That conception of democracy as a cooperative undertaking was doubtless the source of Dewey's great appeal; his apparent blindness to the pervasiveness and persistence of power was the principal reason his critics judged his political ideas naive.

Given the emphasis on flexibility that linked him with other Progressives such as Croly and Lippmann, Dewey's views on particular issues shifted in ways that can be characterized as supple or opportunistic. Unlike Croly and Lippmann, both of whom endorsed Roosevelt in 1912, Dewey judged both Roosevelt and Wilson too timid and voted instead for Eugene Debs. By 1916, however, he admitted admiring Wilson for the reforms passed during his administration. Writing in the *New Republic* in 1916, Dewey acknowledged that Wilson "has appreciated the moving forces of present industrial life and has not permitted the traditional philosophy to stand in the way of doing the things that need to be done." Against all odds, Wilson had freed the Democratic Party from nostalgia and reoriented it toward progressivism. "A party which is in effect as nationalistic as the Republican, but which allies its nationalism with the interests of the masses and not of the privileged pecuniary classes, is what, in my judgment, this country most needs."[17] Roosevelt's New Nationalism, which emphasized accommodating and regulating concentrations of private power by counterposing public power, was widely believed to have been inspired by Croly. Wilson's New Freedom, which emphasized decentralization of all power, was widely believed to have been inspired by "the people's attorney," Louis Brandeis, who feared that concentrations of power in large-scale organizations, either private or public, necessarily threatened democracy. When the assumed dichotomy between Croly's and Brandeis's agendas seemed to dissolve in practice, Dewey, committed as a Pragmatist to revising his views on the basis of experience, shifted his allegiance—and his hopes for democratic reform—to Wilson in 1916. Together with many Progressives, the events that were to unfold during Wilson's second term would prompt him to think again.[18]

American Individualism: Rethinking Democratic Culture, 1918–1932

World War I brought progressive democracy to an end. The sources of prewar reformist ideas seemed to run dry, as the Progressives' enthusiasm for democracy soured into disillusionment. A more careful look back at those sources, though, indicates that the developments of the 1920s flowed directly from submerged elements already present in progressive political thinking.

First, social science, which some Progressives had seen as a weapon to be wielded for the cause of democratic reform, had from the beginning attracted others for a quite different reason, because it promised new and sophisticated techniques that could be used to achieve more effective social control. The study of politics in particular shifted from the broad, nineteenth-century focus on culture and zeroed in on institutions and administration. The resulting discipline of political science employed different tools of analysis to reach a different objective: the successful management, or adjustment, of social and political conflicts that were assumed to be inevitable.

Second, the religious enthusiasm that fed the social gospel could lead away from radical progressive reforms and toward the affirmation of more conservative positions in theology and politics. The fateful division of American Protestantism into its liberal and fundamentalist/Pentecostal wings in the 1920s marked the beginning of a division that would give religious arguments a very different resonance for American Progressives and Social Democrats than they ever had before.

Third, the spirit of voluntarism and democratic idealism that motivated many early settlement house workers was from the outset at odds with an equally deep-seated moralism that saw the purpose of reform as the assimilation of outcasts into American middle-class culture. As social work developed into a profession, new notions of providing "services" to "clients" supplanted the earlier reformist ideals of Jane Addams and her generation.

Fourth, the broad-ranging cultural critique of early twentieth-century feminism narrowed to concentrate on winning the vote. The rationale for woman suffrage shifted from the insistence on women's rights as human beings to the claim that women's unique sensibilities would transform and purify American public life. The "new woman" of the 1920s, although liberated from constraints of many kinds, was scarcely the new woman that thinkers such as Addams, Gilman, and Taft had envisioned.

Finally, pragmatism was transformed by social scientists in the 1920s into something almost completely unrecognizable. Psychologists, inspired by John B. Watson, and political scientists, following the lead of Arthur Bentley and Wesley Clair Mitchell, detached James's and Dewey's functionalism from their ethical and democratic convictions and christened the result behaviorism. In the words of Lord Kelvin, which William F. Ogburn had chiseled into stone on the wall of the Social Science Research Building at the University of Chicago, "If you cannot measure, . . . your knowledge . . . is meager." Drawn to that conception of knowledge, or bewitched by the lure of power, social scientists developed sophisticated technologies of behavioral modification and management, techniques antithetical to the voluntarism that was at the heart of pragmatism. The science of behaviorism dispensed with one of the pragmatists' most important insights, their understanding of the normative dimension of all human experience and activity. Behaviorists instead flattened the rich complexity of James's and Dewey's ideas into scientistic methods of conditioning, administration, and social engineering. Such methods could be used to manage well-adjusted workers and

soothe happy consumers instead of contributing to the creation of the autonomous democratic citizens James and Dewey envisioned.

The anesthetizing effect of these developments was intensified by the consequences of the postwar red scare and its lingering aftereffects. The populace
seemed lost in the mindless celebration of an American culture that had turned
its back on the democratic potential of progressivism and embraced its most anti-
democratic manifestations. Many writers went into exile; many political thinkers
turned away in disgust. Harold Stearns's *Civilization in the United States* (1922)
brought together commentators who shared Stearns's contempt for a barbaric civilization overwhelmed by vulgar materialism. In 1922 the *Nation* ran a series of
articles, These United States, in which writers such as H. L. Mencken, Sinclair
Lewis, Sherwood Anderson, and William Allen White competed to produce the
most savage satire. They offered a state-by-state survey of the crass, smug, ugly,
conformist, dogmatic, lethargic, provincial, ignorant, and, worst of all, contented
American people. In this desolate landscape, filled with hicks and yokels, what
had happened to that hardy perennial of American political discourse, "the people," and who could lead them out of this desert and toward the promised land?[19]

In 1922, a reviewer for the *New York Times* hailed the appearance of just such
a prophet, whose new book ranked "among the few great formulations of American political theory. It bears much the same relation to the problems of the present and the future that the essays of Hamilton, Madison, Jay, and Noah Webster
bore to the problems that occupied men's minds when the Constitution was
framed." The book under review was Herbert Hoover's *American Individualism.*
Hoover contrasted the ideology of American individualism with its principal com-
petitors around the world, including communism, socialism, syndicalism, and autocracy. He also distinguished American individualism from capitalism and from
the individualism of European democracies, insisting in good progressive fashion that laissez-faire was irresponsible, and that individualism without equal opportunity was repressive. The only individualism worth having — American individualism — must combine personal initiative with a deep spiritual commitment
to the value of public service and the importance of cooperation. Instead of celebrating an entrepreneurial or consumerist ethos, Hoover celebrated regulation,
equality, and responsibility.[20] But of course that progressive conception of responsible individualism contained a multitude of diverse possibilities, which
Hoover himself embodied. As the great engineer and the savior of Belgium,
Hoover was in 1920 the preferred candidate of democratically inclined progressive intellectuals and corporate capitalists alike, the darling of those drawn to
strikingly inconsistent notions of a "progressive" America. *American Individualism* too was a Rorschach test: it invited and received a wide range of enthusiastic responses from across the political spectrum.

Among Hoover's admirers was Walter Lippmann, who had tried, along with
Franklin D. Roosevelt, to persuade the Democratic Party leadership to nominate
Hoover for the presidency in 1920. Lippmann had also served (rather more qui-
etly) in the American war effort as a part of the Inquiry, the group Wilson charged

first with plotting strategy and then with plotting the boundaries for the new nations that were to spring forth from the Treaty of Versailles. Lippmann himself
wrote most of Wilson's Fourteen Points. Also like Hoover, Lippmann derived from
his wartime experience a new perspective on public life, which he presented in
Public Opinion (1922), a book as celebrated in its day as *American Individualism*.

The people, Lippmann lamented, could no longer be trusted to perform the
tasks democracy demanded of them. Individuals are separated from the complex
modern world by the "pictures" and "fictions" in their heads. They inhabit artificial "pseudo-environments," which are kept in order thanks to the comforting but
distorting "stereotypes" that help them make sense of an otherwise incomprehensible reality. In place of Jefferson's faith in idealized, "omnicompetent" citizens, the
"dogma of democracy," America needed a "specialized class" of experts, operating
with the security of lifetime tenure, to provide reliable information on issues of
public policy. After mounting a devastating critique of the public's capacity to exercise sound critical judgment, Lippmann concluded *Public Opinion* by suggesting
that a reformed educational system, by inculcating a passion for scientific inquiry,
would enable the public to exercise sound critical judgment.[21] Only readers unpersuaded by his diagnosis, however, could have faith in Lippmann's remedy.

Lippmann's former allies could only shake their heads. Reviewing *Public Opinion* in the *New Republic*, John Dewey applauded Lippmann's dissection of the
problems besetting American democracy. But by focusing attention on the role of
public advisers, and suggesting "the enlightenment of administrators and execu-
tives" as the solution, Lippmann had missed the point. Dewey insisted, as he had
done before the war, that the challenge lay in creating citizens capable of the active and intelligent participation that American democracy clearly lacked.[22]

In *The Public and Its Problems* (1927), perhaps the clearest statement of his
political ideas, Dewey responded to Lippmann's challenge. Dewey began by
denying fashionable behaviorist and naturalist conceptions of social science, insisting that normative questions of meaning and value are inescapable in all
human inquiry. Because man is a social and historical being, philosophy and politics alike must remain flexible, attuned to cultural change. Dewey advanced
three arguments that, in other forms, would attract a great deal of attention when
applied by critics to later versions of rights-based liberalism. First, Dewey wrote,
"The idea of a natural individual in his isolation possessed of full-fledged wants,
of energies to be expended according to his own volition, and of a ready-made
faculty of foresight and prudent calculation is as much a fiction in psychology as
the doctrine of the individual in possession of antecedent political rights is one
in politics."[23] Questions of desire, and conceptions of interest, are historical
rather than timeless.

Second, the idea of community needs to be demystified and understood as a
part of everyday experience. Communication creates shared meanings, which engender common purposes and "a community of interest and endeavor." Through
that process arises what Dewey termed, at least metaphorically, "a general will
and social consciousness: desire and choice on the part of individuals in behalf of

activities that, by means of symbols, are communicable and shared by all concerned."[24] Community is not something elusive or romantic; it is forged by individuals through the imperfect process of communication and brought to life through their active participation in joint endeavors.

Third, Dewey challenged the idea of a democracy administered efficiently and benevolently by elites who claim to know better than the public what needs to be done.

> No government by experts in which the masses do not have a chance to inform the experts as to their needs can be anything but an oligarchy managed in the interests of the few. And the enlightenment must proceed in ways which force the administrative specialists to take account of the needs. The world has suffered more from leaders and authorities than from the masses. The essential need, in other words, is the improvement of the methods and conditions of debate, discussion and persuasion. That is *the* problem of the public.[25]

The democratic project involves widespread participation and critical reflection on the constitution of desires, the communication of ideas, the construction of communities, and the shaping of public policy. That democratic ideal derives, Dewey pointed out, from the experience of individuals in their families, their homes, and their neighborhoods; only if we can find ways to extend those experiences to the broader local, state, and national levels can we create a genuinely democratic culture.

As *American Individualism, Public Opinion,* and *The Public and Its Problems* illustrate, the problems addressed by progressive political thinkers did not disappear in the 1920s. Instead, given the consolidation of power in new private and public hierarchies, and the attendant triumph of technocratic values and managerial strategies, those problems changed shape. The alienation exhibited by many American intellectuals in the 1920s reflects their dissatisfaction with the direction in which public life appeared to be developing. But when viewed in a comparative perspective, and placed next to the alternatives being offered by European champions of fascism, corporatism, and communism, the distinctive frameworks of progressive thought remain evident beneath the different solutions proposed by Hoover, Lippmann, and Dewey.

With the onset of the Depression, those frameworks began to fade from view. Hoover's presidency was overwhelmed when his reliance on voluntary cooperation collided with the reality of conflict in conditions of scarcity. Lippmann's *A Preface to Morals* (1929) called for a return to asceticism, stoicism, and disinterestedness. Although the book was published before the stock market crashed, its phenomenal success reflected the uncanny appropriateness of its counsel at a moment when political activity seemed pointless and despair offered a more attractive alternative. Dewey, almost alone, kept the democratic faith. In *The Quest for Certainty* (1929), he updated the history of ideas he had offered a decade earlier in *Reconstruction in Philosophy* (1920), insisting that Western culture would escape its dead ends of dogmatic philosophy and authoritarian politics only when it finally discarded the discredited effort to achieve and enforce certain knowledge. Whereas Lippmann had come to see in that loss of certainty the melancholy acknowledgment of finitude, for Dewey it promised at last the prospect of a new culture designed and built by ordinary people to replace what had been imposed on them from above.

To redeem that promise was the goal of Dewey's *Individualism Old and New* (1930). Dewey believed, as Hoover did, that American individualism differed from earlier, European varieties because it sprang from a different tradition, which "contains within itself the ideal of equality of opportunity and of freedom for all, without regard to birth and status, as a condition for its effective realization of that equality." Although it was the "spiritual element of our tradition" that distinguished this new individualism from the old, in "the pecuniary culture characteristic of our civilization" that "spiritual factor . . . is obscured and crowded out." Dewey believed that emphasis on an ethic of voluntary service did not go far enough. Again the answer lay in democratic participation. We must use "the realities of a corporate civilization to validate and embody the distinctive moral element in the American version of individualism: Equality and freedom expressed not merely externally and politically but through personal participation in the development of a shared culture."[26] The differences between Hoover's and Dewey's ideas are clear enough, but the resonances are nevertheless striking. They shared a common confidence that America's political tradition contained resources rich enough to restore hope where cynics saw only grounds for despair. Both identified that hope with versions of an enlarged individualism. The roots of that idea stretched back beyond the "self-interest properly understood"—individualism refined from egoism by participation in political associations—that so impressed Tocqueville to the ethically charged amalgamation of religious, republican, and liberal ideas in the eighteenth century.

Liberalism and Social Action:
The Paradoxes of the New Deal, 1933–1948

The choice between Hoover and Franklin D. Roosevelt in 1932 struck most intellectuals as unappetizing. A surprising number joined the Committee of One Hundred Thousand, a somewhat optimistic title for what was nevertheless an impressive collection of writers who supported the Socialist Party candidate, Norman Thomas. Among those affiliated with the committee were many of the critics who had been alienated from politics in the 1920s; John Dewey was one of its officers. Both the *Nation* and the *New Republic* endorsed Thomas. During the campaign Hoover seemed lost, Roosevelt inconsistent. But after his victory Roosevelt enlisted bright young intellectuals to design and administer the programs of his New Deal, and many skeptical radicals quickly became fans. Henry Wallace, Rexford Tugwell, Harold Ickes, and Charles Merriam all brought great energy and an apparent—and, to many, inspiring—commitment to social democratic politics. Many writers thought they could make out distinctly communitarian overtones in the rhetoric of the early New Deal, and they waited with eager anticipation to assess the consequences of this new departure.

They did not have to wait long. For a variety of complex institutional and political reasons, the New Deal failed to live up to those early expectations, and the ideal of a national planning state faded. In place of Wallace's and Tugwell's solidaristic rhetoric came more sober reformist calls from Thurmond Arnold and Felix Frankfurter, in the spirit of Louis Brandeis, for decentralizing and regulating the economy. The tacking and veering of the New Deal, although necessitated by choppy political waters, satisfied few political commentators.

Radicals felt themselves pushed further toward varieties of socialism and communism, both of which attracted enthusiastic support among more intellectuals than at any time before or since. Dewey's student Sidney Hook tried valiantly, if vainly, to forge a philosophical alliance between Marxism and pragmatism. But as Max Eastman (among others) pointed out, one could not at the same time both claim to know the plot of history and deny that history has a plot. For young writers such as Irving Howe, the appeal of communism in the early 1930s lay precisely in the confidence it inspired, an invigorating change from the rudderless alienation that so many intellectuals felt in the previous decade.

Conservative reactions to the New Deal predictably ranged from alarm to horror. Hoover abandoned all vestiges of his early interest in cooperation between the private and public spheres. In *The Challenge to Liberty* (1934), he branded the New Deal's tentative experiments with economic planning a dangerous threat to freedom. Lippmann too tried to sever his ties to his progressive past, but he failed to make a clean break. In *The Good Society* (1937), he admitted that America needed to construct a system of social insurance, that the current distribution of wealth was unacceptable, and that government spending would be required to rebuild America and restore economic growth. Despite the resemblance between that program and Roosevelt's, Lippmann saw in the New Deal an ominous foreshadowing of collectivism. The apocalyptic tone of his critique suggested that something odd was happening to American social commentary, an amplification of hopes and fears whose echoes would persist for several decades. Further raising the volume were the raucous appeals of Louisiana Senator Huey Long, Father Charles Coughlin, and Dr. Francis Townsend, who capitalized on personal magnetism to advance a variety of programs hard to place on the political spectrum.

Awakening from the slumber of isolationism, Americans were startled to see that Europe was again slouching toward war. From the mid-1930s onward, American political ideas cannot be understood without reference to European developments. In the 1920s, the idea of planning was discussed openly by politicians as moderate as Hoover and Roosevelt; by the 1940s, it was anathema. In the early 1930s, the Soviet Union represented to many Americans an intriguing experiment in social engineering; by the end of the decade it was the scene of the purge trials and the source of the insurance policy (the Nazi-Soviet Pact) that freed Hitler to unleash his panzers on Poland. In tandem fascism and communism changed everything, and as a result America too began to look quite different.[27]

Dewey's progress through the 1930s illustrates that change. In 1934, he joined the editorial board of *Social Frontier*, a periodical committed to the idea that "an age of collectivism is opening." In 1935, he published *Liberalism and Social Action*, in which he extended his earlier arguments for radical democratic politics and proclaimed that "the cause of liberalism will be lost for a considerable period if it is not prepared to go further and socialize the forces of production." Three years later, explaining "What I Believe" in *Forum* magazine, Dewey admitted a change in emphasis, acknowledging that he had lost his enthusiasm for central economic planning. In *Freedom and Culture* (1939), Dewey stressed the oppressive weight of the Soviet state and contended that Stalin had obliterated any prospects for democracy that communism might once have contained. Also in 1939, Dewey joined with Hook and others to form the Committee for Cultural Freedom. In their founding manifesto, they linked Hitler's Germany with Stalin's Soviet Union, formally repudiating the popular front against fascism that had attracted many American radicals prior to the purge trials and the Nazi-Soviet Pact. Dewey continued to criticize Roosevelt, but his focus shifted from his earlier impatience with the moderation of the New Deal to concern about Roosevelt's inclination to strengthen the power of the federal government.[28]

If Dewey's growing wariness about collectivism reflected an increased sensitivity to developments in Europe, it also reflected an increased sensitivity to developments closer to home. Besides backing Norman Thomas in 1932, Dewey had supported the state senate campaign of fellow New Yorker Reinhold Niebuhr, who as the Socialist Party candidate won 4 percent of the vote. Their political alliance disguised Dewey's and Niebuhr's profoundly different perspectives on politics. In *Moral Man and Immoral Society* (1932), Niebuhr singled out Dewey to illustrate his broader contention that liberals placed unwarranted faith in reason. Because they refused to acknowledge irrationality, liberals such as Dewey overlooked the pervasiveness of sin and the consequent persistence of power. Until Americans confronted conflict realistically, Niebuhr concluded, plans for democratic reform would go nowhere.

Niebuhr's prominence reflected the return of religious voices to the discourse of American reform, as did the appearance of Dorothy Day's *Catholic Worker* and the spread of the Catholic Worker movement. Both Niebuhr and Day scorned the easy pieties of liberalism and hearkened back to sterner, more demanding versions of Christianity that stressed human sinfulness and divine justice. Particularly after the combined impact of the events of the 1930s, and his brother H. Richard's turn toward the astringent theology of Karl Barth, Niebuhr rejected radical politics and called instead for repentance. In *The Nature and Destiny of Man* (1940), he stressed even more emphatically the gulf dividing humanity from God. Religious voices from the Left thus joined the larger chorus denouncing the New Deal, and liberalism more broadly, for its facile confidence in progress and its refusal to admit the intractability of the problems facing American culture.[29]

Intractable those problems proved to be, not least because of the straitjacket that Republicans and Southern Democrats wrapped around the New Deal's few bold initiatives. The constraints imposed by federalism, the separation of powers, and the two-party system, to say nothing of Roosevelt's own instinctive caution, conspired to limit his latitude. Yet given the obvious political perils of social democracy, Roosevelt's continued gestures in that direction are difficult to understand unless he genuinely sought reform. When he commissioned the National Resources Planning Board to draw up blueprints for an extensive, democratically administered welfare state, he hoped they would chart a path between Americans' longstanding distrust of state power and their desire for social welfare programs to ensure equal opportunity for all citizens.

An obscure young graduate student named Hubert H. Humphrey, writing a thesis in politics at Louisiana State University in 1940, understood clearly the limitations within which Roosevelt was forced to operate. Humphrey noted the gap that separated the radical experimentalism of Dewey's pragmatism from the prudence of the New Deal. In *The Political Philosophy of the New Deal*, an essay whose title would have struck many contemporaries—as indeed it strikes later critics—as delicious if unconscious comedy, Humphrey offered a judicious and incisive assessment of Roosevelt's presidency: "The pragmatism of the New Deal stops at the gateway of immediate fundamental change in either the political or economic order." Anticipating and dissolving a later debate, he declared that "the New Deal is neither revolution nor counterrevolution." Instead, it represents "American democracy working within the political and economic limitations of established government and private enterprise."[30] Humphrey understood that Americans were not about to abandon the Constitution or capitalism, despite the severity of the Depression, and for that reason Roosevelt had no choice but to make haste slowly.

Within those boundaries, Roosevelt's desire for change was strong. But by the time the NRPB report was available in 1943, the solidaristic language of Roosevelt's early initiatives had been tarnished by the perceived failures of the experiments with communitarianism and statism in Europe, as well as by the failures of his own administration. Roosevelt had learned a lot. He knew that Henry Wallace had become a political liability for various reasons, including his association with the discredited idea of economic planning, and he was prepared to sacrifice his vice president. FDR knew that his scheme for Social Security was politically safe only because all workers "earned" the benefits they would receive, and he knew that only the plan's contributory principle distinguished Social Security from other "handouts" that came with stigmas attached.

Thus when Roosevelt sought to make the NRPB report the basis for his 1944 State of the Union Address, the dramatic speech in which he pledged economic security, social security, and moral security for all Americans, he felt compelled to frame his unfamiliar agenda in the familiar vocabulary of individual rights. He labeled his plan a "second bill of rights," even though the policies he outlined would have shifted American politics decisively toward economic and social democracy. Roosevelt tried to justify his proposals for full employment, a minimum income, antimonopoly legislation, universal housing, universal health care, and insurance against old age, sickness, accidents, and unemployment—the full social democratic agenda—in terms of their contribution to protecting individual rights. Whereas earlier American champions of such programs had argued in terms of equality or justice, by 1944 the language of rights was the only viable language available. As it turned out, even draped with the ill-fitting robe of rights, Roosevelt's plan for American social democracy failed to command assent. But he had taken a fateful step by abandoning the progressives' ideals of justice and equality. When he stated his most far-reaching call for change in terms of individual rights, Roosevelt shifted the terms of debate and inadvertently sealed the fate of such social democratic initiatives, for himself and for those reformers who followed him. After World War II, calls for reform in American politics, if they were to be effective, would have to be demands for civil rights rather than pleas for social or economic justice. In the history of American political discourse, the difference has proved to be decisive.[31]

The End of Ideology: Celebrating Consensus, 1949–1963

Many of the political thinkers who resisted the nostrums of Dr. New Deal willingly swallowed the remedies of Dr. Win the War. Intellectuals who embraced the Allied cause had reason to celebrate America's contributions, and the celebration continued when the war ended. Particularly when the world again seemed hostile, and the United States found itself facing, as enemies in a cold war, the world's two largest (if hardly most powerful) nations, it made sense to rally around the flag, or at least to appreciate that it was still flying: the world's first constitutional democracy, after all, had survived to become its oldest.

The war had done wonders for America. Unprecedented government spending not only lifted the economy out of depression, at last, but it also persuaded policymakers that Keynesian strategies could deliver lasting prosperity. Without the pressure of scarcity, conflicts could be postponed forever, both planning and regulation could be avoided, and the effects of economic concentration and political lethargy could be endured happily by consumers growing steadily more affluent. Learning those lessons dramatically altered policy makers' views of the American cultural landscape. Both the first and second New Deals looked less like noble failures than like wasteful expenditures of scarce political resources. Keynes had triumphed over both Croly and Brandeis.

Even Reinhold Niebuhr pocketed his scorn for American liberalism. No book better reflected the overwhelming impact of America's wartime experience than *The Children of Light and the Children of Darkness* (1944). Niebuhr simply divided the world in two. The children of darkness included Nazi, fascist, and Stalinist "moral cynics," who admitted no law beyond their own evil wishes. The children of light, by contrast, knew that self-interest must be disciplined. In their number Niebuhr enlisted practically everyone else, including Locke and Rousseau, Adam Smith and Marx, utilitarians and even "educators" (by which he appeared to mean Deweyans). Beneath the shadow cast by totalitarianism, all other political theories appeared to Niebuhr more similar than different, and many other writers shared that judgment. Although Niebuhr himself remained critical of the distance separating America from its democratic aspirations, as *The Irony of American History* (1952) showed, Americans' revulsion toward the defeated children of darkness led most political thinkers to identify their culture with the children of light.

Consistent with such Manichean formulations, those who gloried in the triumph of American democracy found pragmatism unattractive. Compared with the alternatives of natural law, toward which thinkers such as Lippmann had been leaning even before World War II, ascetic Christianity of the sort Niebuhr embodied, and the clear evidence from the natural and behavioral sciences that they could deliver results, the pragmatists' counsel of moderation premised on the awareness of uncertainty seemed pale and unsatisfying. Dewey confronted the challenge in a new preface to his *Reconstruction in Philosophy*, which was published in a new edition in 1948. Denying charges that moral relativism lay beneath the savage outbreaks of totalitarianism, Dewey warned that those who invoked religious, moral, political, or economic absolutes themselves fed a dangerous intolerance that could stifle dissent. Within a few years, that warning would appear prophetic, as Senator Joseph McCarthy's charges would ignite a bonfire of intolerance.[32]

On all sides of this controversy in the late 1940s, though, partisans agreed that America embodied the essential principle necessary for democracy. For champions of Aristotelianism and neo-orthodoxy, that principle was fidelity to unchanging ideals. For champions of science and social science, that principle was hardheaded empiricism. For champions of Deweyan pragmatism, the principle was a democratic commitment to inquiry. Despite their deep disagreements, all of them identified American culture, as they understood it in their very different ways, as the standard by which other nations, and other political systems, could be judged—and found wanting. The threat of totalitarianism loomed so ominously that Americans took shelter in what they judged most familiar. When the European émigré Hannah Arendt proclaimed authoritatively, in *The Origins of Totalitarianism* (1951), that totalitarianism was utterly unprecedented, and that it dissolved all existing political categories, she seemed to validate Americans' impulse to celebrate the culture that had vanquished that threat.[33]

An early indicator of the powerful dynamic at work in postwar American culture was the formation of Americans for Democratic Action in 1947. While sharing a domestic agenda more progressive than that of the Democratic Party, ADA founders emphasized their strident anticommunism to distinguish themselves from Henry Wallace's more sympathetic view of the Soviet Union. Truman's upset reelection in 1948 heartened hard-boiled reformers such as those in the ADA; some even hoped Truman's Fair Deal would at last redeem the promise of Roosevelt's second bill of rights.[34] But Congress greeted Truman's version of an expansive welfare state with the same distrust Roosevelt met. Lacking support from the diverse coalitions of labor, farmers, and professionals that enacted similar social legislation elsewhere in the industrialized world during these years—Roosevelt complained that England's Beveridge Report should have been called the Roosevelt Plan because of its resemblance to the report of his NRPB—American social democrats were defeated by the combination of contentment and the fear of collectivism. Political writing in the postwar years reinforced both of those impulses.

Joining Niebuhr in the ADA were ex-New Dealers, labor leaders, and two writers who would become prominent commentators in the postwar years, Arthur Schlesinger Jr. and John Kenneth Galbraith. In *The Vital Center* (1949), Schlesinger shrewdly appropriated for himself and his moderate allies the American tradition of reform. Chastened realism, commitment to individualism and voluntary associations, and confidence in America's can-do spirit characterized the vital center. To its left as well as its right lay totalitarianism, tyranny, and oppression. Although Schlesinger admitted that industrialization had brought not only affluence but also anxiety, alienation, fear, and even despair, he counseled readers to abandon utopianism and place their faith in America's free society.

Galbraith provided one of the most compelling and influential explanations of America's success in *American Capitalism: The Theory of Countervailing Power* (1952). Although the economy had grown in the ways that Brandeis, for example, had feared, and was now dominated by oligopolies, these economic mammoths had proved in practice to be stabilizing rather than threatening forces. The countervailing powers of big firms, big labor, and of different segments of the economy contributed to achieving a rough equilibrium. Since the system worked, government should exercise restraint in regulating it. Galbraith himself later revised and even rejected this argument, notably in *The Affluent Society* (1958), and even more forcefully in other volumes that followed. But in the 1950s his analysis proved irresistible to many social scientists, because it provided an economic analysis that bolstered the prevailing political theory of pluralism.

Earlier political theorists, including especially James Madison and Alexis de Tocqueville, had emphasized the salutary consequences of individuals' participation in a variety of voluntary organizations. According to pluralists writing in the 1950s, membership in various groups alleviates the potentially destabilizing effects of industrialization and disenchantment associated with the breakdown of stable communities. In addition to providing individuals with the means to escape —or at least cope with—the anomie of life in modern society, such groups contribute to political stability. Multiple group memberships, because they cut across the lines of religion, class, race, and ethnicity, enable elites to manage, rationalize, and moderate political conflict. David Riesman argued in *The Lonely Crowd* (1950) that the strength of group identifications reduced chances of political turmoil in America, even though that peace was purchased at a considerable cultural price. In contrast to the autonomy prized by earlier generations of Americans, modern Americans found satisfaction through others' eyes: they were "other directed" rather than "inner directed." According to Robert Dahl in *A Preface to Democratic Theory* (1956), political power, concentrated in other systems, was in America uniquely diffuse. Whereas typically conflicts emerge from the clash between an overbearing majority and an oppressed minority, in the United States, as Dahl put it, "minorities rule." In addition to offering a description of how American pluralism worked, Dahl offered American practice as the criterion for democratic culture. Dahl, like Galbraith, later changed his mind, but in the 1950s his writings seemed to demonstrate that pluralism assured both order and a rough approximation of justice.

American politics works, pluralists believed, because Americans agree about essential issues and squabble, albeit sometimes boisterously, only about relatively insignificant differences. They agree about the rules of the game, even when they disagree about how it should be played. The widely read and celebrated historian Daniel Boorstin baptized this consensus in *The Genius of American Politics* (1953), and he argued that it was made possible by Americans' admirable ignorance of political theory. Rather than arranging themselves into doctrinaire, ideologically sophisticated, programmatic political parties, as Europeans seemed always to do, Americans accommodated themselves to an imperfect world, clustered around the political center, and disputed questions of policy rather than fundamental— and dangerously divisive—questions of principle. The historian David Potter attributed American consensus to the richness of the nation's resources and the ingenuity of those who exploited them. Together, abundance and technology could explain the distinctive American character: Americans were a *People of Plenty* (1954). Although he came to denigrate consensus, not to praise it, Louis Hartz offered a portrait of *The Liberal Tradition in America* (1955) that paralleled other pluralist accounts but differed sharply in its disappointed, sometimes bitter tone. Lacking a feudal past, Hartz argued, America developed neither a political Right that could cherish aristocracy nor a political Left that could vow to destroy it. Lacking a revolution worthy of the name, America developed neither nostalgic reactionaries nor romantic utopians. Since Americans were born equal, they concerned themselves only with freedom. Blessed with abundant land and resources, Americans were blinded by their own good luck; their "national irrational liberalism" prevented them from understanding the tragic fate of other people in the world.

Although Hartz's narrative of American liberalism now seems too flat and too static because his argument depends more on epigram and allusion than evidence or even analysis, his conceptualization of American liberalism had a deep and lasting effect on scholarly debate and, more indirectly, on political discourse. For if only discussions of liberty, and considerations of rights, had a legitimate place in the American political tradition, then conservatives and radicals alike were justified in claiming that discussions of equality required stepping outside the fundamental American consensus. Conversely, when challenges were launched from extremes against the middle, liberal pluralists felt confident in dismissing them.

McCarthyism presented an obvious test case for pluralist theory, and social scientists proved worthy of the challenge. From an interdisciplinary seminar at Columbia University in the early 1950s emerged an ambitious, collaborative attempt to explain the phenomenon, a book edited by the sociologist Daniel Bell and first published as *The New American Right* (1955). The contributors distinguished between "class politics," which was rational, grounded in economic interest, limited in aspirations, and for all of those reasons typically American, and "mass politics," which was irrational, grounded in psychological maladjustment, utopian, and thus unAmerican. Whereas the former politics was pluralist, the latter—of which extremist, reactionary McCarthyism was a perfect example—tended toward dogmatism at best and toward totalitarianism at worst. Studies of McCarthy's support have since demonstrated that his appeal was instead consistent with old-fashioned rural conservatism. But while such evidence may undercut the liberal pluralists' explanation, it highlights the powerful appeal of consensus as an analytical construct. Any political upheaval that the center could not contain must be irrational. For the historian Richard Hofstadter, one of the contributors to *The New American Right*, what was true of McCarthyism was also true of populism and progressivism. In *The Age of Reform* (1955), Hofstadter portrayed the populists as irrational, xenophobic, and anti-Semitic; the progressives as members of an old middle class anxious about losing their status. Both groups indulged in mass political action best understood as futile, ceremonial gestures against modernity. The New Deal, by contrast, relied on balancing legitimate group interests; it was a model of pluralist accommodation.[35]

If competition among interest groups exhausted the sphere of legitimate political activity, what role was left for political ideas? Disillusioned by the failures of communism, instructed by the findings of liberal pluralist social science, and impressed by the apparent consolidation of social democracy in Western Europe, a group of intellectuals gathered in Milan in 1955 for a conference sponsored by the Congress for Cultural Freedom and quietly subsidized by the CIA. From their discussions, Daniel Bell was inspired to construct a bold interpretation of what had been happening. When the resulting book was published, it bore the title *The End of Ideology: On the Exhaustion of Political Ideas in the Fifties* (1962). Bell described members of his generation as "twice born." They had passed from their first youth, their radicalism in the 1930s, only to emerge from the sobering realities of war and totalitarianism still, or rather again, young, but transformed. They had learned from experience the folly of all "total ideologies" and the real potential of pragmatic social democracy. Their outlook was a chastened skepticism, their political ideas a combination of pluralism, decentralization, and support for mixed economies and more comprehensive welfare states. Beyond that, Bell concluded, his generation was not prepared to go. But incisive as Bell's argument was, and consistent as it was with some of the most widely held political ideas of its day, his timing could hardly have been worse. Almost as soon as the end of ideology was announced, ideology returned with a vengeance.[36]

Whose Justice? Which Rationality?
Confronting Diversity, 1963–1993

In the closing pages of *The End of Ideology*, Bell noted that the lessons learned by his generation assumed special importance because "a new Left with few memories of the past is emerging."[37] As he suspected, members of that New Left resisted his counsel; that they had few memories of the past is less clear. They distanced themselves from the old Left, the more doctrinaire Left of the 1930s, but they drew heavily from other traditions in the American past. Thoreau provided particular inspiration, not only in his essay on civil disobedience but by his example of living the simple life at Walden Pond. When Students for a Democratic Society (SDS) distributed a recommended reading list in 1961, it included (among other things) the Declaration of Independence, Dewey's *The Public and Its Problems*, and Bell's *The End of Ideology*. In 1962, Tom Hayden wrote the Port Huron Statement, which was to become the manifesto of the New Left, while consulting *The Public and Its Problems*. A year earlier he had traveled from the University of Michigan to New York City, where he had met Daniel Bell, discussed *The End of Ideology*, and explained his own hopes for democratic renewal. From its architects' perspective, SDS stood in a proud tradition of radical democratic action. "Participatory democracy" served the New Left as rallying cry and shorthand political theory; its lineage could be traced directly to Dewey's responses to Lippmann's *Public Opinion*. But as its successes and failures would both reflect, the commitment to local democracy continued to present the same challenges familiar from the progressive period: those opposed to change also took seriously the call to participation. Egalitarian democrats had to decide what to do when "the people" did not share the priorities of those who sought to inspire them.

If Dewey was the New Left's grandfather, more proximate influences included C. Wright Mills, the radical sociologist whose critique of American culture stood in sharp contrast to the celebrations of consensus in the postwar years; religious and existentialist philosophers who decried the meaninglessness of lives without commitment; and the electrifying examples of those involved in the civil rights movement, whose lives seemed to embody such commitment. According to Hayden, an interview with Martin Luther King Jr., at the Democratic Party National Convention in 1960, was the transforming moment of Hayden's life because it convinced him to put away his journalist's pen and become a political activist. A beating Hayden received from a white man a year later, while he was in Mississippi helping to register black voters, brought home to him, as similar experiences did to many, the obstacles facing radicals who were committed to social change as well as democratic participation.[38]

The civil rights movement drew on many sources. The tradition of civil disobedience from Thoreau and Mohandas Gandhi provided a strategy. American theologians such as Rauschenbusch and Niebuhr linked religious faith and political action. The scholarship and activism of black writers such as the sociologist

E. Franklin Frazier provided insight into African-American culture. The writings and example of Du Bois, whose Marxist-inspired radicalism in the 1930s led to a prison sentence in 1951 and then exile in Ghana, alerted black Americans to potential contacts, and support, in the third world. In Frantz Fanon's *The Wretched of the Earth* (1961), and in his other writings, they found a contemporary voice passionately condemning oppression. Perhaps the most important sources, though, were biblical stories of bondage and liberation, which King and other civil rights leaders used repeatedly, and the secular tradition of individual rights, which drew on American liberalism and appealed to the central value proclaimed by American political writers in the postwar period.[39]

By far the most significant political ideas of the civil rights movement came from King and from Malcolm X. Although their ideas are usually presented as a study in contrast, their trajectories before their assassinations point toward another conclusion. King's eloquent "Letter from the Birmingham Jail," which was printed in the *Christian Century* on June 12, 1963, and the concluding pages of *The Autobiography of Malcolm X* (1964), suggest such a convergence. King defended his strategy of nonviolent civil disobedience, much as Niebuhr did in *Moral Man and Immoral Society*, by denying the moral force of unjust laws. He admitted the vulnerability of standing "in the middle of two opposing forces in the Negro community." On the one side stood complacent blacks, those either demoralized and "adjusted to segregation" or relatively comfortable and "insensitive to the problems of the masses." On the other side were those driven by "bitterness and hatred" who came "perilously close to advocating violence"; in their vanguard were various militant groups, especially the Black Muslims led by Elijah Muhammad. "I have tried to stand between these two forces," King wrote, "saying that we need emulate neither the 'do-nothingism' of the complacent nor the hatred of the black nationalist. For there is the more excellent way of love and nonviolent protest." King likened the struggle for civil rights to other struggles for justice being fought around the world. He placed himself and his allies in a long tradition of "extremists" fighting for justice, a tradition stretching from Old Testament prophets through Jesus and early Christian martyrs to Jefferson, Lincoln, and the heroes produced by the civil rights movement itself. He concluded with the two most powerful arguments in his arsenal, appealing to shared religious convictions and the American tradition of natural rights.

> We will win our freedom because the sacred heritage of our nation and the eternal will of God are embodied in our echoing demands. . . . One day the South will know that when these disinherited children of God sat down at lunch counters they were in reality standing up for what is best in the American dream and for the most sacred values in our Judeo-Christian heritage, thereby bringing our nation back to those great wells of democracy which were dug deep by the founding fathers in their formulation of the Constitution and the Declaration of Independence.[40]

The Autobiography of Malcolm X begins as a book smoldering with anger, becomes a book of rage, and ends as a book aspiring to brotherhood. Malcolm's impatience with moderation during the years of his most intense radicalism prompted him to dismiss the utility of civil disobedience and mock King's confidence that appeals to assumed common ideals would lead to racial justice. King might have a dream, but singing spirituals and invoking the ghost of Lincoln would never make it a reality or end black Americans' long nightmare. The great March on Washington in 1963 Malcolm described as a "circus," "a monumental farce," which only encouraged blacks to continue waiting for whites to give them what he believed they would have to take for themselves.

After his break with Elijah Muhammad, however, and as a result of his experiences on trips to the Middle East and Africa, Malcolm X began to see things differently. While he remained committed to separatism as a strategy for blacks seeking to alter their subservient status in white America, and he remained cynical about any progress blacks could achieve through the help of a southern white "fox" such as Lyndon Johnson, Malcolm began to see beyond division the dim prospect of cooperation. He realized, as he put it, "that the white man is *not* inherently evil," as he had been taught by Elijah Muhammad, "but America's racist society influences him to act evilly. The society has produced and nourishes a psychology which brings out the lowest, most base part of human beings." Proceeding along their distinct paths, blacks and whites working to end racism "might be able to show a road to the salvation of America's very soul. It can only be salvaged if human rights and dignity, in full, are extended to black men. Only such real, meaningful actions as those which are sincerely motivated from a deep sense of humanism and moral responsibility can get at the basic causes that produce the racial explosions in America today." Although the approaches to justice would remain different—as his strategy remained different from "King's nonviolent marching"—nevertheless the "goal has always been the same."[41]

But the language of rights, necessary and even shrewd as it might have seemed strategically, proved to be a cul-de-sac. Activists had nowhere to turn once the Civil Rights and Voting Rights Laws of 1964 and 1965 were enacted. Many rejected moderation for more violent strategies to effect change. Attention shifted from King's Southern Christian Leadership Conference to the more militant Student Non-Violent Coordinating Committee, and after 1966 to the still more militant Black Panthers. By 1968 even King had lost patience. Radicalized by America's escalation of the Vietnam War and by the limited success of the civil rights movement, by the time of his death King had started a Poor People's Campaign that looked beyond political liberalism toward a more expansive social democracy.[42] It had become apparent that the problems facing black Americans were cultural as much as political, rooted in a racism that proved stubbornly resistant to change.

Feminists faced a similar problem. The second wave of American feminism began with the publication of Betty Friedan's *The Feminine Mystique* in 1963. By challenging the ideology of domesticity, Friedan offered a rationale for changes that were already under way in American culture. Large numbers of women, many with college educations, were postponing marriage, or at least childbearing, and entering the workforce. They were refusing to play the parts scripted for them by their male-dominated culture, and justified by social scientists' arguments for women's separate sphere, such as those advanced by Ferdinand Lundberg and Marynia Farnham in *Modern Woman: The Lost Sex* (1947). Such disaffected women formed the core supporters of the National Organization for Women (NOW), which was founded in 1966 to support enforcement of the antidiscrimination clause of the 1964 Civil Rights Act. Patterning their efforts on the New Left and the civil rights movement, the women's movement faced some of the same strategic and cultural problems.

Like black activists, women splintered into more and less militant camps. The upper middle-class professionals of NOW did not seek so much to change the American system as to be permitted to enter it and succeed by its rules. A more radical feminism, announced by Kate Millett in *Sexual Politics* (1970), challenged the adequacy of the NOW approach. Moderate and radical feminists disagreed about philosophical as well as strategic issues. Radical feminists questioned the longstanding assumption, accepted by earlier champions as well as critics of feminism, that because women are biologically different from men, they are destined to play different cultural roles as well. Earlier feminists grounded their arguments on women's special nature, arguing that women's unique gift for nurturing would help to purify male-dominated culture. Radical feminists, borrowing a phrase from the New Left, insisted that "the personal is the political," by which they meant that questions of power infect all social relations. For that reason gender must be examined critically. Assumptions about women's difference effectively legitimated their subjection inside as well as outside the family. Gender, such feminists argued, is a complex cultural construction rather than a brute biological fact. When feminist theorists showed that basic concepts such as "authority" and "the public" contain implicit gender biases, they concluded that considerations of gender must henceforth be central to all discussions of political ideas. Such arguments have proved profoundly unsettling for male thinkers across the political spectrum, and their ultimate effect on political discourse remains impossible to assess.[43]

Like black activists since the mid-1960s, however, feminist theorists have been hamstrung by their own preferred discourse of rights. Couching their demands for change in the vocabulary of rights has been doubly dangerous for women, since it carries an implicit challenge to the ethic of service that has been a profoundly powerful force in American culture since early in the nineteenth century. When feminists call for the right to work, their critics—female as well as male—fear the abandonment of children. When feminists call for the right to choose abortion, their critics—female as well as male—fear a selfish disregard for human life. Because no other group in American culture has been assumed to embody the ethic of care, no other group has faced equivalent responses when it demanded its rights. Finding ways to defuse those conflicts, as the feminist legal theorist Joan Williams has argued, remains the principal political challenge women face as they try to resolve our culture's "gender wars."[44]

Together with the New Left, feminism had the additional misfortune of arriving on the American scene at the same time, and for some of the same reasons, as the counterculture. When egocentric male or female hedonists mouthed the same slogans of commitment to high ideals that their own commitment to self-indulgence only mocked, they managed to make those few who were genuinely devoted to political activity appear foolish. With friends like the hippies of San Francisco's Haight-Ashbury district, feminists and the New Left were guaranteed plenty of enemies. When feminists' demands became amalgamated in the public mind with the bottomless desires of consumer culture, it was difficult to invest them with the same moral purpose attached to the civil rights movement. Guilt by association is unfair but difficult to suppress. Widespread public reaction against the perceived self-indulgence of cultural radicals helped fuel one of the most powerful developments of recent American politics, the resurgence of conservatism.

Champions of conservative ideas have had a rough time in America. Ever since the eighteenth century, when in the wake of the Revolution most Loyalists left the country, and aristocrats who remained had to learn to speak the language of republicanism, American public discourse has prized equality above privilege. The American economic system has rewarded innovation, and relentlessly subverted tradition, in its relentless march forward. Lacking a coherent case for hierarchy and stasis, conservatives have learned from experience that they are most convincing when they invoke the Constitution as their ally and portray their opponents as unAmerican. The perceived threat of communism made such arguments plausible in the 1920s and the 1950s, and the enthusiasm of many radicals in the 1960s for Fanon, Fidel Castro, Mao Zedong, and Ho Chi Minh lent added force to such claims. Civil rights activists were widely characterized as communist sympathizers. The New Left was pilloried for its passionate opposition to America's anticommunist crusade in Vietnam. Feminists were accused of betraying the sacred ideals of motherhood and domesticity.

The political triumph and consolidation of New Deal liberalism left the Right without much in the way of a positive political alternative. Opposing the power of big government seemed one attractive option. According to Frederick von Hayek's influential *The Road to Serfdom* (1944), a steep downward path led directly from economic planning to totalitarianism. But as the New Deal, and then postwar social scientists and the Democratic administrations of John F. Kennedy and Lyndon Johnson, abandoned planning and embraced Keynesian fiscal policy, the federal government became a less convincing bogeyman. To complicate matters, most conservatives rather liked the Defense Department. Moreover, opinion polls indicated widespread support for such programs as Social Security. Conservative thinkers instead sought to exploit public anxieties about civil rights, the New Left, and feminism. In the pages of William F. Buckley's magazine the *National Review*, a wide variety of conservatives targeted the radicalism of such groups and, even more fervently, railed against the excesses of the counterculture.

The rebirth of American conservatism is inexplicable without Herbert Marcuse, Angela Davis, and Abbie Hoffmann, who were from conservatives' perspectives the king, queen, and clown prince of the 1960s revolution. When radicals challenged all cultural as well as political authority, when they defied civility and sang the praises of pleasure, when they championed drugs, sex, and subversive music, even many who considered themselves liberals began to be alarmed. The *Public Interest*, a journal founded by and for mainstream social scientists in 1966, gradually changed from a source of progressive ideas on public policy to a source of warnings about the dangers of cultural and political excess. Many of the journal's principal contributors, including Daniel Bell, Irving Kristol, Nathan Glazer, and Seymour Martin Lipset, had moved from 1930s radicalism through 1950s liberalism and had arrived, with Bell, at the end of ideology. In response to the irrationality and utopianism of 1960s radicals, however, the *Public Interest* slid from chastened liberalism into what came to be known as neoconservatism. Kristol in particular became increasingly suspicious about radicalism and increasingly sympathetic toward capitalism.

Successful exploitation of racial, religious, and cultural anxieties lay behind the conservative resurgence that dominated American presidential politics from 1968 to 1992. Voters feared that the Democratic Party had been captured by a combination of uncouth radicals, racial minorities, and elitist technocrats, which together fed conservative uneasiness about cultural change and rightwing populist resentments toward sophisticated cosmopolitans. But this new conservatism lacked a coherent body of ideas. At least for Ronald Reagan, its central value seemed to be the sanctity of the free-market economy, and through his most lasting legacy, a massive national debt, he hoped to guarantee that the federal government would be unable to mount expensive programs of the sort Reagan and his allies opposed. But as always, the economy as it swept forward in the 1980s eroded the traditional values and destroyed the traditional communities that conservatives claimed to cherish. Conservatives also claimed to value the principle of liberty, but they worried that the practice of freedom, especially by women, too often led to self-indulgence.[45]

In *The Cultural Contradictions of Capitalism* (1976), Daniel Bell tried to explain why things seemed to be falling apart. Bell argued that the principles behind the market (functional rationality), the polity (equality), and the culture (self-fulfillment) had become hopelessly inconsistent. He called for a renewed religiosity and a renewed sense of civic responsibility as the solution, but from his reading of Max Weber he seemed aware that the very cultural contradictions he hoped such virtues would resolve militated against their return. A decade later, in the widely read *Habits of the Heart: Individualism and Commitment in American Life* (1985), Robert Bellah, Richard Madsen, William Sullivan, Ann Swidler, and Steven Tipton likewise urged Americans to reach beneath their obsession with "expressive individualism" for the buried religious and civic republican resources that together could redeem American culture.

There are signs that the secular, rights-based discourse that has dominated American politics since the New Deal may be changing. When John Rawls's *A Theory of Justice* (1971) appeared, it was hailed as providing a persuasive statement of the blend of individualist and egalitarian principles underlying the liberal welfare state. Rawls tried to imagine what principles of justice would be chosen by free and equal individuals who came together artificially blind to their own abilities and values. In such circumstances, he argued, individuals would opt for two principles to ensure "justice as fairness." First, all individuals would enjoy as extensive a set of equal rights as would be compatible with the existence of such rights for everyone. Second, any inequalities would be attached to positions and offices open to everyone, and such inequalities would have to benefit the least advantaged members of the society. But Rawls's robust conception of individual rights, and his "thin theory of the good," did not command universal assent. Libertarians such as Robert Nozick wanted even firmer guarantees for individual rights. Communitarians such as Michael Sandel worried that Rawls undervalued community. Feminists such as Susan Okin complained that Rawls's theory of justice — like the theories of his critics and his defenders — is gendered male. Others disputed Rawls's procedures, wondering where such abstract individuals, bereft of history or culture, learned to reason as American professors of philosophy would do.[46]

Oddly enough, just before Rawls's *Theory of Justice* was published, philosophers had been lamenting the sorry state of political theory. Overshadowed by the mass of empirical studies that dominated the discipline of political science, and buried under proclamations of the end of ideology, by 1970 political theory appeared to have vanished. Such reports, as it turned out, were exaggerated; the last two decades have witnessed a resurgence of interest in political theory.[47] Although it is difficult, as well as risky, to attempt a historical assessment of contemporary developments, it seems clear that both Rawls's version of rights-based liberalism and his deductive style of argument now represent only one choice among many.

One of the most arresting developments is the relative decline of enthusiasm for a universal science of politics or a universal theory of justice. Political thinkers, including Rawls himself, increasingly admit that they are writing from premises, and according to procedures, that derive from, and are suitable for, our culture rather than all cultures. The arguments of historians of science such as Thomas Kuhn, philosophers from the tradition of hermeneutics such as Charles Taylor and Paul Ricoeur, cultural anthropologists such as Clifford Geertz and James Clifford, and poststructuralist theorists such as Jacques Derrida and Michel Foucault have all alerted political theorists to the ubiquity of interpretation, which has made them wary of claims to certainty.

American political theorists are now more inclined to stress the incommensurability of different ideals. Michael Walzer argued in *Spheres of Justice: A Defense of Pluralism and Equality* (1983) that our conceptions of rights and obligations do not extend beyond the "shared understandings" of our own cultural tradition. Alasdair MacIntyre has examined that problem in a series of important books, notably *Whose Justice? Which Rationality?* (1988) and *Three Rival Versions of Moral Enquiry* (1992), in which he contrasted distinctive liberal and Nietzschean traditions to his preferred Aristotelian/Thomist tradition of moral reasoning. As such studies illustrate, we have come a long way from consensus.[48]

In this climate, the renewal of the philosophy of pragmatism is hardly surprising. Renewed emphasis on the centrality of questions of meaning, and the provisional status of all interpretations, returns thinkers to the arguments that Dewey made repeatedly concerning the inescapability of normative considerations in all inquiry. Renewed emphasis on the inadequacy of rights talk, and growing awareness of the difficulties involved in moving toward justice from a lopsided concern with individualism, returns thinkers to the arguments Dewey made repeatedly concerning the social nature of experience and the need to recognize the inseparability of individuals and communities.

But pragmatism is currently moving along several different axes.[49] Richard Rorty, the most widely read and controversial of contemporary pragmatists, insists in *Contingency, Irony, and Solidarity* (1989) that philosophy cannot provide philosophical foundations for political arguments. Rorty stresses the need to protect a precious private realm within which individuals may pursue their own ideals or passions without causing pain to any others. Cornel West yokes his pragmatism to the traditions of Marxism and Christianity in *The American Evasion of Philosophy: A Genealogy of Pragmatism* (1989), offering what he calls a "prophetic pragmatism" that aspires to make common cause with oppressed minorities in America and elsewhere. Joan Williams and Thomas Grey, writing in *Pragmatism in Law and Society* (1991), advance varieties of feminist and pragmatic legal theory that rule out all essentialist arguments and look to earlier as much as contemporary pragmatists for inspiration. Richard J. Bernstein, although sympathetic with much of the postmodernism that Rorty champions, accurately points out in *The New Constellation: The Ethical-Political Horizons of Modernity/ Postmodernity* (1992) that Rorty's dichotomy between the public and private spheres is inconsistent with Dewey's pragmatism. In a passage that deftly summarizes the situation in political theory as well, Bernstein acknowledges that cacophony prevails today in philosophical writing. "Philosophy has been decentered. There is no single paradigm, research program, or orientation that dominates philosophy. The fact is that our situation is pluralistic." Given that diversity, "the pragmatic legacy is especially relevant, in particular the call to nurture the type of community and solidarity where there is an engaged fallibilistic pluralism —one that is based upon mutual respect, where we are willing to risk our own prejudgments, are open to listening and learning from others, and we respond to others with responsiveness and responsibility."[50]

During the last century the United States has become a multicultural society, and it will continue to become more rather than less diverse. Political discourse will continue to revolve around the central issue of accommodating differences. Our current political environment does not provide very effective ways of solving that problem. As Mary Ann Glendon argues persuasively in *Rights Talk: The Impoverishment of Political Discourse* (1991), contemporary political argument locks us into polarized positions that make compromise and even conversation increasingly difficult. Compared with political discourse in other industrial democracies, she argues that our rights talk is distinctive because of "its starkness and simplicity, . . . its exaggerated absoluteness, its hyperindividualism, its insularity, and its silence with respect to personal, civic, and collective responsibilities."[51] As Bernstein points out, Dewey's conception of pragmatic democracy offers an escape from those dead ends.

The recognition of difference and uncertainty, and awareness of the need to balance rights against responsibilities, might alter the terms in which we talk about politics. E. J. Dionne, in *Why Americans Hate Politics* (1992), describes the false choices that distort our political perception and blind us to what we share as Americans. No one, he correctly points out, really wants—or needs—to choose between feminism and the family, between reform and traditional values, or between racial justice and individual accountability. Our fondness for stark dichotomies has led us to transform practically all the difficult political issues we face into questions of constitutional law. The more we focus attention on such either/ or formulations as the right to choose *or* the right to life, the presence *or* absence of prayer in school, affirmative action *or* meritocracy, the more rigidly we lock ourselves into a politics of false choices.

The alternatives that Bernstein, Glendon, and Dionne suggest will not automatically resolve such problems. But they return us to the more promising approach of earlier generations of political thinkers, who understood that rights talk obscures more than it clarifies. As Dewey in particular understood, we must examine critically how we as individuals develop our preferences and interests, how we understand and communicate political ideas, how we construct the small and large communities that we prize, and how we can shape public policy on the basis of our experience and our aspirations rather than according to the false choices we are fed.

The problems of politics are perennial, and every provisional solution we attempt will generate a new set of problems. It is difficult now to muster Dewey's confidence that all problems can be resolved neatly through participation and cooperative community building; we know how deeply conflicts divide us. Yet democracy, like the "engaged fallibilistic pluralism" that Bernstein recommends, remains attractive precisely because no final answers are available to political questions. The search for justice will continue to require, as it has for the last century, political ideas that refine the delicate balance between freedom and equality, between rights and responsibilities. Our culture will not escape that condition. Perhaps together pragmatism and democracy will help cure us of our desire for a cure.

NINE

WHY HISTORY MATTERS TO
POLITICAL THEORY

F OR MUCH OF THE twentieth century, American philosophers and social scientists have thirsted for certainty. The natural sciences provided an attractive model for inquiry of all sorts, generating through systematic, rigorous research a reliable body of knowledge commanding respect and assent from specialists and nonspecialists alike. Not only were scientists sure of themselves and their findings but they also seemed capable of providing blueprints for social reform that promised results every bit as predictable as their laboratory experiments. Philosophers, dissatisfied with interminable squabbles about ethics and metaphysics, eagerly joined the crusade for truth organized by logical positivists and linguistic analysts. Students of society and politics, unhappy with the disorder of merely descriptive accounts, struggled to construct a temple of social science that would contain quantifiable, verifiable, and above all, value-free knowledge capable of providing reliable guidance for social engineers. Most historians who noticed such efforts at all viewed them with a mixture of bewilderment and dismay. For their part, analytic philosophers and empirical social scientists considered historians something of an embarrassment, quaint but probably harmless storytellers who could safely be ignored if they refused to go away.

Times have changed.[1] The natural sciences, whose claims to objectivity had intimidated humanists and inspired philosophers and social scientists—and whose hold on solid knowledge had seemed so secure—fell before the historicist analysis of Thomas Kuhn. Many of the schemes for social engineering hatched by enthusiasts for science led to results ranging from disappointing to disastrous, as research findings and their application to social problems were shown to be grounded in questionable assumptions and susceptible to appropriation for ideological purposes antithetical to the scientific ideal of value neutrality.[2] Social scientists then began to admit what practitioners of the *Geisteswissenschaften* such as Wilhelm Dilthey had known since the nineteenth century: because human experience is meaningful, understanding both behavior and expression requires interpreting the complex and shifting systems of symbols through which individuals encounter the world and with which they try to cope with it.[3] Meanings and intentions change over time and across cultures; as that realization spread, hopes of finding a universal logic or a general science of social organization faded.[4]

Marching behind the banner of hermeneutics came an influential band of scholars who challenged the ideal of objectivity—Peter Winch, Clifford Geertz, Charles Taylor, Anthony Giddens, Paul Ricoeur, Michel Foucault, Jacques Derrida, Hans-Georg Gadamer, and Jürgen Habermas. This was a new litany of saints proclaiming variations on a revolutionary gospel of interpretation. They spoke a different language from those scientists, philosophers, and social scientists who sought to escape the clutter of history. Instead of timeless principles and truth, they spoke in a dizzying new language of revolutionary paradigm shifts, incommensurable forms of life, complexities of thick description, competing communities of discourse, archaeologies of knowledge, universal undecidability of texts, inescapability of prejudices, and colonization of life-worlds by an omnivorous technostructure. Each of these moves opened new possibilities for fruitful interaction between social theory and history. Unfortunately, however, as Peter Novick's study of American historians illustrates, most practicing historians have remained as oblivious to these promising developments as they had been to the threats implicit in earlier programs aspiring to achieve scientific status by escaping the confines of history.[5]

The reluctance of many historians to face the consequences of these diverse developments is unfortunate, because the many-pronged attack on natural scientists' claims to certainty, objectivity, and utility present important if seldom appreciated opportunities for developing an alternative to science as a model for social investigation and political argument. Especially since social scientists on both sides of the Atlantic failed to anticipate the most significant events of the last fifty years—the collapse of communism in Eastern Europe and the disintegration of the Soviet Union—the limitations of predictive social science are now almost universally acknowledged.

In this essay, I examine some developments in philosophy and political theory that reflect both growing dissatisfaction with science as a model and renewed interest in historical inquiry, and I indicate why, paradoxically, the more prudent and limited claims of history continue to offer an attractive, if unsteady, source of knowledge. Recent challenges to the possibility of objective truth do not, as might be assumed, diminish the value of history for political theory. Such challenges instead magnify its importance.

BRIDGES BUILT BETWEEN history and politics have clearly altered the field of political theory. Claims characterized as "foundationalist," Don Herzog has suggested, are those "grounded on principles that are (1) undeniable and immune to revision and (2) located outside society and politics." While the canon in political theory has traditionally comprised texts unapologetically premised on just such principles, foundationalism these days seems increasingly unattractive. Contextualism, which emphasizes the intimate relations between ideas and their environment, and between theory and both linguistic and political practice, now exerts an almost irresistible appeal for theorists of both liberal and communitarian persuasions. For example, two notable efforts to establish the primacy of freedom as a political value, Joseph Raz's *The Morality of Freedom* and Richard Flathman's *The Philosophy and Politics of Freedom*, both concede that rights can now be discussed not in the abstract but only in the context of particular social institutions. The validity of all political principles, in Raz's words, "is limited by their background. In this way, institutions shape the principles which are designed for the guidance and remolding of these institutions."[6]

These days few political theorists are content to leave their ideals lying idle in space. Instead they are becoming adept at contextualist and historicist maneuvers. Communitarians no less frequently than liberals have been turning away from the abstract and toward the concrete, away from the general and toward the particular, away from the universal and toward the historical. William Sullivan, for example, tried, however schematically, to relate to American historical development the criticisms of liberalism advanced in the widely read *Habits of the Heart*. William Connolly, attempting to blend elements from Foucault's and Habermas's writings, emphasized the difficulties facing any political system— including our own—that would seek to encourage rather than stifle differences of the sort usually suppressed by structures of power. Connolly traced that difficulty to continuing assaults on private life by the institutionalization of instrumental rationality; his analysis seems to owe as much to a reading of twentieth-century social history as it does to the reading of Foucault and Habermas. Finally, Richard J. Bernstein and Thomas McCarthy have grown increasingly enthusiastic about the attractiveness of Habermas's theory of communicative rationality as Habermas has adopted more self-consciously pragmatist ideas and explicitly repudiated appeals to a transcendental form of argument.[7]

Surely the most striking example of the increasing appeal, if not the pervasiveness, of contextualism in liberal theory, though, is John Rawls's revision of the arguments originally advanced in his *Theory of Justice*. In a series of essays and in *Political Liberalism*, Rawls now admits that all any theory can provide are principles appropriate "for us" rather than for all people at all times. He concedes that such principles derive from "our public political culture itself, including its main institutions and the historical traditions of their interpretation." He acknowledges that political theorists can now offer no more than "provisional fixed points," a deliberately oxymoronic phrase that removes his principles of justice from a disembodied moment of purportedly "rational" reflection and places them firmly in the context of our contemporary liberal democratic culture. Because Rawls now admits that he is writing "to help us work out what we now think," he emphasizes that our understanding of our history, our awareness of "the plurality of incommensurable conceptions of the good" characteristic of our liberal culture, will necessarily shape our ideas about justice.[8]

By thus historicizing his project, by removing it from the realm of universality and locating it in our time and our place, Rawls has pulled the rug out from under the communitarian critics inspired by Hegel or Marx who challenged the abstract nature of his rights-bearing individuals and his thin theory of the good. Moreover, the new and improved constructivist Rawls provides ammunition his champions can use. Amy Gutmann and Stephen Holmes, for example, not only declare Rawls not guilty of committing metaphysics but also charge his fuzzy-minded Hegelian critics with foundationalism and an even deadlier sin of omission, the refusal to do history. In a similar vein, Richard Rorty has quite properly criticized the "terminal wistfulness" that marks the conclusions of studies such as Michael Sandel's *Liberalism and the Limits of Justice*, Roberto Unger's *Knowledge and Politics*, and Alasdair MacIntyre's *After Virtue*. In the words of Jeffrey Stout, "The main problem with communitarian criticism of liberal society . . . is its implicitly utopian character. . . . When you unwrap the utopia, the batteries aren't included."[9]

One of the most powerful recent statements of liberal political theory, Stephen Holmes's double-barreled attack on the critics of liberalism in *The Anatomy of Antiliberalism* and his defense of his own version in *Passions and Constraint: On the Theory of Liberal Democracy* relies explicitly on historical analysis. Holmes demonstrates that, whereas liberal theory is criticized by leftists and celebrated by libertarians because both consider it incompatible with a strong state and redistributionist or regulatory policies, such assumptions derive from historically inaccurate characteristics of liberalism.

Carefully explicating the writings of liberal theorists such as Locke, Montesquieu, Adam Smith, Madison, and Mill, Holmes demonstrates that "liberal principles are compatible with any form of state provision that fosters individual autonomy." Historically, if not in the caricatured version of their ideas presented by their contemporary critics, eighteenth- and nineteenth-century liberals appreciated the capacity of positive state action. They embraced a normative rather than a reductionist concept of individual interest, and they articulated a view of rights more nuanced than the false polarity between negative and positive liberty. Finally, Holmes shows that liberal theorists valued democracy but wanted to make sure popular government would survive. Liberals' efforts to ensure the security of individuals expanded gradually from their resistance to arbitrary state power to their endorsement of social insurance measures consistent with those provided by twentieth-century welfare states. Holmes's argument for liberalism, in other words, depends not on thought experiments akin to Rawls's original position but on the detailed analysis of historical evidence.[10]

The liberal theorist with the most acute sense of history's importance is Michael Walzer. Walzer argues in *Spheres of Justice* for a pluralistic conception because our competing values are "the inevitable product of historical and cultural particularism." "Every substantive account of justice," he concludes, "is a local account." Without a detailed understanding of our tradition, we cannot understand our experience, our institutions, or our ideals. In his recent book *Thick and Thin: Moral Argument at Home and Abroad*, Walzer contrasts richly textured political and ethical arguments ("thick"), which are rooted in a particular historical tradition, with more universal principles ("thin"), which aspire to appeal across different cultures. Attractive as the latter form of argument has been since the Enlightenment, such principles transcend the details, and thus also the reality, of actual human experience. Political ideals must be connected to the meanings people actually attach to that experience. "Social meanings are not just *there*, agreed on once and for all," Walzer sensibly concludes. "Meanings change over time as a result of internal tension and external example; thence, they are always subject to dispute." Walzer denies the possibility of defining for members of our tradition a single form of human excellence or source of satisfaction. We cherish too many competing values, and even inconsistent kinds of activity, including the love of our families, the satisfaction of work well done, the respect of our professional peers, the pleasures of consumption, the rewards of religious and cultural affiliation, and the meaningfulness of our participation in voluntary associations and civic life.[11]

Too often, Walzer notes, political theorists have insisted that the deepest satisfaction for humans comes from one of those activities—work for Marxists, politics for republicans, consuming for capitalists, or civic pride for nationalists— but he disputes such claims. The diversity of choices available to individuals distinguishes our culture from others, and there are solid, historical reasons why we cherish our ability to choose the lives we want to live. Unless we look critically at our own culture instead of taking its values for granted, we will not recognize that even the fundamental procedural rules of our democratic way of life, including the right of free speech and the duty of mutual respect, derive from centuries of hard cultural work. From Walzer's perspective values such as deliberation, often associated with Habermas's "ideal speech situation," are not universal human ideals but the products of particular historical development.[12]

Even though some critics have questioned whether such moves are genuine conversions or merely convenient professions of faith in a currently fashionable historicism,[13] the tendency of theorists to advance their arguments in the more modest tones of historicism and contextualism is undeniable. Particularly clear are the commitments of two leading communitarian theorists, Charles Taylor and his former student Michael Sandel, and that of the Trojan horse of postanalytic philosophy, the liberal pragmatist Richard Rorty.

Taylor was among the leaders of the turn toward hermeneutics, as I have noted, and he has consistently denied the philosophical coherence of attempts to escape historical analysis for either an ostensibly scientific or "rational" alternative. He rejects even the possibility of creating overarching political principles of justice appropriate for all cultures: "the judgment of what is just in a particular society involves combining mutually irreducible principles in a weighting that is appropriate for the particular society, given its history, economy, and degree of integration." In *Sources of Self: The Making of the Modern Identity*, his brilliant explanation of how the sense of individual selfhood developed in modern Western cultures, Taylor has undertaken to provide just such a historical account of the process whereby a sense of "inwardness," an "affirmation of ordinary life," and a view of the creative potential of self-expression together yielded a modern Western sensibility.

We moderns are capable of great depth when we connect with the sources of our commitments, the goods that lie beyond the self. Unfortunately, Taylor laments, we are deflected from our richest philosophical resources by a shallow subjectivism, an uncritical scientism, and an empty instrumentalism. Our widely shared commitments to justice and benevolence, Taylor argues, have become detached from the religious belief in the worth of human beings that undergirded those commitments from the date of their appearance in Western culture, and for that reason their hold on our politics has become increasingly tenuous. "Adopting a stripped-down secular outlook," in Taylor's words, "involves stifling the response in us to some of the deepest and most powerful spiritual aspirations that humans have conceived." Rather than asserting that reason alone can provide an irrefutable argument on behalf of his ideals, Taylor rests his case on a historical account of the way that ancient Christian virtues were transformed by, but nevertheless continue to undergird, modern ideas of the self and its moral and political obligations.[14]

Sandel's recent account of American political thought and practice, *Democracy's Discontent: America in Search of a Public Philosophy*, represents an attempt to bring his communitarian critique of Rawls, originally launched in *Liberalism and the Limits of Justice*, down from the realm of abstraction to the firmer ground of historical analysis by making two distinct arguments. In part one, Sandel claims that judges in the United States since World War II have adopted a false and debilitating view of individual citizens. Whether the issue is individual rights to free speech or privacy or religious expression, or decisions concerning abortion or divorce, courts have increasingly tended to bracket conflicts between substantive values. It is now the sovereign individual self, conceived as something separate from, and prior to, its freely chosen ends (rather than constituted by those values, as Sandel, following Taylor, would have it), whose preferences rule in the "procedural republic" that has emerged in America in the last few decades. Because the Supreme Court is now committed to a conception of the Constitution as "a neutral framework of rights within which persons can pursue their own ends," as Sandel phrases it, the American judicial system refuses to privilege any conception of the good over any other that individuals may claim to cherish as their own, and it refuses to allow communities to restrict individuals in their exercise of those rights. Sandel argues that the Supreme Court's view of individuals as "self-originating sources of valid claims," as persons whose rights cannot be restricted by appeal to any community standards beyond personal preferences, elevates the value of toleration to the point that America is locked into a moral vacuum and forced to allow individuals to pursue their own ends regardless of what those ends might be. This fairly standard—and convincing—critique of the culture of rights attracts adherents from across the intellectual spectrum; commentators ranging from right and left have commended Sandel for the persuasiveness of this part of his book.

In part two of *Democracy's Discontents*, Sandel emphasizes the centrality in American history of what he calls the "formative project of republican citizenship," which has served as an alternative to the liberal emphasis on individual rights. Sandel reconstructs early American history as an unbroken succession of republican quests after the grail of civic virtue. He passes from prerevolutionary republicans through Jeffersonians and Federalists, presenting Madison and Hamilton alike as friends of republican ideals, then portrays as republicans Jacksonian craftsmen and Whig statesmen, then Lincoln Republicans and labor radicals.

In the twentieth century, though, Sandel argues, this tradition of republicanism began to unravel. First the AFL surrendered the ideal of autonomous workers in exchange for better wages, shorter hours, and greater security. Then the New Deal surrendered the republican civic project and embraced a Keynesianism that valued economic growth more than the republican commitment to a public good beyond the preferences of individual consumers. Finally, in the 1950s and especially the 1960s Americans stopped worrying about virtue and learned to be imperturbably "nonjudgmental" about everything—except the claims of those who thought they could identify the values that all Americans should prize.

In Sandel's view, the tension between the desires of the liberal self and the demands of republican citizenship in contemporary America is to be resolved by recovering the republican tradition that defined American culture from the nation's founding until the early twentieth century. Sandel's dissection of the contemporary procedural republic in part one of *Democracy's Discontent* is persuasive, but his account of America's republican tradition is not—although not because, as some of his critics have charged, Sandel has invented a mythology of American history.

Instead the three central problems with Sandel's account show why, if we want to understand the relation between rights and responsibility, or between self and community, in American history, we must resist the temptation to replace one simplification with another. If Sandel is mistaken about the dominance of republican ideas in America prior to the New Deal, it is equally mistaken simply to dismiss the mountain of evidence that has accumulated in the last three decades demonstrating that concern with civic virtue and the public good has been a *part* of American political discourse since the seventeenth century. But exaggerating the role of republicanism helps us no more than exaggerating the role of liberalism; we merely replace the overemphasis on the individual self with an overemphasis on community. We need instead a more balanced view that sees the continuous presence of rights talk and the continuous presence of competing ideals of the common good.

The three main problems with Sandel's republicanism show why the idea of democracy, in which arguments for freedom and arguments for community have jostled against each other, provides a better framework for understanding how the struggles in American public life have almost always involved *balancing* individual rights and civic ideals. First, Sandel's republicanism is too sanitized. He overlooks earlier republicans' willingness to countenance racial oppression, including the greatest abomination of American history, chattel slavery. He overlooks the militarism of the republican tradition, which since the Italian Renaissance has identified virtue not only with autonomous citizens but with national glory of the sort attained by the Roman Empire. He overlooks the longstanding republican assumption that hierarchies of class and gender are perfectly acceptable, even necessary, because they make possible the leisure that enables virtuous male citizens to pursue the public good.

Second, Sandel's republicanism is deaf to the pervasive religiosity of American political discourse. Invocations of the public good in America have until quite recently been embedded in the language of covenant or in a commitment to the Christian ideal of universal human fellowship. To cite only one example, when Samuel Adams challenged his listeners to rally to the patriots' cause, he emphasized that theirs was to be a Christian Sparta, and to most Americans in the 1770s and afterward, that adjective mattered.

Finally, Sandel's republicanism overlooks the reasons *why* twentieth-century rights talk replaced earlier Americans' invocations of civic virtue. Nineteenth-century abolitionists and women's rights advocates could not find within the republican tradition arguments that justified their demands for equality, and in their more recent struggles, from the civil rights movement onward, marginalized Americans have likewise found in the language of rights rather than civic virtue the weapons that have enabled them to plead their case for equality. Within the republican tradition such challenges could be—and usually were—silenced. Within the traditions of natural rights, and especially within religious traditions that envisioned a universal community encompassing all of God's children, the marginalized had powerful resources indeed.

The awareness of these problematical dimensions of republicanism has led some critics to dismiss republican ideas altogether as a kind of wishful thinking, a projection of wistful leftist dreams backward into a world that never was. But admitting that some historians and political theorists got carried away—that at some moments in the 1980s republicanism became an analytical night in which all cows are black—need not lead us back to the one-dimensional portrayals of individualism that necessitated rediscovering the discourse of republicanism in the first place.

Historians of eighteenth- and nineteenth-century American culture were not simply making up the evidence concerning the complex interplay between ideas of rights and ideas of the common good in American discourse. Instead of continuing to wrestle over the relative importance of liberal and republican ideas, we should recognize their joint presence and persistence. For reasons that Willi Paul Adams made abundantly clear in *The First American Constitutions: Republican Ideology and the Making of the State Constitutions in the Revolutionary Era*, we must acknowledge the *diversity* of ideas, the *particular* conflicts of American politics, and the *collision* between the genuine appeal of abstract ideals and the stubborn resistance of hard facts in the forging of government institutions in the late eighteenth century.[15]

Despite the problems with part two of *Democracy's Discontent*, Sandel's approach in this book differs markedly from that of his earlier work. Instead of concentrating on the conceptual inadequacy of Rawls's view of the individual self, Sandel traces a strand of American political discourse from the eighteenth century to the present, seeking to demonstrate with historical evidence the presence of republican concerns in the writings of thinkers from Jefferson and Madison through Jackson and Lincoln to Croly and Brandeis. Although historians will find parts of Sandel's account unconvincing, there can be no mistaking the importance of history for his argument: Sandel's case for a renewed civic project depends on his ability to show convincingly the embeddedness of republican ideals of virtuous citizenship in America's past.

The almost simultaneous appearance of Holmes's spirited defense of liberalism and Sandel's equally spirited attack on it, both of which rely on the historical record despite their dramatically different interpretations of the evidence it contains concerning the relative centrality and current attractiveness of liberal and republican ideas, illustrates the change in perspective among American political theorists from abstract to historical analysis. That shift is equally apparent in the saga of the philosopher Richard Rorty, who has moved from what he called a "postmodern bourgeois liberalism" in the early 1980s to a more historically attuned and politically engaged social democracy.

Rorty's historicism has had such explosive force within the profession of philosophy because he attacked the citadel from within. His insistence that philosophy could never attain scientific status was troubling enough, but perhaps even more troubling was Rorty's judgment that the grail of objective knowledge will likewise continue to elude the natural and social sciences. Rorty first established his credentials with papers discussing standard topics in the analytic tradition, and in 1967 he edited *The Linguistic Turn*, which contains a variety of essays in the prevailing styles of linguistic and logical analysis. In his introduction to that volume, however, he suggested that the conflicts between J. L. Austin's "ordinary-language" philosophy and Rudolph Carnap's logical positivism were so fundamental that they could not be resolved. When *Philosophy and the Mirror of Nature* appeared in 1979, Rorty was widely acknowledged as one of the most incisive critics of twentieth-century Anglo-American philosophy. Here, Rorty insisted that problems such as mind-body dualism, the correspondence theory of truth, theories of knowledge, theories of language, and ultimately the entire conception of a systematic philosophy devoted to finding foundations for objective knowledge rest on misconceptions. Because we make up the questions we ask, Rorty argued, we also make up the answers. In the provocative titles of his two concluding chapters, Rorty urged his fellow philosophers to move "from epistemology to hermeneutics" and to begin practicing "philosophy without mirrors." "Systematic philosophers" such as Locke and Kant, Austin and Carnap, who sought a science of knowledge that would disclose objective truth, should give way to "edifying philosophers" such as James and Dewey, who would contribute to the "conversation of the West" without promising results that philosophy can never deliver. Although others such as Hilary Putnam, Nelson Goodman, and Richard J. Bernstein have offered variations on this theme of "historicist undoing," to use Ian Hacking's phrase, Rorty's assault seemed especially dramatic because it held out no alternative solutions.

In the conclusion of *Philosophy and the Mirror of Nature*, Rorty staked out his heretical position: "To drop the notion of the philosopher as knowing something about knowing which nobody else knows so well would be to drop the notion that his voice always has an overriding claim on the attention of the other participants in the conversation." In his introduction to *The Consequences of Pragmatism*, a collection of essays published in 1982, Rorty refused to back down. There can be no "extra-historical Archimedean point," he wrote. We must face the unsettling realization that "there is nothing deep down inside us except what we have put there ourselves, no criterion that we have not created in the course of creating a practice, no standard of rationality that is not an appeal to such a criterion, no rigorous argumentation that is not obedience to our own conventions." Science, to put the point bluntly, is only "one genre of literature," and all of our efforts to find solid, unchanging knowledge are futile attempts to escape the contingency of the ongoing conversation in which we all participate.[16]

As Rorty realized, little in these claims was really new. Even the gasps from his critics inside and outside the academy only echoed the responses that had greeted the writings of Nietzsche and James. But because the twentieth-century enthusiasm for science had overshadowed the writings of that earlier generation of radical critics, and because Anglo-American philosophers in particular had marched down a road marked "Truth" only to find James and Dewey waiting there for them, Rorty's revival of pragmatism seemed revolutionary.

Despite Rorty's penetrating critique, both *Philosophy and the Mirror of Nature* and *The Consequences of Pragmatism* were, at that time, assimilable. The attack on objectivity had by then established beachheads in the sciences and the social sciences; continental philosophers had been coping with hermeneutics and existential phenomenology for decades. Moreover, the mood of Rorty's writings was encouraging if not downright upbeat. " 'Pragmatism,' " he proclaimed, is "the chief glory of our country's intellectual tradition." Its pioneers James and Dewey wrote, as such dark pessimists as Nietzsche and Heidegger did not, "in a spirit of social hope. They asked us to liberate our new civilization by giving up the notion of 'grounding' our culture, our moral lives, our politics, our religious beliefs, upon 'philosophical bases.' They asked us to give up the neurotic Cartesian quest for certainty."[17]

Against critics from all sides who assailed him with charges of relativism, Rorty responded that the entire notion of relativism becomes incoherent when we appreciate the contingent status of all knowledge. From the perspective of his pragmatism, there is nothing for "truth" to be relative to except our tradition, our purposes, and our linguistic conventions. When we have come to that realization, a calm acceptance of our condition becomes possible, and we can once again take up the conversation. While pragmatism cannot offer objectivity, neither does it threaten the survival of civilization as we know it. Pragmatism, Rorty wrote in an essay entitled "Solidarity or Objectivity," is "a philosophy of solidarity rather than despair." There is no reason to discard our beliefs about the natural world— or to discard our social, moral, and political values—just because we realize we have made them rather than found them. Faith in science, like our other faiths, helps us get things done. Science helps us muddle through, and it will continue to help us even after we have stopped trying to "divinize" it. In his most recent philosophical writings, notably in the introduction to *Objectivity, Relativism, and Truth*, Rorty has reiterated this argument. When he suggests that antirepresentationalists like himself "see no sense in which physics is more independent of our human peculiarities than astrology or literary criticism," it seems clear he has no more patience with the pretensions of critics presuming to dispense wisdom in the shopworn slogans of postmodernism than he has for natural scientists who carry on as before three decades after Kuhn's bombshell burst.[18]

In the absence of foundations, Rorty recommended in *Consequences of Pragmatism* that we look instead to history. We must accept "our inheritance from, and our conversation with, our fellow-humans as our only source of guidance." This is our defense against the nihilism that realists fear will follow from pragmatism. "Our identification with our community—our society, our political tradition, our intellectual heritage—is heightened when we see this community as ours rather than *nature's*, *shaped* rather than found, one among many which men have made." Rorty continued to emphasize the crucial role of history in his provocative and widely read book *Contingency, Irony, and Solidarity*, published in 1989. If we were to surrender our aspirations to certainty, he wrote, we "would regard the justification of liberal society simply as a matter of historical comparison with other attempts at social organization." Rorty advanced an argument that historians should find intriguing, even though it may prove as unsettling for unrepentant objectivists as other species of poststructuralist criticism: "I have been urging in this book that we try *not* to want something which stands beyond history and institutions. The fundamental premise of the book is that a belief can still regulate action, can still be thought worth dying for, among people who are quite aware that this belief is caused by nothing deeper than contingent historical circumstances." In Rorty's "liberal utopia," the charge of relativism loses its force and the claim that there is "'something that stands beyond history'" becomes unintelligible."[19]

Many historians, especially those most troubled by the "historicist undoing" sweeping across philosophy and political theory, will perhaps be surprised to find the burden of providing our culture with guidance dumped in their laps. How is history going to meet this challenge? What can historians offer philosophers such as Rorty and political theorists such as Holmes and Sandel, who now seem to have given up the search for timeless truths and have embraced the particularity of history? Historians who suppose that history can still offer objective truths concerning human affairs have not been paying attention for the past few decades. There are two problems with historians' confident assumption that they can offer an account of the past "as it really happened," in Leopold von Ranke's familiar phrase. First, and incidentally, Ranke's meaning was almost diametrically opposed to the meaning we usually impose on his words, as Georg Iggers explains. Ranke's German contemporaries scoffed at Ranke's romanticism, because he aimed to enable the divine spirit, manifesting itself in history, to flow directly through its conduit, the historian, without any interference on the historian's part. So when Ranke referred to the past "as it really happened," he was inhabiting a thought world closer to the idealism of Hegel than to the commonsense realism of most twentieth-century historians.[20]

The second problem with historians' veneration of objectivity is more fundamental than a simple problem of translation. The unsettling developments that eroded the confidence of Kuhn in science, Geertz in anthropology, Taylor in social theory, and Rorty in philosophy left many historians untouched. Many historians on the left as well as the right generally refuse to question, or even to think seriously about, the status of historical knowledge. While there are of course exceptions, radicals no less often than conservatives continue to assume that historians' access to truth is unproblematical. Many historians seem to have missed the hermeneutic turn that has revolutionized scholarship, from the sciences to philosophy. If even physicists and ethicists can concede that inquiry inescapably involves interpretation, historians need to realize that we, too, cannot escape the hermeneutic circle. The past we study and the present we inhabit exhibit the same characteristics of multidimensionality, meaningfulness, and opacity that prevent natural scientists and political theorists from disclosing universal principles embedded in the world or imposed by the structure of human reason. History always involves interpretation; it never reveals simple truths.

Does that mean history has nothing to offer? If all historical knowledge is subject to revision, it might seem that any hopes for history as an alternative to science are misplaced. But just as physicists who realize they are working within a particular paradigm can still productively do what Kuhn calls "normal science," so historians need not be disabled by the realization that they are engaged in a species of hermeneutics. We historians should learn to see our study of the past as pragmatists and other postanalytic philosophers have taught us to see the present —as an effort to solve problems. The nature of the problems, the range of possible solutions, and the degree of success attained are all questions that require interpretation. They require making the effort to recover the past as it was lived as well as trying to understand how and why things have turned out as they have. Although we cannot escape our own historical context and enter another any more than an anthropologist can become a member of another culture, we must try to penetrate the evidence of behaviors and expressions to understand the experience of those who shaped our past. This historical sensibility, as I call it elsewhere, begins in admitting the uncertainty of our own experience and ends in the provisional interpretations that historians can offer their cultures.[21]

Earlier pragmatists turned to history for precisely the same reasons Rorty now offers. In the words of Wilhelm Dilthey, "The totality of human nature is only to be found in history." The individual "can only become conscious of it and enjoy it when he assembles the mind of the past in himself." If we can attain in the present only provisional understandings that are culturally shaped, an indispensable source of those understandings is a detailed and sophisticated knowledge of the past. As pragmatists and other philosophers and political theorists turn increasingly to "our tradition" as the source and the testing ground for our ideas and our ideals, historians should become alert not only to the limits of historical knowledge but also to its potential role in the construction of a pragmatic cultural self-understanding.[22]

The role of historians in such a pragmatic conception of culture is to insist on the diversity of voices, and the centrality of conflict, in the shaping of our tradition. In contrast to a familiar argument, I suggest that we emphasize the absence of consensus in America. The very origins of liberal tolerance, as Hume argued and as contemporary scholars confirm, can be traced to the religious wars of early modern Europe. The institutionalization of human rights emerged from pragmatic compromises among groups that could not agree on the nature of the good; the language of rights that grew up to contend with older languages of virtue reflects the inability to agree on substantive conceptions of the good. In America, the sometimes competing, sometimes complementary vocabularies of Christianity, republicanism, and liberalism were present throughout the eighteenth century, and the differences among them were masked but not erased under the pressure of fighting for independence and launching the republic. Throughout the nineteenth and twentieth centuries as well, competing conceptions of freedom and justice have drawn strength from the continuing vitality of contradictory and incompatible religious and political traditions. Those conflicts have prevented any single vision from dominating public life in the United States, thereby making impossible the dramatic transformation that marks European polities, in which power can be consolidated around unitary conceptions of the right and the good. The diversity of American politics rather than any liberal consensus defines "our tradition."

For that reason, efforts to derive a single meaning from our past, whether Holmes's expansive liberalism or Sandel's civic republicanism, however plausible and attractive they may be when viewed in isolation, are nevertheless bound to be unpersuasive. Readers who encounter both Holmes's and Sandel's books together might well rub their eyes in wonder, puzzled that two clear-eyed observers examining the history of political discourse come to such diametrically opposite conclusions about its meaning. Those differences indicate the dangers involved in using the past for partisan purposes.[23]

Both Holmes and Sandel insightfully explicate the writings of those within their preferred traditions. But Holmes ignores the role of civic republican and religious language; Sandel ignores the importance of natural rights in American politics prior to World War II. Although both aspire to Walzer's "thick" description, neither quite achieves it. For as the most successful studies of American political thought and behavior published during the last decade have demonstrated, our history has been marked by the blending of different vocabularies and traditions and has shown the shaping pressure exerted on the abstractions of political theory by political experience.[24]

Noting the peculiar tendency of contemporary radical as well as conservative Americans to invoke the idea of universal rights (although they do so for strikingly different purposes), Thomas Haskell has thoughtfully examined "the curious persistence of 'rights talk' in an age of interpretation." One could just as persuasively call attention to the equally curious persistence of "community talk," which attracts communitarians such as Sandel and conservatives such as Newt Gingrich, who wax rhapsodic about churches and other voluntary associations, since if we take seriously the evidence presented in recent historical scholarship, the intermingling of these discourses has been as clear as their competition. A liberalism without any responsibilities accompanying rights, and a communitarianism without any concern for individual liberties, are projected fantasies lacking historical grounding.

The trajectories of historical change, moreover, have been as unanticipated as these competing positions have been interdependent. The American Revolution, ostensibly fought to secure autonomy for virtuous citizens, unleashed a passion for individual rights that eventually threatened to trample the virtue it was intended to facilitate. The welfare state, constructed to preserve and expand the effective liberty of those whose autonomy was compromised by others' exercise of their freedom, eventually culminated in new and perhaps even more deadening forms of dependency.[25] The American tradition is one of struggles waged by partisans of competing ideals who agree only to disagree about the adequacy of every provisional compromise. Endlessly changing circumstances, needs, values, and people have generated new forms of subjugation and new schemes of reform. The unintended consequences of countless individual choices have created new problems in an endless and dizzying spiral.

All the truths of American history and politics have been, as the title of a valuable study by Daniel Rodgers has it, "contested truths." Given the centrality of diversity, and given the tendency of some commentators such as Alasdair MacIntyre and Robert Bellah to despair of such fragmentation, and of others such as Michael Walzer, Jeffrey Stout, and Don Herzog to celebrate it, the widespread dissatisfaction with Rorty's early-1980s conception of a "postmodern bourgeois liberalism" grounded in "our tradition" (singular) is hardly surprising. Of the numerous critics who have discussed this aspect of Rorty's work, Richard J. Bernstein offered perhaps the most pointed challenge. Bernstein charged that Rorty

> tends to gloss over what appears to be the overwhelming "fact" of contemporary life —the breakdown of moral and political consensus, and the conflicts and incompatibility among competing social practices. . . . It is never clear why Rorty, who claims that there is no consensus about competing conceptions of the good life, thinks there is any more consensus about conceptions of justice or liberal democracy.[26]

Because Rorty's early responses to such criticism tended to focus on cold war themes that no longer seem relevant, I will concentrate instead on two aspects of Rorty's writings on politics that are important but inconsistent: his characterization of social democracy and his separation of the spheres of public and private philosophy, the latter of which he has begun to question in his most recent writings.

Rorty has argued, quite reasonably, that dogmas concerning free enterprise and nationalization are no longer helpful in political debate. He accepts Habermas's open-ended characterization of socialism as "overcoming the . . . rise to dominance of cognitive-instrumental" interests. In Rorty's words, "We have to find a definition that commits us to both greater equality and a change in moral climate, without committing us to any particular economic setup." He insists, sensibly enough, that "there is nothing sacred about either the free market or about central planning; the proper balance between the two is a matter of experimental tinkering." That is a definition that not only Habermas but also Rawls would accept, as Rorty points out. It seems likely that William James and John Dewey would have endorsed it as well. Contemporary social democrats, Rorty argues, "think that Dewey and Weber absorbed everything useful Marx had to teach, just as they absorbed everything useful Plato and Aristotle had to teach, and got rid of the residue."[27]

In *Contingency, Irony, and Solidarity*, Rorty was more pessimistic about what we can learn from this earlier generation: "I do not think that we liberals can now imagine a future of 'human dignity, freedom and peace.' That is, we cannot tell ourselves a story about how to get from the actual present to such a future." He concluded soberly, "We have no analogue of the scenario which . . . our grandfathers had for changing the world of 1900." Rorty dedicated *Contingency, Irony, and Solidarity* to "six liberals": his parents and grandparents. His maternal grandfather was Walter Rauschenbusch, a champion of the social gospel who contributed most powerfully to the creation of a social democratic alternative in America. Rauschenbusch understood that the abuse of power and the tendency toward oppression do not spring from, and cannot entirely be dissolved by, structures of economic, social, and political organization. Yet he insisted that personal benevolence alone is not sufficient "to offset the unconscious alienation created by the dominant facts of life which are wedging entire classes apart." Only a far more egalitarian and cooperative economic system would make possible an American culture embodying "the principle of solidarity and fraternity in the fundamental institutions of our industrial life."[28] Rauschenbusch did not know precisely what that ideal would look like in practice, but he knew that a long struggle stood between the injustices of the world he experienced and the achievement of his goals, and he devoted his efforts as a scholar and activist toward that ideal of evolutionary Christian socialism.

Dewey likewise cherished an egalitarian and democratic ideal, and throughout his extraordinarily productive career he insisted that we would reach that goal only if we found ways not only to think pragmatically but also to reorganize our culture so that it is more receptive to demands for equality and less responsive to the will of those with power. Max Weber shared many of the ideals and aspirations that motivated Rauschenbusch and Dewey and was more sympathetic to social democracy than is usually acknowledged.[29] Yet the differences between Dewey and Weber are also important, especially in this context, because their different perspectives shed light on some of the issues that divide Rorty from Habermas, the contemporary thinker who, as much as any other, seems to me to embody the spirit of pragmatic social democratic scholarship.

Rorty has insisted that his philosophical disagreement with Habermas "is not reflected in any political disagreement." He has explicitly endorsed Habermas's pragmatic version of a socialist ideal. The difference between them, until recently, centered on Rorty's defense of a privatized sphere in which liberal ironists pursue personal visions without any implications for public life. Philosophers such as Nietzsche, Heidegger, and Derrida are useless for politics, Rorty admits, but they provide fertile insights for the cultivation of individual aesthetic sensibilities. Rorty stated this contrast bluntly in *Contingency, Irony, and Solidarity*: his utopia, a " 'poeticized' culture," would give up "the attempt to unite" one's private ways of dealing with one's finitude and one's sense of obligation to other human beings.[30]

There is a problem here, which Weber perceived more clearly than Dewey, and it demonstrates clearly why history matters to political theory. The problem stems from the centrality of instrumental rationality — or means-ends reasoning in which the means overshadow consideration of the ends to be achieved — in twentieth-century culture. Given the tendency of this process of rationalization to sweep beneath it all other considerations, given — to use again the phrase Rorty adopted from Habermas — "the rise to dominance of cognitive-instrumental" interests and the need to resist those interests in order to preserve and advance the different sets of values that different groups in our culture cherish in addition to efficiency, it seems clear that the autonomy of the private sphere that Rorty cherishes is more vulnerable than he has been willing to admit. Given the expanding domain of instrumental reason, the separation of public from private philosophy facilitates what Habermas calls the further "colonization of the lifeworld," the invasion of private realms of imagination by an omnivorous technical spirit unsympathetic to private purposes and intolerant of the creativity and diversity that Rorty wants to protect.[31] Dewey and Weber differed on the likelihood that democratic cultures could resist the rule of this cognitive-instrumental rationality, but they agreed on its centrality and the dangers accompanying it.

For strictly pragmatic reasons, therefore — and not because of a commitment to Enlightenment rationalism or an irresistible urge to "go transcendental" and ascend to the realm of Habermas's ideal speech situation — I am as suspicious as some of Rorty's other critics of the idea of a privatized and poeticized utopia. Viewed historically, the institutions that make possible such privacy and poetry appear to be fragile creations that emerged not only from the imaginations of creative artists but also from the struggles of political activists. The survival of these

institutions likewise depends on our culture's continuing resistance to the challenges to individual experimentation that cognitive-instrumental rationality will
inevitably pose.

Rorty concluded the discussion of his poeticized ideal by rejecting Habermas's
rationalist metanarrative, which privileges "communicative reason" and dis-
counts the private imagination:

> I should like to replace both religious and philosophical accounts of a suprahistor-
> ical ground or an end-of-history convergence with a historical narrative about the
> rise of liberal institutions and customs—the institutions and customs which were
> designed to diminish cruelty, make possible government by the consent of the gov-
> erned, and permit as much domination-free communication as possible to take
> place. . . . That shift from epistemology to politics, from an explanation of the rela-
> tion between "reason" and reality to an explanation of how political freedom has
> changed our sense of what human inquiry is good for, is a shift which Dewey was
> willing to make but from which Habermas hangs back.[32]

Dewey was indeed willing to make that move, and Rorty was quite right that
Dewey emphasized the role of art, and the instrumental value of creativity, in
shaping a democratic and pragmatic culture. But Dewey did not believe that such
an aesthetic sensibility could be cultivated, or should be exercised, in isolation
from the public sphere. Dewey thought the new form of individualism that would
emerge in a thoroughly democratized culture would require the participation of
every citizen in the creative and cooperative shaping of public life. It was his democratic faith in the possibility of integrating private and public life that immu-
nized Dewey from Weber's despair. Where Weber saw only bureaucratization and
instrumental rationality trailing disenchantment, Dewey envisioned the lively interaction of personal imagination and political experimentation. Rorty has insisted that philosophers should discard the dualisms that stand in the way of
pragmatism. On pragmatic grounds, it seems reasonable to extend that denial of
dualism to Rorty's own conception of public and private spheres and the cultural
role philosophers should play.

One year after the publication of Dewey's *Art and Experience*, from which
Rorty quoted in the conclusion of his defense of a privatized sphere for liberal
ironists and strong poets, Dewey's *Liberalism and Social Action* appeared. There
he wrote,

> If the early liberals had put forth their special interpretation of liberty as something
> subject to historic relativity they would not have frozen it into a doctrine to be ap-
> plied at all times under all social circumstances. Specifically, they would have rec-
> ognized that effective liberty is a function of the social conditions existing at any
> time. If they had done this, they would have known that as economic relations be-
> came dominantly controlling forces in setting the pattern of human relations, the
> necessity of liberty for individuals which they proclaimed will require social con-
> trol of economic forces in the interest of the great mass of individuals. Because the
> liberals failed to make a distinction between purely formal and legal liberty and ef-
> fective liberty of thought and action, the history of the last one hundred years is the
> history of non-fulfillment of their predictions.[33]

If we value "effective liberty of thought and action," as Dewey did, and if we value "domination-free communication," as Rorty does, we should realize how difficult it has been historically to make progress toward these ideals. We should further realize, as Rauschenbusch did when his dissent was silenced during World War I, as Weber did when he saw how easily the nationalism he cherished could be transformed into a militarism he detested, and as Dewey did when he stood to the left of America's "vital center," effective liberty and domination-free communication remain goals to be achieved rather than achievements to be celebrated. This knowledge does not require stepping into a transhistorical metanarrative, it requires only the pragmatic historical understanding that reaching our goals requires more than exercises of imagination. The resurgence of pragmatism does not mark the end of philosophy but only the return to an older and richer tradition of practical philosophy that traces its roots to Aristotle rather than Plato. Although our historicism has removed from the pragmatic perspective any confidence in a single teleology, the touchstones of pragmatism should continue to be *phronesis* and *praxis*.[34]

The forces that have slowly gathered momentum during recent decades and that have culminated in antifoundationalism, hermeneutics, contextualism, and pragmatism originated in the gradual broadening of perspectives that began, paradoxically enough, at the same time that rationalism was being enthroned by the champions of Enlightenment. As Haskell has argued, the shift in causal attribution that emerged over the course of the eighteenth century was among the cultural developments that eventuated over time in the abolitionist crusade. As individuals came to see themselves and their cultures as enmeshed in webs of interdependency stretching beyond the narrow boundaries of personal experience, some of them began to draw connections between themselves and suffering strangers. That realization flowed in unexpected ways from the rise of a market economy. Thus through a process so rich in irony that it has obscured a crucial relation between the rise of a market for goods and the end of a market for persons, the emergence of capitalism not only created new forms of domination to replace those of feudalism but also contributed indirectly to the sensibility that eventually put an end to slavery. Not merely a new sense of responsibility, however, but agitation, persuasion, and ultimately war made the difference.[35]

If we want to "create a more expansive sense of solidarity than we presently have," as Rorty has urged us to do, if we want to expand the realm of those to whom we do not want to be cruel, the study of our tradition indicates that we should not be content with altering the contours of our imaginations. I am not suggesting that we should try to collapse the private sphere into the public, or vice versa. To the contrary, the distinction between the two, the significance of which Rorty has sometimes exaggerated and Sandel sometimes underestimates, is fundamental to American culture for reasons Walzer has made clear enough. Nor am I suggesting, as some readers might infer, that history can provide detailed road maps leading us from the problems we now face into some utopia designed this time by historians. To the contrary, I want to insist on the manifold difficulties imposed by the recognition of diversity in our tradition and the inescapability of interpretation as the means to understanding it. Both of these features of our current situation complicate enormously any effort to replace science with history as a source of blueprints for social reform, and it would be a mistake to conclude that a historical sensibility can succeed where a scientific sensibility failed to provide adequate guidance.

One of the notable features of the American tradition, as the Bill of Rights illustrates, has been this culture's persistent mistrust of all attempts to provide authoritative and binding statements of principle, whether drawn from religion, natural law, science, or history. We cherish the chance to amend our Constitution, repeal or alter our legislation, and appeal judicial decisions to a higher level. But neither does that realization reduce all knowledge claims to the status of opinion. We must work to keep the tenacity of our inclination toward the either/or of objectivity and relativism from blinding us to the possibility of escaping that abstract dichotomy in practice, through the cultivation of a critical perspective alert to the contested nature of all knowledge but nevertheless aware of the possibility of making judgments on the basis of pragmatic tests and democratic procedures. Between the discredited claims to certainty, on the one hand, and the paralyzing nihilism that reduces all knowledge to willfulness, on the other, lies the fertile ground that earlier pragmatists discovered. In our enthusiasm to cultivate it, however, we should not value the privacy of strong poets above the activity of social reformers. We should resist the impulse to separate their roles rigidly, just as we should resist the other forms of dualism that historicism has taught us to mistrust.

Pragmatists in our past have been content with neither an isolated self nor a self that seeks all its satisfactions in science, art, or politics. They have sought to unite independent thinking with effective and undogmatic social action. That insurgent spirit has been the most important contribution of pragmatism to shaping American culture, and Rorty has recently shown a refreshing willingness to extend that tradition of social criticism. As he wrote in *The Consequences of Pragmatism*, "one can say something useful about truth" only in "the vocabulary of practice rather than theory, of action rather than contemplation."[36] I think Rauschenbusch, Dewey, and Habermas would agree, and I think the historical study of our tradition, and of the complicated interplay between the aspiration to scientific certainty and the impulse to reform, confirms that judgment.

In Rorty's most recent writings he has criticized the academic Left for ignoring poverty and increasing inequality and wallowing in questions of identity irrelevant to the most urgent problems facing Americans today. Although he applauds the progress made on campuses thanks to the efforts of activists who have made the academic world more tolerant of diversity in the categories of race, gender, and sexuality, he has joined other social democrats in emphasizing the importance of reconnecting forms of cultural protest to the issues of social and economic injustice from which they have too often been detached owing to academic radicals' distrust of political and labor leaders and their impatience with the coalition building democracy requires. Such arguments signal a new commitment by Rorty to addressing questions of politics, which I find consistent with Dewey's own stance. Striking too are Rorty's recent admission of the contested terrain of "our tradition" and his observation that we are likelier to find in American history than in contemporary political philosophy or critical theory arguments on behalf of equality and justice that will prove useful for those engaged in the struggles against sadism and selfishness.[37]

Unfortunately, as Rorty has effectively bridged the gap that divided the private from the public spheres in his earlier writings, another gap—that separating those he considers enlightened secularists from narrow-minded religious believers— seems to have widened in his work. That gap deserves attention. Many contemporary Americans, including sophisticated cosmopolitan intellectuals outside as well as within universities, share with Rorty a similar, often implicit assumption that commitments to the ideals of tolerance and justice separate them from benighted theists who may mean well but do not really understand the world they inhabit. One of the most important reasons why history matters to political theory is that it reveals the error of that assumption. Before sketching, in the conclusion of this essay, an alternative perspective on the split between religious and secular Americans, I will take a detour to discuss briefly a way of thinking about questions of race and ethnicity with implications for the problem facing secular intellectuals on the topic of religious belief.

Thanks in part to their commitment to the liberal ideals of tolerance and diversity, some of America's universities (such as the campuses of the University of California at Berkeley and Los Angeles) have become not only sites of debate on the issue of multiculturalism but also outposts for what David Hollinger has called "postethnic America." As the nation's ethnic mixtures have become increasingly rich and complex as a result of generations of intermarriage, earlier assumptions about distinct ethnic communities of descent have come under pressure from reality and from a new view of identity. Since Americans increasingly do not fit into the standard categories of white, black, Hispanic, Asian, or native, the conceptual frameworks of cultural pluralism and multiculturalism, which rest on assumptions about the homogeneity and integrity of different ethnic groups, have been exposed as inadequate for understanding many Americans' lives and their interaction with each other. As Hollinger has argued, ideas have begun to change along with experience. For some Americans at least, "postethnicity" has emerged as an attractive ideal—even if it remains a reality for only a small minority, of which the self-described "Cablinasian" professional golfer Tiger Woods can perhaps serve as an avatar.

The postethnic ideal incorporates and depends on recognizing the historicity and artificiality of the concepts of race and culture and celebrating the positive value of mingling diverse races and cultures. Although the hard facts of continuing ethnoracial ascription still circumscribe the options open to millions of Americans—especially African Americans—thereby demonstrating the gulf that separates reality from this postethnic ideal, the emergence of the ideal itself is significant. In Hollinger's words, "the postethnic ideal embodies the hope that the United States can develop a democratic and egalitarian culture enabling it to be more than a site for a variety of diasporas and of projects in colonization and conquest."[38] In principle, at least, the legacy of its tortured past could enable the United States to become a cosmopolitan postethnic democracy premised on the virtues of liberalism, not only freedom and equality but also tolerance and generosity.

The ideal of postethnic America suggests an attractive alternative to racism and ethnoracial tribalism. As a culture we have a long way to go before it is achieved, but articulating new ideals of racial or gender equality has always been a precondition to their achievement. The obstacles standing in the way—especially the deep, high, and thick barrier of racism between whites and blacks—should not obscure our vision of the ideal; to the contrary, such obstacles should serve only to clarify how important it is for us to begin work removing them.

I believe we should adopt a similar strategy for renegotiating the boundaries dividing religious from nonreligious Americans. As Hollinger and others such as Kwame Anthony Appiah, Michael Walzer, and Charles Taylor have argued in different ways, it is as important to understand what unites people of all races and cultures within a single polity as it is to understand what divides them.[39] Likewise those of us committed to the virtues of liberalism must find ways to connect what we share across the divide between religion and secularism. Liberalism will not flourish again in the United States if it remains locked in a cul-de-sac of anticlericalism, as it is—and perhaps more important, as it is perceived to be—on many American campuses and in many American journals of opinion.

Since the seventeenth century, the source of most Americans' moral convictions has been, and continues to be, religious belief. Unless liberals can connect their political, social, and economic projects with the spirituality that remains the most vibrant source of personal commitment in contemporary America, liberalism will not soon invigorate American politics. Is that alliance possible?

From Judith Sargent Murray and John Adams to Dorothy Day and Martin Luther King Jr., American reformers have drawn inspiration and ammunition from the resources of their religious traditions. The current divide between secular and religious activists is a recent phenomenon, dating only from the fracturing of American Protestantism into liberal and fundamentalist wings in the 1920s, and its consequences have been disastrous to the American Left. Prior to that fissure Christians often and without difficulty allied themselves with science and with liberal reform movements; both nineteenth-century abolitionism and twentieth-century progressivism relied heavily on Christian denominations for leadership and support. After World War I, however, the ideal of science as a dispassionate quest for objective truth came to be identified with the ideal of secular cosmopolitanism. Consequently secular intellectuals characterized religious faith as an anachronism typical of uneducated, unsophisticated, and unscientific Americans whose credulity also made them vulnerable to fascism abroad and irrational conspiracy theories at home.[40]

For fifty years now leading American philosophers and political theorists have focused their energies on battles fought between the heirs of eighteenth-century Enlightenment rationalism and those fought against their diverse scientific and postmodern critics. All sides in these struggles, intent on mapping (and occupying) the contested terrains of reason, power, and language, ignored the inconvenient fact that over 95 percent of Americans still profess belief in God and that a large majority actively participates in religious activities ranging from daily prayer to weekly or monthly attendance at religious services. Most academic discussions of feminism ignore female piety; participants in the wars over multiculturalism ignore the importance of religious beliefs in shaping the identity of ethnic communities.

Considering, first, the tradition of interaction between communities of religious faith and liberal politics; second, the possibility of a postethnic culture that would draw strength from the multiple voluntary affiliations of its citizens; and third, the debilitating isolation of academic philosophical and political discourse from the conversations and concerns of most Americans, contemporary liberals can find good reasons to build bridges across the chasm separating agnostics and atheists from religious believers. Such bridges cannot be built on dogmatic proclamations of moral certainty, and those—on both sides of the chasm—who insist they have found truth will therefore reject such suggestions as heretical. But in addition to the antifoundationalists, pragmatists, liberals, and communitarians who have been urging us to take a hermeneutic turn as we think about politics, confess our own historicity, and admit the particularity of our own convictions, there are many equally circumspect, chastened theists in American religious history. From Jefferson and Madison to William James and Jane Addams and on to Reinhold Niebuhr and John Courtney Murray, noteworthy believers have emphasized the moral consequences of their faith and muted their theological convictions (or doubts) to make persuasive arguments why their fellow citizens should rethink their selfishness and embrace the virtues of liberalism.

Niebuhr in particular, as Richard Fox has shown, urged Americans to assume an ironic posture quite different from the cynicism that infects contemporary American culture. Niebuhr thought irony could shield people from certainty and help them understand that they cannot always control the consequences of the choices they make. In *The Irony of American History* Niebuhr showed how the nation's past demonstrates not only the importance of moral convictions and devotion to liberal virtues but also the impossibility of guaranteeing that justice will be secured by such efforts.[41] Such an ironic sensibility might enable religious believers who share Niebuhr's self-criticism to join together with antifoundationalists such as Rorty, but that alliance would require tolerance across the divide between religious and secular Americans. Those whose moral commitments spring from nonreligious ideals would have to be willing to make common cause with those whose moral commitments derive from their faith, and vice versa. Some of those moral commitments overlap, others conflict. The likelihood of forging such an alliance seems to me as unclear as the likelihood of achieving a postethnic America, and for some of the same reasons. But if liberalism is to return from the margins of American politics to the central position it held for most of the twentieth century, such an alliance will be necessary. The powerful example of religious dissidents in Eastern Europe, who spearheaded democratic revolutions and recovered traditions suppressed for decades, indicates that such alliances are possible and potentially fruitful. The experience of such nations in recent years indicates that maintaining such alliances is also problematical.

The history of the United States, as I have noted, is filled with such efforts, which might be renewed if we were to adopt the strategy of earlier pragmatic liberals such as William James, his student W. E. B. Du Bois, and Walter Rauschenbusch. James urged his contemporaries to resist "pronouncing on the meaninglessness of forms of existence other than our own." He argued that we should instead "tolerate, respect, and indulge those whom we see harmlessly interested and happy in their own ways, however unintelligible these may be to us. Hands off: neither the whole of truth nor the whole of good is revealed to any single observer, although each observer gains a partial superiority of insight from the peculiar positions in which he stands."[42] Du Bois, examining the problem of the color line that bedeviled his generation as it does our own, argued that its solution "depends on the ability of the representatives of these opposing views to see and appreciate and sympathize with each other's position. . . . Only by a union of intelligence and sympathy across the color-line in this critical period of the Republic shall justice and right triumph."[43] Writing four years after *The Souls of Black Folk* was published, and as if in conversation with Du Bois, Rauschenbusch went a step further: "Individual sympathy and understanding has been our chief reliance in the past for overcoming the differences between the social classes. The feelings and principles implanted by Christianity have been a powerful aid in that direction." Reformers such as Jane Addams and others involved in settlement houses were working to "increase that sympathetic intelligence." But, Rauschenbusch asked, "if this sympathy diminishes by the widening of the social chasm, what hope have we?"[44]

American liberal democrats today must face that question. Just as James, Du Bois, Addams, and Rauschenbusch did, we must encourage and facilitate communication, intelligence, and sympathy across the lines of race, gender, and class. But we must realize that beyond advocating such tolerance and generosity, we must once again address the hard facts of greed and poverty, "the widening of the social chasm," which Americans historically have considered a betrayal of the nation's promise.

Liberal democrats should not surrender to the New Right or conservative Christians the civic resources available to us from egalitarian reform crusades in our nation's past. Nor should we concede to free-market economists and the capitalists they serve the claim that the rising inequality of Americans since 1980 is inevitable. Adam Smith understood—more clearly than those who cite his *Wealth of Nations* without bothering to consult his *Theory of Moral Sentiments*—that inequality is always a moral and political choice that reflects a nation's willingness to allow those with power to dominate those without it. Inequality in the United

States decreased from the 1930s through the 1970s because of deliberate decisions to invest in education and fund social programs through progressive taxation; it has increased as we have abandoned those commitments. Liberal democrats need not concede to a band of social scientists the claim that "rational
choice" is always and everywhere self-serving. The entire history of American
social reform screams out against that claim; in a different key, so does the historicism of leading contemporary social and political theorists and philosophers.
We should invoke the example of those in our tradition who have fought for the
ideals of tolerance, generosity, and democracy. Balancing rights and responsibilities has been a persistent theme in American history; the former have not simply trumped the latter. Clashing ethical principles have until recently resounded
in American public discourse; proclamations of the market's inviolability have
never been permitted to silence the demands of justice.

James Madison wrote passionately to James Monroe in 1786 that he would
"never be convinced" that any policy—no matter how popular—could be considered expedient if it is not just.

> There is no maxim in my opinion which is more liable to be misapplied and which
> therefore needs more elucidation than the current one that the interest of the ma-
> jority is the political standard of right and wrong. Taking the word "interest" as syn-
> onymous with "ultimate happiness," in which sense it is qualified with every neces-
> sary moral ingredient, the proposition is no doubt true. But taking it in the popular
> sense, as referring to immediate augmentation of property and wealth, nothing can
> be more false. In the latter sense, it would be the interest of the majority in every
> community to despoil and enslave the minority.

Such a policy, Madison concluded, "is only reestablishing under another name a
more specious form, force as the measure of right."[45]

From Plato's Thrasymachus to his contemporary heirs, people eager to define
justice as the will of the stronger have sprung up in every culture. But in American history, those who cherish political ideals of tolerance and economic ideals
of equal opportunity have always challenged, admittedly with varying degrees
of success, the maxim that force should be allowed to prevail. Our nation's history makes clear that from Madison's day to our own, and from both sides of the
religious-secular divide, the most potent and effective responses to that maxim
have drawn strength from the "moral ingredient" of American political discourse,
the virtues of liberalism.

NOTES

Chapter 1

For thoughtful responses to this introductory chapter, I am grateful to Richard Wightman Fox, Timothy Peltason, Thomas Bender, Thomas Haskell, David Hollinger, Peter Hansen, and the members of the Brandeis faculty seminar on inequality: Anne Carter, Gary Jefferson, Jacqueline Jones, Sidney Milkis, Robert Reich, and Deborah Stone.

1. Langston Hughes, "Freedom's Plow," *The Collected Poems of Langston Hughes*, ed. Arnold Rampersad and David Roessel (New York: Knopf, 1995), pp. 263–68.

2. James Madison to James Monroe, October 5, 1786, in *The Papers of James Madison*, ed. William T. Hutchinson et al. (Chicago and Charlottesville: University of Chicago Press and University Press of Virginia, 1962–), 9: 140–141; quoted in the most detailed and incisive study of Madison's ideas and political activity during the crucial years from 1780–1792, Lance Banning, *The Sacred Fire of Liberty: James Madison and the Founding of the Federal Republic* (Ithaca, N.Y.: Cornell University Press, 1995), p. 72.

3. This apt phrase comes from the editors' introduction to a fine collection of essays illustrating the revival of virtue ethics in Anglo-American philosophy, *Virtue Ethics*, ed. Roger Crisp and Michael Slote (Oxford: Oxford University Press, 1997), p. 18.

4. William James, "The Moral Philosopher and the Moral Life," in *The Will to Believe and Other Essays in Popular Philosophy*, ed. Edward H. Madden, in *The Works of William James*, ed. Frederick H. Burkhardt et al. (1897; Cambridge: Harvard University Press, 1979), p. 158. See also Henry Sidgwick, *The Methods of Ethics*, 7th edition (1907; Indianapolis: Hackett, 1981); and the discussion of Sidgwick's role as mediator rather than classical exponent of utilitarianism, and his influence on James and Dewey, in James T. Kloppenberg, *Uncertain Victory: Social Democracy and Progressivism in European and American Thought, 1870–1920* (New York: Oxford University Press, 1986), pp. 115–144.

5. The most persuasive of these has been William A. Galston. See William A. Galston, *Liberal Purposes: Goods, Virtues, and Diversity in the Liberal State* (Cambridge: Cambridge University Press, 1991); and his contributions to two instructive collections of essays, which contain numerous thoughtful contributions to the debate over virtue and liberalism: *Virtue*, ed. John W. Chapman and William A. Galston (New York: New York University Press, 1992); and *Seedbeds of Virtue: Sources of Competence, Character, and*

179

Citizenship in American Society, ed. Mary Ann Glendon and David Blankenhorn (Lanham, Md.: Madison Books, 1995).

6. William James, "The Moral Philosopher and the Moral Life," in *The Will to Believe and Other Essays in Popular Philosophy*, ed. Edward H. Madden, in *The Works of William James*, ed. Frederick H. Burkhardt et al. (1897; Cambridge: Harvard University Press, 1979), p. 154. For a more detailed treatment of this tragic sensibility, see also the discussion of the contrast between Max Weber and John Dewey in James T. Kloppenberg, "Democracy and Disenchantment: From Weber and Dewey to Habermas and Rorty" in *Modernist Impulses in the Human Sciences*, ed. Dorothy Ross (Baltimore: Johns Hopkins University Press, 1994), pp. 69–90, reprinted as chapter 6 in this volume.

7. See William J. Bennett, ed., *The Book of Virtues: A Treasury of Great Moral Stories* (New York: Simon and Schuster, 1993); and William J. Bennett, ed., *The Moral Compass: Stories for a Life's Journey* (New York: Simon and Schuster, 1995); and compare Michael Lerner, *The Politics of Meaning: Restoring Hope and Possibility in an Age of Cynicism* (Reading, Mass.: Addison-Wesley, 1996). For more irreverent views, compare Jon Katz, *Virtuous Reality: How America Surrendered Its Discussion of Moral Values to Opportunists, Nitwits, and Blockheads Like William Bennett* (New York: Random House, 1997); and the diverse definitions of virtue offered by contemporary Americans ranging from Oliver North and Candice Bergen to Howard Stern and Norma Kamali in "Who's Winning the Culture Wars?" *George*, April/May 1996, pp. 102–143.

8. James Madison to Archibald Stuart, October 30, 1787, in *The Papers of James Madison*, ed. William T. Hutchinson et al. (Chicago and Charlottesville: University of Chicago Press and University Press of Virginia, 1962–), 10: 232; quoted in Banning, *The Sacred Fire of Liberty*, pp. 232, 477n. 126.

9. Louis Hartz, *The Liberal Tradition in America* (New York: Harcourt, Brace and World, 1955). Despite the availability of evidence to demonstrate, and the willingness of specialists to concede, that practically every one of Hartz's specific claims about American history has been disproved by recent scholarship showing the depth and persistence of basic conflicts in American society and politics, the reputation of this book somehow endures. To cite but a single recent example, the political theorist Bob Pepperman Taylor, in his thoughtful study *America's Bachelor Uncle: Thoreau and the American Polity* (Lawrence: University of Kansas Press, 1996), p. ix, describes Hartz's *Liberal Tradition* as "the greatest book ever written about the American political tradition," a not uncommon assessment. For a more detailed examination of the shortcomings of Hartz's analysis of American history, see James T. Kloppenberg, "In Retrospect: Louis Hartz and *The Liberal Tradition in America*," *Reviews in American History*, forthcoming.

10. See Reinhold Niebuhr's remarks in "Transcript of Proceedings," State Department Policy Planning Staff Meeting, November 20, 1950, pp. 2, 40; National Archives, Washington D.C., quoted in Richard Wightman Fox, *Reinhold Niebuhr: A Biography*, with a new introduction and afterword (Ithaca, N.Y.: Cornell University Press, 1996), p. 357.

11. For "A Model of Christian Charity," Winthrop's address to the Puritans sailing to Massachusetts in 1630, see *Winthrop Papers*, II (Boston: Massachusetts Historical Society, 1931), pp. 282–295; reprinted in Edmund Morgan, ed., *Puritan Political Ideas, 1558–1794* (Indianapolis: Bobbs-Merrill, 1965), pp. 75–93. See also the fine discussion of the immediate context of Winthrop's address in Jane Kamensky, *Governing the Tongue: The Politics of Speech in Early New England* (New York: Oxford University Press, 1997), pp. 43–70; and more generally, Stephen Foster, *The Long Argument: English Puritanism and the Shaping of New England Culture, 1570–1700* (Chapel Hill: University of North Carolina Press, 1991).

12. Among the many books devoted to the conceptual relation between freedom and

equality in liberal political theory, see especially the brilliant study by Joseph Raz, *The Morality of Freedom* (Oxford: Oxford University Press, 1986); and Steven Lukes, "Equality and Liberty: Must They Conflict?" in Lukes, *Moral Conflict and Politics* (Oxford: Oxford University Press, 1991).

13. Isaiah Berlin, "Two Concepts of Liberty," in Berlin, *Four Essays on Liberty* (Oxford: Oxford University Press, 1969), pp. 118–172. Although the distinction between negative and positive liberty seems to me untenable conceptually, I want to argue here only that most of the American thinkers discussed in this book could not be fitted into Berlin's framework without distorting their ideas beyond recognition. During the last year of his life, Berlin was asked by Jack Rakove what he thought about Jefferson and Madison, to which Berlin replied, regretfully, that he had never read them. See Jack N. Rakove, "Re: Isaiah Berlin," (H-OEAHC@NET.MSU.EDU, November 11, 1997). On the compatibility between liberalism and government regulation of the economy, see Stephen Holmes, *Passions and Constraint: On the Theory of Liberal Democracy* (Chicago: University of Chicago Press, 1995); and Ira Katznelson, *Liberalism's Crooked Circle: Letters to Adam Michnik* (Princeton: Princeton University Press, 1996).

14. Winthrop, "A Model of Christian Charity," pp. 75–93. Stephen Innes, in his incisive and informative study *Creating the Commonwealth: The Economic Culture of Puritan New England* (New York: Norton, 1995), emphasizes the Puritans' intense commitments to religious ideals, economic activity, and self-government, which combined to prohibit "cruelty and unmercifulness to the poor" (p. 309). In his conclusion Innes writes, "The same religious precepts and civil institutions that systematized and amplified the virtues likely to produce commercial success checked their free play on behalf of the common good" (p. 312).

In *Commerce and Culture: The Maritime Communities of Colonial Massachusetts* (New York: Norton, 1984), Christine Heyrman makes a similar point about early settlers in the towns of Marblehead and Gloucester: "[T]he drive for profit did not dominate social relationships to redefine attitudes toward governing economic behavior. Forbearance toward local debtors, a cautious approach to investment, limited aspirations for expansion and innovation, and a concern for communal welfare characterized the outlook of all participants in local commerce, even major merchants and entrepreneurs" (p. 19).

Important as understanding that dynamic is, exaggerating its importance would be a mistake. Christian principles of mercy clearly mattered less in the murderously cruel slave economies that developed in the southern colonies. Nevertheless, casting ruthless Virginian planters in the role of prototypical "Americans" is no more accurate than it would be to so characterize the most pious Puritans. I want only to emphasize that addressing the problem of poverty, and expressing dissatisfaction with the exercise of freedom in economic activity unregulated by principles of "liberallity," is an authentic American tradition that dates back to the early seventeenth century.

15. On these issues, see the brilliant work of William J. Novak, *The People's Welfare: Law and Regulation in Nineteenth-Century America* (Chapel Hill: University of North Carolina Press, 1996), which uncovers a previously unknown universe of "by-laws, ordinances, statutes, and common law restrictions regulating nearly every aspect of early American economy and society, from Sunday observance to the carting of offal." As Novak accurately observes, these regulations "explode tenacious myths about nineteenth-century government (or its absence) and demonstrate the pervasiveness of regulation in early American versions of the good society" (p. 1). For my understanding of antebellum America, I am deeply indebted to Novak's outstanding scholarship.

16. For a dazzling account of the diverse sources of abolitionist sentiment and how they developed, see Elizabeth B. Clark, " 'The Sacred Rights of the Weak': Pain, Sympa-

thy, and the Culture of Individual Rights in Antebellum America," *Journal of American History* 82 (September 1995): 463–493. For the provocative debates between David Brion Davis, Thomas L. Haskell, and John Ashworth concerning the relation between antislavery sentiment and capitalism, see Thomas J. Bender, ed., *The Antislavery Debate: Capitalism and Abolitionism as a Problem in Historical Interpretation* (Berkeley: University of California Press, 1992).

J. David Greenstone, in *The Lincoln Persuasion: Remaking American Liberalism* (Princeton: Princeton University Press, 1993), argues for the "bipolarity" of American political thought, a division between thinkers concerned principally with individuals' self-interest and those devoted to more perfectionist ideals. Lincoln's genius, in Greenstone's view, was his ability to combine the two traditions. Greenstone argues persuasively that "Lincoln began to move away from a primary concern with economic modernization toward a political humanitarianism in which he joined instrumental calculation with a perfectionist ethic, and political obligation with moral duty." Lincoln's response to the crisis of the 1850s, then to the Civil War, was "a new statement of the Puritans' Augustinian piety. Gripped by a sense of responsibility for the nation's suffering, Lincoln articulated the connection between his perfectionist ethic and the final inexplicable character of human affairs. In his Second Inaugural, in an eloquent invocation of God's ineluctable judgments, as well as in his repeated calls for days of national fasting, Lincoln connected the duties of citizenship with moral dedication, in language that both recalled and extended Puritan rhetoric" (p. 283).

17. See Robert Shalhope, *Bennington and the Green Mountain Boys: The Emergence of Liberal Democracy in Vermont, 1760–1850* (Baltimore: Johns Hopkins University Press, 1996); Christopher Lasch, *The True and Only Heaven: Progress and Its Critics* (New York: Norton, 1991); and Brad J. Clarke, "Natural Rights Republicanism: Anti-Monopolism from the Jeffersonians through the Populists," unpublished Ph.D. dissertation, Brandeis University, 1996.

18. W. E. B. Du Bois, *The Souls of Black Folk*, in Du Bois, *Writings*, ed. Nathan Huggins (New York: Library of America, 1986), p. 491. For an incisive treatment of the cultural, ethical, political, and economic dimensions in Du Bois's analysis of race in *The Souls of Black* Folk and afterward, see Thomas Holt, "The Political Uses of Alienation," *American Quarterly* 42 (1990): 301–323. See also Arnold Rampersad, *The Art and Imagination of W. E. B. Du Bois* (1976; New York: Schocken Books, 1990), pp. 68–90; David Levering Lewis, *W. E. B. Du Bois: Biography of a Race, 1869–1919* (New York: Henry Holt, 1993), pp. 265–286. On the role of religion in the civil rights movement, see Richard H. King, *Civil Rights and the Idea of Freedom* (New York: Oxford University Press, 1992); Taylor Branch, *Parting the Waters: America in the King Years, 1954–1963* (New York: Simon and Schuster, 1988); and James T. Kloppenberg, "Religion and Politics in American Thought Since the Enlightenment," in *Knowledge and Belief in America*, ed. William M. Shea and Peter A. Huff (New York: Cambridge University Press, 1995), reprinted as chapter 3 in this volume. On the crippling effects of racial, ethnic, gender, and religious characteristics ascribed to some Americans by others seeking—often successfully—to deny their status as citizens, see Rogers M. Smith, "Beyond Tocqueville, Myrdal, and Hartz: The Multiple Traditions in America," *American Political Science Review* 87 (1993): 549–566; and Rogers M. Smith, *Civic Ideals: Conflicting Visions of Citizenship in American Public Law* (New Haven: Yale University Press, 1997).

19. See Jill Quadagno, *The Color of Welfare: How Racism Undermined the War on Poverty* (New York: Oxford University Press, 1994); Jacqueline Jones, *The Dispossessed: America's Underclasses from the Civil War to the Present* (New York: Basic Books, 1992); Margaret Weir, Ann Shola Orloff, and Theda Skocpol, eds., *The Politics of Social Policy*

in the United States (Princeton: Princeton University Press, 1988); Steve Fraser and Gary Gerstle, eds., *The Rise and Fall of the New Deal Order, 1930–1980* (Princeton: Princeton University Press, 1989).

20. See E. J. Dionne Jr., *Why Americans Hate Politics* (New York: Touchstone, 1991); Kathleen Hall Jamieson, *Packaging the Presidency: A History and Criticism of Presidential Campaign Advertising*, 2nd ed. (New York: Oxford University Press, 1992); Christopher Lasch, *The Revolt of the Elites and the Betrayal of Democracy* (New York: Norton, 1995); and Jeffrey C. Goldfarb, *The Cynical Society: The Culture of Politics and the Politics of Culture* (Chicago: University of Chicago Press, 1991).

21. For a brilliant characterization of Reagan's historical significance and his legacy for the Republican Party, see Garry Wills, "It's His Party," *New York Times Sunday Magazine*, August 11, 1996, pp. 29–37, 55–59. For a surprisingly uncynical perspective on government from an experienced public servant who spent nine years working in two spots unlikely to be associated with the phrase "public virtue"—Cook County, Illinois, and the FBI—and who found in his personal experience and in his study of the U.S. Congress evidence of efforts to identify and advance the common good, see Joseph M. Bessette, *The Mild Voice of Reason: Deliberative Democracy and American National Government* (Chicago: University of Chicago Press, 1996).

22. Adam Michnik, "Gray is Beautiful: Thoughts on Democracy in Central Europe," *Dissent*, Spring 1997, pp. 14–18.

23. Ralph Ellison, *Invisible Man* (1952; New York: Vintage, 1972), pp. 559–568.

Chapter 2

For comments offered on an earlier version of this essay, I am grateful to Joyce Appleby, Lance Banning, Hendrik Hartog, James Henretta, James Hoopes, Richard L. McCormick, Drew McCoy, J. R. Pole, David Thelen, and Gordon Wood. They bear a share of the responsibility for whatever virtues the essay may have; I take credit for any vices that remain.

1. Dante Alighieri, *The Divine Comedy*, Cantica 1: *Hell (L'Inferno)*, trans. Dorothy L. Sayers (Harmondsworth: Penguin, 1949), Canto XXVIII, pp. 246–250; John Patrick Diggins, "Comrades and Citizens: New Mythologies in American Historiography," *American Historical Review* 90 (June 1985): 614–638; Paul Conkin, "Comment," ibid., pp. 639–643; John Patrick Diggins, "Reply," ibid., pp. 644–649; Lance Banning, "Jeffersonian Ideology Revisited: Liberal and Classical Ideas in the New American Republic," *William and Mary Quarterly* 43 (January 1986): 3–19; Joyce Appleby, "Republicanism in Old and New Contexts," ibid., pp. 20–34. See also the essays collected in the special issue "Republicanism in the History and Historiography of the United States," ed. Joyce Appleby, *American Quarterly* 37 (Fall 1985): 461–598.

2. Louis Hartz, *The Liberal Tradition in America: An Interpretation of American Political Thought since the Revolution* (New York: Harcourt, Brace and World, 1955); Daniel Boorstin, *The Genius of American Politics* (Chicago: University of Chicago Press, 1953); Bernard Bailyn, *The Ideological Origins of the American Revolution* (Cambridge: Harvard University Press, 1967); Gordon Wood, *The Creation of the American Republic, 1776–1787* (Chapel Hill: University of North Carolina Press, 1969); Henry F. May, *The Enlightenment in America* (New York: Oxford University Press, 1976); Morton White, *The Philosophy of the American Revolution* (New York: Oxford University Press, 1978); Garry Wills, *Inventing America: Jefferson's Declaration of Independence* (Garden City: Doubleday, 1978); D. H. Meyer, *The Democratic Enlightenment* (New York: Putnam, 1976); the essays collected in the special issue "An American Enlightenment," Joseph Ellis, ed., *American Quarterly* 28 (Summer 1976): 147–293; J. G. A. Pocock, *The Machiavellian*

Moment: Florentine Political Thought and the Atlantic Republican Tradition (Princeton: Princeton University Press, 1975); J. G. A. Pocock, *Virtue, Commerce, and History* (Cambridge: Cambridge University Press, 1985), see esp. pp. 48, 79, for particularly sharp formulations of this argument; and cf. John Patrick Diggins, *The Lost Soul of American Politics: Virtue, Self-Interest, and the Foundations of Liberalism* (New York: Basic Books, 1984), see esp. pp. 3–145, 345.

3. Recent discussions include Richard J. Bernstein, *Beyond Objectivism and Relativism: Science, Hermeneutics and Praxis* (Philadelphia: University of Pennsylvania Press, 1983); Richard Rorty, J. B. Schneewind, and Quentin Skinner, eds., *Philosophy in History* (Cambridge: Cambridge University Press, 1984); Quentin Skinner, ed., *The Return of Grand Theory in the Human Sciences* (Cambridge: Cambridge University Press, 1985); Pocock, *Virtue, Commerce, and History*, pp. 1–34; James A. Henretta, "Social History As Lived and Written," *American Historical Review* 84 (December 1979): 1293–1322. For a critique of such ideas, see John Patrick Diggins, "The Oyster and the Pearl: The Problem of Contextualism in Intellectual History," *History and Theory* 23 (1984): 151–169; and esp. Diggins, *Lost Soul of American Politics*, pp. 347–365. Two collections of essays that not only discuss methodology but also provide splendid examples of how the methodology works are Dominick LaCapra and Steven L. Kaplan, eds., *Modern European Intellectual History: Reappraisals and New Perspectives* (Ithaca, N.Y.: Cornell University Press, 1982); and David A. Hollinger, *In the American Province: Studies in the History and Historiography of Ideas* (Bloomington: Indiana University Press, 1985). For more detailed discussion of these issues, see James T. Kloppenberg, "Deconstruction and Hermeneutics as Strategies for Intellectual History: The Recent Work of Dominick LaCapra and David Hollinger," *Intellectual History Newsletter* 9 (April 1987): 3–22.

4. Norman Fiering, *Moral Philosophy at Seventeenth-Century Harvard: A Discipline in Transition* (Chapel Hill: University of North Carolina Press, 1981); Norman Fiering, *Jonathan Edwards's Moral Thought and Its British Context* (Chapel Hill: University of North Carolina Press, 1981). See also Bruce Kuklick, *Churchmen and Philosophers: From Jonathan Edwards to John Dewey* (New Haven: Yale University Press, 1985), pp. 5–111; and Elizabeth Flower and Murray G. Murphey, *A History of Philosophy in America*, 2 vols. (New York: Capricorn, 1977), I: 3–361.

5. For emphasis on the "paganism" of the Enlightenment, see Peter Gay, *The Enlightenment: An Interpretation*, 2 vols. (New York: Knopf, 1966). On the American side, see esp. May, *Enlightenment in America*. Recent discussions of the Enlightenment emphasizing its multidimensionality include Lester Crocker, "Interpreting the Enlightenment: A Political Approach," *Journal of the History of Ideas* 46 (April-June 1985): 211–230; and Roy Porter and Mikulas Teich, eds., *The Enlightenment in National Context* (Cambridge: Cambridge University Press, 1981).

For a seminal discussion of Puritanism and politics, see Perry Miller, *Errand into the Wilderness* (Cambridge: Belknap Press of Harvard University Press, 1956), pp. 16–47; see esp. p. 47. The overly ambitious claims of Alan Heimert, *Religion and the American Mind: From the Great Awakening to the Revolution* (Cambridge: Harvard University Press, 1966), have been moderated, and the role of religion carefully assessed, in several recent studies. See Richard L. Bushman, *From Puritan to Yankee: Character and the Social Order in Connecticut, 1690–1765* (Cambridge: Harvard University Press, 1967); William G. McLoughlin, "The Role of Religion in the Revolution: Liberty of Conscience and Cultural Cohesion in the New Nation," in *Essays on the American Revolution*, ed. Stephen G. Kurtz and James H. Hutson (Chapel Hill: University of North Carolina Press, 1973), pp. 197–255; William G. McLoughlin, *Revivals, Awakenings, and Reform: An Essay on Revolution and Social Change in America, 1607–1977* (Chicago: University of Chicago Press, 1978), pp. 24–97; Nathan O. Hatch, *The Sacred Cause of Liberty: Republican Thought and the Millenium in Revolutionary New England* (New Haven: Yale University Press, 1977); Patricia U. Bonomi, "'A Just Opposition': The Great Awakening as a Radical Model," in *The Origins of Anglo-American Radicalism*, ed. Margaret Jacob and James Jacob (London: George Allen and Unwin, 1984), pp. 243–256; Rhys Isaac, "Radicalised Religion and Changing Lifestyles: Virginia in the Period of the American Revolution," ibid., pp. 257–267; and David D. Hall, "Religion and Society: Problems and Reconsiderations," in *Colonial British America: Essays in the New History of the Early Modern Era*, ed. Jack P. Greene and J. R. Pole (Baltimore: Johns Hopkins University Press, 1984), pp. 317–344. On declension and the jeremiad, cf. Gene Wise, "Implicit Irony in Perry Miller's New England Mind," *Journal of the History of Ideas* 29 (October-December 1968): 579–600; Robert G. Pope, "New England versus the New England Mind: The Myth of Declension," *Journal of Social History* 3 (Winter 1969–70): 95–108; and Sacvan Bercovitch, *The American Jeremiad* (Madison: University of Wisconsin Press, 1978).

6. Caroline Robbins, *The Eighteenth-Century Commonwealthman: Studies in the Transmission, Development and Circumstances of English Liberal Thought from the Restoration of Charles II until the War with the Thirteen Colonies* (Cambridge: Harvard University Press, 1959); Bailyn, *Ideological Origins*; Bernard Bailyn, ed., *Pamphlets of the American Revolution, 1750–1776* (Cambridge: Harvard University Press, 1965); Wood, *Creation*; Robert E. Shalhope, "Toward a Republican Synthesis: The Emergence of an Understanding of Republicanism in American Historiography," *William and Mary Quarterly* 29 (January 1972): 49–80; Pocock, *Machiavellian Moment*; and J. G. A. Pocock, "*The Machiavellian Moment* Revisited: A Study in History and Ideology," *Journal of Modern History* 53 (March 1981): 49–72.

7. A recent study of Machiavelli that challenges Pocock's view is Mark Hulliung, *Citizen Machiavelli* (Princeton: Princeton University Press, 1983). See also Robert Shackleton, *Montesquieu: A Critical Biography* (Oxford: Oxford University Press, 1961); Mark Hulliung, *Montesquieu and the Old Regime* (Berkeley: University of California Press, 1976); Marvin Meyers, ed., *The Mind of the Founder: Sources of the Political Thought of James Madison* (Hanover: University Press of New England, 1981), pp. xi–xli; John R. Howe Jr., *The Changing Political Thought of John Adams* (Princeton: Princeton University Press, 1966); and Alasdair MacIntyre, *After Virtue* (Notre Dame: University of Notre Dame Press, 1981), pp. 210–221.

8. C. B. Macpherson, *The Political Theory of Possessive Individualism* (Oxford: Oxford University Press, 1962); Joyce Appleby, "Ideology and Theory: The Tension between Political and Economic Liberalism in Seventeenth-Century England," *American Historical Review* 81 (June 1976): 512, 515. For an especially pointed formulation of her critique of Pocock, see Joyce Appleby, "Response to J. G. A. Pocock," *Intellectual History Newsletter* 4 (Spring 1982): 20–22.

9. Locke quoted in John Dunn, *Rethinking Modern Political Theory: Essays, 1979–83* (Cambridge: Cambridge University Press, 1985), 194 n. 43. Cf. this passage: "In January 1698, in a letter to his friend William Molyneux, Locke summed up the convictions of a lifetime: 'If I could think that discourses and arguments to the understanding were like the several sorts of cates [foodstuffs] to different palates and stomachs, some nauseous and destructive to one, which are pleasant and restorative to another; I should no more think of books and study, and should think my time better imploy'd at push-pin than reading or writing. But I am convinc'd of the contrary: I know there is truth opposite to falsehood, that it may be found if people will, and is worth the seeking, and is not only the most valuable, but the pleasantest thing in the world'"; John Dunn, *Locke* (Oxford: Oxford University Press, 1984), p. 87. See also John Dunn, *The Political Thought*

of John Locke: An Historical Account of the "Two Treatises of Government" (Cambridge: Cambridge University Press, 1969). In his most recent work Dunn has continued to emphasize the necessity of understanding Locke's conception of rights in the context of his religious belief. In John Dunn, "What is Living and What is Dead in the Political Theory of John Locke?" paper delivered in Cambridge, Mass., in 1986 (in the possession of James T. Kloppenberg), pp. 10–11, he wrote, "For Locke all the rights human beings have (and which they certainly do possess prior to and independently of all human political authority) derive from, depend upon and are rigidly constrained by a framework of objective duty: God's requirements for human agents. Within this setting, but as he supposed only within this setting, the claims of right are indeed decisive and all human beings have a duty to observe them and to enforce them." Dunn's interpretation relies in important respects on Peter Laslett's brilliant essay on Locke: Peter Laslett, introduction, in John Locke, *Two Treatises of Government*, ed. Peter Laslett (Cambridge: Cambridge University Press, 1960), pp. 15–168; this interpretation has been extended in James Tully, *A Discourse on Property: John Locke and His Adversaries* (Cambridge: Cambridge University Press, 1980). Morton White incorporated this view of Locke in his analysis of Jefferson; see White, *Philosophy of the American Revolution*, pp. 57–60. The possibility that Locke himself provided the best arsenal of arguments against C. B. Macpherson's critique is explored in Patrick Riley, *Will and Political Legitimacy: A Critical Exposition of Social Contract Theory in Hobbes, Locke, Rousseau, Kant, and Hegel* (Cambridge: Harvard University Press, 1982), pp. 61–97.

10. David Hume, *An Enquiry concerning the Principles of Morals* (La Salle: Open Court, 1938), p. 67; see also the discussion of this passage in Gertrude Himmelfarb, *The Idea of Poverty: England in the Early Industrial Age* (New York: Knopf, 1984), p. 35. The critical literature on the Scottish moral philosophers is vast and growing rapidly. A thoughtful review of recent work is Nicholas Phillipson, "The Scottish Enlightenment," in *The Enlightenment in National Context*, ed. Porter and Reich, pp. 19–40. An early exploration of the similarities between Scotland and the American colonies was John Clive and Bernard Bailyn, "England's Cultural Provinces: Scotland and America," *William and Mary Quarterly* 11 (April 1954): 200–213; more extensive investigations of Scottish ideas in America include May, *Enlightenment in America*; White, *Philosophy of the American Revolution*; Wills, *Inventing America*; D. H. Meyer, *The Instructed Conscience: The Shaping of the American National Ethic* (Philadelphia: University of Pennsylvania Press, 1972); Meyer, *Democratic Enlightenment*; and Terence Martin, *The Instructed Vision: Scottish Common Sense Philosophy and the Origins of American Fiction* (Bloomington: Indiana University Press, 1961). For a balanced assessment of the impact of Scottish common sense on American thought, see J. R. Pole, "Enlightenment and the Politics of American Nature," in *The Enlightenment in National Context*, ed. Porter and Teich, p. 209.

11. Adam Smith, *The Theory of Moral Sentiments* (Indianapolis: Bobbs-Merrill, 1969), p. 47. Cf. the following passage: "There can be no proper motive for hurting our neighbor, there can be no incitement to do evil to another which mankind will go along with, except just indignation for evil which that other has done to us. To disturb his happiness merely because it stands in the way of our own, to take from him what is of real use to him merely because it may be of equal or of more use to us, or to indulge, in this manner, at the expense of other people, the natural preference which every man has for his own happiness above that of other people, is what no impartial spectator can go along with"; ibid., p. 160. For a splendid discussion of Smith's attempt to integrate his political economy with the philosophy of moral sense he derived from his mentor Francis Hutcheson, who had tried to unify the competing strands of natural law represented by Grotius's radical individualism and Pufendorf's responsible communitarianism, see Richard Teichgraeber III,

'Free Trade' and Moral Philosophy: Rethinking the Sources of Adam Smith's "Wealth of Nations" (Durham, N.C.: Duke University Press, 1986); and introduction, in Adam Smith, *An Inquiry into the Nature and Causes of the Wealth of Nations*, ed. Richard Teichgraeber III (New York: Modern Library, 1985), pp. ix–xlviii. Teichgraeber also emphasizes Smith's debts to the seventeenth-century British economists who were impatient both with mercantilism and with what E. P. Thompson and others have called the tradition of "moral economy." See E. P. Thompson, "The Moral Economy of the Crowd in Eighteenth-Century England," *Past and Present* 50 (February 1971): 76–136. Cf. the following passage: "For Smith political economy was not an end in itself but a means to an end, that end being the wealth and well being, moral and material, of the 'people,' of whom the 'laboring poor' were the largest part. And the poor themselves had a moral status in that economy—not the special moral status they enjoyed in a fixed, hierarchic order, but that which adhered to them as individuals in a free society sharing a common human, which is to say, moral, nature"; Himmelfarb, *Idea of Poverty*, p. 63. This interpretation of Adam Smith, first advanced by Jacob Viner in the 1920s, has since become less revisionist than orthodox. See Jacob Viner, "Adam Smith and Laissez-Faire," in *The Long View and the Short: Studies in Economic Theory and Policy* (Glencoe, Ill.: Free Press, 1958), pp. 213–245. An influential presentation of this view is Donald Winch, *Adam Smith's Politics: An Essay in Historiographic Revision* (Cambridge: Cambridge University Press, 1978); see also the range of perspectives in Istvan Hont and Michael Ignatieff, eds., *Wealth and Virtue: The Shaping of Political Economy in the Scottish Enlightenment* (Cambridge: Cambridge University Press, 1983). On the roots of liberal political economy in the tradition of natural law, see Richard Tuck, *Natural Rights Theories: Their Origin and Development* (Cambridge: Cambridge University Press, 1979).

12. See Dunn, *Locke*, pp. 36–44, for a brief discussion of this problem, and Tully, *Discourse on Property*, for a more extended treatment. On Adam Smith and the consequences of political economy, cf. Istvan Hont and Michael Ignatieff, "Needs and Justice in the Wealth of Nations: An Introductory Essay," in *Wealth and Virtue*, ed. Hont and Ignatieff, pp. 1–44; and Nicholas Phillipson, "Adam Smith as Civic Moralist," ibid., pp. 179–202. Max Weber's most straightforward discussion of the varieties of rational action appears in Max Weber, *Economy and Society*, eds. Guenther Roth and Claus Wittich, trans. Ephraim Fischoll et al., 2 vols. (Berkeley: University of California Press, 1978), I: 24–26.

13. Two collections of essays provide extremely helpful overviews of recent work in American colonial social history, and both are transatlantic in focus. The phrase "inadvertent pluralism" appears in an essay in the first collection; see Joyce Appleby, James Jacob, and Margaret Jacob, "Introduction," in *Origins of Anglo-American Radicalism*, ed. Jacob and Jacob, p. 11. The other collection is *Colonial British America*, ed. Greene and Pole. Comparative analyses of Europe and America have transformed the study of colonial intellectual life. Discussions of recent work reflecting that influence include Daniel Walker Howe, "European Sources of Political Ideas in Jeffersonian America," *Reviews in American History* 10 (December 1982): 28–44; Robert E. Shalhope, "Republicanism and Early American Historiography," *William and Mary Quarterly* 39 (April 1982): 334–356; and Pole, "Enlightenment and the Politics of American Nature," pp. 192–214.

14. See John Dunn, "The Politics of Locke in England and America in the Eighteenth Century," in *John Locke: Problems and Perspectives*, ed. John W. Yolton (Cambridge: Cambridge University Press, 1969), pp. 45–80; May, *Enlightenment in America*, pp. 3–101, 153–304; White, *Philosophy of the American Revolution*; and Wills, *Inventing America*.

15. Joyce Appleby, "The Social Origins of American Revolutionary Ideology," *Journal of American History* 64 (March 1978): 939–958, esp. pp. 955–956. See also Joyce Appleby, "Liberalism and the American Revolution," *New England Quarterly* 49 (March

1976): 3–26; Joyce Appleby, "What Is Still American in the Political Philosophy of Thomas Jefferson?" *William and Mary Quarterly* 39 (April 1982): 287–304; Joyce Appleby, "Commercial Farming and the 'Agrarian Myth' in the Early Republic," *Journal of American History* 68 (March 1982): 833–849; Joyce Appleby, "The Radical *Double-Entendre* in the Right to Self-Government," in *Origins of Anglo-American Radicalism*, ed. Jacob and Jacob, pp. 275–283; and Joyce Appleby, *Capitalism and a New Social Order: The Republican Vision of the 1790s* (New York: New York University Press, 1984).

16. Thomas Jefferson, *Writings*, ed. Merrill D. Peterson (New York: Library of America, 1984), pp. 1335–1339. Cf. the similar discussion in Thomas Paine, *The Rights of Man*, ed. Eric Foner (New York: Penguin, 1984), p. 163. On Jefferson, see John P. Diggins, "Slavery, Race, and Equality: Jefferson and the Pathos of the Enlightenment," *American Quarterly* 28 (Summer 1976): 206–228; and Pole, "Enlightenment and the Politics of American Nature," pp. 200–203. On the anti-utilitarian thrust of Jefferson's ethics, see White, *Philosophy of the American Revolution*, pp. 97–141. His account is more persuasive than that of Adrienne Koch, *The Philosophy of Thomas Jefferson* (New York: Columbia University Press, 1943), pp. 15–43.

17. John E. Crowley, *"This Sheba, Self": The Conceptualization of Economic Life in Eighteenth-Century America* (Baltimore: John Hopkins University Press, 1974), p. 84. For evidence of the diverse ideas animating Americans from different backgrounds during the Revolution, see Alfred E. Young, ed., *The American Revolution: Explorations in the History of American Radicalism* (DeKalb, Ill.: Northern Illinois University Press, 1976); Eric Foner, *Tom Paine and Revolutionary America* (New York: Oxford University Press, 1976); and Gary B. Nash, "Artisans and Politics in Eighteenth-Century Philadelphia," in *Origins of Anglo-American Radicalism*, ed. Jacob and Jacob, pp. 162–182. The contrast between these ideas and the interpretation Appleby has advanced in her essays on the Revolution is discussed by Shalhope, "Republicanism and Early American Historiography," p. 343 n. 24. Although it finally dissolves into a polemical division of the American political world between heroic "nationalists" and dastardly "ideologues," there is a wealth of valuable material, particularly on American and English law, in Forrest McDonald, *Novus Ordo Seclorum: The Intellectual Origins of the Constitution* (Lawrence: University Press of Kansas, 1985).

18. The concept of autonomy, most carefully formulated by Immanuel Kant but also crucial for John Locke and Jean Jacques Rousseau, filtered into American thought largely through the influence of Francis Hutcheson and Thomas Reid, the Scottish philosophers whose ideas most nearly resembled Kant's.

19. J. G. A. Pocock, "Radical Criticisms of the Whig Order in the Age between Revolutions," in *Origins of Anglo-American Radicalism*, ed. Jacob and Jacob, p. 44; Robert R. Palmer, *The World of the French Revolution* (New York: Harper and Row, 1971), pp. 269–270; J. R. Pole, *Political Representation in England and the Origins of the American Republic* (London: Macmillan, 1966), pp. 503–539; Wood, *Creation*, pp. 344–389, 605–615; and McDonald, *Novus Ordo Seclorum*, pp. 260, 280–293. For the contention that the idea of popular sovereignty can be traced to Locke's writings, see Julian Franklin, *John Locke and the Theory of Sovereignty* (Cambridge: Cambridge University Press, 1978), pp. 97, 104, 123–126.

20. Michael Kammen, *Deputyes & Libertyes: The Origins of Representative Government in Colonial America* (New York: Knopf, 1969); Timothy H. Breen, *The Character of the Good Ruler: Puritan Political Ideas in New England, 1630–1730* (New Haven: Yale University Press, 1970); John M. Murrin, "Political Development," in *Colonial British America*, ed. Greene and Pole, pp. 439–440; Edmund S. Morgan, *American Slavery, American Freedom: The Ordeal of Colonial Virginia* (New York: Norton, 1975); J. R. Pole,

Paths to the American Past (New York: Oxford University Press, 1979), pp. 55–74; Jack P. Greene, *The Quest for Power: The Lower Houses of Assembly in the Southern Royal Colonies, 1689–1776* (Chapel Hill: University of North Carolina Press, 1963); Jack P. Greene, "An Uneasy Connection: An Analysis of the Preconditions of the American Revolution," in *Essays on the American Revolution*, ed. Kurtz and Hutson, pp. 32–80; Pole, *Political Representation*, pp. 508–513; Martyn P. Thompson, "The History of Fundamental Law in Political Thought from the French Wars of Religion to the American Revolution," *American Historical Review* 91 (December 1986): 1103–1128.

21. McLoughlin, *Revivals, Awakenings, and Reform*, pp. 98–140; Bercovitch, *American Jeremiad*, pp. 132–175. My understanding of the recreation of revolutionary fervor in the revivals of the Second Great Awakening rests on conversations with Christine Heyrman, who is exploring the process as it occurred in the Carolinas. On the formation of the genteel tradition, see May, *Enlightenment in America*, pp. 307–362. On the Federalists, see James M. Banner, *To the Hartford Convention* (New York: Knopf, 1970); Linda Kerber, *Federalists in Dissent* (Ithaca, N.Y.: Cornell University Press, 1970); and Gerald Stourzh, *Alexander Hamilton and the Idea of Republican Government* (Stanford: Stanford University Press, 1970). For the suggestion that in the early nineteenth century, party loyalty emerged as yet another (mutant) species of civic virtue, see David Hackett Fischer, *The Revolution of American Conservatism: The Federalist Party in the Era of Jeffersonian Democracy* (New York: Harper and Row, 1965).

22. John Ashworth, "The Jeffersonians: Classical Republicans or Liberal Capitalists?" *Journal of American Studies* 18 (December 1984): 425–435; and cf. Drew McCoy, *The Elusive Republic: Political Economy in Jeffersonian America* (Chapel Hill: University of North Carolina Press, 1980), p. 10; Lance Banning, *The Jeffersonian Persuasion: Evolution of a Party Ideology* (Ithaca, N.Y.: Cornell University Press, 1978), p. 193; and Appleby, *Capitalism and a New Social Order*, p. 80.

23. Banning, "Jeffersonian Ideology Revisited," pp. 6–8; see also McCoy, *Elusive Republic*, esp. pp. 49, 61, 90–100. Pocock has hammered this theme repeatedly; for a particularly sharp statement of his position, see Pocock, *Virtue, Commerce, and History*, pp. 66–67, 69–71.

24. Madison's speech of June 29, 1788, is in *The Papers of James Madison*, ed. Robert A. Rutland and Charles E. Hobson (Charlottesville: University Press of Virginia, 1977) 11: 163. See also James Madison, Alexander Hamilton, and John Jay, *The Federalist*, ed. Jacob E. Cooke (Middletown: Wesleyan University Press, 1961), pp. 56–65, 384–390.

25. Ralph Ketcham, *Presidents above Party: The First American Presidency, 1789–1829* (Chapel Hill: University of North Carolina Press, 1984). See also the insightful review by Gordon Wood, "Politics without Party," *New York Review of Books*, October 11, 1984, pp. 18–21.

26. McCoy, *Elusive Republic*, p. 68.

27. Appleby, *Capitalism and a New Social Order*, p. 104. Even Pocock now concedes that he has underestimated the importance of the tradition of natural jurisprudence as a factor shaping—and perhaps ultimately combining with—classical republicanism. See Pocock, "*The Macchiavellian Moment Revisited*," p. 54. The impulse to identify *the* Jeffersonians, unfortunately, appears to be as irresistible to Banning as to Appleby: "The presence of such variety, however, does not exclude the possibility of identifying a core of belief that held Jeffersonians together, and I remain willing to argue both that the Republicans were bound together by the concepts explored in *The Jeffersonian Persuasion* and *The Elusive Republic* and that the thought of the great party leaders should be placed somewhere toward the middle of the party's spectrum"; Banning, "Jeffersonian Ideology

Revisited," p. 19 n. 46, pp. 12–13, 16, 33. The realization of diversity has rendered this sort of argument unhelpful and unnecessarily contentious, as several historians have pointed out. See, for example, Shalhope, "Republicanism and Early American Historiography," p. 350; John Zvesper, *Political Philosophy and Rhetoric: A Study of the Origins of American Party Politics* (Cambridge: Cambridge University Press, 1977), pp. 39–44, 87–131; and Richard Twomey, "Jacobins and Jeffersonians: Anglo-American Radical Ideology, 1790-1810," in *Origins of Anglo-American Radicalism*, ed. Jacob and Jacob, pp. 291–297. See especially the conclusion drawn by John Ashworth: "As far as virtue and self-interest are concerned, then, neither party was wholly classical—and neither was unambiguously liberal. The labels cannot be made to stick." Ashworth, "The Jeffersonians," p. 430. This is not to say that all of these competing interpretations are equally correct, instead they seem to me almost equally incomplete. Perhaps historians of the early Republic should follow the lead of historians of the American progressive period, who have abandoned the search for the quintessential progressives and now examine the various elements that cooperated to form various progressive coalitions. See, for example, John Buenker's essay in John Buenker, John Burnham, and Robert Crunden, *Progressivism* (Cambridge, Mass.: Schenkman, 1977), pp. 31–69; and Daniel T. Rodgers, "In Search of Progressivism," *Reviews in American History* 10 (December 1982): 113–132.

28. Albert H. Smyth, ed., *The Writings of Benjamin Franklin*, 10 vols. (New York: 1905–07), IX: 80. See also Pole, *Political Representation*, pp. 531–532; Rowland Berthoff, "Independence and Attachment, Virtue and Interest: From Republican Citizen to Free Enterpriser, 1787-1837," in *Uprooted Americans: Essays to Honor Oscar Handlin*, ed. Richard L. Bushman et al. (Boston: Little, Brown, 1979), pp. 97–124. Berthoff's essay elaborates on a theme suggested by Berthoff and John M. Murrin: "Other reforms of the post-Revolutionary half century also promised to make men more equal, on the model of the yeoman freeholder, but instead made them free to become unequal, and on a far grander scale than was possible through land speculation." Rowland Berthoff and John M. Murrin, "Feudalism, Communalism, and the Yeoman Freeholder: The American Revolution Considered as a Social Accident," in *Essays on the American Revolution*, ed. Kurtz and Hutson, p. 284.

29. See Samuel Harrison Smith, "Remarks on Education: Illustrating the Close Connection between Virtue and Wisdom," in *Essays on Education in the Early Republic*, ed. Frederick Rudolph (Cambridge: Belknap Press of Harvard University Press, 1965), esp. p. 216. See also David M. Post, "Jeffersonian Revisions of Locke: Education, Property Rights, and Liberty," *Journal of the History of Ideas* 47 (January-March 1986): 147–157. As Appleby writes, "The attribution of autonomy to the individual members of society also suggested a moral and material self-sufficiency, and this self-sufficiency conveyed new meaning to the idea of self-interest"; Appleby, "The Radical *Double-Entendre* in the Right to Self-Government," p. 276.

30. James Wilson quoted in Wood, *Creation*, p. 614. For a complementary discussion of Wilson and the idea of popular sovereignty, see Pole, "Enlightenment and the Politics of American Nature," pp. 209–211. On bicameralism and popular sovereignty, see Appleby, "America as a Model for the Radical French Reformers of 1789," *William and Mary Quarterly* 28 (April 1971): 267–286; Appleby, *Capitalism and a New Social Order*, pp. 61–67; Wood, *Creation*, pp. 576–615; Robert R. Palmer, *The Age of the Democratic Revolution*, 2 vols. (Princeton: Princeton University Press, 1959–64), I: 282. Commentators from Tom Paine to Robert R. Palmer have noted the striking similarities among the Virginia Declaration of Rights, Jefferson's Declaration of Independence, and the French Declaration of the Rights of Man and Citizen. See Paine, *Rights of Man*, ed. Foner, pp. 110–115; and Palmer, *Democratic Revolution*, I: 518–521.

31. My reading of Rousseau has been influenced primarily by the writings of Roger Masters. See Roger Masters, *The Political Philosophy of Rousseau* (Princeton: Princeton University Press, 1968); Roger Masters, introduction, in Jean Jacques Rousseau, *The First and Second Discourses* (New York: St. Martin's, 1964); and Roger Masters, introduction, in Jean Jacques Rousseau, *On the Social Contract* (New York: St. Martin's, 1978). For a detailed examination of Rousseau's debts to the tradition of natural law, see Robert Derathé, *Jean-Jacques Rousseau et la science politique de son temps* (Paris: Presses universitaire de France, 1979). For a contrasting view, see Judith Shklar, *Men and Citizens: A Study of Rousseau's Social Theory* (Cambridge: Cambridge University Press, 1969). Recent studies concentrating on the tension between the tradition of absolute authority and the assertion of individual rights include Nannerl O. Keohane, *Philosophy and the State in France: The Renaissance to the Enlightenment* (Princeton: Princeton University Press, 1980); and Stephen Holmes, *Benjamin Constant and the Making of Modern Liberalism* (New Haven: Yale University Press, 1984). See also François Furet, *Interpreting the French Revolution*, trans. Elborg Forster (Cambridge: Cambridge University Press, 1981), pp. 28–79. Cf. the discussions of Furet in Keith Michael Baker, "Enlightenment and Revolution in France: Old Problems, Renewed Approaches," *Journal of Modern History* 53 (June 1981): 281–303; and Lynn Hunt, *Politics, Culture, and Class in the French Revolution* (Berkeley: University of California Press, 1984). The passage from Gustave Laurent, ed., *Oeuvres complètes de Robespierre*, vol. V (Paris: Presses universitaires de France, 1961), p. 207, is discussed in Norman Hamson, "The Enlightenment in France," in *The Enlightenment in National Context*, ed. Porter and Teich, p. 49. For a provocative consideration of Rousseau's relation to the other *philosophes* and to the Revolution, which emphasizes the revolutionaries' need to legitimate a *droit public* for the Republic, see Keith Michael Baker, "On the Problem of the Ideological Origins of the French Revolution," in *Modern European Intellectual History*, ed. LaCapra and Kaplan, pp. 197–219.

32. In the larger study of democracy in America and Europe since 1680 that I am preparing, I will emphasize the extent to which certain ideas in American political thought parallel Rousseau's—and perhaps even more controversially, Kant's—and distinguish between those ideas and the utilitarianism developed by British radicals in the late eighteenth and early nineteenth centuries. For a discussion of the contrast between the ideas of natural law and utilitarianism, see the comparison of Jonathan Edwards's Augustinianism and Benjamin Franklin's utilitarianism in Norman Fiering, "Benjamin Franklin and the Way to Virtue," *American Quarterly* 30 (Summer 1978): 199–223; and Fiering, *Jonathan Edwards's Moral Thought*, pp. 346–361. On the rise of an ethically flattened political economy in Britain, see Isaac Kramnick, "Republican Revisionism Revisited," *American Historical Review* 87 (June 1982): 629–664. On the ideological and moral conflicts such an amoral political economy provoked in Britain, see Himmelfarb, *Idea of Poverty*, p. 101. The conflict was different in Britain and America, but it is important to remember that the idea of laissez-faire encountered resistance in both political cultures.

33. Appleby, *Capitalism and a New Social Order*, pp. ix–x; Wood, *Creation*, pp. 562–564. See also Martin Diamond, "Ethics and Politics: The American Way," in *The Moral Foundations of the American Republic*, ed. Robert H. Horwitz (Charlottesville: University Press of Virginia, 1979), esp. pp. 68–72; Marvin Meyers, "Liberty, Equality, and Constitutional Self-Government," in *Liberty and Equality Under the Constitution*, ed. John Agresto (Washington: American Historical Association, 1983); and Marvin Meyers, *Revolutionary Thoughts in the Founding* (Claremont, Calif.: The Claremont Institute for the Study of Statesmanship and Political Philosophy, 1984). The persistence of the religious, republican, and liberal vocabularies of virtue in nineteenth-century America can be seen by comparing the following: Herbert G. Gutman, "Protestantism and American Labor,"

Work, Culture, and Society in Industrializing America (New York: Vintage, 1977), pp. 79–117; Marvin Meyers, *The Jacksonian Persuasion: Politics and Belief* (Stanford: Stanford University Press, 1960); Daniel Walker Howe, *The Political Culture of the American Whigs* (Chicago: University of Chicago Press, 1979); Dorothy Ross, "The Liberal Tradition Revisited and the Republican Tradition Addressed," in *New Directions in American Intellectual History*, ed. John Higham and Paul K. Conkin (Baltimore: Johns Hopkins University Press, 1979), pp. 116–131; and Sean Wilentz, "On Class and Politics in Jacksonian America," *Reviews in American History* 10 (December 1982): 45–63. For a thoughtful overview, see Dorothy Ross, "Liberalism," in *The Encyclopedia of American Political History*, ed. Jack P. Greene, 3 vols. (New York: Scribner's, 1984), II: 750–763. On the transformation of these ideas in the late nineteenth and early twentieth centuries, see James T. Kloppenberg, *Uncertain Victory: Social Democracy and Progressivism in European and American Thought, 1870–1920* (New York: Oxford University Press, 1986).

Chapter 3

For helpful comments offered on earlier drafts of this essay, I am grateful to Richard J. Bernstein, Jon Butler, Andrew Delbanco, Eldon Eisenach, Giles Gunn, Peter A. Huff, Michael J. Lacey, Nathan Hatch, Mark Noll, William M. Shea, Rogers Smith, and especially Richard Wightman Fox. Whatever cogency the essay has now owes much to their efforts; its idiosyncrasies and inadequacies are entirely my own.

1. An extended discussion of recent developments in social theory, philosophy of science, and epistemology is beyond the scope of this chapter. On these issues see James T. Kloppenberg, "Why History Matters to Political Theory," in *Scientific Authority and Twentieth-Century America*, ed. Ronald Walters (Baltimore: Johns Hopkins University Press, 1997), pp. 185–203, reprinted as chapter 9 in this volume; and James T. Kloppenberg, "Pragmatism: A New Name for Some Old Ways of Thinking?" *Journal of American History* 83 (1996): 100–138.

2. For recent developments in American religion, see the following: "Church Membership Statistics, 1940–1985, for Selected U.S. Denominations," in *Yearbook of American and Canadian Churches 1987*, ed. Constant H. Jacquet (Nashville: Abington Press, 1987); Andrew M. Greeley, *American Catholicism since the Council: An Unauthorized Report* (Chicago: Thomas More Press, 1985); Robert Wuthnow, *The Restructuring of American Religion: Society and Faith since World War II* (Princeton: Princeton University Press, 1988); and George M. Marsden, *Religion and American Culture* (New York: Harcourt Brace Jovanovich, 1990).

3. David Tracy, "Afterword: Theology, Public Discourse, and the American Tradition," in *Religion and Twentieth-Century American Intellectual Life*, ed. Michael J. Lacey (Cambridge: Cambridge University Press, 1989), p. 201.

4. For further discussion of these trends, see Peter Novick, *That Noble Dream: The "Objectivity Question" and the American Historical Profession* (Cambridge: Cambridge University Press, 1988); and cf. James T. Kloppenberg, "Objectivity and Historicism: A Century of American Historical Writing," *The American Historical Review* 94 (1989): 1011–1030.

5. For an incisive discussion of Williams, see Garry Wills, *Under God: Religion and American Politics* (New York: Simon and Schuster, 1990), pp. 345–353; on Williams's use of Augustine, see Perry Miller, *Roger Williams: His Contribution to the American Tradition* (1953; reprint New York: Atheneum, 1974), pp. 22–38.

6. David Hackett Fischer, *Albion's Seed: Four British Folkways in America* (New York: Oxford University Press, 1989), p. 795; David D. Hall, "Religion and Society: Problems

and Reconsiderations," in *Colonial British America: Essays in the New History of the Early Modern Era*, ed. Jack P. Greene and J. R. Pole (Baltimore: Johns Hopkins University Press, 1984), p. 336.

7. See Henry F. May, *The Enlightenment in America* (New York: Oxford University Press, 1976); Donald H. Meyer, *The Democratic Enlightenment* (New York: G.P. Putnam's Sons, 1976); J. R. Pole, "Enlightenment and the Politics of American Nature," in *The Enlightenment in National Context*, ed. R. Porter and M. Teich (Cambridge: Cambridge University Press, 1981); and James T. Kloppenberg, "North America," in *The Blackwell Companion to the Enlightenment*, ed. John W. Yolton (Oxford: Blackwell Publishers, 1991).

8. Merrill D. Peterson, in *The Jefferson Image in the American Mind* (New York: Oxford University Press, 1960), traced the ups and downs of Jefferson's reputation, and the ebb and flow of popular and scholarly writing about him, from his death through the 1950s. The 250th anniversary of Jefferson's birth provided the occasion for a scholarly conference that yielded the volume *Jeffersonian Legacies* (Charlottesville: University Press of Virginia, 1993), a splendid collection of essays edited by Peter S. Onuf that continues Peterson's account into the 1990s. Just as Jefferson's first memorialists found symbolic significance in the coincidence that both Jefferson and his long-time friend and rival John Adams died on July 4, 1826, the fiftieth anniversary of the signing of the Declaration of Independence, so have generations of commentators tried to take stock of American democracy by coming to terms with the meaning of Jefferson.

9. Jefferson, *Writings*, ed. Merrill D. Peterson (New York: Library of America, 1984), pp. 122, 118.

10. Ibid., p. 1301. The most recent study of Jefferson's religious ideas is Edwin S. Gaustad, *Sworn on the Altar of God: A Religious Biography of Thomas Jefferson* (Grand Rapids: Eerdmans, 1996), which demonstrates the depth as well as the unconventionality of Jefferson's religiosity. See also the thoughtful essay by Paul K. Conkin, "The Religious Pilgrimage of Thomas Jefferson," in *Jeffersonian Legacies*, pp. 19-49.

11. J. C. D. Clark, *The Language of Liberty, 1660-1832; Political Discourse and Social Dynamics in the Anglo-American World* (Cambridge: Cambridge Univeristy Press, 1994); Ruth H. Bloch, "Religion and Ideological Change in the American Revolution," in *Religion and American Politics from the Colonial Period to the 1980s*, ed. Mark A. Noll (New York: Oxford University Press, 1990), p. 47; see also the following discussions of the central role of religion in the Revolution; Ruth H. Bloch, *Visionary Republic: Millennial Themes in American Thought, 1756-1800* (New York: Cambridge University Press, 1985); Nathan O. Hatch, *The Sacred Cause of Liberty: Republican Thought and the Millennium in Revolutionary New England* (New Haven: Yale University Press, 1977); Patricia Bonomi, *Under the Cope of Heaven: Religion, Society, and Politics in Colonial America* (New York: Oxford University Press, 1986); and James T. Kloppenberg, "The Virtues of Liberalism: Christianity, Republicanism, and Ethics in Early American Political Discourse," *Journal of American History* 74 (1987): 9-33, reprinted as chapter 2 in this volume.

12. Harry S. Stout, "Rhetoric and Reality in the Early Republic: The Case of the Federalist Clergy," in Noll, *Religion*, pp. 62-76; Daniel T. Rodgers, "Natural Rights," *Contested Truths: Keywords in American Politics Since Independence* (New York: Basic Books, 1987), pp. 45-79; Akhil Amar, "The Bill of Rights as a Constitution," *Yale Law Journal* (1991); Donald S. Lutz, *The Origins of American Constitutionalism* (Baton Rouge: Louisiana State University Press, 1988); John F. Wilson, "Religion, Government, and Power in the New Nation," in Noll, *Religion*, pp. 77-91; Guyora Binder, "Revolution as a Constitutional Concept," a paper delivered at the Annual Meeting of the American Society for Legal History, February 1990, copy in the possession of James T. Kloppenberg.

13. *The Papers of James Madison*, ed. William T. Hutchinson et al. (Chicago: Univer-

sity of Chicago Press, 1962–77), 8: 295–305. On this issue, see also the essays in *The Virginia Statute for Religious Freedom: Its Evolution and Consequences*, ed. Merrill D. Peterson and Robert C. Vaughan, Cambridge Studies in Religion and American Public Life (Cambridge: Cambridge University Press, 1988); and Wills, *Under God*, pp. 373–380. On the Antifederalists' interest in religious tests and state religions, see Isaac Kramnick, "'The Great National Discussion': The Discourse of Politics in 1787," in Kramnick, *Republican and Bourgeois Radicalism: Political Ideology in Late Eighteenth-Century England and America* (Ithaca, N.Y.: Cornell University Press, 1990), pp. 260–288.

14. In addition to Gordon Wood, *The Creation of the American Republic, 1776–1787* (New York: Norton, 1969); see Robert E. Shalhope, *The Roots of Democracy: American Thought and Culture, 1760–1800* (Boston: Twayne, 1990); the fine, brief discussion in Daniel Walker Howe, "Anti-Federalist/Federalist Dialogue and Its Implications for Constitutional Understanding," *Northwestern University Law Review* 84 (1989): 1–11; and John L. Brooke, *The Heart of the Commonwealth: Society and Political Culture in Worcester County, Massachusetts, 1731–1861* (Cambridge: Cambridge University Press, 1989).

15. Jon Butler, *Awash in a Sea of Faith: Christianizing the American People* (Cambridge: Harvard University Press, 1990); James Turner, *Without God, Without Creed: The Origins of Unbelief in America* (Baltimore: Johns Hopkins University Press, 1985), pp. 100–101; Nathan O. Hatch, "The Democratization of Christianity and the Character of American Politics," in Noll, *Religion*, pp. 92–120; Gordon Wood, "Ideology and the Origins of a Liberal America," *William and Mary Quarterly*, 3rd series, 44 (1987): 628–640; and R. Laurence Moore, "Religion, Secularization, and the Shaping of the Culture Industry in Antebellum America," *American Quarterly* 41 (1989): 216–242.

16. See Elizabeth B. Clark, "'The Sacred Rights of the Weak': Pain, Sympathy, and the Culture of Individual Rights in Antebellum America," *Journal of American History* 82 (1995): 463-593; Daniel Walker Howe, "Religion and Politics in the Antebellum North," in Noll, *Religion*, pp. 121–145; Daniel Walker Howe, "The Evangelical Movement and Political Culture in the North during the Second Party System," *Journal of American History* 77 (1991): 1216–1239, an especially valuable discussion of these themes; Daniel Walker Howe, *The Political Culture of the American Whigs* (Chicago: University of Chicago Press, 1979); Martin J. Wiener, ed., "Humanitarianism or Control? A Symposium on Aspects of Nineteenth-Century Social Reform in Britain and America," *Rice University Studies* 67 (1981): 1–84; Alexis de Tocqueville, *Democracy in America*, ed. J. P. Mayer (Garden City, N.Y.: Anchor Books, 1969), p. 508; and James T. Kloppenberg, "Life Everlasting: Tocqueville in America," *La Revue Tocqueville/The Tocqueville Review* 17 (1996): 119–136, reprinted as chapter 5 in this volume.

17. Lois Banner, "Religious Benevolence as Social Control: A Critique of an Interpretation," *Journal of American History* 60 (1973): 34–41; Joan Williams, "Domesticity as the Dangerous Supplement of Liberalism," *Journal of Women's History* 2 (1991): 69–88; Carroll Smith-Rosenberg, *Disorderly Conduct: Visions of Gender in Victorian America* (New York: Oxford University Press, 1985); Butler, *Awash in a Sea of Faith*, pp. 129–163.

18. J. David Greenstone, "Political Culture and American Political Development: Liberty, Union, and the Liberal Bipolarity," in *Studies in American Political Development* (New Haven: Yale University Press, 1986) I: 1–49; John P. Diggins, *The Lost Soul of American Politics: Virtue, Self-Interest, and the Foundations of Liberalism* (New York: Basic Books, 1984), pp. 277–333; Andrew Delbanco, "Lincoln and Modernity," in *Knowledge and Belief in America*, pp. 247–269; Andrew Delbanco, *The Death of Satan: How Americans Have Lost the Sense of Evil* (New York: Farrar, Straus and Giroux, 1995), pp. 131–138; and Reinhold Niebuhr, *The Irony of American History* (New York: Charles Scribner's Sons, 1952), pp. 171–174.

19. Leon Fink, "The New Labor History and the Powers of Historical Pessimism: Consensus, Hegemony, and the Case of the Knights of Labor," *Journal of American History* 75 (1988): 115–136; William McGuire King, "An Enthusiasm for Humanity: The Social Emphasis in Religion and its Accommodation in Protestant Theology," in Lacey, *Religion*, pp. 49–77; Robert T. Handy, "Protestant Theological Tensions and Political Styles in the Progressive Period," in Noll, *Religion*, pp. 281–301; Richard L. McCormick, *The Party Period and Public Policy* (New York: Oxford University Press, 1986), part 3. For a view of progressivism as explicitly religious, see Robert M. Crunden, *Ministers of Reform: The Progressives' Achievement in American Civilization, 1889–1920* (New York: Basic Books, 1982). On Rauschenbusch and Ely, see James T. Kloppenberg, *Uncertain Victory: Social Democracy and Progressivism in European and American Thought, 1870–1920* (New York: Oxford University Press, 1986), chaps. 6–7.

20. Jane Addams, *Twenty Years at Hull House* (1910; reprint New York: Signet, 1960), pp. 68–69, 307–308.

21. Wills, *Under God*, p. 106. See also Ferenc Morton Szasz, *The Divided Mind of Protestant America* (Tuscaloosa: University of Alabama Press, 1982); and George Marsden, *Fundamentalism and American Culture: The Shaping of Twentieth-Century Evangelicalism, 1870–1925* (New York: Oxford University Press, 1980).

22. This analysis draws on a wide variety of materials, including the rapidly proliferating secondary literatures on academic professionalization and twentieth-century politics that are impossible to discuss adequately here. For especially useful treatments of these related phenomena, see Bruce Kuklick, *Churchmen and Philosophers: From Jonathan Edwards to John Dewey* (New Haven: Yale University Press, 1985); Julie A. Reuben, *The Making of the Modern University: Intellectual Transformation and the Marginalization of Morality* (Chicago: University of Chicago Press, 1996); Edward A. Purcell, *The Crisis of Democratic Theory: Scientific Naturalism and the Problem of Value* (Lexington: University of Kentucky, 1973); and *The Culture of Consumption: Critical Essays in American History, 1880–1980*, ed. Richard Wightman Fox and T. J. Jackson Lears (New York: Pantheon, 1983). I explore the political dimension of these developments in two recent essays, "Who's Afraid of the Welfare State," *Reviews in American History* 18 (1990): 395–405; and "Deliberative Democracy and the Problem of Poverty in America," chapter 7 in this volume. Recent discussions of religion and politics in contemporary America include James E. Findlay, "Religion and Politics in the Sixties: The Churches and the Civil Rights Act of 1964," *Journal of American History* 77 (1990): 66–92; all the essays in Lacey, *Religion*; the essays by Martin Marty, Robert Wuthnow, and George Marsden in Noll, *Religion*; and Marsden, *Religion and American Culture*, pp. 167–278.

23. Adolph Reed, *The Jesse Jackson Phenomenon: The Crisis of Purpose in Afro-American Politics* (New Haven: Yale University Press, 1986). For a spirited response to Reed's analysis, see Wills, *Under God*, pp. 237–241. The religious dimension of the civil rights movement is one of the central themes in Taylor Branch, *Parting the Waters: America in the King Years, 1954–63* (New York: Simon and Schuster, 1988); and in Richard H. King, *Civil Rights and the Idea of Freedom* (New York: Oxford University Press, 1992). A thoughtful review essay illuminating recent developments, particularly the role played in recent political and cultural controversies by theological conservatives (Fundamentalists, evangelicals, Pentecostals, and charismatics) is Leo P. Ribuffo, "God and Contemporary Politics," *Journal of American History* 79 (1993): 1515–1533.

24. William James, *The Varieties of Religious Experience* (1902; New York: Modern Library, 1929), pp. 498–516; Gerald E. Myers, *William James: His Life and Thought* (New Haven: Yale University Press, 1986), pp. 446–480; John E. Smith, *Purpose and Thought:*

The Meaning of Pragmatism (New Haven: Yale University Press, 1978), pp. 159–166; William A. Clebsch, *American Religious Thought: A History* (Chicago: University of Chicago Press, 1973), pp. 125–170; and Kloppenberg, *Uncertain Victory*, chaps. 1–5, on James's epistemology and his ethics.

25. *Dialogues of Alfred North Whitehead: As Recorded by Lucien Price* (Boston: Little, Brown & Co., 1954), pp. 337–338, quoted in Myers, *William James*, p. 614 n. 82.

26. John Dewey, *A Common Faith*, in *The Later Works, 1925–1953*, vol. 9: 1933–1934, ed. Jo Ann Boydston (Carbondale: Southern Illinois University Press, 1986), pp. 8, 23; Stephen C. Rockefeller, *John Dewey: Religious Faith and Democratic Humanism* (New York: Columbia University Press, 1991); John E. Smith, *Purpose and Thought*, p. 191.

27. John Dewey, *Reconstruction in Philosophy*, in *The Middle Works, 1899–1924*, vol. 12: 1920, ed. Jo Ann Boydston (Carbondale: Southern Illinois University Press, 1982), pp. 200–201. See also Bruce Kuklick, *Churchmen and Philosophers: From Jonathan Edwards To John Dewey* (New Haven: Yale University Press, 1985); and Kuklick, "John Dewey, American Theology, and Scientific Politics," in Lacey, ed., *Religion*, pp. 78–93; and Kloppenberg, *Uncertain Victory*.

28. Richard Rorty, *Contingency, Irony, and Solidarity* (Cambridge: Cambridge University Press, 1989), p. 45; James T. Kloppenberg, "Pragmatism: A New Name for Some Old Ways of Thinking?" *Journal of American History* 83 (1996): 100–138; Kloppenberg, "Why History Matters to Political Theory," in *Scientific Authority and Twentieth-Century America*, ed. R. Walters (Baltimore: Johns Hopkins Univ. Press, 1997, reprinted as chapter 9 in this volume); R. J. Bernstein, "One Step Forward, Two Steps Back: Richard Rorty on Liberal Democracy and Philosophy," *Political Theory* 15 (1987): 548–550; Bernstein, "Rorty's Liberal Utopia," *Social Research* 57 (1990): 31–72; N. Fraser, "Solidarity or Singularity: Richard Rorty between Romanticism and Technocracy," *Unruly Practices: Power, Discourse, and Gender in Contemporary Social Theory* (Minneapolis: University of Minnesota Press, 1989), pp. 93–110; and Cornel West, *The American Evasion of Philosophy* (Madison: University of Wisconsin Press, 1989), pp. 194–210.

29. Giles Gunn, "Enamored Against Thee by These Strange Minds: Recovering the Relations Between Religion and the Enlightenment in Nineteenth- and Twentieth-Century American Literary Culture," in *Knowledge and Belief in America: Enlightenment Traditions and Modern Religious Thought*, ed. William M. Shea and Peter A. Huff (Cambridge: Cambridge University Press, 1995), pp. 52–87.

30. William James, *Pragmatism*, in *The Works of William James*, ed. Frederick Burkhardt (Cambridge: Harvard University Press, 1975), pp. 102–103; John Dewey, *The Public and Its Problems*, in *The Later Works*, vol. 2: 1925-1927, ed. Jo Ann Boydston (Carbondale: University of Southern Illinois Press, 1984), p. 331. For fuller discussion of Dewey's argument, see James T. Kloppenberg, "Democracy and Disenchantment: From Weber and Dewey to Habermas and Rorty," in *Modernist Impulses in the Human Sciences*, ed. Dorothy Ross (Baltimore: Johns Hopkins University Press, 1994), reprinted as chapter 6 in this volume.

31. See Robert B. Westbrook, "Politics as Consumption: Managing the Modern American Election," in Fox and Lears, eds., *The Culture of Consumption*, pp. 143–173; Thomas Byrne Edsall, "The Changing Shape of Power: A Realignment in Public Policy," in *The Rise and Fall of the New Deal Order, 1930–1980*, ed. Steve Fraser and Gary Gerstle (Princeton: Princeton University Press, 1989), pp. 269–293; and Kathleen Hall Jamieson, *Eloquence in an Electronic Age: The Transformation of Political Speechmaking* (New York: Oxford University Press, 1988).

32. Friedrich Nietzsche, *On the Advantage and Disadvantage of History for Life*, trans. Peter Preuss (Indianapolis: Hackett, 1980), p. 40. For an incisive updating of this argu-

ment, and a spirited response to some religious thinkers' effort to make postmodern skepticism work for them in their denials of the adequacy of Enlightenment rationalism, see David A. Hollinger, *Science, Jews, and Secular Culture: Studies in Mid-Twentieth-Century American Intellectual History* (Princeton: Princeton University Press, 1996), pp. 28–33.

33. Daniel Bell, *The Cultural Contradictions of Capitalism* (New York: Basic Books, 1976); Robert Bellah et al., *Habits of the Heart: Individualism and Commitment in American Life* (Berkeley: University of California Press, 1985). See also two fine studies, Jeffrey Stout, *Ethics After Babel: The Languages of Morals and Their Discontents* (Boston: Beacon Press, 1988); and George Armstrong Kelly, *Politics and Religious Consciousness in America* (New Brunswick, N.J.: Transaction Books, 1984), pp. 258, 261. On the Niebuhrs, see Richard Wightman Fox, "The Niebuhr Brothers and the Liberal Protestant Heritage," in Lacey, ed., *Religion*, pp. 94–115; and Fox, "H. Richard Niebuhr's Divided Kingdom," *American Quarterly* 42 (March 1990): 93–101.

34. The most comprehensive presentation of this analysis is Jürgen Habermas, *The Theory of Communicative Action*, trans. Thomas McCarthy, 2 volumes (Boston: Beacon Press, 1984, 1987); among the many discussions of Habermas, see especially Stephen K. White, *The Recent Work of Jürgen Habermas: Reason, Justice, and Modernity* (Cambridge: Cambridge University Press, 1988).

35. On these issues see the incisive discussion in two fine books: Isaac Kramnick and R. Laurence Moore, *The Godless Constitution: The Case Against Religious Correctness* (New York: Norton, 1996); and Ira Katznelson, *Liberalism's Crooked Circle: Letters to Adam Michnik* (Princeton: Princeton University Press, 1996), pp. 101–185, esp. 141–149.

36. Charles Taylor, *Sources of the Self: The Making of the Modern Identity* (Cambridge: Harvard University Press, 1989); William James, "What Makes a Life Significant?" in *Talks to Teachers on Psychology, and to Students on Some of Life's Ideals*, in *The Works of William James*, ed. Frederick Burkhardt (Cambridge: Harvard University Press, 1983).

37. Taylor, *Sources of the Self*, p. 520; the passage from Madison's "Detached Memoranda," originally published in the *William and Mary Quarterly*, 3rd series, 3 (1946): 555, is quoted in a thoughtful essay by Leo Pfeffer, "Madison's 'Detached Memoranda': Then and Now," in Peterson and Vaughan, eds., *The Virginia Statute for Religious Freedom*, p. 307.

38. The relation between postfoundationalism, faith, and political action that I am suggesting thus differs in its insistence on circumspection from those recommended in recent studies that are somewhat more optimistic than I am about the consequences of forging a strong union between religion and politics. See Glenn Tinder, *The Political Meaning of Christianity: An Interpretation* (Baton Rouge: Louisiana State University Press, 1989); and Cornel West, *The American Evasion of Philosophy*, pp. 226–239, in which he recommends a "prophetic pragmatism" balanced with Niebuhr "on the tightrope between Promethean romanticism and Augustinian pessimism," a position I consider attractive but precarious. Much as I admire West's ambitions in this book, I believe his enthusiasm for the potential of organic intellectuals such as those Antonio Gramsci described needs to be tempered not only by the counsel of Augustine but also by the wisdom, if not by the patience, of Job.

Chapter 4

For critical comments and conversations that helped shape my understanding of these issues, I am grateful to Joyce Appleby, Lance Banning, Thomas Bender, Mark Hulliung, Denis Lacorne, Christopher Lasch, Drew McCoy, Henri Mendras, Marvin Meyers, J. R. Pole, Daniel Rodgers, Robert Shalhope, Rogers Smith, Shannon Stimson, Robert Westbrook, and Olivier Zunz. Since all of them would, I suspect, still disagree with at least part of my argument, this acknowledgment of my gratitude for their assistance should not be understood to implicate them.

1. Alexis de Tocqueville, *Democracy in America*, trans. George Lawrence, ed. J. P. Mayer (Garden City, N.Y.: Anchor Books, 1969), pp. 46–47.

2. Although earlier historians had noted the connection between American political thought and the classical tradition, the most important studies for recent historians have been those by Carolyn Robbins and J. G. A. Pocock. See Robbins, *The Eighteenth-Century Commonwealthman: Studies in the Transmission, Development, and Circumstances of English Liberal Thought from the Restoration of Charles II until the War with the Thirteen Colonies* (Cambridge: Harvard University Press, 1959); and Pocock, *The Machiavellian Movement: Florentine Political Thought and the Atlantic Republican Tradition* (Princeton: Princeton University Press, 1975).

3. Bernard Bailyn, *The Ideological Origins of the American Revolution* (Cambridge: Belknap Press of Harvard University Press, 1967); Gordon S. Wood, *The Creation of the American Republic, 1776–1787* (Chapel Hill: University of North Carolina Press, 1969).

4. Bernard Bailyn, "The Central Themes of the American Revolution: An Interpretation," in *Essays on the American Revolution*, ed. Stephen G. Kurtz and James H. Hutson (Chapel Hill: University of North Carolina Press, 1973), p. 9.

5. On the question of methodology, I have outlined an alternative to these binary opposites that I call pragmatic hermeneutics. See James T. Kloppenberg, "Why History Matters to Political Theory," in *Scientific Authority and Twentieth-Century America*, ed. Ronald Walters (Baltimore: Johns Hopkins University Press, 1997), pp. 185–203, reprinted as chapter 9 in this volume; and "Objectivity and Historicism: A Century of American Historical Writing," *American Historical Review* 94 (1989): 1011–1030. On the substantive issues, I have tried to show the interplay of distinguishable ideas and vocabularies in "The Virtues of Liberalism: Christianity, Republicanism, and Ethics in Early American Political Discourse," *Journal of American History* 74 (1987): 9–33, reprinted as chapter 2 in this volume; and "Knowledge and Belief in American Public Life," in *Knowledge and Belief in America: Enlightenment Traditions and Modern Religious Thought*, ed. William M. Shea and Peter A. Huff (New York: Cambridge University Press, 1995), pp. 27–51, reprinted as chapter 3 of this volume. The notes to these essays provide a more thorough guide to the secondary literature than it is possible to offer here.

6. Ruth Bloch, "Religion and Ideological Change in the American Revolution," in *Religion and American Politics From The Colonial Period to the 1980s*, ed. Mark A. Noll (New York: Oxford University Press, 1990), p. 47. On this issue see also Bloch, *Visionary Republic: Millennial Themes in American Thought, 1756–1800* (New York: Cambridge University Press, 1985); Nathan O. Hatch, *The Sacred Cause of Liberty: Republican Thought and the Millennium in Revolutionary New England* (New Haven: Yale University Press, 1977); and Patricia Bonomi, *Under the Cope of Heaven: Religion, Society, and Politics in Colonial America* (New York: Oxford University Press, 1986).

7. Adams quoted in Wood, *Creation of the American Republic*, p. 407.

8. Thomas Paine, *Common Sense*, ed. Isaac Kramnick (New York: Penguin, 1982), p. 99. Kramnick has written one of the best recent assessments of Paine in his essay "Tom Paine: Radical Liberal," reprinted in Kramnick, *Republicanism and Bourgeois Radicalism: Political Ideology in Late Eighteenth-Century England and America* (Ithaca, N.Y.: Cornell University Press, 1990), pp. 133–160. Eric Foner places greater emphasis on Paine's debt to republicanism in his *Tom Paine and Revolutionary America* (New York: Oxford University Press, 1976).

9. John E. Crowley, *"This Sheba, Self": The Conceptualization of Economic Life in*

Eighteenth-Century America (Baltimore: Johns Hopkins University Press, 1974); and Forrest McDonald, *Novus Ordo Seclorum: The Intellectual Origins of the Constitution* (Lawrence: University Press of Kansas, 1985).

10. Donald Lutz, *The Origins of American Constitutionalism* (Baton Rouge: Louisiana State University Press, 1988); and John F. Wilson, "Religion, Government, and Power in the New Nation," in Noll, ed., *Religion and American Politics*, pp. 77–91.

11. *The Papers of James Madison*, ed. William T. Hutchinson et al. (Chicago: University of Chicago Press, 1962-1977) 8: 295–305. On this issue, see also the essays in *The Virginia Statute for Religious Freedom: Its Evolution and Consequences*, ed. Merrill D. Peterson and Robert C. Baughan, Cambridge Studies in Religion and American Public Life (Cambridge: Cambridge University Press, 1988); and on the Antifederalists' interest in religious tests and state religions, Kramnick, "'The Great National Discussion': The Discourse of Politics in 1787," in Kramnick, *Republicanism and Bourgeois Radicalism*, pp. 260–288.

12. John L. Brooke, *The Heart of the Commonwealth: Society and Political Culture in Worcester County, Massachusetts, 1731–1861* (New York: Cambridge University Press, 1989).

13. Madison's speech of June 20, 1788, which has become a touchstone for those who emphasize his affinities with republicanism, is in *The Papers of James Madison*, ed. Robert A. Rutland and Charles F. Hobson (Charlottesville: University of Virginia Press, 1977) 11: p. 163. Among those who have challenged the liberal pluralists' adoption of Madison are Marvin Meyers, *The Mind of the Founder: Sources of the Political Thought of James Madison*, revised ed. (Hanover: University Press of New England, 1981), pp. xi–xlvii; and Drew McCoy, *The Elusive Republic: Political Economy in Jeffersonian America* (Chapel Hill: University of North Carolina Press, 1980).

14. Robert E. Shalhope, *The Roots of Democracy: American Thought and Culture, 1760–1800* (Boston: Twayne, 1990), pp. 157–158. See also the quite different interpretations in Lance Banning, *The Jeffersonian Persuasion: Evolution of a Party Ideology* (Ithaca, N.Y.: Cornell University Press, 1978), who sees the Jeffersonians as essentially republican; and Joyce Appleby, *Capitalism and a New Social Order: The Republican Vision of the 1790s* (New York: New York University Press, 1984), who stresses their liberalism. Helpful attempts to clarify these issues are Shalhope, "Republicanism and Early American Historiography," *William and Mary Quarterly*, 3rd series, 39 (1982): 334–356; Kramnick, "Republican Revisionism Revisited," in *Republicanism and Bourgeois Radicalism*, pp. 163–199; John Ashworth, "The Jeffersonians: Classical Republicans or Liberal Capitalists?" *Journal of American Studies* 18 (1984): 425–435; Banning, "Jeffersonian Ideology Revisited: Liberal and Classical Ideas in the New American Republic," *William and Mary Quarterly* 43 (1986): 3–19; and Appleby, "Republicanism in Old and New Contexts," ibid., pp. 20–34. I discuss these controversies in greater detail in "The Virtues of Liberalism," reprinted as chapter 2 in this volume.

15. Marvin Meyers, *The Jacksonian Persuasion: Politics and Belief* (Stanford: Stanford University Press, 1957); Daniel Walker Howe, *The Political Culture of the American Whigs* (Chicago: University of Chicago Press, 1979); and for incisive discussions of the relation between republicanism and changing conceptions of women's sphere, Ruth Bloch, "The Gendered Meanings of Virtue in Revolutionary America," *Signs* 13 (1987): 37–57, which brings together a large literature; and the challenging interpretation of Joan Williams, "Domesticity as the Dangerous Supplement," *Journal of Women's History* 2 (1991): 69–88.

16. See Eric Foner, *Free Soil, Free Labor, Free Men: The Ideology of the Republican Party Before the Civil War* (New York: Oxford University Press, 1970); Howe, *The Political Culture of the American Whigs*; and Brooke, *The Heart of the Commonwealth*.

17. Kevin Thornton, "The *Nation* and the Decline and Fall of Republican Virtue, 1865–1876," unpublished Ph.D. dissertation, University of Michigan, 1996.

18. Philip Ethington, *The Public City: The Political Construction of Urban Life in San Francisco, 1850–1900* (New York: Cambridge University Press, 1994). Chief among the studies that have stressed the importance of republicanism for American workers are Sean Wilentz, *Chants Democratic: New York City and the Rise of the Working Class, 1788–1850* (New York: Oxford University Press, 1984); Wilentz, "Against Exceptionalism: Class Consciousness and the American Labor Movement, 1790-1920," *International Labor and Working Class History* 26 (1984): 1–24; Leon Fink, *Workingmen's Democracy: The Knights of Labor and American Politics* (Urbana: University of Illinois Press, 1983); Fink, "The New Labor History and the Powers of Historical Pessimism: Consensus, Hegemony, and the Case of the Knights of Labor," *Journal of American History* 75 (1988): 115–136; and Lawrence Goodwyn, *Democratic Promise: The Populist Moment in America* (New York: Oxford University Press, 1976). An incisive study of the transformation of the American labor movement in the early twentieth century is David Montgomery, *The Fall of the House of Labor: The Workplace, the State, and American Labor Activism, 1865–1925* (New York: Cambridge University Press, 1987).

19. James T. Kloppenberg, *Uncertain Victory: Progressivism and Social Democracy in American and European Thought, 1870–1920* (New York: Oxford University Press, 1986). These ideas did not entirely disappear, however, thanks largely to the efforts of John Dewey. For a thorough analysis of Dewey's political thought and activities, see Robert B. Westbrook, *John Dewey and American Democracy* (Ithaca, N.Y.: Cornell University Press, 1991).

20. Two fine collections of recent work on the New Deal and its aftermath, which demonstrate the problems of politics by coalition and the relation between the Democratic Party's difficulties and the shortcomings of the American welfare state, are Steve Fraser and Gary Gerstle, eds., *The Rise and Fall of the New Deal Order, 1930–1980* (Princeton: Princeton University Press, 1989); and Margaret Weir, Ann Shola Orloff, and Theda Skocpol, eds., *The Politics of Social Policy in the United States* (Princeton: Princeton University Press, 1988).

21. Jennifer Nedelsky, *Private Property and the Limits of American Constitutionalism: The Madisonian Framework and Its Legacy* (Chicago: University of Chicago Press, 1991).

22. Robert N. Bellah et al., *Habits of the Heart: Individualism and Commitment in American Life* (Berkeley: University of California Press, 1985); Bellah et al., *The Good Society* (New York: Alfred A. Knopf, 1991).

23. Daniel T. Rodgers, "Republicanism: The Career of a Concept," *Journal of American History* 79 (1992): 11–38. Rodgers has developed a parallel argument concerning the importance of looking beneath the rhetoric of popular sovereignty to see the ubiquitous struggles for power that are at the center of American political culture. See Daniel T. Rodgers and Sean Wilentz, "The Languages of Power in the United States," in *Language, History and Class*, ed. Penelope J. Corfield (Oxford: Basil Blackwell, 1991), pp. 240–263. In this essay Rodgers and Wilentz tacitly indicate the inappropriateness of using republicanism as a tool for understanding conflict in American history, precisely the argument Ethington advances in *Public City*.

24. William J. Novak, *The People's Welfare: Law and Regulation in Nineteenth-Century America* (Chapel Hill: University of North Carolina Press, 1996).

25. Bailyn, "The Ideological Fulfillment of the American Revolution," in *Faces of Revolution: Personalities and Themes in the Struggle for American Independence* (New York: Alfred A. Knopf, 1991), pp. 225–278, is a masterful overview of the central issues in late-eighteenth-century American politics and ideas in general and the ratification of the Con-

stitution in particular. It is worth noting that neither Bailyn nor Wood has been guilty of the blindness to liberalism and religion that some champions of republican interpretations have shown.

26. Mary Ann Glendon, *Rights Talk: The Impoverishment of Political Discourse* (New York: Free Press, 1991); Jane Mansbridge, ed., *Beyond Self-Interest* (Chicago: University of Chicago Press, 1990).

Chapter 5

For the invitation to participate, with Françoise Mélonio, in the symposium on Tocqueville in France and America at which I first delivered an early version of this essay, I am grateful to Christine Zunz and the Maison Française of the University of Virginia. For their comments and their encouragement, I am grateful also to Françoise Mélonio, Henri Mendras, Simon Langlois, and Olivier Zunz, my colleagues on the editorial board of *La Revue Tocqueville/The Tocqueville Review*, who have helped me appreciate the depth and complexity of Tocqueville's perspective on democracy in America.

1. Among the many overviews of this subject, the most valuable include Lynn Marshall and Seymour Drescher, "American Historians and Tocqueville's *Democracy*," *Journal of American History* 55 (1968): 512–532; Robert Nisbet, "Many Tocquevilles," *American Scholar* 46 (1976): 59–75; and Sean Wilentz, "Many Democracies: On Tocqueville and Jacksonian America," in Abraham S. Eisenstadt, ed., *Reconsidering Tocqueville's "Democracy in America"* (New Brunswick, N.J.: Rutgers University Press, 1988), pp. 207–228.

2. Tocqueville's February, 1835, letter to Eugène Stoffels in John Bigelow's introduction to his edition of *Democracy in America*, trans. Henry Reeve (New York: D. Appleton and Company, 1899), p. xiii.

3. Ibid., p. xiv.

4. Daniel Walker Howe, *The Political Culture of the American Whigs* (Chicago: University of Chicago Press, 1979). See also the discussion of this theme in Howe's more wide-ranging study of self-discipline in American thought, *Virtue, Passion, and Politics: The Construction of the Self in American Thought, From Jonathan Edwards to Abraham Lincoln and Beyond* (Cambridge: Harvard University Press, forthcoming); and the discussion of "ordered freedom" in early New England in David Hackett Fischer, *Albion's Seed: Four British Folkways in America* (New York: Oxford University Press, 1979).

5. John C. Spencer's preface to *Democracy in America*, trans. Henry Reeve (New York: Dearborn, 1838), p. xii.

6. Bigelow's introduction, p. xii.

7. Frances Trollope, *Domestic Manners of the Americans* (London, 1832). The best compilation of travelers' accounts remains the collection *Abroad in America: Visitors to the New Nation, 1776–1914*, ed. Marc Pachter and Frances Stevenson Wein (Reading, Mass.: Addison-Wesley, 1976); see especially Marcus Cunliffe's delightful essay on Trollope, pp. 33–42.

8. Robert H. Wiebe, *Self-Rule: A Cultural History of American Democracy* (Chicago: University of Chicago Press, 1995), pp. 61–85.

9. The anonymous assessment published in *The United States Magazine and Democratic Review* is quoted by Thomas Bender in an excellent introduction written for his recent edition of *Democracy in America* (New York: The Modern Library, 1981), p. xli. See also Bender's judicious article on Tocqueville in *A Companion to American Thought*, ed. Richard Wightman Fox and James T. Kloppenberg (Oxford: Blackwell Publishers, 1995), pp. 676–678.

10. Nisbet, "Many Tocquevilles"; Wilfred McClay, *The Masterless: Self and Society in Modern America* (Chapel Hill: University of North Carolina Press, 1994), pp. 42ff., 235f., 252ff.

11. Marshall and Drescher, "American Historians and Tocqueville's *Democracy*," p. 514 n. 7, point out that Adams drew heavily from Tocqueville in his *History of the United States during the Administrations of Thomas Jefferson and James Madison* (1891–98): "'I have learned to think De Tocqueville my model,' wrote Adams in a letter of 1863, 'and I study his life and works as the Gospel of my private religion.'"

12. George-Wilson Pierson, *Tocqueville and Beaumont in America* (New York: Oxford University Press, 1938). The first mass-market edition of *Democracy in America* appeared in 1945 with a revised translation and an extensive introduction by Phillips Bradley and a foreword by Harold Laski (New York: Knopf, 1945). A second, even less expensive abridged edition was published two years later with an introduction by Henry Steele Commager (New York: Oxford University Press, 1947). It is in this form, or in subsequent abridgments including that edited by Richard Heffner (New York: Mentor Books, 1956), that generations of students have encountered *Democracy in America* in its guise as, in Heffner's phrase, "a tract for our times" (p. 9).

13. Dwight Macdonald's "A Theory of Mass Culture" was reprinted, along with a variety of post-World War II commentaries and earlier sources—including of course an excerpt from *Democracy in America*—in *Mass Culture: The Popular Arts in America*, ed. David Manning White and Bernard Rosenberg (New York: Free Press, 1957). On Bell, see *The End of Ideology*, revised edition with a new afterword (1962; Cambridge: Harvard University Press, 1988); and Howard Brick, *Daniel Bell and the Decline of Intellectual Radicalism: Social Theory and Political Reconciliation in the 1940s* (Madison: University of Wisconsin Press, 1986).

14. Clinton Rossiter, *The American Presidency* (New York, 1956), quoted by Marshall and Drescher, "American Historians and Tocqueville's *Democracy*," pp. 515–516; Louis Hartz, *The Liberal Tradition in America* (New York: Harcourt, Brace, and World, 1955); Marvin Meyers, *The Jacksonian Persuasion: Politics and Belief* (Stanford: Stanford University Press, 1957). On the normative status of American democracy in the post-World War II period, see especially Edward A. Purcell Jr., *The Crisis of Democratic Theory: Scientific Naturalism and the Problem of Value* (Lexington: University Press of Kentucky, 1973).

A still common misperception of Tocqueville's analysis of American democracy stems from an error contained in the epigraph to the original printing of Hartz's *Liberal Tradition in America*, an error whose survival, even after it was corrected in later editions of Hartz's book, underscores the power of the image of Tocqueville as a champion of individual freedom created in the 1940s and 1950s. Whereas Tocqueville wrote that "Americans have this great advantage, that they attained democracy without the sufferings of a democratic revolution and that they were born equal instead of becoming so," Hartz's epigraph read "they are born free, instead of becoming so." [See *Democracy in America*, ed. J. P. Mayer, trans. George Lawrence (Garden City, N.Y.: Anchor Books, 1969), p. 509. All further quotations from *Democracy in America* are from this now-standard edition.] Illustrating the continuing vitality of this misunderstanding, John Patrick Diggins, in his widely read *The Lost Soul of American Politics: Virtue, Self-Interest, and the Foundations of Liberalism* (New York: Basic Books, 1984), pp. 35, 345, twice misquotes Tocqueville as having written that Americans were "born free."

15. David Riesman et al., *The Lonely Crowd: A Study of the Changing American Character* (New Haven: Yale University Press, 1969). For an excellent discussion of Riesman and his use of Tocqueville in the context of post-World War II American social science, see McClay, *The Masterless*, pp. 226–268.

16. Vincent E. Starzinger, *Middlingness: Juste Milieu Theory in France and England, 1815–1848* (Charlottesville: University Press of Virginia, 1965); Herbert Marcuse, *One-Dimensional Man: Studies in the Ideology of Advanced Industrial Society* (Boston: Beacon Press, 1964); Marcuse, *An Essay on Liberation* (Boston: Beacon Press, 1969).

17. Meyers, *The Jacksonian Persuasion*, pp. 33–56; Roger Boesche, *The Strange Liberalism of Alexis de Tocqueville* (Ithaca, N.Y.: Cornell University Press, 1988); Alan Kahan, *Aristocratic Liberalism: The Social and Political Thought of Jacob Burckhardt, John Stuart Mill, and Alexis de Tocqueville* (New York: Oxford University Press, 1992).

18. For a Tocquevillean account of deliberation as the democratic means toward the end of reaching unanimous verdicts, see Jeffrey Abramson, *We, the Jury: The Jury System and the Ideal of Democracy* (New York: Free Press, 1994).

19. This remains a common misunderstanding of Tocqueville's assessment. At the conclusion of a film shown immediately before Bill Clinton's speech accepting his party's nomination for president at the Democratic Party Convention in Chicago on August 29, 1996, the president explained that his political career had helped him see again a truth he traced to Tocqueville: "America is great," Clinton proclaimed, "because America is good." Although familiar, and perhaps effective as election-year rhetoric, such claims are quite distant from Tocqueville's sober denial of Americans' superior civic or moral virtue.

20. Tocqueville, *Democracy in America*, pp. 524, 572.

21. See Marvin Meyers, ed., *The Mind of the Founder: Sources of the Political Thought of James Madison* (Hanover, N.H.: University Press of New England, 1981); Drew R. McCoy, *The Elusive Republic: Political Economy in Jeffersonian America* (New York: Norton, 1980); and especially Lance Banning, *The Sacred Fire of Liberty: James Madison and the Founding of the Federal Republic* (Ithaca, N.Y.: Cornell University Press, 1995). I have discussed these issues in "The Virtues of Liberalism: Christianity, Republicanism, and Ethics in Early American Political Discourse," *Journal of American History* 74 (1987): 9–33, reprinted as chapter 2 in this volume; and "The Republican Idea in American History and Historiography," *La Revue Tocqueville/The Tocqueville Review* 13 (1992): 119–136, reprinted as chapter 4 in this volume.

22. Robert Bellah et al., *Habits of the Heart: Individualism and Commitment in American Life* (Berkeley: University of California Press, 1985); and the later volume by Bellah et al., *The Good Society* (New York: Knopf, 1991). See also the work of William Sullivan, the member of the Bellah group most concerned with questions of philosophy and political theory, *Reconstructing Public Philosophy* (Berkeley: University of California Press, 1982).

23. Mary Ann Glendon, *Rights Talk: The Impoverishment of Political Discourse* (New York: Free Press, 1991).

24. Thomas Bender, *Toward an Urban Vision: Ideas and Institutions in Nineteenth-Century America* (Baltimore: Johns Hopkins University Press, 1975); Bender, *Community and Social Change in America* (New Brunswick, N.J.: Rutgers University Press, 1978).

25. William Galston, *Liberal Purposes: Goods, Virtues, and Diversity in the Liberal State* (Cambridge: Cambridge University Press, 1991); Jane Mansbridge, ed., *Beyond Self-Interest* (Chicago: University of Chicago Press, 1990); and Jean Bethke Elshtain, *Democracy on Trial* (New York: Basic Books, 1995).

26. See Robert D. Putnam, "Bowling Alone: America's Declining Social Capital," *Journal of Democracy* 6 (1995): 64–79; and Putnam, "Bowling Alone, Revisited," *The Responsive Community* 5 (1995): 18–33.

27. André Jardin, *Alexis de Tocqueville, 1805–1859* (Paris: Hachette, 1984), pp. 493–504.

28. Tocqueville, *The European Revolution and Correspondences with Gobineau*, trans.

John Lucacs (Gloucester, Mass.: Peter Smith, 1968), pp. 190f.; Tocqueville, *Selected Letters on Politics and Society*, ed. Roger Boesche, trans. James Toupin and Roger Boesche (Berkeley: University of California Press, 1985), pp. 342-344; and Joshua Mitchell, *The Fragility of Freedom: Tocqueville on Religion, Democracy, and the American Future* (Chicago: University of Chicago Press, 1995).

29. Tocqueville, *Democracy in America*, pp. 289, 445, 294.

30. See for example Wilentz, "Many Democracies," pp. 209-210.

31. Spencer's preface to *Democracy in America*, p. xi.

32. I have discussed these issues in greater detail in "Knowledge and Belief in American Public Life," in *Knowledge and Belief in America: Enlightenment Traditions and Modern Religious Thought*, ed. William M. Shea and Peter A. Huff (Cambridge: Cambridge University Press, 1995), pp. 27-51, reprinted as chapter 3 in this volume.

33. According to Allan Megill's comment at the symposium on Tocqueville at the University of Virginia on November 3, 1995, at which this essay was first discussed, in a forthcoming study of postmodernism and historiography Frank Ankersmit singles out Tocqueville's work as exemplifying the unresolved tensions that postmodernists should strive to preserve in their work. Although contrasting Tocqueville's perspective with that of French and American historians who have affiliated themselves with liberalism, Marxism, or other identifiable political positions seems promising, the anguished tone of *Democracy in America* suggests that Tocqueville accepted ambiguity, complexity, and irony not so much as positive virtues but *faute de mieux*. For an earlier statement of Ankersmit's reading of Tocqueville, see his thoughtful and challenging essay "Tocqueville and the Sublimity of Democracy," Part 1: "Content," *La Revue Tocqueville/The Tocqueville Review* 14 (1993): 173-200; and Part 2: "Form," *La Revue Tocqueville/The Tocqueville Review* 15 (1994): 193-217.

Chapter 6

I have discussed the ideas in this essay with so many friends and colleagues that even the following lengthy list leaves out the names of many who helped me formulate and refine my argument—often by disagreeing sharply with it. For their comments and generosity I am grateful to Richard J. Bernstein, Stefan Collini, Jean Heffer, David Hollinger, Stephen Kalberg, Ruth Leys, Philip Pauly, Timothy Peltason, Theodore Porter, Paul Robinson, Alan Ryan, Ian Shapiro, Rogers Smith, Shannon Stimson, James Turner, Cheryl Welch, and Robert Westbook. A special word of thanks to Richard Rorty, whose creative misreadings of Dewey and Habermas helped inspire this essay, whose response to my argument has heightened my awareness of the importance of studying ideas historically, and whose efforts to renew American pragmatism continue to challenge those of us interested in the connections between pragmatic philosophy and democratic politics. Finally, I am indebted to Dorothy Ross, Peter Weingart, and Olivier Zunz for organizing the conferences in Bellagio and Bielefeld at which these ideas matured, and to Hans Joas for organizing the conference at Bad Homburg that confirmed my commitment to the continuing vitality of Dewey's philosophy.

1. Ernest Jones, *The Life and Work of Sigmund Freud*, ed. Lionel Trilling and Steven Marcus (New York: Basic Books, 1961), p. 270; see also pp. 265-271 on Freud's American visit.

2. Marianne Weber, *Max Weber: A Biography*, trans. Harry Zohn (New York: John Wiley and Sons, 1975), p. 304; see also pp. 279-304 on Weber's American visit.

3. This is not the place for a bibliographical essay on Dewey and Weber. I discuss the literature in *Uncertain Victory: Social Democracy and Progressivism in European and*

American Thought, 1870–1920 (New York: Oxford University Press, 1986). See pp. 425–426 nn. 47–54 on Weber; and pp. 491–494 nn. 51–64 on Dewey.

4. See especially the work of Richard J. Bernstein, *The Restructuring of Social and Political Theory* (New York: Harcourt Brace Jovanovich, 1976), and *Beyond Objectivism and Relativism: Science, Hermeneutics and Praxis* (Philadelphia: University of Pennsylvania Press, 1983); and the collection of essays edited by Richard Rorty, Jerome Schneewind, and Quentin Skinner, *Philosophy in History: Essays on the Historiography of Philosophy* (Cambridge: Cambridge University Press, 1984). I discuss these issues in "Deconstruction and Hermeneutics as Strategies for Intellectual History: The Recent Work of Dominick LaCapra and David Hollinger," *Intellectual History Newsletter* 9 (1987): 3–22; "Objectivity and Historicism: A Century of American Historical Writing," *American Historical Review* 94 (1989): 1011–1030; and "Why History Matters to Political Theory," in *Scientific Authority and Twentieth-Century America*, ed. Ronald Walters (Baltimore: Johns Hopkins University Press, 1997), pp. 185–203, reprinted as chapter 9 in this volume.

5. Weber, *Roscher and Knies: The Logical Problems of Historical Economics*, ed. and trans. Guy Oakes (New York: Charles Scribner's Sons, 1975), pp. 160–161, 176, and esp. pp. 264–266; "'Objectivity' in Social Science," and "The Meaning of 'Ethical Neutrality,'" in *The Methodology of the Social Science*, ed. and trans. Edward A. Shils and Henry A. Finch (Glencoe, Ill.: Free Press, 1949), pp. 66–69, 33, 40; *The Protestant Ethic and the Spirit of Capitalism*, trans. Talcott Parsons (New York: Charles Scribner's Sons, 1958), p. 183; and *Economy and Society*, ed. Guenther Roth and Claus Wittich, trans. Ephraim Fischoll et al. (1968; reprint Berkeley: University of California Press, 1978) 1: 4, 19–20; 2: 1375–1380. Discussions of Weber's methodology that stress its hermeneutical quality include Thomas Burger, *Max Weber's Theory of Concept Formation: History, Laws, and Ideal Types* (Durham: Duke University Press, 1976); Hans Henrick Bruun, *Science, Values, and Politics in Max Weber's Methodology* (Copenhagen: Munksgaard, 1972); Jose Casanova, "Interpretations and Misinterpretations of Max Weber: The Problem of Rationalization," in *Max Weber's Political Sociology: A Pessimistic Vision of a Rationalized World*, ed. Ronald Glassman and Vatro Murvar (Westport, Conn.: Greenwood Press, 1984), pp. 141–153; Robert J. Antonio, "Values, History, and Science: The Metatheoretic Foundations of the Weber-Marx Dialogue," and Jürgen Kocka, "The Social Sciences between Dogmatism and Decisionism: A Comparison of Karl Marx and Max Weber," in *A Weber-Marx Dialogue*, ed. Robert J. Antonio and Ronald Glassman (Lawrence: University Press of Kansas, 1985), pp. 20–43, 134–166. For an overview and examples of recent work on Weber that addresses these questions, see Scott Lash and Sam Whimster, eds., *Max Weber, Rationality and Modernity* (London: Allen & Unwin, 1987).

6. Dewey, *Experience and Nature* (Chicago: Open Court, 1925), in Dewey, *The Later Works, 1925–1953* (hereafter cited as *LW*), ed. Jo Ann Boydston et al. (Carbondale: Southern Illinois University Press, 1981–90), 1: 230; *How We Think*, in Dewey, *The Middle Works, 1899–1924* (hereafter cited as *MW*), ed. Jo Ann Boydston et al. (Carbondale: Southern Illinois University Press, 1976–83), 6: 272; see also pp. 273–285. Robert Westbrook emphasizes this seldom acknowledged dimension of Dewey's philosophy in chap. 10 of *John Dewey and American Democracy* (Ithaca, N.Y.: Cornell University Press, 1991).

7. Dewey, "The Reflex Arc Concept in Psychology," *The Early Works, 1882–1898* (hereafter cited as *EW*), ed. Jo Ann Boydston et al. (Carbondale: Southern Illinois University Press, 1967–72), 5: 96–109; and "Nature and Its Good," *MW*, 4: 29.

8. *John Dewey: Lectures in China, 1919–1920*, ed. Robert W. Clopton and Tsuin-Chen Ou (Honolulu: University Press of Hawaii, 1973), pp. 57, 59. For discussion of the attraction of scientistic approaches in American social sciences in the 1920s, see Westbrook, *John Dewey and American Democracy*, pp. 281–300; and four more general studies, Ed-

ward Purcell, *The Crisis of Democratic Theory: Scientific Naturalism and the Problem of Value* (Lexington: University Press of Kentucky, 1973); David M. Ricci, *The Tragedy of Political Science: Politics, Scholarship, and Democracy* (New Haven: Yale University Press, 1984); Raymond Seidelman, *Disenchanted Realists: Political Science and the American Crisis, 1884–1984* (Albany: State University of New York Press, 1985); and Dorothy Ross, *The Origins of American Social Science* (Cambridge: Cambridge University Press, 1991).

9. As Ted Porter points out in "The Death of the Object: *Fin de siècle* Philosophy of Physics," in *Modernist Impulses in the Human Sciences, 1870–1930*, ed. Dorothy Ross (Baltimore: Johns Hopkins University Press, 1994), pp. 128–151, the contemporary understanding of the meaning of these physicists' contribution was at variance with their own. For a classic statement of the reaction of those nonscientists who tended to understand the significance of critical positivism as Dewey did, see Henry Adams, *The Education of Henry Adams* (Boston: Massachusetts Historical Society, 1918), chap. 31.

10. James Gouinlock, introduction to Dewey, *LW*, 2: xxiv.

11. Dewey, *The Public and Its Problems*, *LW*, 2: 344–345.

12. Dewey, *The Quest for Certainty*, *LW*, 4: 232. For a thoughtful discussion of the enduring value of Dewey's "thoroughly 'pragmatist' account of science and philosophy" in *The Quest for Certainty*, see Stephen Toulmin's Introduction to *LW*, 4: vii–xxii, in which he indicates the reasons why it is a mistake to confuse Dewey's instrumentalism with the unreflective naturalism of some self-styled empiricists in the physical and the social sciences.

13. Despite the many virtues of her comprehensive study *The Origins of American Social Science*, Dorothy Ross minimizes the significance of this crucial aspect of Dewey's thinking in her discussion of his ideas and their significance on pp. 327–330. Moreover, the cogent and persuasive critique of scientism that she offers on pp. 471–473 of her epilogue recapitulates Dewey's own critique of the mechanistic positivism of social science. Compare her discussion with Dewey's in *The Quest for Certainty*, *LW*, 4: 196, where the hermeneutical dimension of his ideas is particularly apparent: "The doctrine that knowledge is ideally or in its office a disclosure of antecedent reality resulted, under the impact of the results of natural science, in relegating purpose to the purely subjective, to states of consciousness. An unsolved problem then developed out of the question as to how purpose could be efficacious in the world. Now intelligent action is purposive action; if it is a natural occurrence, coming into being under complex but specifiable conditions of organic and social interaction, then purpose like intelligence is within nature; it is a 'category' having objective standing and validity. It has this status in a direct way through the place and operation of human art within the natural scene; *for distinctively human conduct can be interpreted and understood only in terms of purpose* [emphasis mine]. Purpose is the dominant category of anything truly denominated history, whether in its enacting or in the writing of it, since action which is *distinctively* human is marked by intent" [emphasis in original].

14. For a splendid discussion of this controversial issue in Weber's work, see Stephen Kalberg, "The Role of Ideal Interests in Max Weber's Comparative Historical Sociology," in *A Marx-Weber Dialogue*, pp. 46–67. Whether or not Weber believed such meanings could be generated under conditions of disenchantment has been the subject of considerable debate. See for example the discussion in Jürgen Habermas, *The Theory of Communicative Action*, vol. 2, *Lifeworld and System: A Critique of Functionalist Reason* (1st German edition 1981), trans. Thomas McCarthy (Boston: Beacon Press, 1989), pp. 303–331. If Kalberg is correct, Habermas is building on Weber's own ideas rather than revising or supplementing them.

15. Dewey, *Studies in Logical Theory*, *MW*, 2: 298–315; see also "The Significance of the Problem of Knowledge," in *The Influence of Darwin and Other Essays on Contemporary Thought*, in Dewey, *EW*, 5: 20–21; and Weber, *Economy and Society*, 1: 24–26. Recent discussions of Weber's concept of rationality include Ann Swidler, "The Concept of Rationality in the Work of Max Weber," *Sociological Inquiry* 43 (1973): 35–42; Stephen Kalberg, "Max Weber's Types of Rationality: Cornerstones for the Analysis of Rationalization Processes in History," *American Journal of Sociology* 85 (1980): 1145–1179; Jeffrey C. Alexander, *Theoretical Logic in Sociology*, vol. 3: *The Classical Attempt at Synthesis: Max Weber* (Berkeley: University of California Press, 1983), pp. 24–29, 134–135; and Wolfgang Schluchter, "The Paradox of Rationalization: On the Relation of Ethics and World," in Schluchter and Guenther Roth, *Max Weber's Vision of History: Ethics and Methods* (Berkeley: University of California Press, 1979), pp. 11–64.

16. Weber, "Science as a Vocation," *From Max Weber: Essays in Sociology*, ed. and trans. Hans Gerth and C. Wright Mills (New York: Oxford University Press, 1946), p. 143. For competing discussions of Weber's own attitude toward instrumental rationality, cf. Wolfgang Mommsen, *The Age of Bureaucracy: Perspectives on the Political Sociology of Max Weber* (New York: Harper & Row, 1974); and Alexander, *Theoretical Logic in Sociology*, 3: 202–204, n 89.

17. Dewey, "Self-Realization as the Moral Ideal," *EW*, 4: 52n; *Reconstruction in Philosophy*, *MW*, 12: 173. For recent discussions of the development of Dewey's ethics, see Bruce Kuklick, *Churchmen and Philosophers: From Jonathan Edwards to John Dewey*, (New Haven: Yale University Press, 1985), pp. 230–253; and James Gouinlock, *John Dewey's Philosophy of Value* (New York: Humanities Press, 1972).

18. Weber, "The Meaning of 'Ethical Neutrality,'" *Methodology*, pp. 15–18. See also Marianne Weber, *Weber*, pp. 89–90, 156–157, 322. In "The Application of the Weberian Concept of Rationalization to Contemporary Conditions," in *Max Weber, Rationality and Modernity*, pp. 164–170, Martin Albrow contends that Weber incorporated a Kantian ethics so thoroughly into his conception of rational action that Anglo-American scholars have missed the mark in their treatments of instrumental rationality in relation to utilitarianism. As the passage quoted suggests, Weber himself occasionally distinguished will from consequences.

19. For Dewey's understanding of the development of democracy, see *The Public and Its Problems*, *LW*, 2: 235–372; cf. Weber, "Capitalism and Rural Society in Germany," *From Max Weber*, pp. 363–385; *The Protestant Ethic*, pp. 47–78; and *Economy and Society*, pp. 971, 961; see also Wolfgang Mommsen, *Max Weber and German Politics, 1890–1920*, 2nd ed., trans. Michael S. Steinberg (1974; Chicago: University of Chicago Press, 1984), p. 323; David Beetham, *Max Weber and the Theory of Modern Politics* (London: George Allen and Unwin, 1974), pp. 152–164; and Guenther Roth, epilogue, *Max Weber's Vision of History*, pp. 200–201.

20. Dewey, *The Public and Its Problems*, *LW*, 2: 369–372; see also Dewey's review of Lippmann's *Public Opinion* reprinted in *MW*, 13: 337–344. On the centrality of this idea for a number of American progressives, see Jean B. Quandt, *From the Small Town to the Great Community: The Social Thought of Progressive Intellectuals* (New Brunswick, N.J.: Rutgers University Press, 1970).

21. Marianne Weber, *Weber*, p. 293; see also Weber, *Economy and Society*, 2: 949–952, 1414–1415; and the fine essay by Ernest Kilker, "Max Weber and the Possibilities for Democracy," in *Max Weber's Political Sociology*, pp. 55–65.

22. Weber, "Parliament and Government in a Reconstructed Germany," *Economy and Society*, 2: 1401–1402; "Speech for the General Information of Austrian Officers in Vienna," trans. D. Hÿtch, in *Max Weber: The Interpretation of Social Reality*, ed. J. E. T. El-

dridge (New York: Charles Scribner's Sons, 1971), pp. 203–204. See also Kalberg, "The Role of Ideal Interests in Max Weber's Historical Sociology," p. 59; Wolfgang Schluchter, *The Rise of Western Rationalism: Max Weber's Developmental History*, trans. Guenther Roth (Berkeley: University of California Press, 1981), pp. 115–117; and Jürgen Habermas, *The Philosophical Discourse of Modernity: Twelve Lectures*, trans. Frederick Lawrence (Cambridge: MIT Press, 1987), p. 70.

23. Weber, "Science as a Vocation," *From Max Weber*, p. 139. The resolution of that paradox is, as I will suggest below, central to Habermas's project in *The Theory of Communicative Action*.

24. Cf. the contrasting interpretations of Weber's speech before the Protestant Social Congress in Beetham, *Max Weber and the Theory of Modern Politics*, pp. 43–44; Mommsen, *Max Weber and German Politics*, pp. 91–123; and Lawrence A. Scaff. *Fleeing the Iron Cage: Culture, Politics, and Modernity in the Thought of Max Weber* (Berkeley: University of California Press, 1989), pp. 65–72.

25. Weber, "The Prospects for Liberal Democracy in Tsarist Russia," in *Weber: Selections in Translation*, ed. W. G. Runciman, trans. Eric Matthews (Cambridge: Cambridge University Press, 1978), pp. 281–282.

26. Weber, *Economy and Society*, 2: 1459–1460; and cf. Mommsen, *Max Weber and German Politics*, pp. 34–43, 355–356, for Weber's emphasis on the difficulties facing Germany in the post-war period, and pp. 382–389, for Mommsen's controversial and tendentious comparison of Weber with Karl Schmitt. See Stephen Turner and Regis Factor, "Decisionism and Politics: Weber as Constitutional Theorist," in *Max Weber, Rationality and Modernity*, pp. 334–354, for a thoughtful discussion of these issues.

27. Weber, "Politik als Beruf," *Gesammelte Politische Schriften*, ed. Johannes Winckelmann (Tubingen: Mohr, 1958), pp. 536, 547. In this case I have not followed the translation by Gerth and Mills because I believe it muddles the distinction Weber wanted to draw; cf. *From Max Weber*, pp. 117, 127. For a fine discussion of Weber's 1919 lectures on *Wissenschaft* and *Politik* as vocations, see Schluchter, "Value-Neutrality and the Ethic of Responsibility," in *Max Weber's Vision of History*, pp. 65–116.

28. Most of Weber's critics have considered his ethical ideas inadequate because he does not resolve the conflict between the ethics of conviction and responsibility. Cf. especially Wolfgang Schluchter, "The Paradox of Rationalization: On the Relation of Ethics and World," in *Max Weber's Vision of History*, pp. 50–59; and Mommsen, *Max Weber and German Politics*, pp. 440–445. Efforts to "go beyond" Weber on this point seem to me unpersuasive, for reasons discussed in *Uncertain Victory*, pp. 340–348.

29. Dewey's presidential address to the American Psychological Association, 1899, *MW*, 1: 130–150.

30. Dewey, *Reconstruction in Philosophy*, in *MW*, 12: 201.

31. Dewey, "Individuality, Equality, and Superiority," in *MW*, 13: 295–300; *John Dewey: Lectures in China*, p. 98.

32. Dewey, *The Public and Its Problems*, in *LW*, 2: 331.

33. Dewey, *Experience and Nature*, in *LW*, 1: 139, 140–146; Westbrook, *John Dewey and American Democracy*, pp. 336–337.

34. Jürgen Habermas, *The Theory of Communicative Action*, vol. 1: *Reason and the Rationalization of Society* (1st German edition 1981), trans. Thomas McCarthy (Boston: Beacon Press, 1984), pp. 398–399; and vol. 2: *Lifeworld and System*, p. 330. McCarthy emphasizes in his introduction the extent to which Habermas has moderated his earlier criticism of Weber and now relies heavily on Weber's understanding of the process of rationalization. Discussions of Habermas in English include Thomas McCarthy, *The Critical Theory of Jürgen Habermas* (Cambridge: MIT Press, 1978); Raymond Geuss, *The Idea*

of a Critical Theory: Habermas and the Frankfurt School (Cambridge: Cambridge University Press, 1981); Richard J. Bernstein, ed., Habermas and Modernity (Cambridge: Polity Press, 1985); Martin Jay, Marxism and Totality: The Adventures of a Concept from Lukacs to Habermas (Berkeley: University of California Press, 1984); Stephen K. White, The Recent Work of Jürgen Habermas (Cambridge: Cambridge University Press, 1988); Jane Braten, Habermas's Critical Theory of Society (Albany: State University of New York Press, 1991); and Robert C. Holub, Jürgen Habermas: Critic in the Public Sphere (London: Routledge, 1991). As Mommsen has pointed out, and Habermas himself now seems willing to concede, Habermas's earlier critique of capitalist rationality did not so much contradict Weber as follow his lead. Cf. Habermas, Toward a Rational Society, trans. Jeremy J. Shapiro (Boston: Beacon Press, 1970), pp. 81–90; Theory and Practice, trans. John Viertel (Boston: Beacon Press, 1973), pp. 82–86; and Mommsen, The Age of Bureaucracy, pp. 95–115. Habermas's recent writings reflect his continuing attempt to come to terms with Weber's legacy. See for example the apparently inconsistent comments on Weber in The Philosophical Discourse of Modernity, pp. 70, 115, and 315–316.

35. Richard Rorty, "Postmodernist Bourgeois Liberalism," Journal of Philosophy 80 (1983): 583–589. See also Rorty, Philosophy and the Mirror of Nature (Princeton: Princeton University Press, 1979), pp. 315–394, and Consequences of Pragmatism (Minneapolis: University of Minnesota Press, 1982), pp. 160–175, 191–230.

36. Rorty, "Habermas and Lyotard on Postmodernity," Habermas and Modernity, pp. 161–175.

37. Habermas, "Questions and Counterquestions," Habermas and Modernity, p. 198.

38. John Dewey: Lectures in China, pp. 84, 90. Westbrook discusses Dewey's visit to China, and surveys the considerable literature on his significance in the New China movement, in John Dewey and American Democracy, pp. 240–260. On Dewey's challenge to the reduction of ethics to "taste," see Michael J. Perry, Morality, Politics, and Law: A Bicentennial Essay (Oxford: Oxford University Press, 1988), pp. 36–54. Richard J. Bernstein's comment appears in his essay "What is the Difference that Makes a Difference? Gadamer, Habermas, and Rorty," in his Philosophical Profiles: Essays in a Pragmatic Mode (Cambridge: Polity Press, 1986), p. 91. See also Bernstein's fine essay "Rorty's Liberal Utopia," Social Research 57 (1990): 31–72, in which he persuasively contrasts Rorty's ideas with those of Dewey and Habermas.

39. Weber, Economy and Society, 1: 85–86; 2: 655–657.

40. Weber, Economy and Society, 1: 601.

41. Weber, "National Character and the Junkers," From Max Weber, p. 393. See the insightful discussion of these issues in Scaff, Fleeing the Iron Cage, pp. 158–185.

42. If Rorty's claim to Dewey's legacy is mistaken, it is at least an understandable mistake, since Dewey himself at times tried to minimize the significance of the dimension of his ideas that distinguished his philosophy from Weber's. Charles Frankel has pointed out, in "John Dewey's Social Philosophy," New Studies in the Philosophy of John Dewey, ed. Steven M. Cahn (Hanover, N.H.: University Press of New England, 1977), p. 34, "It might be said, indeed, that Dewey often neglected his own counsel. His methodological point, presumably, was that all distinctions are contextual in significance"—as Rorty accurately contends. "But in books like Experience and Nature, in which he tried to develop a metaphysics, or in the concept of 'the situation' which he put forward in his Logic, he seemed to have forgotten the contextualism of his own attack on dualism and to have put a sweeping experimental monism and egalitarianism in its place." Democracy likewise functioned for Dewey as an unvarying regulative ideal, whose possibility and desirability he took for granted independent of particular historical contexts. Dewey used the idea of democracy in much the same way that Habermas uses the ideal speech situation. Rorty has been re-

sponsible, perhaps more than any American philosopher except possibly Richard J. Bernstein, for reawakening interest in Dewey's thought. Yet in his recent incarnation as a champion of "liberal ironists" such as Nietzsche and Derrida, Rorty has drawn the fire of several self-styled pragmatists. See for example Jeffrey Stout, *Ethics After Babel* (Boston: Beacon Press, 1988); Cornel West, *The American Evasion of Philosophy* (Madison: University of Wisconsin Press, 1989); and especially Westbrook, *John Dewey and American Democracy.* Referring to Rorty's view that "'no such discipline as "philosophical anthropology" is required as a preface to politics,'" Westbrook concedes (on p. 367 n. 37) that such a position may be correct, but he correctly notes that "it is not, as a matter of intellectual history, 'the Deweyan view.'" In a detailed review of Westbrook's *Dewey* published in *The Intellectual History Newsletter* 13 (1991): 48–55, Richard J. Bernstein emphasized the crucial difference between this "Deweyan view," as Westbrook accurately presents it, and Rorty's dismissal of such attempts to ground democratic politics on a philosophical foundation. Westbrook writes even more pointedly, in his epilog, that "it is simply dead wrong to read Dewey's liberalism, as Rorty has done, as celebrating a politics centered on 'our ability to leave people alone'" (p. 542). I have discussed the critical literature on Rorty and expressed my own similar misgivings about his recent work, particularly *Contingency, Irony, and Solidarity* (Cambridge: Cambridge University Press, 1989), in "Why History Matters to Political Theory," a paper first delivered at the annual meeting of the Organization of American Historians in April 1989 (see note 4 above; this essay is reprinted as chapter 9 of this volume). As Rorty made clear in his initial response to that paper, and as he makes clear in his essay "Dewey between Hegel and Darwin," in Ross, ed., *Modernist Impulses in the Human Sciences, 1870–1930*, pp. 54–68, his understanding of Dewey and mine remain far apart. "Sometimes," Rorty wrote in *New Republic*, June 19, 1989, p. 38, "when we think that we are rediscovering the mighty dead, we are just inventing imaginary playmates." "This danger," Rorty conceded, "is extreme for us philosophers." Perhaps it is, but none of us is immune. As historians, we must remain alert to that danger and to the difference between our desire to think imaginatively and our duty to think historically. To his credit, Rorty has recently shown encouraging signs of a willingness to exchange his liberal ironism for liberal engagement. See especially his essay "Intellectuals in Politics," *Dissent*, Fall 1991, pp. 483–490; and his reply to Andrew Ross in *Dissent*, Spring 1992, pp. 265–267.

Chapter 7

A shorter version of this paper was originally delivered as the keynote address at a conference on the topic "Self and Community in America" sponsored by the Graduiertenkolleg of the John F. Kennedy-Institut für Nordamerikastudien at the Free University of Berlin, December 12, 1996.

For their critical comments on this and earlier versions of this essay, I am grateful to Willi Paul Adams, Bernard Bailyn, Timothy Breen, Michael Ermarth, David Hollinger, Morton Keller, David Kennedy, Alan Lawson, Sidney Milkis, James Oakes, Deborah Stone, Margaret Weir, and Heidi Whelan.

1. Claus Offe and Ulrich Preuss, "Democratic Institutions and Moral Resources," in *Political Theory Today*, ed. David Held (Stanford: Stanford University Press, 1991), pp. 143–171. This article is discussed in James T. Kloppenberg, "Democracy in Social Theory," *Problems of Democracy in the United States*, Symposium of the Gradiuertenkolleg at the John F. Kennedy-Institut für Nordamerikastudien, Freie Universität Berlin (Berlin: Zentrale Universitätsdruckerei, 1993), pp. 20–25.

2. On these developments, see James T. Kloppenberg, "The Virtues of Liberalism:

Christianity, Republicanism, and Ethics in Early American Political Discourse," *Journal of American History* 74 (1987): 9–33, reprinted as chapter 2 in this volume; and James T. Kloppenberg, "The Republican Idea in American History and Historiography," *La Revue Tocqueville/The Tocqueville Review* 13 (1992): 119–136, reprinted as chapter 4 in this volume.

3. Michael Sandel, *Democracy's Discontent: America in Search of a Public Philosophy* (Cambridge: Harvard University Press, 1996), p. 28. For a more detailed discussion of this book, see chapter 9 in this volume.

4. Seyla Benhabib, *Situating the Self: Gender, Community, and Postmodernism in Contemporary Ethics* (New York: Routledge, 1992), pp. 4–6. Benhabib has been criticized by Judith Butler for endorsing an ideal of discursivity that Butler considers inherently and inevitably exclusionary; Nancy Fraser has faulted Benhabib for sometimes underestimating the value of historical narratives that could situate her own idea of the situated self. Fraser's variety of feminism, which rests on and integrates the ideas of democracy and pragmatism, is very close to my own. For Butler's and Fraser's critiques and Benhabib's responses, see Seyla Benhabib, Judith Butler, Drucilla Cornell, and Nancy Fraser, *Feminist Contentions: A Philosophical Exchange* (New York: Routledge, 1995). For recent discussions of Habermas and discourse ethics, see Stephen White, *The Cambridge Companion to Habermas* (Cambridge: Cambridge University Press, 1995); Seyla Benhabib and Fred Dallmayr, eds., *The Communicative Ethics Controversy* (Cambridge: MIT Press, 1990); Craig Calhoun, ed., *Habermas and the Public Sphere* (Cambridge: MIT Press, 1992); and Jürgen Habermas, *Moral Consciousness and Communicative Action*, trans. Christian Lenhardt and Shierry Weber Nicholsen, with an introduction by Thomas McCarthy (Cambridge: MIT Press, 1990). For discussion of these ideas in the controversies over recent American pragmatism, see James T. Kloppenberg, "Pragmatism: An Old Name for Some New Ways of Thinking?" *Journal of American History* 83 (1996): 100–138.

5. Benhabib, *Situating the Self*, pp. 7–19, 225–230.

6. On this dimension of Madison's thought, see Marvin Meyers, ed., *The Mind of the Founder: Sources of the Political Thought of James Madison* (Hanover, N.H.: University Press of New England, 1981); Drew R. McCoy, *The Elusive Republic: Political Economy in Jeffersonian America* (New York: Norton, 1980); and especially Lance Banning, *The Sacred Fire of Liberty: James Madison and the Founding of the Federal Republic* (Ithaca, N.Y.: Cornell University Press, 1995). I have discussed these issues in "The Virtues of Liberalism: Christianity, Republicanism, and Ethics in Early American Political Discourse," *Journal of American History* 74 (1987): 9–33, reprinted as chapter 2 in this volume; and "The Republican Idea in American History and Historiography," *La Revue Tocqueville/ The Tocqueville Review* 13 (1992): 119–136, reprinted as chapter 4 in this volume.

7. Roosevelt's Oct. 28, 1944, speech, "We Are Not Going to Turn the Clock Back, Campaign Address at Soldiers' Field, Chicago, Illinois," is in Samuel Rosenman, ed., *Public Papers and Addresses of Franklin D. Roosevelt*, vol. 13, 1944–45 (New York: Russell and Russell, 1969), pp. 369–378. On this speech and the discussions that preceded it, see Sidney Milkis, "Franklin D. Roosevelt, Progressivism, and the Limits of Popular Leadership," unpublished manuscript in author's possession.

8. There is nothing unique about the peculiarities of the welfare programs adopted in the United States. The Whiggish assumption that all roads lead to Stockholm, implicit in much of the literature on the welfare state until fairly recently, now seems untenable. Stein Ringen has expressed this perspective in *The Possibility of Politics* (Oxford: Oxford University Press, 1987), p. 48: "There never was a consensus over the welfare state. Social policy reforms have always had to be fought through against opposition, at times against fierce opposition. This was as true in the now idealized 1950s and 1960s as it had been pre-

viously, and it is as true for those nations which have developed large welfare states as it is for nations with less encompassing social policy systems." Abram De Swaan has also put the point well: "Creating social security was hard political work. It demanded strategic coalition building and tactical parliamentary and bureaucratic maneuvering. The coalitions that carried social security though parliament, and made it acceptable to the workers and employers concerned, very much determined the nature of the arrangement. . . . The *moment and the momentum* of these episodes is explained by identifying both the coalition that carried the scheme and the opposition against it." See de Swaan, *In Care of the State* (New York: Oxford University Press, 1988), pp. 156–157; and cf. the similar views expressed in Adam Przeworski and John Sprague, *Paper Stones: A History of Electoral Socialism* (Chicago: University of Chicago Press, 1986); and Richard Rose, "Is American Public Policy Exceptional?" in *Is America Different? A New Look at American Exceptionalism*, ed. Byron E. Shafer (Oxford: Clarendon Press of Oxford University Press, 1991), pp. 187–221.

9. Marion Clawson, *New Deal Planning: The National Resources Planning Board* (Baltimore: Johns Hopkins University Press, 1981), provides a chronological list of the major reports published by the NRPB on pp. 322–347. On the NRPB, see also Barry D. Karl, *Charles E. Merriam and the Study of Politics* (Chicago: University of Chicago Press, 1974); Philip W. Warken, *A History of the National Resources Planning Board* (New York: Garland Publishing, 1979); and Alan Brinkley, *The End of Reform: New Deal Liberalism in Recession and War* (New York: Knopf, 1995), pp. 245–264.

10. National Resources Planning Board, *Security, Work, and Relief Policies* (Washington, D.C.: U.S. Government Printing Office, 1943), pp. 4, 345–349. See also Clawson, *New Deal Planning* pp. 136–142; Karl, *Merriam*, pp. 276–280; and Warken, *National Resources Planning Board*, pp. 215–235.

11. NRPB, *Security*, pp. 400, 405, 410–412, 420, 424. Alan Brinkley suggested the more down-to-earth interpretation of the board's language in a telephone conversation with the author on August 29, 1989. Further research may help resolve this question, but as should become apparent, the significance of the point remains even if one prefers to read the board's emphasis on democracy as a defensive tactic rather than evidence of genuine conviction.

12. On the role of reciprocity and participation in civic life in Tocqueville's analysis of democracy, see James T. Kloppenberg, "Life Everlasting: Tocqueville in America," *La Revue Tocqueville/The Tocqueville Review* 17 (1996): 19–36, reprinted as chapter 5 in this volume.

13. NRPB, *Security*, p. 544; emphasis in original. Cf. NRPB, *Report for 1943* (Washington, D.C.: U.S. Government Printing Office, 1943), p. 81: "Greater efforts must be made by administrators to take the public into their confidence, and all techniques for enlisting lay participation, such as advisory committees and representation of citizens on appeal boards, must be exploited to the full. In this venture, the private social agencies have an important role to play. The sphere of their activities has been changed by the increasing assumption by government of responsibility for maintenance of the needy, but their opportunities for experimentation in the improvement of service and for leadership in evaluation and understanding of policies and programs have been correspondingly increased."

14. Congressman John Rankin of Mississippi called the NRPB's report "the most fantastic conglomeration of bureaucratic stupidity ever sent to Congress. . . . It would wreck this Republic, wipe out the Constitution, destroy our form of government, set up a totalitarian regime, eliminate private enterprise, regiment our people indefinitely, and pile up on their backs a burden of expenditures that no nation on earth could bear." Rankin's editor-

ial from the *New York Times*, March 14, 1943, is quoted in Warken, *The National Resources Planning Board*, p. 233. For other equally restrained judgments, see pp. 231–233, and cf. the discussion of popular reaction to the board's report in Edwin Amenta and Theda Skocpol, "Redefining the New Deal: World War II and the Development of Social Provision in the United States," in *The Politics of Social Policy in the United States*, ed. Margaret Weir, Ann Shola Orloff, and Theda Skocpol (Princeton: Princeton University Press, 1988), pp. 86–94; and Brinkley, *The End of Reform*, pp. 254–258.

15. NRPB, *Report for 1943*, p. 18.

16. Comprehensive accounts include Abram de Swaan, *In Care of the State*; Douglas Ashford, *The Emergence of Welfare States* (Oxford: Blackwell, 1986); François Ewald, *L'Etat providence* (Paris: Bernard Grasset, 1986); Walter I. Trattner, *From Poor Law to Welfare State: A History of Social Welfare in America*, 3rd ed. (New York: Free Press, 1984); Michael Katz, *In the Shadow of the Poorhouse: A Social History of Welfare in America* (New York: Basic Books, 1986); James T. Patterson, *America's Struggle Against Poverty, 1900–1980* (Cambridge: Harvard University Press, 1981); Douglas Ashford and E. W. Kelley, eds., *Nationalizing Social Security in Europe and America* (Greenwich, Conn.: Jai Press, 1986); and Peter Flora and Arnold J. Heidenheimer, eds., *The Development of Welfare States in Europe and America* (New Brunswick, N.J.: Transaction Books, 1981).

17. Katz, *In the Shadow of the Poorhouse*, p. 36; James T. Kloppenberg, "The Virtues of Liberalism," reprinted as chapter 2 in this volume; Daniel T. Rodgers, *The Work Ethic and Industrial America* (Chicago: University of Chicago Press, 1978).

18. Morton Keller, *Affairs of State: Public Life in Late Nineteenth Century America* (Cambridge: Harvard University Press, 1977); Stephen Skowronek, *Building a New American State: The Expansion of National Administrative Capacities, 1877–1920* (Cambridge: Harvard University Press, 1982); William R. Brock, *Investigation and Responsibility: Public Responsibility in The United States, 1865–1900* (Cambridge: Cambridge University Press, 1984); Ira Katznelson, " 'The Burdens of Urban History': Comment," in *Studies in American Political Development* 3 (1989): 30–51; Ann Shola Orloff, "The Political Origins of America's Belated Welfare State," in *The Politics of Social Policy*, pp. 37–80; Theda Skocpol and John Ikenberry, "The Political Formation of the American Welfare State in Historical and Comparative Perspective," *Comparative Social Research* 6 (1983): 87–148; and Amenta and Skocpol, "Redefining the New Deal."

19. Richard L. McCormick, *The Party Period and Public Policy: American Politics From the Age of Jackson to the Progressive Era* (New York: Oxford University Press, 1986), pp. 197–227, 263–288, 311–356; Orloff, "The Political Origins of America's Belated Welfare State"; and James T. Kloppenberg, *Uncertain Victory: Social Democracy and Progressivism in European and American Thought, 1870–1920* (New York: Oxford University Press, 1986), pp. 199–297.

20. Barry D. Karl, *The Uneasy State: The United States from 1915 to 1945* (Chicago: University of Chicago Press, 1983), pp. 46–69; Ellis Hawley, "The New Deal State and the Anti-Bureaucratic Tradition," in *The New Deal and Its Legacy: Critique and Appraisal*, ed. Robert Eden (New York: Greenwood Press, 1989), pp. 77–92.

21. This is not the place for an extended bibliographical essay on the New Deal. Some recent studies that have shaped my interpretation include Alan Lawson, *Ideas in Crisis: The New Deal and the Great Depression* (Baltimore: Johns Hopkins University Press, forthcoming); Sidney M. Milkis, "The New Deal, Administrative Reform, and the Transcendence of Partisan Politics," *Administration and Society* 18 (1987): 433–472; Sidney M. Milkis, "New Deal Party Politics, Administrative Reform, and the Transformation of

the American Constitution," in Eden, ed., *The New Deal and Its Legacy*, pp. 123–154; Sidney M. Milkis, "The Presidency, Policy Reform, and the Rise of Administrative Politics," in *Remaking American Politics*, ed. Sidney M. Milkis and Richard A. Harris (Boulder: Westview Press, 1989), pp. 146–187; Barry D. Karl, "Constitution and Central Planning: The Third New Deal Revisited," *Supreme Court Reviews* 1988, ed. Philip B. Kurland, Gerhard Casper, and Dennis J. Hutchenson (Chicago: University of Chicago Press, 1989), pp. 163–201. In that essay, Karl writes, "Contrary to what I argued some years ago, the Reorganization Act of 1939 did not give Roosevelt what he wanted in 1937 by a long shot. What he wanted in 1937 would have involved a dramatic transformation in American presidential administration. It would have placed in the White House a planning board charged with the responsibility for directing the actions of a regional system of planning boards" (p. 188). Karl's argument in this essay thus revises his earlier work on Roosevelt in the New Deal, particularly *The Uneasy State*. For other useful reappraisals of the New Deal in light of recent scholarship, see Harvard Sitkoff, ed., *Fifty Years Later: The New Deal Evaluated* (New York: Knopf, 1985).

22. Harry Hopkins, "Beyond Relief: The Larger Task," *New York Times*, August 19, 1931.

23. For Roosevelt's 1944 State of the Union Address, see Samuel I. Rosenman, ed., *The Public Papers and Addresses of Franklin D. Roosevelt*, vol. 13: 1944–45 (New York: Russell and Russell, 1969), pp. 32–44. James MacGregor Burns, *Roosevelt: The Soldier of Freedom* (New York: Harcourt Brace Jovanovich, 1970), pp. 425–426. For contrasting interpretations of Roosevelt's speech and his attitude toward the NRPB during these years, cf. Karl, *Merriam*, pp. 270–283; Clawson, *New Deal Planning*, pp. 237–241; David Brody, "The New Deal and World War II," in *The New Deal: The National Level*, ed. John Braeman et al. (Columbus: Ohio State University Press, 1975), pp. 300–305; John M. Blum, *V Was For Victory: Politics and American Culture During World War II* (New York: Harcourt Brace Jovanovich, 1976), pp. 245–254, all of whom suggest that FDR was genuinely committed to the NRPB and its vision of the postwar world. For an interpretation with a different emphasis, see John W. Jeffries, "Franklin D. Roosevelt and the 'America of Tomorrow,'" in *Power and Responsibility: Case Studies in American Leadership*, ed. David M. Kennedy and Michael E. Parrish (New York: Harcourt Brace Jovanovich, 1986), pp. 29–86, a fine essay that I find persuasive on many issues, but not on this one.

Jeffries argues that FDR endorsed the "second bill of rights" because his pollster Hadley Cantril warned him that "bold and courageous steps" would be necessary to solidify public support on domestic policy. Jeffries then contends that FDR dropped the issue for reasons that I find altogether adequate to explain this development: his concern shifted back to the war, his health began to decline, and he realized that these measures were politically too controversial while the war was still to be won. Given that final assessment in particular, which also explains why FDR reluctantly agreed to drop Henry Wallace from the 1944 ticket, the most plausible explanation of the State of the Union Address, in the absence of evidence pointing toward a different conclusion, remains the simplest one: Roosevelt believed what he said. He backed off only because the path to the domestic support he required as Commander in Chief did not lead in the direction of the welfare state.

24. Jeffries, "Franklin D. Roosevelt and the 'America of Tomorrow,'" p. 44.

25. William Beveridge, *Social Insurance and Allied Services* (London: Macmillan, 1942); Jose Harris, *William Beveridge: A Biography* (Oxford: Clarendon Press of Oxford University Press, 1977); Jose Harris, "Some Aspects of Social Policy in Britain During the Second World War," in *The Emergence of the Welfare State in Britain and Germany, 1850–1950*, ed. Wolfgang J. Mommsen (London: Croom Helm, 1981), pp. 247–262.

26. Churchill quoted in Derek Fraser, *The Evolution of the British Welfare State: A His-*

tory of Social Policy Since the Industrial Revolution, 2nd ed. (London: Macmillan, 1984), p. 218. See also G. C. Peden, *British Economic and Social Policy: Lloyd George to Margaret Thatcher* (Oxford: Philip Allan, 1985), pp. 135–163.

27. Richard Titmuss, *Problems of Social Policy*, History of the Second World War, United Kingdom Civil Series, ed. W. H. Hancock (London: HMSO, 1950), p. 508.

28. This reassessment began with Paul Addison, *The Road to 1945: British Politics and the Second World War* (London: Jonathan Cape, 1975), who demonstrated that the wartime consensus derived as much from Conservative politicians' willingness to cooperate with Labour in the coalition government as it did from changes in deeply rooted convictions. Bolstering that skeptical position were Jose Harris, "Some Aspects of Social Policy"; and Kenneth O. Morgan, *Labour in Power, 1945–1951* (Oxford: Clarendon Press of Oxford University Press, 1984), pp. 142–187, who discussed the social policies of the postwar Atlee government without any reference to Titmuss's views on national solidarity. See also the fine discussion of the role of politics in the shaping of European welfare states in Peter Baldwin, *The Politics of Social Solidarity: Class Bases of the European Welfare State, 1875–1975* (Cambridge: Cambridge University Press, 1990). For Baldwin's account of the Beveridge Report and its role in postwar politics, see pp. 107–134, 232–247.

29. Beveridge, *Social Insurance and Allied Services*, pp. 6–7, 293.

30. Ibid.; see also the discussion of Beveridge's earlier manifesto, *Insurance for All and Everything*, published in 1924, in Michael Freeden, *Liberalism Divided: A Study in British Political Thought, 1914–1939* (Oxford: Clarendon Press of Oxford University Press, 1986), p. 98.

31. William Beveridge, *Full Employment in a Free Society* (New York: Norton, 1945), pp. 257–258.

32. Ibid., p. 16. See also William Beveridge, *Causes and Cures of Unemployment* (London: Longmans, Green, 1931).

33. De Swaan, *In Care of the State*, pp. 143–151; Fraser, *British Welfare State*, pp. 11–177. A thorough account of the Liberal Party's efforts is Bentley B. Gilbert, *The Evolution of National Insurance in Great Britain: The Origins of the Welfare State* (London: Michael Joseph, 1966). For the philosophy and politics of the new liberalism, see chaps. 8, 9, and 10 of Kloppenberg, *Uncertain Victory*. On the interwar years, see Michael Freeden, *Liberalism Divided*.

34. See the discussion of these ideas in Francis G. Castles, "Introduction: Puzzles of Political Economy," in *The Comparative History of Public Policy*, ed. Francis G. Castles (New York: Oxford University Press, 1989), pp. 8–13.

35. See especially the essays collected in Peter B. Evans, Dietrich Reuschemeyer, and Theda Skocpol, eds., *Bringing the State Back In* (New York: Cambridge University Press, 1985); Weir, Orloff, and Skocpol, *The Politics of Social Policy*; and Edwin Amenta and Theda Skocpol, "Taking Exception: Explaining the Distinctiveness of American Public Policies in the Last Century," in Castles, ed., *The Comparative History of Public Policy*, pp. 292–333.

36. In a letter to Felix Frankfurter written February 9, 1937, Roosevelt wrote, "it is the same old story of those who have property to fail to realize that I am the best friend the profit system ever had, even though I add my denunciation of unconscionable profits." Frankfurter Papers, Library of Congress, Washington, D.C., quoted in Milkis, "The Presidency, Policy Reform, and the Rise of Administrative Politics," p. 185, n 76; see also Richard Polenberg, *War and Society: The United States, 1941–1945* (New York: Lippincott, 1972). On labor's apostasy from social and industrial democracy, see David Montgomery, *The Fall of the House of Labor: The Workplace, The State, and American Labor Activism, 1865–1925* (New York: Cambridge University Press, 1987); Ira Katznelson, *City*

Trenches: Urban Politics and the Patterning of Class in the United States (Chicago: University of Chicago Press, 1981); Steve Fraser, *Labor Will Rule: Sidney Hillman and the Rise of American Labor* (New York: Free Press, 1991); Steve Fraser, "The 'Labor Question'";
Nelson Lichtenstein, "From Corporatism to Collective Bargaining: Organized Labor and the Eclipse of Social Democracy in the Postwar Era," in *The Rise and Fall of the New Deal Order, 1930–1980*, ed. Steve Fraser and Gary Gerstle (New York: Basic Books, 1989), pp. 55–84, 122–152; Nelson Lichtenstein, *The Most Dangerous Man in Detroit: Walter Reuther and the Fate of American Labor* (New York: Basic Books, 1995); Beth Stevens, "Blurring the Boundaries: How the Federal Government Has Influenced Welfare Benefits in the Private Sector," in *The Politics of Social Policy*, pp. 123–148; and David Brody, "The New Deal and World War II." In *The Politics of Social Solidarity*, Baldwin argues that British and European labor movements have shown a similar tendency to endorse universal programs of social provision when the working class lacks benefits, then to prefer more narrow programs after they had won benefits themselves, rather than agreeing to pay taxes so benefits might be extended to include other groups.

37. Hawley, "The New Deal State and the Anti-Bureaucratic Tradition," and Karl, *The Uneasy State*, both stress the ambivalence of business leaders toward planning. On agriculture, see Kenneth Finegold, "Agriculture and the Politics of U.S. Social Provision: Social Insurance and Food Stamps," in *The Politics of Social Policy*, pp. 199–234. On Keynesianism in America, see Alan Lawson, *The Failure of Independent Liberalism 1930–1941* (New York: Capricorn, 1971), p. 221; Margaret Weir, "Ideas and Politics: The Acceptance of Keynesianism in Britain and the United States," draft in my possession; Alan Brinkley, "The New Deal and the Idea of the State," in *The Rise and Fall of the New Deal Order*, pp. 85–121; and, for the most detailed account of the rise of Keynesian thinking and its effect on social democratic initiatives, Brinkley, *The End of Reform*.

38. Mark Leff, "The Politics of Sacrifice on the American Home Front in World War II," *Journal of American History* 77 (1991): 1296–1318. On this issue see also Blum, *V Was For Victory*.

39. Karl, *Uneasy State*, p. 214. For a more detailed account of the responses to the NRPB report, see Brinkley, *End of Reform*, pp. 254–258. Even John Dewey admitted to a "change of emphasis" toward individualism in the face of dictatorships and totalitarianism. See Lawson, *Independent Liberalism*, p. 246.

40. Morgan, *Labour in Power*, pp. 18–44; see also the comparative analysis of Britain and America in Amenta and Skocpol, "Redefining the New Deal," pp. 95–122, which examines critically various explanations scholars have offered to account for developments in Britain.

41. Addison, *The Road to 1945*, pp. 42–44; Morgan, *Labour in Power*, pp. 20–64; Freeden, *Liberalism Divided*, pp. 356–363, T. H. Marshall, "The Welfare State: A Sociological Interpretation," quoted in Ringen, *The Possibility of Politics*, p. 35.

42. T. O. Lloyd, *Empire to Welfare State: English History, 1906–1967* (Oxford: Oxford University Press, 1970), pp. 266–269; Morgan, *Labour in Power*, pp. 34–44; Addison, *The Road to 1945*, pp. 258–269; and for the efforts of the Thatcher government, see Patrick Dunleavy, "The United Kingdom: Paradoxes of an Ungrounded Statism," in *The Comparative History of Public Policy*, pp. 281–287; and Hall, *Governing the Economy*, pp. 100–136.

43. This feature of American social policy has received a great deal of attention. See for example Katz, *In the Shadow of the Poorhouse*, pp. 230–234; the essays by Beth Stevens, by Margaret Weir, and by Theda Skocpol in *The Politics of Social Policy*, pp. 123–148, 149–198, 293–311; the essays by Steve Fraser, by Nelson Lichtenstein, and by Ira Katznelson in *The Rise and Fall of the New Deal Order*, pp. 55–84, 122–152, 185–211;

NOTES TO PAGES 119-124   217

and Skocpol and Ikenberry, "The Political Formation of the American Welfare State in Historical and Comparative Perspective."

44. In the face of almost two decades of welfare bashing, it is worth noting two conclusive results of recent research: first, welfare states do indeed decrease the amount of poverty; and second, recent attacks on public assistance programs have slowed the growth of the welfare state but have not led to actual declines in public spending—even in the United States and Great Britain. Recent comparative studies by Stein Ringen, Abram de Swaan, and Robert Morris, and studies of American programs by Sheldon Danziger and his associates, all point to the same conclusion: welfare works. There is simply less inequality after direct transfers than there is in gross income, and the overall qualitative effect of indirect transfers is similarly positive. In Ringen's words, "The thesis that poverty has remained at more or less the same level in spite of economic growth and redistributive efforts is rejected on theoretical, methodological, and empirical grounds. Instead, the proportion of the population living in poverty is shown to be low and to have been reduced" as a result of social programs. Ringen, *The Possibility of Politics*, p. 198; cf. de Swaan, *In Care of the State*; Robert Morris, ed., *Testing the Limits of Social Welfare: International Perspectives on Policy Changes in Nine Countries* (Boston: University Press of New England, 1988); and Sheldon Danziger and D. H. Weinberg, eds., *Fighting Poverty* (Cambridge: Harvard University Press, 1986).

45. Joseph Harris, "Outline for the New York Conference," May 9 and 10, 1936, Franklin D. Roosevelt papers, Hyde Park, New York, quoted in Milkis, "The New Deal, Administrative Reform, and the Transcendence of Partisan Politics," p. 445.

46. Jeremy Waldron, "Welfare and the Images of Charity," *Philosophical Quarterly* 36 (1986): 463–482; Joseph Raz, *The Morality of Freedom* (Oxford: Clarendon Press of Oxford University Press, 1986), p. 409; Robert E. Goodin, *Reasons for Welfare: The Political Theory of the Welfare State* (Princeton: Princeton University Press, 1988), pp. 183, 368. In contrast to these neo-Kantian arguments, a neo-Hegelian rationale is developed in Richard Dien Winfield, *The Just Economy* (London: Routledge, 1988). For an ambitious attempt to reconcile these traditions of negative and positive liberty, which likewise concentrates on the importance of the universality of "situated" freedom, see Richard E. Flathman, *The Philosophy and Politics of Freedom* (Chicago: University of Chicago Press, 1987).

47. Cf. Skocpol, "The Limits of the New Deal System."

48. Michael Walzer, "Socializing the Welfare State," in *Democracy and the Welfare State*, ed. Amy Gutmann (Princeton: Princeton University Press, 1988), pp. 13–26.

49. De Swaan, *In Care of the State*, p. 11.

50. Eveline Burns, Comparison of the Beveridge and the NRPB Reports, December 3, 1942, Franklin D. Roosevelt papers, Hyde Park, New York.

51. W. E. B. Du Bois, *The Souls of Black Folk* in Du Bois, *Writings*, ed. Nathan Huggins (1903; New York: Library of America, 1986); David A. Hollinger, *Postethnic America: Beyond Multiculturalism* (New York: Basic Books, 1995).

Chapter 8

As originally published in the *Encyclopedia of the United States in the Twentieth Century*, ed. Stanley Kutler, 4 vols. (New York: Charles Scribner's Sons, 1996), this chapter was followed by an essay on sources rather than end notes. I have added notes here to bring this chapter into conformity with the others in this volume, but these notes do not begin to provide comprehensive guidance to the primary or secondary sources on twentieth-century American political thought. Readers seeking more detailed information should consult *A Companion to American Thought*, ed. Richard Wightman Fox and James T. Kloppenberg (Oxford: Blackwell Publishers, 1995); and, for well chosen primary sources and reliable guides to the secondary literature, *The American Intellectual Tradition*, ed. David A. Hollinger and Charles Capper, 3rd ed. (New York: Oxford University Press, 1997).

1. Recent interpretive overviews of American political thought include the brilliant, unclassifiable study by Christopher Lasch, *The True and Only Heaven: Progress and Its Critics* (New York: Norton, 1991); and the mordant, encyclopedic work by John P. Diggins, *The Rise and Fall of the American Left* (New York: Norton, 1992). Daniel T. Rodgers, *Contested Truths: Keywords in American Politics* (New York: Basic Books, 1987), is a wide-ranging and provocative interpretation of political discourse. On the strange career of democratic theory, see the indispensable analysis by Edward A. Purcell Jr., *The Crisis of Democratic Theory: Scientific Naturalism and the Problem of Value* (Lexington: University Press of Kentucky, 1973), which encompasses the entire period from the 1890s to the 1960s.

On a central theme in American intellectual life, see Wilfred M. McClay, *The Masterless: Self and Society in Modern America* (Chapel Hill: University of North Carolina Press, 1994); on a central site of American intellectual life, see Thomas Bender, *New York Intellect* (New York: Knopf, 1987); for a challenge to standard ideological and chronological categories, see Michael Kazin, *The Populist Persuasion: An American History* (New York: Basic Books, 1995).

2. Walter Lippmann, *Drift and Mastery: An Attempt to Diagnose the Current Unrest*, ed. William E. Leuchtenburg (1911; Madison: University of Wisconsin Press, 1985), p. 106. Perhaps the most widely read and influential book published in the United States in the post–Civil War years was Edward Bellamy, *Looking Backward: 2000–1887*; it is currently available in a splendid, annotated edition, with an introduction by Daniel Borus (Boston: Bedford Books of St. Martin's Press, 1995).

On late nineteenth-century American thought, see the essays by Daniel Walker Howe, David Hall, and Geoffrey Blodgett in *Victorian America*, ed. Daniel Walker Howe (Philadelphia: University of Pennsylvania Press, 1976); John Sproat, *"The Best Men": Liberal Reformers in the Gilded Age* (New York: Oxford University Press, 1968); and John L. Thomas, *Alternative America: Henry George, Edward Bellamy, Henry Demarest Lloyd, and the Adversary Tradition* (Cambridge: Belknap Press of Harvard University Press, 1983).

3. Among recent studies of progressive-era thought, different interpretations are available in Robert Crunden, *Ministers of Reform: The Progressives' Achievement in American Civilization, 1889–1920* (New York: Basic Books, 1982), which stresses the importance of religion; Eldon Eisenach, *The Lost Promise of Progressivism* (Lawrence: University Press of Kansas, 1994), which differentiates the progressives' vision of the public good from the interest-group liberalism that replaced it; and James T. Kloppenberg, *Uncertain Victory: Social Democracy and Progressivism in European and American Thought, 1870–1920* (New York: Oxford University Press, 1986), which emphasizes the connection between philosophy and political theory for selected thinkers on both sides of the Atlantic.

On the rise of social science, compare Dorothy Ross, *The Origins of American Social Science* (Cambridge: Cambridge University Press, 1991), which highlights the role played by the ideology of American exceptionalism; Thomas L. Haskell, *The Emergence of Professional Social Science: The American Social Science Association and the Nineteenth-Century Crisis of Authority* (Urbana: University of Illinois Press, 1977), which explores early American social scientists' efforts to establish the authority of their discursive communities as an alternative to naive voluntarism and reductionist positivism; Mary O. Furner, *Advocacy and Objectivity: A Crisis in the Professionalization of American So-*

cial Science, 1865–1905 (Lexington: University Press of Kentucky, 1975), which examines the conflict between scholars' views of their responsibilities; and Julie A. Reuben, *The Making of the Modern University: Intellectual Transformation and the Marginalization of Morality* (Chicago: University of Chicago Press, 1996), which traces the shift of focus in higher education from religion to science.

4. Richard T. Ely, *Socialism and Social Reform* (New York: Thomas Crowell & Co., 1894), pp. 255–257, 175f. The most detailed study of Ely remains Benjamin G. Rader, *The Academic Mind and Reform: The Influence of Richard T. Ely in American Life* (Lexington: University Press of Kentucky, 1966).

5. Walter Rauschenbusch, *Christianizing the Social Order* (New York: Macmillan Co., 1912), p. 9. On the social gospel, see Henry F. May, *Protestant Churches and Industrial America* (New York: Oxford University Press, 1949); William R. Hutchinson, *The Modernist Impulse in American Protestantism* (Cambridge: Harvard University Press, 1976); Susan Curtis, *A Consuming Faith: The Social Gospel and Modern American Culture* (Baltimore: Johns Hopkins University Press, 1991); and Richard Wightman Fox, "The Culture of Liberal Protestantism," *Journal of Interdisciplinary History* 23 (1993): 639–660.

6. Jane Addams, *Twenty Years at Hull House* (1910; New York: Signet, 1961), pp. 76, 89. Compare the treatments of Addams in Allen F. Davis, *American Heroine: The Life and Legend of Jane Addams* (New York: Oxford University Press, 1973); and Rivka Shpak Lissak, *Pluralism & Progressives: Hull House and the New Immigrants, 1890–1919* (Chicago: University of Chicago Press, 1989). The most comprehensive study of the settlement house movement remains Allen F. Davis, *Spearheads for Reform: The Social Settlements and the Progressive Movement, 1890–1914* (New York: Oxford University Press, 1967).

7. On feminist theory, three fine studies are Rosalind Rosenberg, *Beyond Separate Spheres: Intellectual Roots of Modern Feminism* (New Haven: Yale University Press, 1982); Nancy Cott, *The Grounding of Modern Feminism* (New Haven: Yale University Press, 1987); and Ellen Fitzpatrick, *Endless Crusade: Women Social Scientists and Progressive Reform* (New York: Oxford University Press, 1990). The principal contribution to feminist theory by Charlotte Perkins Gilman, *Women and Economics*, ed. Carl N. Degler (1898; New York: Harper Torchbooks, 1966), should be supplemented by her fiction, a sampling of which—including her haunting classic "The Yellow Wallpaper"—is available in *The Charlotte Perkins Gilman Reader*, ed. Ann J. Lane (New York: Pantheon, 1980). See also Ann J. Lane, *To "Herland" and Beyond: The Life and Work of Charlotte Perkins Gilman* (New York: Pantheon, 1990) and, on another influential feminist and activist, Kathryn Kish Sklar, *Florence Kelley and the Nation's Work: The Rise of Women's Political Culture, 1830–1900* vol. 1, *Doing the Nation's Work* (New Haven: Yale University Press, 1995).

8. Studies of James's political ideas include George Cotkin, *William James: Public Philosopher* (Baltimore: Johns Hopkins University Press, 1990); and Joshua I. Miller, *Democratic Temperament: The Legacy of William James* (Lawrence: University Press of Kansas, 1997). On the relation between James's philosophy and his politics, and an assessment of his significance for other American progressives and social democrats, see Kloppenberg, *Uncertain Victory* pp. 145–195.

9. Jesse Taft, *The Woman's Movement from the Point of View of Social Consciousness* (Chicago: University of Chicago Press, 1916), pp. 55, 57, quoted in Rosenberg, *Separate Spheres*, pp. 139, 142. See also Charlene Haddock Seigfried, *Pragmatism and Feminism: Reweaving the Social Fabric* (Chicago: University of Chicago Press, 1996); and, on a leading feminist educator, Joyce Antler, *Lucy Sprague Mitchell* (New Haven: Yale University Press, 1987).

10. W. E. B. Du Bois quoted in Cornel West, *The American Evasion of Philosophy* (Madison: University of Wisconsin Press, 1989), p. 139.

11. W. E. B. Du Bois, *The Souls of Black Folk*, in Du Bois, *Writings*, ed. Nathan Huggins (1903; New York: Library of America, 1986), p. 365. On the young Du Bois, see the authoritative biography by David Levering Lewis, *W. E. B. Du Bois: Biography of a Race, 1868–1919* (New York: Henry Holt & Co.,1993); Thomas A. Holt, "The Political Uses of Alienation: W. E. B. Du Bois on Politics, Race, and Culture," *American Quarterly* 42 (1990): 301–323; and Richard Cullen Rath, "Echo and Narcissus: The Afrocentric Pragmatism of W. E. B. Du Bois," *Journal of American History* 84 (1997): 461–495.

12. Walter Lippmann, *A Preface to Politics* (1913; Ann Arbor: University of Michigan Press, 1962), p. 29; Lippmann, *Drift and Mastery*, pp. 147–148, 141, 18. On Lippmann, see Ronald Steel, *Walter Lippmann and the American Century* (Boston: Atlantic–Little, Brown, 1980).

13. Herbert Croly, *The Promise of American Life*, ed. John William Ward (1909; Indianapolis: Bobbs-Merrill, 1965), pp. 453–454; Croly, *Progressive Democracy* (New York: Macmillan, 1914), p. 378. A splendid biography is David W. Levy, *Herbert Croly of "The New Republic"* (Princeton: Princeton University Press, 1985); see also Edward A. Stettner, *Shaping Modern Liberalism: Herbert Croly and Progressive Thought* (Lawrence: University Press of Kansas, 1993); and Charles Forcey, *The Crossroads of Liberalism: Croly, Weyl, Lippmann, and the Progressive Era, 1900–1925* (New York: Oxford University Press, 1961).

14. Croly, *Progressive Democracy*, pp. 358, 424–425.

15. Jane M. Dewey, "Biography of John Dewey," in *The Philosophy of John Dewey*, 2nd ed., ed. Paul A. Schilpp (New York: Tudor, 1951), p. 30. The outstanding work on Dewey is Robert B. Westbrook, *John Dewey and American Democracy* (Ithaca, N.Y.: Cornell University Press, 1991), which, given Dewey's centrality and his longevity, also provides a remarkably comprehensive guide to twentieth-century American political discourse. Other recent studies of Dewey include Steven C. Rockefeller, *John Dewey: Religious Faith and Democratic Humanism* (New York: Columbia University Press, 1991); Alan Ryan, *John Dewey and the High Tide of American Liberalism* (New York: Norton, 1995); and James T. Kloppenberg, "Democracy and Disenchantment: From Weber and Dewey to Habermas and Rorty," in *Modernist Impulses in the Human Sciences, 1870–1930*, ed. Dorothy Ross (Baltimore: Johns Hopkins University Press, 1994) reprinted as chapter 6 in this volume. A sympathetic treatment of some of Dewey's critics is Casey Nelson Blake, *Beloved Community: The Cultural Criticism of Randolph Bourne, Van Wyck Brooks, Waldo Frank, and Lewis Mumford* (Chapel Hill: University of North Carolina Press, 1990).

16. John Dewey, *The Ethics of Democracy* (Ann Arbor: Andrews & Co., 1888), in Dewey, *The Early Works, 1882–1898*, ed. Jo Ann Boydston et al. (Carbondale: Southern Illinois University Press, 1967), 1: 248–249.

17. John Dewey, "The Hughes Campaign," *New Republic* 8 (1916): 319–321, in Dewey, *The Middle Works, 1899–1924*, ed. Jo Ann Boydston et al. (Carbondale: Southern Illinois University Press, 1980), 10: 254.

18. Of the many fine works on Louis Brandeis and his influence on Wilson's New Freedom, see especially Philippa Strum, *Louis D. Brandeis: Justice for the People* (New York: Schocken, 1984); and Philippa Strum, *Brandeis: Beyond Progressivism* (Lawrence: University Press of Kansas, 1993).

19. See the discussion of Harold Stearns, *Civilization in the United States*, and its context in the comprehensive and detailed account by Richard Pells, *Radical Visions and American Dreams: Culture and Social Thought in the Depression Years* (New York: Harper, 1973), pp. 16–42.

20. Herbert Hoover, *American Individualism* (Garden City, N.Y.: Doubleday, 1923).

The review in *The New York Times* is quoted in Joan Hoff Wilson, *Herbert Hoover: Forgotten Progressive* (Boston: Little, Brown, 1975), p. 55.

21. Walter Lippman, *Public Opinion* (1922; New York: Free Press, 1965), pp. 3, 10, 53, 158, 180, 195.

22. John Dewey's review of Lippmann's *Public Opinion*, originally published in the *New Republic* 30 (1922): 286–288, in Dewey, *Middle Works*, 13: 337–344.

23. John Dewey, *The Public and Its Problems* (New York: Henry Holt, 1927), in Dewey, *The Later Works, 1925–1953*, ed. Jo Ann Boydston et al. (Carbondale: Southern Illinois University Press, 1984), 2: 299.

24. Ibid., 331.

25. Ibid., 365.

26. John Dewey, *Individualism Old and New* (New York: Capricorn, 1930), in Dewey, *Later Works*, 5: 48–49, 57.

27. Reliable overviews of the 1930s include Arthur Ekirch, *Ideologies and Utopias: The Impact of the New Deal on American Thought* (New York: Quadrangle, 1969), which stresses the positive achievements of liberal reform; the more critical but still sympathetic study by Alan Lawson, *The Failure of Independent Liberalism, 1930–1941* (New York: Capricorn, 1971); Pells, *Radical Visions and American Dreams*; and Purcell, *The Crisis of Democratic Theory*. For the writings of New Deal intellectuals, see the selections in Howard Zinn, ed., *New Deal Thought* (Indianapolis: Bobbs-Merrill, 1966).

On the impact of European ideas in America, see Martin Jay, *The Dialectical Imagination: A History of the Frankfurt School and the Institute of Social Research, 1923–1950* (Boston: Little, Brown, 1973); and H. Stuart Hughes, *The Sea Change: The Migration of Social Thought, 1930–1965* (New York: Harper & Row, 1977); on American perceptions of European developments, John P. Diggins, *Mussolini and Fascism: The View from America* (Princeton: Princeton University Press, 1972). On American critics outside the mainstream, see the graceful studies by Daniel Aaron, *Writers on the Left* ((New York: Oxford University Press, 1961); and Alan Brinkley, *Voices of Protest: Huey Long, Father Coughlin, and the Great Depression* (New York: Knopf, 1982).

28. John Dewey, *Liberalism and Social Action* (New York: G. P. Putnam's Sons, 1935), in Dewey, *The Later Works*, 11: 61–62. The most reliable treatment of Dewey's evolving ideas during these years is Westbrook, *John Dewey and American Democracy*, pp. 377–523.

29. The best study of Reinhold Niebuhr is Richard Wightman Fox, *Reinhold Niebuhr: A Biography*, with a new introduction and afterword (Ithaca, N.Y.: Cornell University Press, 1996). On Dorothy Day and other Catholic radicals, see James Terence Fisher, *The Catholic Counterculture in America, 1933–1962* (Chapel Hill: University of North Carolina Press, 1989). On the general issue of religion and politics in twentieth-century America, see Leo Ribuffo, "God and Contemporary Politics," *Journal of American History* 79 (1993): 1515–1533; Robert Wuthnow, *The Restructuring of American Religion: Society and Faith Since World War II* (Princeton: Princeton University Press, 1988); and Garry Wills, *Under God: Religion and American Politics* (New York: Simon & Schuster, 1990).

30. Hubert Humphrey, *The Political Philosophy of the New Deal* (1940; Baton Rouge: Louisiana State University Press, 1970), p. 17.

31. Two outstanding collections of essays examine the interaction among ideas, institutions, and political pressures in shaping the New Deal and the postwar American welfare state: *The Rise and Fall of the New Deal Order*, ed. Steve Fraser and Gary Gerstle (Princeton: Princeton University Press, 1989); and *The Politics of Social Policy in the United States*, ed. Margaret Weir, Ann Shola Orloff, and Theda Skocpol (Princeton: Princeton University Press, 1988). For more detailed discussion of these issues, see James T.

Kloppenberg, "Deliberative Democracy and the Problem of Poverty in America," chapter 7 in this volume.

32. The best treatment of these developments is Purcell, *The Crisis of Democratic Theory*. A provocative analysis that emphasizes the reorientation of some American liberals toward economic issues is Gary Gerstle, "The Protean Character of American Liberalism," *American Historical Review* 99 (1994): 1043–1073. On the post–World War II years more generally, see Richard Pells, *The Liberal Mind in a Conservative Age: American Intellectuals in the 1940s and 1950s* (New York: Harper and Row, 1985); Stephen J. Whitfield, *The Culture of the Cold War* (Baltimore: Johns Hopkins University Press, 1990); and John Patrick Diggins, *The Proud Decades: America in War and Peace* (New York: Norton, 1988).

33. On Arendt's widely influential interpretation of totalitarianism, see Stephen J. Whitfield, *Into the Dark: Hannah Arendt and Totalitarianism* (Philadelphia: Temple University Press, 1980); and more generally, Elizabeth Young-Bruehl, *Hannah Arendt, For the Love of the World* (New Haven: Yale University Press, 1982).

34. Steven M. Gillon, *Politics and Vision: The ADA and American Liberalism, 1947–1985* (New York: Oxford University Press, 1987).

35. For a brilliant study of pluralism and its consequences for social and political theory, see Michael Paul Rogin, *The Intellectuals and McCarthy: The Radical Specter* (Cambridge: MIT Press, 1967).

36. Howard Brick, *Daniel Bell and the Decline of Intellectual Radicalism: Social Theory and Political Reconciliation in the 1940s* (Madison: University of Wisconsin Press, 1986), illuminates Bell's early career; Bell offered his own reflections on the controversy his argument engendered in a revised edition of *The End of Ideology: On the Exhaustion of Political Ideas in the 1950s* (1962; Cambridge: Harvard University Press, 1988). On the New York intellectuals more generally, see Alexander Bloom, *Prodigal Sons: The New York Intellectuals and Their World* (New York: Oxford University Press, 1986); Terry A. Cooney, *The Rise of the New York Intellectuals: "Partisan Review" and Its Circle* (Madison: University of Wisconsin Press, 1986); Neil Jumonville, *Critical Crossings: The New York Intellectuals in Postwar America* (Berkeley: University of California Press, 1991); and Alan M. Wald, *The New York Intellectuals: The Rise and Decline of the Anti-Stalinist Left from the 1930s to the 1980s* (Chapel Hill: University of North Carolina Press, 1987).

37. Bell, *The End of Ideology*, p. 405.

38. An outstanding analysis of the ideas of the New Left is Jim Miller, *"Democracy Is in the Streets": From Port Huron to the Siege of Chicago* (New York: Simon and Schuster, 1987). Other accounts include Maurice Isserman, *If I Had a Hammer . . . : The Death of the Old Left and the Birth of the New Left* (New York: Basic Books, 1987); and Todd Gitlin, *The Sixties: Years of Hope, Days of Rage* (New York: Bantam, 1987).

39. Of particular value for the ideas of the civil rights movement are the brilliant study by Richard H. King, *Civil Rights and the Idea of Freedom* (New York: Oxford University Press, 1992); Taylor Branch, *Parting the Waters: America in the King Years, 1954–1963* (New York: Simon and Schuster, 1988), which pays particular attention to the role of religious leaders; and, on the movement's more militant wing, Clayborne Carson, *In Struggle: SNCC and the Black Awakening of the 1960s* (Cambridge: Harvard University Press, 1981).

40. Martin Luther King Jr., "Letter from a Birmingham Jail," *The Christian Century*, June 12, 1963, pp. 769–775, in King, *Why We Can't Wait* (New York: New American Library, 1964). On the development of King's thought, see John J. Ansbro, *Martin Luther King Jr.: The Making of a Mind* (Maryknoll, N.Y.: Orbis, 1982).

41. Malcolm X, with Alex Haley, *The Autobiography of Malcolm X* (1964; New York: Ballantine, 1973), pp. 371, 377. See also James Cone, *Martin and Malcolm and America: A Dream or a Nightmare?* (Maryknoll, N.Y.: Orbis, 1991).

42. On King's attempt to carry the civil rights movement into northern cities, see James Ralph Jr., *Northern Protest: Martin Luther King Jr., Chicago, and the Civil Rights Movement* (Cambridge: Harvard University Press, 1993).

43. On second-wave feminism generally, see Sara Evans, *Personal Politics: The Roots of Women's Liberation in the Civil Rights Movement and the New Left* (New York: Knopf, 1979); and Alice Echols, *Daring to Be Bad: Radical Feminism in America, 1967–1975* (Minneapolis: University of Minnesota Press, 1989). On Friedan in particular, see Daniel Horowitz, "Rethinking Betty Friedan and *The Feminine Mystique*: Labor Union Radicalism and Feminism in Cold War America," *American Quarterly* 48 (1996): 1–42. On the paradoxical relation between second-wave feminism and psychology, see Ellen Herman, *The Romance of American Psychology: Political Culture in the Age of Experts* (Berkeley: University of California Press, 1995), pp. 276–303.

44. Joan Williams, "Gender Wars: Selfless Women in the Republic of Choice," *New York University Law Review* 66 (1991): 1559–1634; see also Seigfried, *Pragmatism and Feminism*, pp. 111–276. A spirited set of essays and rejoinders by Seyla Benhabib, Judith Butler, Drucilla Cornell, and Nancy Fraser, which suggests the wide range of contemporary feminist theoretical perspectives, is *Feminist Contentions: A Philosophical Exchange* (London: Routledge, 1996); another illuminating overview of these issues is Lori J. Kenschaft, "Feminism," in *A Companion to American Thought*, pp. 232–235.

45. For an introduction to these issues, see Alan Brinkley, "The Problem of American Conservatism," with responses by Susan M. Yohn and Leo Ribuffo and Brinkley's rejoinder, *American Historical Review* 99 (1994): 409–452. Studies of American conservatism include George H. Nash, *The Conservative Intellectual Movement in America: Since 1945* (New York: Basic Books, 1976); John Patrick Diggins, *Up from Communism: Conservative Odysseys in American Intellectual History* (New York: Harper & Row, 1975); Patrick Allitt, *Catholic Intellectuals and Conservative Politics in America* (Ithaca, N.Y.: Cornell University Press, 1993); Eugene D. Genovese, *The Southern Tradition: The Achievements and Limitations of an American Conservatism* (Cambridge: Harvard University Press, 1994); Peter Steinfels, *The Neo-Conservatives: The Men Who Are Changing America's Politics* (New York: Simon & Schuster, 1979); and David Hoeveler Jr., *Watch on the Right: Conservative Intellectuals in the Reagan Era* (Madison: University of Wisconsin Press, 1991).

46. On Rawls and *A Theory of Justice*, see *Reading Rawls*, ed. Norman Daniels (New York: Basic Books, 1975); and *Liberalism and Its Critics*, ed. Michael Sandel (Oxford: Blackwell, 1984).

47. On the discipline of political science in the middle decades of the twentieth century, see David Ricci, *The Tragedy of Political Science: Politics, Scholarship, and Democracy* (New Haven: Yale University Press, 1984); and the comprehensive review essay by John S. Dryzek and Stephen T. Leonard, "History and Discipline in Political Science," *American Political Science Review* 82 (1988): 1245–1260.

To understand why things have changed, and why we are currently seeing a revival of political theory in American scholarship, see Thomas Bender, "Politics, Intellect, and the American University, 1945–1995," *Daedalus* 126 (Winter 1997): 1–38; and Rogers Smith, "Still Blowing in the Wind: The American Quest for a Democratic, Scientific Political Science," *Daedalus* 126 (Winter 1997): 253–288. Richard J. Bernstein, *The Restructuring of Social and Political Theory* (New York: Harcourt Brace Jovanovich, 1976), explains how and why the value-free empiricism of mainstream social science collapsed in the 1960s and 1970s.

Volumes harvesting recent work include *Liberalism and the Moral Life*, ed. Nancy Rosenblum (Cambridge: Harvard University Press, 1989), which contains essays that chal-

lenge the frequently assumed identification of liberalism with a narrow and shallow possessive individualism; *Beyond Self-Interest,* ed. Jane J. Mansbridge (Chicago: University
of Chicago Press, 1990), which includes essays from leading social scientists who agree
about the inadequacy of the common view that human behavior is driven by self-interest;
Democracy and the Welfare State, ed. Amy Gutmann (Princeton: Princeton University
Press, 1988), which includes thoughtful reflections on the ethics and the political status
of social welfare programs in America; and *Political Theory Today,* ed. David Held (Stanford: Stanford University Press, 1991), which surveys recent work from a variety of critical perspectives.

48. For further discussion of recent developments in political theory, see James T. Kloppenberg, "Why History Matters to Political Theory," in *Scientific Authority and Twentieth-
Century America,* ed. Ronald Walters (Baltimore: Johns Hopkins University Press, 1997),
pp. 185-203, reprinted as chapter 9 in this volume. The best way to follow the development of contemporary political ideas is to read such journals as *Political Theory, Dissent,
Ethics, The American Prospect, The Public Interest, Commonweal, Commentary, Tikkun,*
and *The Responsive Community.*

49. Two attempts to explain and assess the recent revival of pragmatism are Richard
J. Bernstein, "The Resurgence of Pragmatism," *Social Research* 59 (1992): 813-840; and
James T. Kloppenberg, "Pragmatism: An Old Name for Some New Ways of Thinking?"
Journal of American History 83 (1996): 100-138.

50. Richard J. Bernstein, *The New Constellation: The Ethical-Political Horizons of
Modernity/Postmodernity* (Cambridge: MIT Press, 1992), pp. 338-339.

51. Mary Ann Glendon, *Rights Talk: The Impoverishment of Political Discourse* (New
York: Free Press, 1991), p. xi. Two theorists working in a similar vein are William Sulli-
van, one of the contributors to *Habits of the Heart,* who was explicit about his debts to
Dewey in his *Reconstructing Public Philosophy* (Berkeley: University of California Press,
1982); and William A. Galston, who argued in *Justice and the Human Good* (Chicago:
University of Chicago Press, 1980), and in a collection of essays, *Liberal Purposes: Goods,
Virtues, and Diversity in the Liberal State* (Cambridge: Cambridge University Press,
1991), that liberals need not claim to be neutral about what constitutes the good, and what
liberal virtues are; in Galston's judgment, which I share, such proclamations of neutrality
impoverish liberal discourse and weaken progressive politics.

Chapter 9

1. I do not mean to suggest that analytic philosophy and objective social science are
dead; to the contrary, they obviously remain very much alive. For guides to recent developments, see "American Academic Culture in Transformation: Fifty Years, Four Disciplines," *Daedalus,* Winter 1997, especially the following: Robert M. Solow, "How Did
Economics Get That Way and What Way Did It Get?" pp. 39-58; David M. Kreps, "Economics—The Current Position," pp. 59-86; William J. Barber, "Reconfigurations in
American Academic Economics: A General Practitioner's Perspective," pp. 87-104; Hilary Putnam, "A Half Century of Philosophy, Viewed from Within," pp. 175-208; Alexander Nehamas, "Trends in Recent American Philosophy," pp. 209-224; and Rogers M.
Smith, "Still Blowing in the Wind: The American Quest for a Democratic, Scientific Political Science," which surveys the avalanche of historical studies of the discipline that
have been published in the last decade. See also the thoughtful introductory overview of
this collection of essays by Thomas Bender, "Politics, Intellect, and the American University, 1945-1995," pp. 1-38.

2. Thomas S. Kuhn, *The Structure of Scientific Revolutions* (Chicago: University of

Chicago Press, 1962). See also Ellen Herman, *The Romance of American Psychology: Political Culture in the Age of Experts* (Berkeley: University of California Press, 1995); Ronald Walters, ed., *Scientific Authority and Twentieth-Century America* (Baltimore: Johns Hopkins University Press, 1997); and especially David A. Hollinger, *Postethnic America: Beyond Multiculturalism* (New York: Basic Books, 1995).

3. The best study of Dilthey in English is Michael Ermarth, *Wilhelm Dilthey: The Critique of Historical Reason* (Chicago: University of Chicago Press, 1978).

4. Even though conceptions of reason and human preferences have varied dramatically over time and space, reflecting the enormous variations of history and culture, some social scientists have clung to an abstract theory of "rational choice." But as the failures of rational-choice models to explain, let alone predict, the messy data of human behavior accumulate, the promise of a unified theory capable of generating a predictive science of human behavior is revealed as a mirage. An incisive critical guide to the literature surrounding rational choice theories is Donald P. Green and Ian Shapiro, *Pathologies of Rational Choice: A Critique of Applications in Political Science* (New Haven: Yale University Press, 1994).

5. Peter Novick, *That Noble Dream: The "Objectivity Question" and the American Historical Profession* (Cambridge: Cambridge University Press, 1988). For overviews of these complex developments, see Richard J. Bernstein, *The Restructuring of Social and Political Theory* (New York: Harcourt Brace Jovanovich, 1976); Fred R. Dallmayr and Thomas A. McCarthy, eds., *Understanding and Social Inquiry* (Notre Dame: University of Notre Dame Press, 1977); Quentin Skinner, ed., *The Return of Grand Theory in the Human Sciences* (Cambridge: Cambridge University Press, 1985); Ralph Cohen and Michael S. Roth, eds., *History And. . . : Histories Within the Human Sciences* (Charlottesville: University Press of Virginia, 1995); and Terrence J. McDonald, ed., *The Historic Turn in the Human Sciences* (Ann Arbor: University of Michigan Press, 1996).

6. Don Herzog, *Without Foundations: Justification in Political Theory* (Ithaca, N.Y.: Cornell University Press, 1985), p. 20; Joseph Raz, *The Morality of Freedom* (Oxford: Clarendon Press of Oxford University Press, 1986), p. 3; Richard Flathman, *The Philosophy and Politics of Freedom* (Chicago: University of Chicago Press, 1987). Flathman elaborates his position in his collection of essays *Toward a Liberalism* (Ithaca, N.Y.: Cornell University Press, 1989). The contextualist approach to the study of political thought is usually associated with the work of Quentin Skinner. For a useful compilation of Skinner's work, his critics' arguments, and his response, see James Tully, ed., *Meaning and Context: Quentin Skinner and His Critics* (Princeton: Princeton University Press, 1988).

7. William Sullivan's contributions to Robert N. Bellah, Richard Madsen, William M. Sullivan, Ann Swidler, and Steven M. Tipton, *Habits of the Heart: Individualism and Commitment in American Life* (Berkeley: University of California Press, 1986), are especially apparent in chaps. 2 and 10; compare his *Reconstructing Public Philosophy* (Berkeley: University of California Press, 1982). Charles Taylor, *Philosophy and the Human Sciences: Philosophical Papers* (Cambridge: Cambridge University Press, 1985), 2: 312–313; see also Taylor, *Sources of the Self: The Making of the Modern Identity* (Cambridge: Harvard University Press, 1989); the quotation is from p. 520. Compare William Galston, *Liberal Purposes: Goods, Virtues, and Diversity in the Liberal State* (Cambridge: Cambridge University Press, 1991), who argues convincingly that liberalism itself, independent of the religious convictions that animated its early champions, contains adequate resources to sustain a conception of the good and virtuous life. See also William E. Connolly, *Politics and Ambiguity* (Madison: University of Wisconsin Press, 1987); Richard J. Bernstein, *Beyond Objectivism and Relativism* (Philadelphia: University of Pennsylvania Press, 1983); Richard J. Bernstein, *Habermas and Modernity* (Cambridge: Polity, 1985); Richard J. Bernstein, *The New Constellation: The Ethical-Political Horizons of Modernity/*

Postmodernity (Cambridge: MIT Press, 1992); and Thomas McCarthy, *The Critical Theory of Jürgen Habermas*, 2nd ed. (Cambridge: MIT Press, 1985). I am aware of the difficulties involved in grouping disparate thinkers under the unwieldy labels "liberal" and "communitarian." On this division, see John R. Wallach, "Liberals, Communitarians, and the Tasks of Political Theory," *Political Theory* 15 (1987): 581-611; and cf. Richard J. Bernstein, "One Step Forward, Two Steps Back: Richard Rorty on Liberal Democracy and Philosophy," *Political Theory* 15 (1987): 561, nn 12, 14.

8.   John Rawls, "Kantian Constructivism in Moral Theory," *Journal of Philosophy* 77 (1980): 515-572; John Rawls, "Justice as Fairness: Political, Not Metaphysical," *Philosophy and Public Affairs* 14 (1985): 223-251; the quotations are from pp. 228, 238, and 249. For the full statement of his revised position, see John Rawls, *Political Liberalism* (New York: Columbia University Press, 1993). On Rawls's constructivism, see Richard Rorty, "The Priority of Democracy to Philosophy," in *The Virginia Statute for Religious Freedom: Its Evolution and Consequences in American History*, ed. Merrill D. Peterson and Robert C. Vaughan (Cambridge: Cambridge University Press, 1988). For a critical assessment of the adequacy of Rawls's historicist turn, see Patrick Neal, "Justice as Fairness: Political or Metaphysical?" *Political Theory* 18 (1990): 24-50; for a defense of Rawls, cf. Amy Gutmann, "The Central Role of Rawls's Theory," *Dissent* (1989): 338-342.

9.   Amy Gutmann, "Communitarian Critics of Liberalism," *Philosophy and Public Affairs* 14 (1985): 308-322; Stephen Holmes, "The Community Trap," *New Republic*, November 28, 1988, pp. 24-28; Rorty, "The Priority of Democracy," p. 272; Jeffrey Stout, *Ethics after Babel: The Languages of Morals and Their Discontents* (Boston: Beacon, 1988), p. 229.

10.   Stephen Holmes, *The Anatomy of Antiliberalism* (Cambridge: Harvard University Press, 1993); Stephen Holmes, *Passions and Constraint: On the Theory of Liberal Democracy* (Cambridge: Harvard University Press, 1995); the quotation is from p. xii.

11.   Michael Walzer, *Spheres of Justice: A Defense of Pluralism and Equality* (New York: Basic Books, 1983), pp. 6, 314; Michael Walzer, *Thick and Thin: Moral Argument at Home and Abroad* (Notre Dame: University of Notre Dame Press, 1994); the quotation is from p. 27. Introducing a series of state-of-the-art essays in *Dissent* in 1989, Walzer noted "a series of convergences: between liberals and socialists, Marxists and pluralists, defenders of community and defenders of individual autonomy." In his estimation, "a renewed sense of the value of liberalism and social democracy is their single most important cause." While I too would emphasize that factor in explaining this reorientation, the contributors of several of the essays, including notably Alan Ryan on communitarianism, Don Herzog on liberalism, David Plotke on Marxism, and Sanford Levinson on critical legal studies, also note the importance of an increased awareness of historicity and resistance to foundationalism in accounting for the convergences Walzer stresses. See Walzer, "The State of Political Theory," *Dissent* (1989): 337-370.

12.   Walzer, *Thick and Thin*, pp. 12-13. Walzer's way of advocating democratic procedures thus deflects criticism of the ideal of deliberation advanced by some skeptics who worry that it necessarily privileges articulate, educated persons who are skilled at argument and discriminates against those lacking such skills. Acknowledging the roots of the practice of deliberation in the preferences of aristocratic and educated elites should help us guard against the potential exclusion of less privileged persons and encourage sympathetic listening to those less inclined or trained to develop reasoned, abstract arguments than to "testify" on the basis of their own lived experience. Admitting the imperfections of deliberation need not cause democrats to dismiss it; after all testimony has been heard and understood, some procedure remains necessary for deciding what is to be done. On this issue, see Lynn M. Sanders, "Against Deliberation," *Political Theory* 25 (1997): 347-376. On the importance of traditions of participation in civic affairs, see the influential work of

Robert Putnam et al., *Making Democracy Work: Civic Traditions in Modern Italy* (Princeton: Princeton University Press, 1993); and Robert Putnam, "Bowling Alone," *Journal of Democracy* 6 (1995): 64–79.

13. J. Donald Moon, for example, chided Richard Flathman for replacing the early Rawls's foundationalism with an equally suspicious claim that rights are, after all, "elemental," in his review of *The Philosophy and Politics of Freedom*, in *Political Theory* 16 (1988): 650–654. Jeffrey Stout suggested, in *Ethics After Babel*, p. 227, that Rawls probably would not have labored so diligently on the original position if he were concerned only to validate it on thoroughly contextualist grounds; other critics have found evidence in *Political Liberalism* of Rawls's earlier inclination to treat certain modern Western ideals as "human." William A. Galston contended, in "Community, Democracy, Philosophy: The Political Thought of Michael Walzer," *Political Theory* 17 (1989): 119–130, that despite Walzer's many invocations of the concrete, particular, and historical, a "lurking universalism" pervades his analysis of democratic politics. *Thick and Thin* can be read as Walzer's response to such criticism. Finally, Habermas's continuing reliance on the notion of an ideal speech situation suggests to many of his critics that, despite his pragmatist rhetoric, he ultimately retreats to the supposedly universalist rationalism of the Enlightenment. See for example Bernstein, introduction to *Habermas and Modernity*, pp. 1–32; and John B. Thompson and David Held, eds., *Habermas: Critical Debates* (Cambridge: MIT Press, 1982).

14. Taylor, *Sources of the Self*, p. 520. For its conceptual depth, its nuanced analysis of several centuries of intellectual history, and its remarkable erudition, I consider this book one of the monuments of twentieth-century thought. For a decidedly less enthusiastic assessment, see Judith Sklar's biting critique in *Political Theory* 19 (1991): 105–109, in which she takes the standard skeptical view of Taylor's position that I suggest, in the conclusion of this essay, we should try to move beyond. Taylor offers a condensed version of part of his larger argument in *The Ethics of Authenticity* (Cambridge: Harvard University Press, 1992), but in my judgment it lacks the persuasive power of *Sources of the Self*.

15. Compare Michael Sandel, *Liberalism and the Limits of Justice* (Cambridge: Cambridge University Press, 1982); and Michael Sandel, *Democracy's Discontent: America in Search of a Public Philosophy* (Cambridge: Harvard University Press, 1996), p. 28. Willi Paul Adams, *The First American Constitutions: Republican Ideology and the Making of the State Constitutions in the Revolutionary Era*, trans. Robert Kimber and Rita Kimber (Chapel Hill: University of North Carolina Press, 1980). On these issues see also chapters 2 and 4 in this volume.

16. Richard Rorty, ed., *The Linguistic Turn: Recent Essays in Philosophical Method* (Chicago: University of Chicago Press, 1967); Richard Rorty, *Philosophy and the Mirror of Nature* (Princeton: Princeton University Press, 1979), p. 392; and Richard Rorty, *The Consequences of Pragmatism* (Minneapolis: University of Minnesota Press, 1982), pp. xl, xliii. I discuss Rorty's work in greater detail, and place it in the context of the broader revival of pragmatism in recent American thought, in Kloppenberg, "Pragmatism: An Old Name for Some New Ways of Thinking?" *Journal of American History* 83 (1996): 100–138. The phrase "historicist undoing" is from Ian Hacking, "Two Kinds of 'New Historicism' for Philosophers," in *History and. . . : Histories within the Human Sciences*, pp. 296–316.

17. Rorty, *Consequences*, pp. xviii, 160, 161.

18. Richard Rorty, *Objectivity, Relativism, and Truth* (Cambridge: Cambridge University Press, 1991), p. 8. Rorty's essay "Solidarity or Objectivity," in John Rajchman and Cornel West, *Post-Analytic Philosophy* (New York: Columbia University Press, 1985), together with many others Rorty wrote in the 1980s, are collected in two volumes published

in 1991 by Cambridge University Press: *Objectivity, Relativism, and Truth* and *Essays on Heidegger and Others*. On the incoherence of the problem of relativism from a pragmatic perspective, see especially Donald Davidson, "On the Very Idea of a Conceptual Scheme," in Rajchman and West, *Post-Analytic Philosophy*, pp. 129–144.

19. Richard Rorty, *Contingency, Irony, and Solidarity* (Cambridge: Cambridge University Press, 1989), pp. xvi, 53, 189–190. See also Rorty, *Consequences*, p. 166.

20. Georg Iggers, introduction to Leopold von Ranke, *The Theory and Practice of History*, discussed in Novick, *Noble Dream*, pp. 27–28.

21. James T. Kloppenberg, *Uncertain Victory: Social Democracy and Progressivism in European and American Thought, 1870–1920* (New York: Oxford University Press, 1986), pp. 107–114. For an account that reflects the gradual emergence of this sensibility from its roots in the scientific revolution, see Joyce Appleby, Lynn Hunt, and Margaret Jacob, *Telling the Truth about History* (New York: W. W. Norton, 1994).

22. The quotation from Wilhelm Dilthey is from his *Selected Writings*, ed. and trans. H. P. Rickman (Cambridge: Cambridge University Press, 1976), p. 120. The writings of John Dunn and Quentin Skinner were seminal in resurrecting the historical analysis of political ideas. Among recent examples emphasizing the importance of the historicist turn in political theory, see Alasdair MacIntyre, "The Indispensability of Political Theory," in *The Nature of Political Theory*, ed. David Miller and Larry Siedentop (Oxford: Oxford University Press, 1983); Herzog, *Without Foundations*, pp. 218–243; Don Herzog, "Approaching the Constitution," *Ethics* 99 (1988): 147–154; Stout, *Ethics after Babel*, pp. 47, 72–73, 120. For a more detailed discussion of historicism, see James T. Kloppenberg, "Objectivity and Historicism: A Century of American Historical Writing," *American Historical Review* 94 (1989): 1011–1030.

23. A partial list of recent works by historians who have demonstrated the inadequacy of attempts to characterize American political thought as straightforwardly "liberal" or "republican" begins with Jack N. Rakove, *Original Meanings: Politics and Ideas in the Making of the Constitution* (New York: Knopf, 1996); and Donald S. Lutz, *A Preface to American Political Theory* (Lawrence: University Press of Kansas, 1992), both of whom make clear the role of Americans' experience in shaping our characteristic form of political expression, constitution writing, and institution building. Robert Shalhope, *The Roots of Democracy: American Thought and Culture, 1760–1800* (Boston: Twayne, 1990); and Lance Banning, *The Sacred Fire of Liberty: James Madison and the Founding of the Federal Republic* (Ithaca, N.Y.: Cornell University Press, 1995) both see the blending of religious, republican, and liberal ideas in the founding more clearly than do Gordon Wood, who minimizes the role of religion in *The Radicalism of the American Revolution* (New York: Knopf, 1991); and J. C. D. Clark, who treats the Revolution as the last war of religion waged by anti-Catholic zealots in *The Language of Liberty, 1660–1832: Political Discourse and Social Dynamics in the Anglo-American World* (Cambridge: Cambridge University Press, 1994).

Studies acknowledging that an interest in securing individuals' supposedly "liberal" property rights was not incompatible with a supposedly "republican" interest in justice include Joyce Appleby, *Liberalism and Republicanism in the Historical Imagination* (Cambridge: Harvard University Press, 1992); Isaac Kramnick, *Republicanism and Bourgeois Radicalism: Political Ideology in Late Eighteenth-Century England and America* (Ithaca, N.Y.: Cornell University Press, 1990); Richard F. Teichgraeber III, *Sublime Thoughts/ Penny Wisdom: Situating Emerson and Thoreau in the American Market* (Baltimore: Johns Hopkins University Press, 1995); Richard Ellis, *American Political Cultures* (New York: Oxford University Press, 1993); and especially William J. Novak, *The People's Welfare: Law and Regulation in Nineteenth-Century America* (Chapel Hill: University of North

Carolina Press, 1996), which argues convincingly that nineteenth-century America's supposedly liberal courts embraced, and enforced, an ideal of the public good that drew on various sources and incorporated ideas of virtue, freedom, and social responsibility.

For my own arguments concerning the multiple sources and complex varieties of American political thought and behavior, which cannot be reduced to a conflict between "liberalism" and "republicanism" without serious distortion, see chapters 2, 3, 4, and 8 in this volume.

24. The problems involved in simplifying history for political purposes rather than deriving from it an understanding of the complexity of the past are equally apparent in the recent surge of interest in legal history and the diverse appropriations of historical evidence by lawyers across the political spectrum. On this issue, see Laura Kalman, *The Strange Career of Legal Liberalism* (New Haven: Yale University Press, 1996); and James T. Kloppenberg, "Deliberative Democracy and Judicial Supremacy," *Law and History Review* 13 (1995): 393–411.

25. Thomas Haskell, "The Curious Persistence of Rights Talk in the 'Age of Interpretation,'" *Journal of American History* 74 (1987): 984–1012; Amy Gutmann, ed., *Democracy and the Welfare State* (Princeton: Princeton University Press, 1988), especially the essays by Michael Walzer, J. Donald Moon, and Jon Elster. See also my discussion of the rise of the American and British welfare states in chapter 7 in this volume.

26. Daniel T. Rodgers, *Contested Truths* (New York: Basic Books, 1987); Bernstein, "One Step Forward," reprinted in Richard J. Bernstein, *The New Constellation: The Ethical-Political Horizons of Modernity/Postmodernity* (Cambridge: MIT Press, 1992); the quotation is from p. 245. See also Rorty's response to Bernstein, "Thugs and Theorists," *Political Theory* 15 (1987): 564–580; Richard Rorty, "Postmodern Bourgeois Liberalism," in *Hermeneutics and Praxis*, ed. Robert Hollinger (Notre Dame: University of Notre Dame Press, 1985); MacIntyre, "Indispensability of Political Theory"; Bellah, *Habits of the Heart*; Walzer, *Spheres of Justice*; Stout, *Ethics after Babel*; Herzog, *Without Foundations*; and Nancy Fraser, "Solidarity or Singularity? Richard Rorty between Romanticism and Technocracy," in Fraser, *Unruly Practices* (Minneapolis: Minnesota University Press, 1989).

27. Rorty, "Thugs and Theorists," pp. 565, 571, 577, n. 19.

28. Rorty, *Contingency*, pp. 181–182. Walter Rauschenbusch, *Christianity and the Social Crisis* (1907; New York: Harper-Torchbooks, 1964), pp. 408, 252.

29. Compare James T. Kloppenberg, "Democracy and Disenchantment: From Weber and Dewey to Habermas and Rorty," in *Modernist Impulses in the Human Sciences, 1870–1930*, ed. Dorothy Ross (Baltimore: Johns Hopkins University Press, 1994), pp. 185–203, reprinted as chapter 6 in this volume; and Richard Rorty, "Dewey between Hegel and Darwin," in *Modernist Impulses in the Human Sciences, 1870–1930*, pp. 54–68.

30. Rorty, *Contingency*, pp. 67–68. On the similarities between Habermas and Dewey, see Bernstein, *Philosophical Profiles*, p. 91; and Rorty, "Thugs and Theorists," p. 580 n. 31.

31. Peter Dews, ed., *Habermas, Autonomy and Solidarity: Interviews* (London: Verso, 1986), p. 91, quoted in Rorty, "Thugs and Theorists," pp. 565 575 n. 6. For Habermas's conception of the relation between cognitive-instrumental rationality and the life world, see Habermas, *The Theory of Communicative Action*, trans. Thomas McCarthy, 2 vols. (Boston: Beacon, 1984, 1987).

32. Rorty, *Contingency*, p. 68.

33. John Dewey, *Liberalism and Social Action*, The Page-Barbour Lectures, in Dewey, *The Later Works, 1925–1953*, ed. Jo Ann Boydston (Carbondale: Southern Illinois Uni-

versity Press, 1987) 11: 27. Cf. Dewey, *Art as Experience*, in ibid., 10: 350, quoted in Rorty, *Contingency*, p. 69.

34. See Kloppenberg, "Pragmatism: An Old Name for Some New Ways of Thinking?"; Stephen Toulmin, "The Recovery of Practical Philosophy," *American Scholar* 57 (1988): 337–352; and the elaboration of this argument in Stephen Toulmin, *Cosmopolis: The Hidden Agenda of Modernity* (New York: Free Press, 1990).

35. Thomas Haskell, "Capitalism and the Origins of the Humanitarian Sensibility," parts 1 and 2, *American Historical Review* 90 (1985): 339–361, 457–466; Thomas Haskell,"Convention and Hegemonic Interest in the Debate over Antislavery: A Reply to Davis and Ashworth," *American Historical Review* 92 (1987): 829–879. The contributions of Haskell, David Brion Davis, and John Ashworth to this exchange on the sources of antislavery sentiment, together with a valuable introduction by Thomas Bender, are available in Thomas Bender, ed., *The Antislavery Debate: Capitalism and Abolitionism as a Problem of Historical Interpretation* (Berkeley: University of California Press, 1992). For further illumination of the diverse sources of antebellum reformist sentiment, see the brilliant essay by Elizabeth B. Clark, " 'The Sacred Rights of the Weak': Pain, Sympathy, and the Culture of Individual Rights in Antebellum America," *Journal of American History* 82 (1995): 463–493; and Daniel Walker Howe, *Virtue, Passion, and Politics: The Construction of the Self in American Thought, from Jonathan Edwards to Abraham Lincoln and Beyond* (Cambridge: Harvard University Press, 1997).

36. Rorty, *Contingency*, p. 196; Rorty, *Consequences*, p. 162. On the question of dualism in Rorty's writings during the 1980s, see Stout's parallel formulation in *Ethics after Babel*, pp. 241, 261–263, 292.

There is a paradoxical and incongruous relation between the distinction Rorty insisted upon between the private and public spheres and his stiff resistance to the genre distinction between what Habermas calls the "world-disclosing" and "problem-solving" capacities of "art and literature on the one hand, and science, morality, and law on the other." When Rorty offered historical knowledge of our tradition as the source of the only standard of comparison we can offer to persuade others of the value of our values, he seemed to rely on precisely the genre distinction he refused to allow Habermas to make. It is, after all, not the quality of the literature but the quality of the lives our culture makes possible that Rorty offered as evidence of the superiority—for us—of liberal democracy. Cf. Jürgen Habermas, "Excursus on Leveling the Genre Distinction between Philosophy and Literature," in Habermas, *The Philosophical Discourse of Modernity: Twelve Lectures*, trans. Frederick Lawrence (Cambridge: MIT Press, 1986); Rorty, "Thugs and Theorists," p. 579 n. 26; Rorty, "Solidarity and Objectivity," p. 11; and Rorty, *Contingency*, pp. 53, 84–85.

37. See for example Richard Rorty, "The Intellectuals at the End of Socialism," *Yale Review* 80 (1992): 1–16; Richard Rorty, "Human Rights, Rationality, and Sentimentality," *Yale Review* 81 (1993): 1–20; Richard Rorty, "The Intellectuals and the Poor," a lecture delivered at Pomona College on February 19, 1996; and Richard Rorty, "Back to Class Politics," *Dissent*, Winter 1997, pp. 31–34.

38. David A. Hollinger, "Cultural Pluralism and Multiculturalism," in *A Companion to American Thought*, ed. Richard Wightman Fox and James T. Kloppenberg (Oxford: Blackwell Publishers, 1995), pp. 162–166. For Hollinger's brilliant, full-scale articulation of his argument, see David A. Hollinger, *Postethnic America: Beyond Multiculturalism* (New York: Basic Books, 1995).

39. Kwame Anthony Appiah, *In My Father's House: Africa in the Philosophy of Culture* (New York: Oxford University Press, 1992); Michael Walzer, "What Does It Mean to Be an American?" *Social Research* 57 (Fall 1990): 591–614; Michael Walzer, "Multiculturalism and Individualism," *Dissent*, Spring 1994, pp. 185–191; Charles Taylor et al.,

Multiculturalism: Examining the Politics of Recognition, ed. Amy Gutmann (Princeton: Princeton University Press, 1994).

40. For clear road maps through the complicated transformations of American Protestantism, see the following essays in *A Companion to American Thought* ed. Richard Wightman Fox and James T. Kloppenberg (Oxford: Blackwell, 1995): Mark A. Noll, "Evangelicalism," pp. 221–223; Mark A. Noll, "Fundamentalism," pp. 260–262; and Richard Wightman Fox, "Liberal Protestantism," pp. 394–397. On the role of American Jewish intellectuals in transforming academic culture, see the essays collected in David A. Hollinger, *Science, Jews, and Secular Culture: Studies in Mid-Twentieth-Century American Intellectual History* (Princeton: Princeton University Press, 1996); and on Catholics, see John T. McGreevy, "Thinking on One's Own: Catholicism in the American Intellectual Imagination, 1928-1960," *Journal of American History* 84 (1997): 97–131. For more extended discussion of these issues, see chapter 3 in this volume.

41. Richard Wightman Fox, "Speak of the Devil: Popular Religion in American Culture," *American Literary History* 9 (1997): 181–195; Richard Wightman Fox, *Reinhold Niebuhr: A Biography* (New York: Pantheon Books, 1985), pp. 243–247, 291–298. See also Andrew Delbanco, *The Death of Satan: How Americans Have Lost the Sense of Evil* (New York: Farrar, Straus, and Giroux, 1995).

42. William James, "On a Certain Blindness in Human Beings," *Talks to Teachers on Psychology, and to Students on Some of Life's Ideals* (1899; New York: Norton, 1958), pp. 149–169.

43. Du Bois, *The Souls of Black Folk*, in Du Bois, *Writings*, ed. Nathan Huggins (1903; New York: Library of America, 1986), p. 492.

44. Walter Rauschenbusch, *Christianity and the Social Crisis*, p. 252.

45. James Madison to James Monroe, October 5, 1786, quoted in Banning, *The Sacred Fire of Liberty*, pp. 72–73.

INDEX

Abolitionism, 46, 175
Adams, Henry, 74
Adams, John, 24, 31, 36, 45, 175
Adams, Samuel, 62, 162
Adams, Willi Paul, 162
Addams, Jane, 49, 83, 127–28, 131, 133, 176, 177
African Americans
  Christianity and, 47
  See also Civil rights movement; Race relations; Slavery
Agriculture, in early America, 28, 32, 33, 42
Allen, Ethan, 15
American Economic Association, 48
American Revolution, 22, 24, 28–29, 30, 32, 44, 45, 60, 62, 150, 168, 188n. 18
Americans for Democratic Action, 142–43
Anderson, Sherwood, 134
Anglicanism, 42, 44
Ankersmit, Frank, 204n. 33
Antifederalists, 45, 63, 65
Antifoundationalism, 172, 176
Antiwar movement, 50
Appiah, Kwame Anthony, 175
Appleby, Joyce, 25, 29, 32, 34, 36, 37, 189n. 27
Aquinas, St. Thomas, 4, 6, 23, 27
Arendt, Hannah, 142
Aristotle, 4, 6, 122, 169, 172
Arnold, Thurmond, 138

Ashworth, John, 32, 189n. 27
Associational life
  pluralism and, 143
  Tocqueville on, 76–80
Augustine, St., 40, 58, 62, 197n. 38

Bailyn, Bernard, 22, 24, 60, 64, 69
Banning, Lance, 32, 34, 77, 189n. 27
Barlow, Joel, 15
Barnes, Harry Elmer, 86
Barth, Karl, 139
Beard, Charles, 74
Beecher, Lyman, 46
Behaviorism, 133–34
Bell, Daniel, 54, 74, 145–46, 151
Bellah, Robert, 55–56, 68, 78, 151, 168
Bellamy, Edward, 125, 126
Bender, Thomas, 78
Benhabib, Seyla, 101, 103–4, 105, 211n. 5
Bennett, William, 8
Bentham, Jeremy, 4, 5, 29, 88
Bentley, Arthur, 133
Berlin, Isaiah, 14, 181n. 13
Bernstein, Richard J., 98, 103, 105, 153, 154, 157, 164, 168–69, 209n. 42
Berthoff, Rowland, 190n. 28
Beveridge Report (Great Britain), 101, 111–14, 116, 117–18, 143
Bigelow, John, 73
Bill of Rights, 18–19, 44–45, 63–64, 173
Black Muslims, 147